Turner and Venice

Turner and Venice

Ian Warrell
With essays by David Laven,
Jan Morris and Cecilia Powell

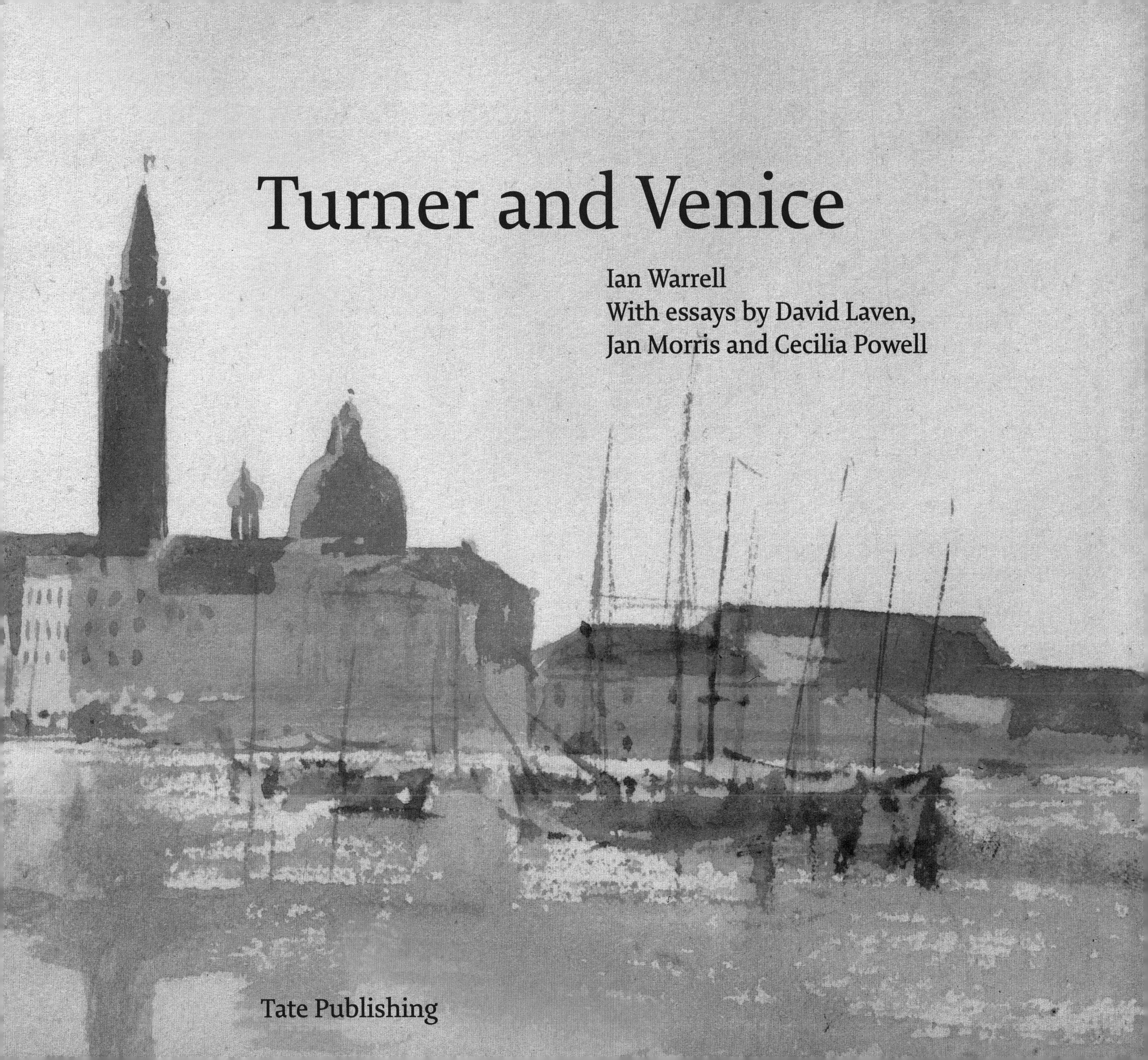

Tate Publishing

First published in 2003 by order of the Tate Trustees
by Tate Publishing, a division of Tate Enterprises Ltd,
Millbank, London SW1P 4RG
www.tate.org.uk
on the occasion of the exhibition at
    Tate Britain, London
    9 October 2003 – 11 January 2004
and touring to
    Kimbell Art Museum, Fort Worth
    15 February – 30 May 2004

© Tate 2003

British Library Cataloguing in Publication Data
A catalogue record for this book is available from the British Library

ISBN 1 85437 463 X (pbk)
ISBN 1 85437 480 X (hbk)

Distributed in the United States and Canada
by Harry N. Abrams, Inc., New York

Library of Congress Cataloging in Publication Data
Library of Congress Control Number: 2003108253

Designed by Lippa Pearce Design Ltd

Printed and bound in Italy by Conti Tipocolor

Measurements of works of art are given in centimetres, height before width

Titles given in the captions are Turner's own for the paintings
exhibited during his lifetime

Standard Abbreviated References

B&J
    Martin Butlin and Evelyn Joll, *The Paintings of J.M.W. Turner*,
    2 vols., London and New Haven 1977, revised 2nd ed. 1984
Finberg 1930
    A.J. Finberg, *In Venice with Turner*, London 1930 (copies in the Tate
    and British Museum Print Rooms have manuscript annotations
    by C.F. Bell)
GPdiV
    Gazzetta Privilegiata di Venezia
    Venice's daily newspaper during the period of Turner's visits
Oxford Companion
    Evelyn Joll, Martin Butlin and Luke Herrmann, *The Oxford
    Companion to J.M.W. Turner*, Oxford 2001
R (plus number)
    W.G. Rawlinson, *The Engraved Work of J.M.W. Turner*, 2 vols., 1908
    and 1913
S (plus number)
    Lindsay Stainton, *Turner's Venice*, London 1985
TB (plus roman numerals)
    Turner Bequest works on paper, as catalogued by A.J. Finberg,
    A Complete Inventory of the Drawings of the Turner Bequest, 2 vols.,
    London 1909
W (plus number)
    Checklist of works on paper outside the Turner Bequest, as
    catalogued by Andrew Wilton, *The Life and Work of J.M.W. Turner*,
    Fribourg and London 1979

Note: The watercolours of the Vaughan Bequest in the collections
of the National Galleries of Scotland, Edinburgh, and the National
Gallery of Ireland, Dublin, cannot be lent. They are exhibited at
these institutions each January

Front cover:
Bridge of Sighs, Ducal Palace and Custom-House, Venice: Canaletti Painting exhibited
Royal Academy 1833 (fig.103, detail)
Back cover:
The Giudecca Canal, looking towards Fusina at Sunset 1840 (fig.210)

Frontispiece:
San Giorgio Maggiore – Early Morning 1819
(fig.74, detail)
Pages 40–1:
Campo Santo, Venice exhibited Royal Academy
1842 (fig.257, detail)

Contents

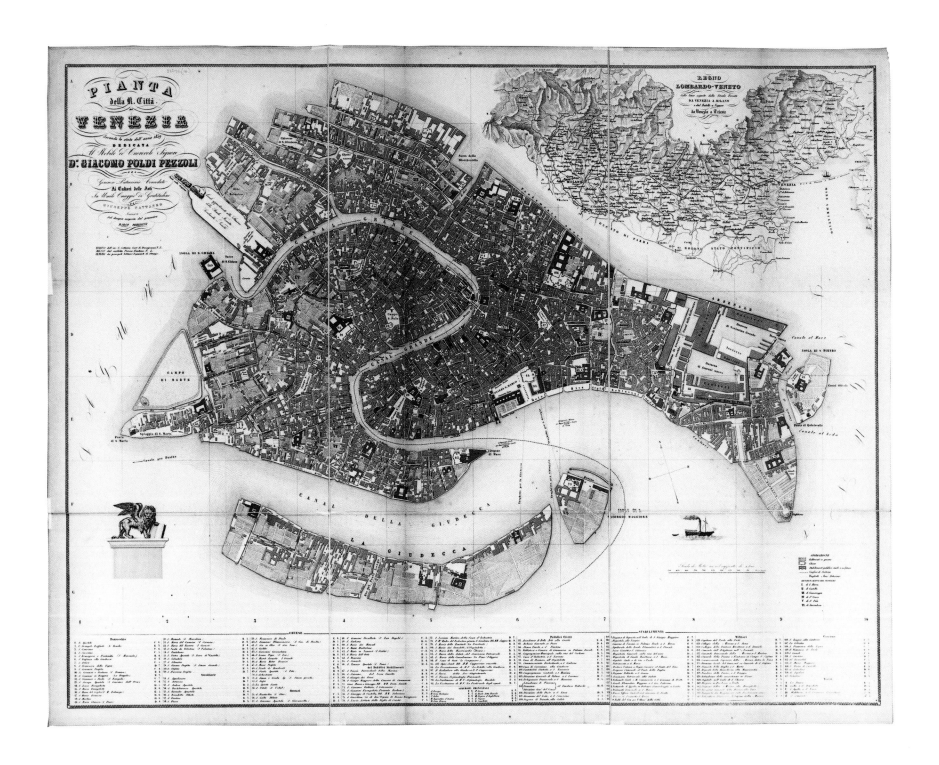

1
M. Peressini
Map of Central Venice 1849
Engraving
The British Library, London

Foreword

No one should be surprised that the visual and cultural allure of Venice repeatedly enveloped an artist like Turner, attuned as he was to both the potency and manifestation of light and the weighty authority of history. What is surprising, perhaps, is that this is the first time his relationship with this city has been explored in an exhibition – even though the Venetian paintings and watercolours have always been one of the most widely accepted foundation stones of his achievement, offering something new to each generation that has encountered them.

Even as the series of canvases began to appear during the last two decades of Turner's working life, these works met with far greater immediate admiration and acceptance than many of the other pictures painted in his 'late' manner. By the early twentieth century they were among his most highly prized images, which prompted A.J .Finberg (subsequently the artist's biographer) to examine the phenomenon in his book *In Venice with Turner* (1930). This was one of the first in-depth studies to approach Turner without the crutch of Ruskin's prose. While Finberg's book considerably surpassed earlier knowledge, it did not entirely resolve the dates of Turner's visits to the city, which made it difficult to date the watercolours precisely. These concerns were not addressed more fully until the end of the 1960s, when intensive but largely unpublished research was undertaken by two scholars: Barbara Reise and Hardy George. It was the latter who finally resolved the date of the third tour that had eluded Finberg.

In the last thirty years, beginning even before the bicentenary of Turner's birth, there has been a sustained re-examination of his whole oeuvre that has delved into byways as well as focusing on the more obvious highlights. Prior to the return to the Tate in 1986–7 of the huge collection of watercolours in the artist's bequest, the British Museum was the centre of much of this scholarly activity. This included the 1975 exhibition in which Andrew Wilton dated many of the Venetian watercolours to 1840 for the first time. Ten years later the museum published Lindsay Stainton's *Turner's Venice*, which introduced the more mysterious studies on toned paper to a wider audience.

Stainton's work in particular prompted the idea of developing an exhibition in which the full range of the artist's response to the city and its artistic traditions could be considered together. The validity of approaching the subject afresh has been rewarded in the research of Ian Warrell, curator of the present show, which has resulted in new titles for many of the sketches and watercolours (all available on the Tate website). These revised identifications have provided many insights into the way Turner worked in Venice, revealing that he reverted to a long-abandoned practice of sketching in colour on the spot, as well as working from memory. Furthermore, the dates and titles of the final six Venetian paintings that Turner exhibited are here reassessed and redistributed, solving a muddle stemming from the elderly artist himself. Finally, it appears that twentieth-century notions of what Turner's vision of Venice should look like sometimes led earlier curators astray in their attempts to assign titles to his unfinished pictures – two of the most atmospheric late canvases long associated with the ethereal mists of the lagoon can now be linked with England, rather than Italy (*figs.276–7*).

Ian Warrell's conception, creation and curatorship of this project has been both a labour of love and a professional *tour de force*. Beyond the show itself, I believe the importance of his Venice research, published for the first time in this catalogue, will be widely recognised. Meanwhile, in addition to his discussion of Turner's individual responses to Venice, we are delighted that it was possible to persuade the distinguished travel writer Jan Morris to provide the animated introductory essay to this volume. Her long connection with Venice as a regular visitor illuminates the hold the city exerted on a sophisticated traveller like Turner, who would similarly have seen beyond the illusion of the city's magical façade, and yet was still enchanted. We are also highly fortunate in the other contributors: Cecilia Powell is well known for her work on Turner, most recently for her investigations into his journeys through Germany, but also for her earlier work on his time in southern Italy; and David Laven, of the University of Reading, who as the author of a recent book on Venice under the Habsburgs is eminently qualified to offer an impression of what the city must have been like at the time of Turner's visits.

Working alongside Ian Warrell in the realisation of this complex project have been assistant curator Louise Hayward and registrar Sionaigh Durrant, who have shared much of the practical responsibilities for the exhibition's organisation. We are hugely grateful to them both, to Judith Nesbitt, head of exhibitions and display at Tate Britain, to installation manager Andy Shiel and to many further staff behind the scenes, including Roy Perry, Piers Townshend, Rosie Freemantle, Brian McKenzie, Lisa Hayes and Catherine Clement, as well as John Jervis, who has overseen the production of the catalogue with immense dedication. We have been fortunate to have the architectural firm of Adam Caruso and Peter St John as the designers of the exhibition.

As always, the exhibition would not have been possible without the generosity of the private collectors and of other museums from which the assembled works have been gathered. Though it is invidious to single out any one institution, we are especially grateful that the National Gallery of Art in Washington has lent three of its major paintings, including the celebrated *Keelmen* (*fig.105*), which has not been seen in London since 1975. We are also pleased that so many of the pictures will be seen at the Kimbell Art Museum, in Fort Worth, to which the exhibition moves after its showing at Tate Britain. We are grateful to our colleagues there, Director Timothy Potts and Chief Curator Malcolm Warner, for their determination to secure this exhibition for presentation to an American audience and for working with us so closely to make it happen.

Another kind of valuable support for the exhibition comes from Barclays PLC. This is the first major show at Tate Britain to be sponsored by Barclays, as part of their Invest and Inspire arts sponsorship programme, which includes support of the National Theatre, the British Museum and the National Gallery. We are delighted to be working with Barclays and thank them for their commitment to Tate Britain.

Stephen Deuchar
Director, Tate Britain

Sponsor's Foreword

Barclays is proud to be supporting the *Turner and Venice* exhibition. Working with Tate Britain is part of Invest and Inspire – our arts sponsorship programme. Barclays has established partnerships with four of Britain's leading arts institutions: the Royal National Theatre, the British Museum, the National Gallery and Tate Britain. The aim of Invest and Inspire is to increase access to the arts. We have worked with each of the arts organisations to create innovative public events from *All Aboard! Sunday in the South Pacific,* a day of free family entertainment in and around the National Theatre, to *A Romantic Journey with the Queen of Sheba,* a concert in the forecourt of the British Museum. It is now a pleasure to be working with Tate Britain on *Turner and Venice,* and partnering them in the creation of *Carnival! A day in Venice at Tate Britain.* This day of free public events will aim to encourage new and diverse audiences to get involved with the gallery. We hope that Invest and Inspire will be an inspiring demonstration of the benefits that imaginative business investment in the arts can bring.

Sir Peter Middleton, Chairman, Barclays PLC

Acknowledgements

The starting point for this project was, of course, Lindsay Stainton's richly insightful book *Turner's Venice*, which my parents gave me before I came to work at the Tate. It was a marvellous stimulus that inspired me to look more closely at Turner. I am consequently especially pleased to thank Lindsay for her generous advice when we discussed the project in outline, at its earliest stage, and for her help with so many things over the years.

Many other people have made invaluable contributions to the development of the exhibition and this accompanying publication. Of these, I should like to start by remembering four people who each offered encouragement as my work got underway, but who are no longer with us to see its realisation: Sir Paul Getty expressed great enthusiasm for the exhibition during his visits to study Turner's Venetian watercolours, which he loved so much; Francis Haskell suggested several areas of study worth pursuing; and, though a Constable specialist, Leslie Parris was unequivocal in lending his support. Finally, the much-missed Evelyn Joll shared his comprehensive knowledge of the whereabouts of pictures in private collections, conveying also his keen anticipation at the prospect of bringing long-separated paintings together.

An immense amount of scholarly and practical assistance, both great and small, has been provided by the following individuals: George d'Almeida; Anthony Bailey; Sir Nicholas and Lady Bacon; Peter Barber; Elizabeth Barker; Toni Booth; Stephen Borys; Peter Bower; Judith Brodie; Martin Butlin; Caroline Campbell; Andrew Clayton-Payne; Maurice Davies; James Dearden; Harriet Drummond; Lucy Ducat-Hammersley; Lord and Lady Egremont; Mrs Embiricos; Mark Evans; Jennie Farmer; Richard Feigen; Kate Fielden; Marianne Ford; Gillian Forrester; Ann Forsdyke; Dr John Gage; Bamber Gascoigne; Hardy George; Constance Gounod; Matthew Green; Alastair Grieve; Antony Griffiths; Colin Harrison; James Harvey; George Hecksher; Elspeth Hector; Luke Herrmann; Robert Hewison; David Hill; Charles Hope; Sarah Horborough; John House; Peter Humfrey; Isobel Hunter; Virginia Ibbott; Raymond Keaveney; Franklin Kelly; Martin Krause; Thomas Krens; Alastair Laing; Lord Lansdowne; Lowell Libson; Kathy Lochnan; Andrew Loukes; Jane MacAvock; Professor Michael Mallett; Chris Michaelides; Sir Oliver Millar; Jane Munro; Patrick Murphy; Kimberly Nichols; Larry Nichols; Charles Nugent; Guy Peppiatt; Jan Piggott; Margaret Plant; Timothy Potts; Earl A. Powell III; Sarah Quill; Paul Raison; Janice Reading; Russell Roberts; Angela Roche; Stephen Rogers; Christopher Rowell; Nick Savage; Valerie Scott; Eric Shanes; Tessa Sidey; Nathaniel Silver; Samantha Sizemore; Janet Skidmore; Greg Smith; Katharine Solender; John Stainton; Lucille Stiger; Akiko Terao; Dodge Thompson; David Thomson; Gary Tinterow; Jennifer Tonkovich; Julian Treuherz; Rosalind Mallord Turner; Malcolm Warner; Henry Wemys; Tim Wilcox; Scott Wilcox; Stephen Wildman; Andrew Wilton; Andrew Wyld. I am also indebted to the staff of the British Library, the London Library, the Fondazione Cini, and the Libreria Marciana in Venice. During the period that the Metropolitan Museum was collaborating on the project, I benefited from the generosity, wisdom and wit of Katharine Baetjer. I would also like to thank Stephen Tate, for his endless patience and astute analytical skills.

My attempts to unearth Turner's painting *Venus and Adonis* for the exhibition sadly proved unsuccessful, but I am, nevertheless, grateful to Sharon Campbell and Cataline de Szegőffy, at the British Embassy in Caracas, who were valiant and dogged in taking up the quest.

At the Tate I have received support in numerous ways from colleagues throughout the institution, in many cases above and beyond the call of duty: John Anderson; Rosie Bass; Anne Beckwith-Smith; Joanne Bernstein; Giorgia Bottinelli; Jane Brehony; David Brown; Celia Clear; Catherine Clement; Nicola Cole; Juliet Cook; Rachel Crome; Meg Duff; Alison Duke; Sionaigh Durrant; Claire Eva; Matthew Flintham; Rosie Freemantle; Adrian Glew; Jo Gracey; Melanie Greenwood; Richard Hamilton; Robin Hamlyn; Lisa Hayes; Louise Hayward; Karen Hearn; Sarah Hyde; Matthew Imms; Chloe Johnson; James Kay; Katharine Lockett; Ben Luke; Anne Lyles; Siobhan McCracken; Brian McKenzie; Tara McKinney; Juliet Mazini; Nicola Moorby; Judith Nesbitt; Nicole Newman; Andrea Nixon; Diane Perkins; Roy Perry; Ruth Rattenbury; Sue Smith; Sarah Taft; Rod Tidnam; Sarah Tinsley; Joyce Townsend; Piers Townshend; Sheena Wagstaff. This catalogue would not have been produced without the meticulous work of Richard Dawes, Rebecca Fortey, Tim Holton, John Jervis, Fran Matheson and Johanna Stephenson.

In Venice itself my requests for assistance were invariably met with great enthusiasm for the project, which makes it all the more regrettable that, as this catalogue goes to press, there is no certainty that the exhibition will be seen in the setting that inspired it, despite repeated attempts to bring this about. For their efforts towards this end, and for help with my research, I would like to thank Caterina Barbini, Professor Alessandro Bettagno, Clarenza Catullo, Giuseppe Donega, Daniela Ferretti, Bozena Anna Kowalczyk, Victoria Press, Philip Rylands, Thomas Sharman, Jasper Sharp, Admiral Lorenzo Sferra and Caterina Bon Valsassina. Special thanks should go to Emmanuele Nasi and Francesca Forni at the Westin Europa and Regina Hotel, for their kind hospitality and interest in the exhibition. Finally, in order to resolve a series of niggling details, I have made many demands on the good will of my friends Davide Battistin and Maria Novella Benzoni, which helped me far more than they knew at the time.

As Stephen Deuchar has already mentioned, it is a real honour to have such a distinguished group of fellow contributors. As a result of our various discussions, Cecilia Powell and David Laven have enriched my understanding of Venetian issues; and both authors greatly illuminate Turner's experience of the city in the essays that follow. I am also grateful to Jan Morris for agreeing with such alacrity to write something for the catalogue. Her wonderful book of 1960 is still the perfect introduction to the colourful vitality of Venice, and it is truly satisfying to be able to include here a coda to that earlier account.

Ian Warrell

Turner, Venice, the Generals and Me Jan Morris

At the end of the Second World War I found myself, for a month or two, helping to run the motor boats of Venice, all of which had been requisitioned by the British Army. One of my duties was to escort very senior officers from our dock near the Piazzale Roma along the Grand Canal to the similarly requisitioned Danieli Hotel, where they were to be luxuriously accommodated, and one of my delights was to observe the expressions on their faces as we chugged down the mostly empty waterway (the war was hardly over) along the towering line of shabby palaces, under the Rialto bridge, past the Salute until, with a showy burst of our engines, we emerged into the great Basin of St Mark and discovered the incomparable sweep of the city laid out for our inspection.

I was nineteen years old, and the generals mostly treated me in an avuncular way. I, on the other hand, felt rather patronising towards them, for I had already passed through the gamut of responses that I saw expressed in their faces, and I knew that they would end their brief voyage with me experiencing a sort of bouillabaisse of emotions. It is a paradox of Venice that, although physically it changes less than any other great city of Europe, it arouses in its foreign visitors such volatile reactions, especially perhaps in the British, especially perhaps in the *English*. England and Venice are morganatically related, as it were, although the English probably recognise the link more often than the Venetians. Both states were born of the same parent, the sea. Both were anomalies among the nations. Both were, during several centuries, proud of their insularity. Both acquired, and lost, immense maritime and commercial empires. Both were intensely conscious of their own decline, and spent the years of their diminishment casting around for new purposes, systems or alliances. Both have relied for their self-esteem upon myth and theatrical display.

Hazily, I am sure, my very English generals contemplated these connections as they were propelled towards the Danieli. Hazily I had contemplated them too, during that first stay in Venice, and I have been influenced by them ever since, as during a lifetime's acquaintance with the city I have been variously seduced, disenchanted, astonished, alienated, bewitched, saddened and supernally elated. Only the other day I was robbed of half my worldly wealth on a vaporetto, and even then my responses were jumbled – the thief was so skilful, the boat was so merrily jammed with polyglot visitors, it was rather comical that after fifty years' experience of Venice I should be so ignominiously deflated, and Harry's Bar gave me a free supper to cheer me up.

Nobody was more thoroughly and complicatedly English than J.M.W. Turner, who made three visits to Venice between 1819 and 1840, and was certainly conscious of the parallels between the two sea states – so beloved of the English Romantic poets, who saw in the fate of the one the possible destiny of the other. He never stayed long in the city, but he produced hundreds of oil paintings, watercolours and sketches of it, some drawn on the spot, some done at home in England from drafts or from memory. Among them, it seems to me, are illustrated all the varying effects that passed through my generals' minds, and through mine at one time or another during my sojourns in the city.

A sense of unreality is what dominates most visitors' first responses to Venice. Charles Dickens, in 1844, was so bemused by it that he wrote his only essay about the city in hallucinatory form: 'I have, many and many a time, thought since of this strange Dream upon the water: half-wondering if it lie there yet, and if its name be VENICE.'

It was certainly like a city of illusion when I first got there, and found myself billeted in a house on the Lagoon side of the island of Giudecca. Venice then seemed to me desolately impotent in the aftermath of conflict. When I looked out from my window across the Lagoon, I thought it was like a dead lake in a fable. There were few boats about. The water struck me as metallically motionless, and the scattered islands looked altogether deserted. The colours I recall as pallid, listless; the atmosphere was habitually opaque; hardly a breath of wind stirred the cypresses in our garden, or disturbed the slumbering cats. The only sound I remember from that stricken Venice was the ceaseless thudding lap of the water against the walls of our boathouse on the shore, with an occasional explosion from a mine being blown up at sea.

Was it really like that? I doubt it. The memory is selective, and there were probably more boats about, and more noises, and Venice was doubtless less ethereally wasted than I imagine it now. But then the meanings of Venice, more than those of most cities, are essentially subjective, and there is nowhere on earth where observation merges more subtly into imagination, especially when an observer is new to the scene. Even the earthiest of my water-borne generals, I do not doubt, found his soldierly assessments clouded over, misted, heightened, magicked, when we first navigated him out of the Grand Canal into the wide Lagoon, and Dickens never pretended for a moment that what he saw that day in 1844 was mere reality.

2
Aerial view of Venice from above the
Isola di San Giorgio Maggiore and the
Giudecca, looking west towards Mestre

Nobody, before or since, in any medium, has ever recorded the first impact of Venetian mystery more exactly – if exactness is quite the right analysis – than Turner did during his first brief visit in 1819 (*figs.74, 75, 77, 78*). The vaporous masterpieces he produced then have been said to represent the dawn of Impressionism. For me they suggest Debussy in paint, and it is Debussy's languorous, limpid cadences that come into my head still when I remember my own original stay in Venice. I suppose most of us, when we first see a great spectacle, whether it be the Manhattan skyline, the white line of the Himalayas or the Changing of the Guard, see it only as a marvellous blur, an instant generalisation, and the generalised blur of Venice is surely the most potent of them all.

The four revelatory watercolours that Turner did in 1819 are not so much pictures of Venice as pictures of the *idea* of Venice, shimmering in the early morning or eerily refulgent in the sun. No matter that at least one of them seems to represent an impossible view – this is not topography. The city looks just as empty, just as evanescent, as it did to me, and perhaps for similar reasons. In 1946 it had emerged saddened and impoverished by war; in 1819 it was debilitated by the years of uncertainty that had followed the fall of the Venetian Republic in 1797 – seized by Napoleon, handed over to the Austrians, taken back by the French, besieged by the Austrians again and finally, in 1815, reincorporated into the Austrian empire. Turner found it enervated and half-empty, just as I did, and that first melancholy limbo feeling evidently seduced him too, for to my mind he never painted the city quite so hauntingly again.

But he certainly painted it differently. After the first disorienting shock of encounter, people generally refocus their vision of Venice, and begin to look at its buildings more precisely. So evidently did Turner. Of course, he already knew the exquisitely detailed *vedute* of Canaletto, and had produced watercolour versions of other people's sketches of the city. Even on that first visit, if he was painting dreams, he was drawing architecture – some of his own pencilled sketches of Venetian buildings look to me almost indistinguishable from Canaletto's. On his later visits to the city he frequently reverted to his mystical mode, but for the most part his vision seems to have been sharper, his images more real. Perhaps he was thinking partly of his market – many of his pictures were later made into engravings.

Besides, eighteen years after its accession to Austrian rule, the city was settling down. It was more prosperous now, it was more populous and more lively – give it another fifteen years and it would be breaking into virile revolution against Vienna's rule. It was perhaps rather like it was in the 1960s, when it seemed to me to have lost most of its tristesse while recovering much of its composure. Most foreigners loved Venice then. There were not too many of them about, the city was not too crowded,

Milanese capitalism had not subverted its style and many of its old traditions, from religious rites to gondoliers' conventions, were still lustily alive. The music I heard in my mind in those days, as I swaggered along the Grand Canal in my own boat, was not Debussyan at all, but much more like something from Mendelssohn's Italian Symphony.

I was very happy in Venice in the 1960s. It is true that much of its fabric was crumbling and leprous-looking, but I rather liked that, just as I cherished a shamefully romantic vision of the whole construction one day sinking into its parental waves. I thought it all just the right mixture of the poignant and the heroic. The bronze horses still stood there, heartrendingly loyal, upon the façade of the Basilica. Monks knocked at our door, looking for alms. The motor traffic on the canals, though certainly noisier and more robust than it had been when I shepherded my brass hats to the Danieli, was not overwhelming. Nobody robbed me on a vaporetto!

Perhaps it is not fanciful to interpret Turner's later pictures of Venice as reflecting rather the same mood. They are far livelier than his earlier paintings. Streets are busy, lights blaze, lovers are rowed in gondolas in the moonlight. We see worshippers at prayer, processions, brightly lit theatres, barrels in a wine shop. We also see buildings more solidly portrayed, and once an early steamboat spouts its smoke all too realistically across the Lagoon (*fig.255*). This is no longer just the suggestion of Venice, it is much more nearly Venice itself – even when it is a Venice intermittently veiled in allegory. When he was away from Venice Turner sometimes worked up paintings of the city which seem to me almost brassily commonplace. The pictures he made on the spot, though, even in the years of his worldly maturity, nearly always managed to infuse the sensations of the time with the esoteric permanence of the setting. To me an oil painting he did in 1837 of the Grand Canal, with the Rialto bridge in the distant background (*fig.58*), a vivid bustle of boats, crowded wharves and an unexplained water-borne ceremony happening at one side of it, absolutely expresses my own mature responses to the muddled stimuli of Venetian life.

Nowadays, at the start of the twenty-first century, the stimuli often seem to have gone too far. To be true to itself, of course, Venice must be crowded – it always was the grandest of tourist attractions, 'a boast, a marvel and a show', and the empty winters we used to know were only intermissions between performances. Even the city's most infatuated lovers, though, must surely admit that the year-round jam-packed exhibition that is Venice now has lost some of its allure. We do not wish its melancholy back, but we miss its dignity, and with it the old civic echoes of grandeur and genius. After fifty years of my own affair with the city, sometimes I feel only like getting the hell out of the place; and as I wheedle and elbow my way on a sticky, drizzly morning through the multitudes staring at the Bridge of

Sighs from the Ponte della Paglia, just occasionally I sympathise with D.H. Lawrence's characterisation of the city as green, slippery and abhorrent. Something cracked in my own addiction to Venice when, twenty-odd years ago, those noble horses of St Mark were bridled at last, put away in a museum stable and replaced by replicas destitute of charisma.

Our responses to any city are necessarily changeable: its history, its economic condition, its political health, its weather, its age – *our* age – all affect our impressions. Turner saw the city in deprivation and in prosperity, but he never saw the horses go, and he never experienced it on a summer weekend in 2003. I can imagine, all the same, that he was prophetically foreseeing its future in his oddly symbolic picture *Juliet and her Nurse* (*fig.*61), which he painted in 1836. Just for once he does not seem to like the Venice he is portraying. The great piazza and its rooftops swarm with preposterously dressed people. Fireworks go off all over the place. Smoke hangs about, and a distant hubbub is palpable. It is a garish scene, as though the city is in a feverishly revengeful or malicious state (and indeed some scholars used to argue that the picture really portrayed the execution of a murderer in the Piazza San Marco).

Ever since Ruskin reputable judges have greatly admired this picture. I very much dislike it. For me it is a picture of distasteful frisson. But wait: behind that frenzied scene in the piazza, beyond the blare of the fireworks, outside the crowd's gossipy racket, serenely the red-brick campanile soars into a realm of silence above, swirled about by clouds of strange colour and gravely supervised by a few pale stars. Turner knew that the truth of Venice lies in its profoundly sensual transcendentalism, to be glimpsed even at the city's most tawdry or depressing moments, and never to be expunged. So in my heart do I, even on the Ponte della Paglia: and so, I suspect, did those battle-hardened generals of mine, when I ushered them ashore so long ago – stumbling shakily from boat to jetty, and returning my farewell salute in a kindly preoccupied way, as though they had seen miracles.

3
The Piazzetta, looking towards San Giorgio Maggiore, with Austrian Soldiers on Duty 1819
Pencil on paper, 11.2 x 18.5
From the 'Milan to Venice' sketchbook
Tate (TB CLXXV f.46v; D14402)

Turner and Venice Ian Warrell

Turner's light-filled images of Venice represent one of the most important strands of his mature work. No other city, with the possible exception of Rome, consistently captivated his imagination over such a long period, or stimulated so many astonishing paintings and watercolours. Between 1833, when he was already fifty-eight, and 1846, there were, in fact, just two years in which he did not send pictures of Venice to the annual Royal Academy exhibitions, and during this period his Venetian paintings constituted a third of his total output.[1] It is just as significant that these canvases, though radical in their handling of paint, frequently found buyers, unlike so many of his critically maligned later works, and that in the second half of his career they account for nearly half of all the paintings he sold soon after they were first exhibited. Remarkably, given the vital role that Venice assumed in stimulating his art and sustaining his livelihood, Turner spent comparatively little time in the city itself. Now that the details of his travels are clearer, it transpires that the combined number of days he passed there during the course of three visits actually amounts to somewhat less than four weeks (in contrast with his two much longer stays in Rome, of nearly six months).[2]

With the benefit of hindsight, it is clear that there was a certain inevitability to the close association that developed between the artist and Venice. As the later sections of this book demonstrate, this arose from various literary and historical ideas, from specific artistic influences and, of course, from the unique beauties of the city itself, all of which combined with Turner's own temperamental affinity for Venice as a subject.

Yet in acknowledging the potency of this rich amalgamation, it is worth observing that the impact on him was not as immediate as has often been suggested. It was in fact nearly fourteen years after he first arrived in Venice in 1819 before he really began to mine its potential on canvas. Other exaggerations about the nature of his response to Venice have arisen by considering the resulting works too much in isolation (a fault perhaps perpetrated by the present volume). Admittedly, this mono-thematic approach is partly induced by the immense volume of material arising from his visits to the city. Even so, the later watercolours of Switzerland and Germany are really not so different in technique or mood from those of Venice. Furthermore, a tendency to identify the loose, atmospheric brushwork of Turner's later canvases as something growing explicitly, or exclusively, from his experience of Venice has tended to blinker a true understanding of the actual subjects of some of his final pictures. In the

case of two radical unfinished works (*figs.276–7*), which have been associated with the wraith-like mists of the lagoon, this has prevented their correct identification as images of the rain-laden skies of the Channel.

One circumstance that seems especially relevant to Turner's appreciation of Venice is that he had begun his career with a series of impressive marine paintings, and such subjects were always crucial to his aims as an artist, earning him the acclaim of his contemporaries as 'the great *sea* painter'.[3] Even at times when he seemed preoccupied with landscape material, he remained in thrall to the difficulties of capturing the nuances of light on water. But his precocious observations of the sea evolved in tandem with his absorption of the British topographical tradition. This combined the objectives of picturesque view-making with antiquarian interests, and was in part indebted to Canaletto, whose well-known views of Venice and London were a spur to any artist attempting to paint townscapes.[4] Inevitably, the familiarity of Canaletto's images meant that the idea of Venice was inextricably bound up for most British artists in the achievement of this great predecessor. But Turner's ambitions were not confined to the range of Canaletto's subject matter. He aimed to imbue landscape with the more distinguished meanings of History Painting, and hence considered the full range of Venetian art, looking for inspiration in the ranks of earlier masters, most notably Titian and Tintoretto, who both had a formative influence on his work.

And yet, as Canaletto had proved before him, Venice offered unparalleled source material to a talented topographer with a passion for light and water. The 'glorious City in the Sea' owes its fame above all else to its dramatic setting: it rises precariously from a series of islands in the middle of a saltwater lagoon, with tidal waterways instead of streets, and is balanced, as it were, between sea and sky. Its unusual geographical situation is also the cause of its celebrated light, an obviously important factor in its eventual appeal to Turner. As Paul Hills has observed, 'No city built on land can offer so brilliant and so strange an intermingling and intensifying of the colour of the sky and the colour of the buildings on the surface of its thoroughfares.'[5] The wide expanses of the lagoon seem to accentuate especially the effects of sunrise and sunset, surpassing in reality what art aspires to achieve. This was plain to the young John Ruskin, who witnessed there a sunset that produced 'a light such as Turner in his maddest moments never came up to'.[6] Few visitors, in fact, have remained unmoved by the seductive visual appeal of the city, with its long, glittering reflections, its apparent insubstantiality and its disorientating labyrinthine interior. Completely overawed, Charles Dickens professed in 1844, 'I never saw the thing before that I should be afraid to describe.'[7]

If the sea was responsible for the distinctive physical characteristics of Venice, it was also the source of its reputation and wealth, both directly attributable to the Venetian Republic's legendary command of the Mediterranean. For Turner, who was steeped in naval lore, this was a tradition that would have undoubtedly increased the city's allure. However, these glories were already fading before he was born in 1775, and by 1797, when he was beginning to establish himself at the Royal Academy, at the pinnacle of the London art world, Venice was generally perceived to be merely a pale and rather decadent imitation of its former self. At this time, as the traditional Grand Tour came to an end, the city was eking out an existence by staging its former pageantry for a trickle of visiting tourists. The fall of its republic that year was consequently acknowledged as the logical outcome of its present moral lassitude, though its submission to the tyranny of France sharpened British fears of a loss of its own liberty.

For much of his early manhood Turner lived through a turbulent era, surrounded by toppling empires, and it is not surprising that the decline of earlier historic civilisations had great fascination for his generation. He would have been aware of the humiliating fate of Venice at the hands of alternating French and Austrian presences in the years after 1797, but its plight did not at this stage specifically engage him. Instead he turned to Carthage, meditating on its rivalry with Rome as a means of addressing the contemporary stand-off between Britain and France. However, as time went on, it became increasingly commonplace to draw comparisons between Venice in its heyday and the thriving commerce of nineteenth-century London. If Rome had been the chief reference point for eighteenth-century London, it was now Venice, the 'Rome of the Ocean', that seemed to offer the closest parallel.[8] But this recognition carried with it an implicit fear that the proud might of Britain's seaborne empire stood at risk of decline if it did not heed the lessons of Venice. In the post-Waterloo era Britain had assumed the position of a restraining umpire on the world stage. But Turner could have learned from a book by Henry Sass in his personal library that a similarly aloof stance had not prevented the loss of Venice's empire or its degradation to a 'petty province'.[9]

For some, the parallels between the two cities went beyond the obvious connection of their prowess as trading centres. Turner's associate the Scottish artist David Wilkie, for example, noted during a trip to Venice in 1826 that it reminded him particularly of the warren of streets around Covent Garden: 'By land and by water the town is full of intricacy, full of St Martin's Courts, of Maiden Lanes, and Cranbourne Alleys, interrupted at every corner with canals and high bridges.'[10] This is an arresting observation, not least because the area in London he describes was Turner's boyhood home. Ironically, Ruskin was later to contrast Turner's early life in this area with that of Giorgione in Venice, and to insist that the ugliness of London's alleys contributed to a stunted vision of the world.[11] But, sadly, we can never know whether Turner himself was struck by any resemblance between Venice and his home town, since he left no comments about what he discovered on his travels, other than the jottings he made in his sketchbooks and incidental remarks in his correspondence.

If there was something inherently analogous in the shared identity of Venice and London as the hubs of maritime empires, there was also a thrilling sense of the alien, or, more specifically, of the oriental about Venice for its visitors.[12] This was perfectly expressed by the American writer James Fenimore Cooper, who observed in his 1838 account: 'It appeared as if we were in the centre of a civilisation entirely novel … I felt as if transported to a scene in the Arabian nights.'[13] East certainly met West in the architecture of San Marco, and the city continued to welcome Greek and Turkish traders. But Cooper's perceptions are at one with the prevailing idea of Venice as a magical city of dreams, which developed during the first half of the nineteenth century, much encouraged by the evocative fourth Canto of Byron's *Childe Harold's Pilgrimage* (1818). This opens with the memorable image of Venice rising from the waters like an eastern goddess, bedecked with jewels, and goes on to lament the city's now ravaged beauty in elegiac lines steeped in Romantic nostalgia. The most important legacy of the poem for Turner was the notion of Venice as a city suspended in time. His biographer A.J. Finberg claimed that he translated this into his own 'ideal Venice, whose past and present are fused into a vague sentiment'.[14]

Venice in 1819

Byron's poem was published less than a year before Turner made the first of his three visits to Venice. Though there was formerly some uncertainty about when these took place, Turner is now known to have been in Venice in 1819, 1833 and 1840. The dates of his first and last sojourns were established in 1930 by Finberg, who was then inclined to think that the second tour had taken place in 1835.[15] This conclusion was subsequently challenged by C.F. Bell, who contended wrongly that there had been visits in both 1832 and 1835.[16] It was only in 1970 that Hardy George provided conclusive evidence for a visit to Venice in 1833, though the shape of that tour was not fully described until comparatively recently.[17]

Although Turner was then forty-four, his Italian trip of 1819 was only the third time he had crossed the Channel. The chief object of his tour was Rome, which had resumed its role as a fulcrum for artistic endeavour, attracting painters from all over Europe. A particular enticement for Turner was the chance to study the countryside outside Rome that had inspired his hero, Claude Gellée (c.1600/5–1682), known also as Claude or Le Lorrain, who was the most enduring influence on his idealised landscapes. It is a point worth stressing, because it partly explains why Venice did not feature more significantly in Turner's plans. Indeed, his stay there was just a brief interlude of perhaps five days in a tour that lasted six months.

His appearance in Venice was recorded in the daily list of arrivals in the *Gazzetta Privilegiata di Venezia*, from which it can be deduced that he was there on Wednesday 8 September.[18] Among those travellers also registered as having come from Milan, there was only one other 'gent. Inglese', as Turner styled himself, but there was also an Italian artist called Goggi. Turner's deliberate ploy of adopting a description that did not attract attention yet asserted his dignity probably suggests that the two artists did not discover their shared profession. In any case, Turner would have been inhibited in striking up spontaneous acquaintances by his inability to master foreign languages.

The crossing to Venice from the mainland was a major rite for all travellers, invariably described in terms of incredulous wonder. So it is surprising that there are no sketches of Turner's journey across the Lagoon, something that could perhaps indicate that he arrived after dark. This seems to have been a common occurrence, experienced by Frances, Lady Shelley in 1838 and a few years later by Dickens, who recalled seeing the city initially as 'a great light, lying in the distance on the sea', which, as he approached, 'began to burn brighter; and from being one light became a cluster of tapers, twinkling and shining out of the water'.[19]

Before leaving England, Turner had benefited greatly from the advice of James Hakewill, author of *A Picturesque Tour of Italy* (see *figs.29–33*), who had filled a small notebook with suggestions for his itinerary. One of these directed Turner to go to the Albergo Leon Bianco after arriving in Venice.[20] This was a distinguished hotel, by then situated to the south of the Rialto bridge, on the Grand Canal (*fig.4*). It was frequented by many notable nineteenth-century British travellers, including artists such as Clarkson Stanfield and the Countess of Blessington. During her stay in 1828 the Countess considered her lodgings 'excellent'. She took special delight in

a sitting room with a bay window that allowed her to survey the Grand Canal (as in *figs.29–31*), but noted that the other apartments were 'spacious and well furnished, and the *cuisine* remarkably good'. Her chief reservation concerned the Austrian rules that prevented the innkeeper from serving French wine with dinner, 'a privation much complained of' by the guests.[21]

As his travel documents would have required him to move on to his next port of call within a fixed number of days, Turner's time in Venice was limited. But it is clear from his sketchbooks that he did not waste a moment. Working in four books, he covered around one hundred and sixty pages with pencil sketches, frequently setting down several studies on each page and occasionally extending a panoramic view across a couple of sheets. He also found time, early one morning, to paint the small group of breathtaking watercolour studies that respond so directly to the special quality of Venetian light, searing the silhouettes of campaniles and domes into the memory (*figs.74–5, 77–8*). In contrast with his later visits, this material was all recorded on paper he had brought from England.[22] The pencil sketches are crisp, linear notations of architecture and shipping, the result of diligent observation and skilled draughtsmanship, demonstrating a fine coordination of hand and eye. From these, it is apparent that Turner had an exacting itinerary, and one made all the more demanding by the difficulties of executing many of his sketches while seated in a rocking gondola. His material covers all the major buildings around the Piazza and the Bacino di San Marco, the famous Arsenale and several viewpoints on the Grand Canal around the Rialto bridge (*figs.3, 72, 76*).

But Turner did not restrict his studies to the city's spectacular public face. Hakewill had indicated where he might find examples of the works

4
Dionisio Moretti (1790–?1834)
The Albergo Leon Bianco and Palazzo Grimani, on the East Side of the Grand Canal 1828
(plate 30 from *Il Canal Grande di Venezia, Descritto da Antonio Quadri*)

of the key triumvirate of sixteenth-century Venetian painting – Titian, Tintoretto and Veronese – and these pointers led him to the Accademia, the Palazzo Pisani and the church of Santa Maria Gloriosa dei Frari.[23] In suggesting the latter, however, Hakewill was providing misinformation, for the picture he told Turner to expect there, Titian's *St Peter Martyr* altarpiece, was actually to be found in the other major gothic church, Santi Giovanni e Paolo (see *figs.40–1*). This was a painting Turner had seen and greatly admired among Napoleon's booty in the Louvre in 1802; it had been returned to its original setting in Venice a year or two before. When Turner eventually located it, he made a copy of various details early in the sequence of his sketches, which seems to indicate that he was particularly keen to renew this acquaintance.[24]

He was drawn to the Accademia by another painting he had first seen in Paris, Tintoretto's *The Miracle of Saint Mark Freeing the Slave* 1548 (see *fig.48*). To ensure he found the art gallery, he made a note in one of his sketchbooks of the correct Italian phrase for asking directions to it.[25] However, his most significant studies of Tintoretto's work occurred not in the Accademia, but in the church and Scuola Grande di San Rocco, with its vast cycle of paintings spread across two floors. This experience was an unexpected revelation, and it is apparent from a number of rudimentary *aide-mémoires* in one of his notebooks that Turner must have stood transfixed by the imaginative ingenuity and powerful chiaroscuro evident in these paintings (see *fig.49*). Months later, after confronting the frescoes of Raphael and Michelangelo, he was prepared to state that Tintoretto's work was the most impressive he had encountered during his travels.[26]

The thumbnail sketches of various other paintings in the book reveal that he also entered the public rooms of the Doge's Palace, and his abiding admiration for Titian was clearly the reason for his visit to the Palazzo Barbarigo, on the Grand Canal not far from the Leon Bianco, which contained some of the artist's last paintings.

In contrast to these records of his untiring labours, his sketchbooks offer few clues as to how he spent his time once night fell. There were few other English residents or visitors at this period with whom he could have passed an evening (had he been of a more sociable disposition). The most notable temporary resident was, of course, Byron, who had lived sporadically in Venice since 1816. As they had friends in common, this would have been one of the rare occasions on which an introduction could have brought the two men together (see *fig.63*). Yet, during the crucial days in September 1819, Byron was away from Venice, and did not come back until the day after Turner departed.[27]

Whether planned, or purely fortuitously, the last day of Turner's stay coincided with the arrival of two Royal Academy colleagues, John Jackson and Francis Chantrey, both of whom were among his circle of friends and

were similarly bound for Rome.[28] Regrettably, the newspaper that records their presence gives no details of where they were planning to stay, but the popularity of the Leon Bianco makes it highly likely that they all met up briefly there.

The following morning, Monday 13 September, Turner moved on towards Rome, the true goal of his journey, and it was to be another fourteen years before he returned to Venice. With the exception of the great inspiration he was to draw from his studies of Titian and Tintoretto, this first visit proved to be no more remarkable in its fundamental character than his stopovers in countless other towns and cities across Europe. Indeed, the visual databank he compiled of the external appearance of Venice contributed to an already vast stock of raw material, which he continued to lay down on the off chance that he might want to develop an idea as a more finished image for the Academy exhibitions, or for other commissioned subjects. But, except in a handful of instances (*figs.64, 67, 94–5*), the concentrated body of first-hand impressions of the city, so painstakingly gathered, was to remain untapped until 1833.

There were, of course, the extraordinary watercolours, but they, too, seem to build on the techniques he had been evolving during the preceding years, rather than representing a complete and radical new direction. If truth be told, their scaled-down simplicity can equally be felt in some of the colour studies Turner made in the next few months at Naples and Tivoli, though neither of those settings stimulated such a perfect union of subject and the means of its representation.[29]

Many claims have been made for the immediate impact of Venetian light on Turner's subsequent work, as if it exerted a kind of palpable transformation. However, though it is difficult to quantify, the startling clarity of the 1819 studies cannot be shown to have been widely applied in his watercolours of the 1820s. If there was a change, it is more perceptible in his oil paintings, though the graduated azure skies that softly illuminate the major paintings of these years are surely principally indebted to the light of southern Italy, which he had greater opportunity to study.[30]

Quite why Turner felt no immediate desire to use his Venetian material for publicly exhibited works remains a puzzle. The popularity of Byron's *Childe Harold's Pilgrimage* and his other Venetian poems, such as *Beppo* (1818) and the *Ode on Venice* (published June 1819), should have lent a depiction of the city the kind of topicality that Turner so often deliberately courted. There is, however, evidence that he embarked on a large-scale view of the Rialto bridge in the early 1820s (*fig.5*). This has roughly the same dimensions as the immense *Rome from the Vatican*, one of his widest canvases, and may have been conceived as a pendant. Only the overarching outline of the bridge and the blank shapes of palaces can now be seen in this badly preserved painting, which was apparently abandoned when the

composition had been little more than sketched out. Presumably when Turner moved on to other new ideas he simply rolled up the canvas and forgot about it. But his failure to make more of his Venetian material during the 1820s may be attributed to the fact that his agenda was most frequently determined by his continuing rivalry with the spectre of Claude, which drew him again to Rome, rather than Venice, in 1828.

Turner's Art and Reputation in the 1830s

As the 1820s came to a close Turner attracted the new patronage of Hugh Andrew Johnstone Munro of Novar, a wealthy Scottish landowner, who became one of the most significant collectors of his mature work.[31] His first acquisition was probably the Titian-inspired painting *Venus and Adonis* (*fig.43*), which hung in his London home at 113 Park Street (near Grosvenor Square) among a range of canvases by, or attributed to, the great Venetians whom Turner sought to imitate. The documented details of Munro's life are regrettably scant, and offer little to explain the close connection that developed with Turner, other than that he was himself an amateur painter. He was notably fortunate in being one of the few people to accompany Turner on his travels.[32] Whether he undertook other European tours independently is not known, but, if the subjects he commissioned and bought from Turner are a fair reflection of his own interests, he seems to have been especially attracted to Italy and its history.

This is a significant point because it appears that it was Munro who provided the incentive for Turner's second trip to Venice, in 1833. Although the date of the tour is not specified, an anecdote included in both the first and the heavily revised second edition of Walter Thornbury's flawed biography of the artist states that Munro agreed to pay the travel expenses on the understanding that Turner would develop a watercolour of Venice for him.[33] He probably had in mind the kind of finished drawings Turner had produced in the late 1820s, which were engraved as illustrations for the *Keepsake* annual, such as those of Florence, Arona and Lake Albano.[34]

Unfortunately, it is not documented precisely when in 1833 Munro put forward his proposal, but clearly it has an interesting bearing on the appearance of two small paintings of Venice by Turner at the Royal Academy's exhibition that spring (*figs.6, 103*). This was the first time he had exhibited views of Venice, which suggests two possibilities. Could it be that it was actually Munro's encouragement that stimulated Turner to delve into his Venetian sketches now that he had evidence of the commercial potential of this material? Or is it more likely that Munro's commission was a response to the exhibits themselves?

By the time of Turner's second visit, Venice was becoming a fashionable subject, not just at the Society of Painters in Water Colours, which tended to display a preponderance of topographical studies, but also

5
*The Rialto c.*1820
Oil on canvas, 177.5 x 335.3
Tate (No5543; B&J 245)

6
William Miller (1796–1882) after Turner's untraced painting *Ducal Palace, Venice* 1833 (B&J 352)
The Piazzetta, Venice 1854
Engraving (R 674)

at the Royal Academy and the British Institution, where the adoption of a literary source, such as Shakespeare or Byron, was the excuse for a Venetian setting (*fig.60*). Similarly, images of Venice began to appear regularly in the hugely popular publications known as the 'annuals'. These handsome volumes were usually issued towards the end of each year, with an eye on the Christmas market, and were composed of images by contemporary artists (*figs.70–1*) alongside an uneven blend of literary pieces, generally tinged with the broad brush of sentimentality.[35] Though other artists played their part in the shift towards an eventual visual saturation of Venetian imagery, much of the groundwork in each of these forums was the achievement of two men: Samuel Prout and Clarkson Stanfield.

By 1833 Stanfield had already secured notable royal and aristocratic patronage, though he was still not a full member of the Academy. His promise of future achievements made him an artist that many were watching closely, not least Turner, who was always acutely observant of his contemporaries, especially those who represented even the remotest threat to his hold on British landscape painting. During these years Turner's jealousy of his status sometimes took the form of playful attempts to outshine the adjacent exhibits of his colleagues in the Royal Academy shows.[36] Although incidents of this kind were a source of resigned amusement among the Academicians, they were not always appreciated by those who felt Turner had landed a direct hit rather than a warning shot across the bows. Thus, in 1833, the critics were inclined to condemn him for his depictions of Venice, as it was felt that these trespassed on a subject more widely associated with Stanfield.

It is illuminating to consider this response in conjunction with contemporary accusations that Turner's dominance of the art world was harmful to other artists (see also p.105). Such concerns were especially relevant in 1833, when a court case was pending in which Turner sought to defend his right to approve reproductions made after his images. Though a valid point was at stake about artistic integrity, it was all too easy for his opponents to imply that Turner was motivated by baser, money-grubbing instincts.[37]

His celebrity as a producer of book illustrations had begun with a set of twenty-four vignettes for the 1830 edition of Samuel Rogers's poem *Italy* (*fig.64*), and the considerable commercial success of that publication forced other publishers to acknowledge that Turner's participation in a project was an indispensable guarantee of enhanced sales. However, the competing demands of publishers during the early 1830s meant that the market was rapidly inundated with images from Turner's hand. In 1833 alone, print collectors were offered the latest instalments of six different publications containing his works, with two other series in the course of preparation.[38]

Significantly, Turner's skilful creation of these detailed designs, which

contrast so dramatically with the extravagantly coloured and bravura finish of his oil paintings, played a vital role in sustaining his reputation throughout the 1830s, while also shoring up his financial independence. For, though he managed to sell around twenty-five of the sixty-two paintings he exhibited between 1830 and 1840, few of these were what Turner himself would have considered major works. This point was grasped by a commentator in the *Athenaeum*, who recognised the necessity of the work for book publishers, and protested in May 1833 that even though Turner was 'the noblest landscape painter of any age, [he] cannot sell one of his poetic pictures: he rolls them up, and lays them aside, after they have been the wonder of the Exhibition'.[39]

By this stage the critics were increasingly vociferous about what they perceived to be the eccentricity of Turner's ever-more imprecise style and his poetic use of colour. His reputation was, therefore, divided between those who were captivated by his painterly alchemy and those who, because they did not understand it, sought only to mock. The latter needed the flimsiest of excuses to attack him, and so in 1833 they seized the opportunity provided by his apparent incursion on Stanfield's territory.

Even though Turner's two 1833 Venetian pictures were the smallest of his exhibits that year, they drew a disproportionate amount of critical attention. And while neither was hung in the same room as Stanfield's painting (*fig.102*), it was widely reported and agreed that Turner completed the larger of the two (*fig.103*) in direct competition with it. Confirmation that Turner's motives were indeed expansionist comes in the second picture (*fig.6*), which can be seen as a deliberate attempt to outdo the work of another contemporary artist, in this case the recently deceased Richard Parkes Bonington (*fig.19*). Thus it seems reasonably clear that it was through these local influences that Turner awoke at last to the potential of Venice for his own art, and at the same time this realisation forced him to address Canaletto's achievement, even as he sought to surpass it.

Venice in 1833

By the time the Academy exhibition closed, Turner was once again on his way to Venice (see pp.31–2). On this occasion the *Gazzetta Privilegiata* recorded only his arrival on 9 September, noting that he had come from Vienna. The date of his departure does not appear in the newspaper, but can be inferred from one of his sketchbooks, which contains an inscription that seems to indicate that he was in Bozen by the 22nd, a circumstance that means he can have spent little more than a week in Venice.[40]

By this date his appearance frequently struck those he encountered as incompatible with their (possibly Romantic) notions of what an artist should look like (see *fig.13*). He was short and seems rarely to have been smartly dressed, apparently having more in common with a sea captain than a member of the Royal Academy. A little earlier in 1833, for example, the *Morning Chronicle* had characterised him as a 'tubby little man' who showed all the 'marks of feeding well', and there are many similar disparaging comments about his lack of physical distinction.[41] However, though his constitution was fundamentally strong, he was increasingly affected by illness. Indeed, one could speculate that he was attracted to some of the places on his itineraries during the 1830s and 1840s because they offered the restorative waters so fashionable as cures in the first half of the nineteenth century.[42] A concern for his well-being may also have been a factor in his decision to choose the comforts of the Grande Albergo l'Europa on his return to Venice in 1833, instead of the Leon Bianco. It has not proved possible to establish the hotel's rates at this date, nor how they compared with those of the Leon Bianco, which Stanfield had considered 'expensive' in 1830. But the Europa's higher grading and its attractive location would undoubtedly have increased the cost of Turner's accommodation. However, though he was travelling at Munro's expense that year, it would be unreasonable to accuse him of being profligate with his patron's funds, as he chose the same hotel in 1840, when he was paying his own way.

The Hotel Europa (*fig.7*) was then situated in the late-fifteenth-century Palazzo Giustinian-Morosini, at the mouth of the Grand Canal, opposite the Punta della Dogana. In the maze of streets immediately behind the building Turner would have found the church of San Moise, while the adjacent Dandolo palace, previously the venue of the gaming salon known as the Ridotto, was at that time used for balls and theatrical spectacles.[43] In 1819 he had made several sketches from the end of the Calle del Ridotto beside the palazzo, and must have noted then its attractive location, looking out across the Bacino towards the island of San Giorgio Maggiore. Instead of offering this classic prospect, the rooms he was given seem to have been high up at the back of the hotel, surveying the city to the north, though this did not deter him from exploring the views from its rooftops (*fig.142*).

Later guests of the Europa included Théophile Gautier, George Eliot, Giuseppe Verdi and Marcel Proust, but in 1833 the dates of Turner's stay partly coincided with those of François-René, Vicomte de Chateaubriand, the French Romantic writer and politician. This was also Chateaubriand's second visit to Venice, and it is interesting to note that he too was more captivated by the city on this later occasion. Though he recorded several fascinating impressions in his posthumously published *Mémoires d'outre-tombe*, his individual concerns seem to have prevented him from taking note of the shabby English artist also resident at the Europa.[44]

As in 1819, Turner's time in Venice was evidently spent in an intensive bout of sightseeing, which took him to parts of the city he had previously neglected, such as the eastern district of Castello, near the church of San Pietro, and the long northern waterfront of the Fondamente Nove.[45]

In seeking out these places, he also penetrated more deeply into the side canals, and these routes introduced him to the churches of San Martino and Santa Giustina as well as to Santa Maria Formosa.[46] Many of his sketches are annotated with the names of the buildings he had recorded, for which information he was presumably indebted to his gondolier.

Another subject Turner had neglected in 1819 was the interior of San Marco, and so this forms the focus of a small sequence of sketches.[47] Some of these attempt to transcribe the rich surface decoration of mosaics and precious stones, but the cursory nature of these studies suggests either that he did not truly engage with the architecture or that he was deterred from giving it greater scrutiny by his habitual dislike of being observed sketching.

Turner's interest in the art of Venice led him to copy a print by Canaletto (*fig.24*), further evidence of his continuing interest in his great predecessor.[48] More predictably, a sketch of the interior of Santi Giovanni e Paolo indicates that he went again to study Titian's altarpiece (*fig.41*), but, surprisingly, the only other painting he transcribed on this visit seems to be by (or after) Van Dyck, an artist who was very much in his mind during the early 1830s because of his prominence in the collection at Petworth House, where Turner was often the guest of Lord Egremont.[49]

During the course of this visit he created a further substantial body of pencil memoranda, covering nearly two hundred sheets, most of which were recorded in the plump 'Venice' sketchbook (*fig.112*), which he had probably bought in Vienna as he travelled southwards.[50] The beginning and end of the visit, however, are documented fleetingly in two further books (*figs.8, 83*). During the late 1820s, instead of depending on a large sketchbook for more complete compositions, Turner seems to have resorted to bundles of loose paper on which to jot down ideas that he developed subsequently in colour. Whether he did this in Venice in 1833 has been the subject of much speculation, and various attempts have been made to link some of the large body of watercolours in the artist's bequest with this tour.[51]

Among the sheets that have most often been associated with 1833 are the batch of nearly forty nocturnal studies on various types of buff, grey and brownish paper,[52] some of which were made from the roof of the Europa hotel (*figs.149–50; see Appendix*). The principal argument for dating them to this year seemed to be that the aerial vantage point can be connected in essence, if not in strict topography, to the 1836 painting *Juliet and her Nurse* (*fig.61*), which looks down on the Piazza and San Marco at night. Moreover, both the studies and the painting feature bursts of light from fireworks.[53] While this conclusion has the advantage of these compositional elements, it has remained somewhat in doubt because of Turner's terse handling of paint, which has more in common with his final style of the 1840s. The argument for dating the 'brown paper' studies to 1833 has now, however,

been crucially undermined by the identification of a group of views of the German riverside town of Hals, which were evidently made on the same sheets, and which have been securely dated by Cecilia Powell to 1840.[54]

To complicate the dating of the watercolours still further, it seems probable that some of those painted on grey paper may have been executed during the 1833 visit. This dove-grey paper would have been ideal for use in bright Italian light: its less reflective surface and flat tone would have assisted the artist by absorbing some of the sun's brilliance. The current 1840 dating for these sheets was arrived at, quite reasonably, by Andrew Wilton, who concluded that, since they sometimes feature scaffolding on the Campanile of San Marco, they must date from 1839–40, when the structure was undergoing restoration.[55] Though this argument still holds true for several items in the group, recent research has shown that Turner was using sheets of grey paper between London and Venice in 1833,[56] which necessitates a reappraisal of whether any of the colour studies may be earlier than previously thought. In fact, at least three of the designs set out the compositions of paintings exhibited at the Royal Academy before the 1840 visit (figs.82, 111, 180), though these could also be interpreted as instances of Turner revisiting a subject he had already treated. More significantly, another of them apparently includes the campanile of Sant'Angelo, which was demolished in 1837 (fig.190), so that this study, at least, must date from 1833. But, if this is correct, it means that stylistic similarities among the watercolours cannot be relied upon as the sole indicator of when they were painted.

Venetian Paintings of the 1830s: Poetry and Pairings

Once Turner was back in London, he seems not to have been in any hurry to complete the promised watercolour for Munro as remuneration for the cost of his travels. In fact, sometime during the winter of 1833–4 he began work instead on a large oil painting (fig.104). This was the first of three Venetian subjects, painted on canvases measuring around 90 x 120 cm, one of which appeared in each of the following annual Academy exhibitions (figs.61, 109). If the 1834 picture Venice was actually intended for Munro, as seems likely in view of Turner's immediate obligations, it is clearly noteworthy that he chose not to acquire it (contemporary anecdotes suggest that Munro was dissatisfied with the Venetian painting he did acquire from Turner, though this was actually the picture of 1835). Venice was actually sold for £350, during the first week of the exhibition, to Henry McConnel, a Manchester-based textile manufacturer and one of the new patrons, mostly self-made men, who supported the final phase of Turner's career.[57]

Like his other Venetian subjects of the 1830s, the picture depicts one of the most famous views of the city in a way that represents another attempt to imitate Canaletto – albeit on Turner's own terms. The viewpoints he

7
Samuel Prout (1783–1852)
Entrance to Grand Canal, with the Palazzo Giustinian (the Hotel Europa) 1824
Pencil, 26.5 x 37
Private collection

8 (cat.80)
Views on the Grand Canal: the steps of Santa Maria della Salute; and a view towards the Rialto bridge 1833
Pencil, 10.9 x 20.3 each
From the 'Venice up to Trento' sketchbook
Tate (TB CCCXII ff.2v, 3; D31600, D31601)

adopts, for example, are generally lower, allowing him to give freer rein to the play of reflections in his limpid washes of colour. But though the pictures are as densely peopled as Canaletto's, there is a sense of suspended animation, of stilted expectancy, about them. There is, furthermore, an element of paradox in Turner's inclusion of the landmarks of contemporary Venice, such as the new lighthouses on the harbour of San Giorgio Maggiore, which seem to conflict with the costumes of his figures, which are more redolent of an unspecific moment in the past, creating an ambiguity about how to interpret the pictures. The effect is cogently described by the historian Margaret Plant: 'For Turner, the city is written in the past – not imaged in a spirit of nostalgia, but through a dialectic of remembering – the present yields to the past and its richness, present-day detail and its sounds are muffled.'[58]

Though this combination of elements seems not to have appealed to Munro in 1834, he acquired the two Venetian exhibits of 1835 and 1836. It is unlikely that either of these was received as part of the understanding covering the 1833 travel expenses. Had Turner parted with an oil painting rather than a watercolour, it would have been an excessively generous means of thanking Munro for his support, for even as commissioned works these paintings would have been worth the considerable sum of £300 (£50 less than anything bought from the Academy exhibitions). It is hard to convert this to an exact contemporary figure, but, to put it into perspective, one of McConnel's mill workers would have been paid a mere eleven shillings for a sixty-nine-hour week and so would have had to work for more than ten and a half years to pay for a £300 painting.[59]

Curiously, Turner seems to have been slightly disdainful of the immediate success of his Venetian paintings. After securing 200 guineas from Robert Vernon for the 1833 picture of Canaletto in Venice (fig.103), he raised the price for the subsequent, admittedly slightly larger canvases, remarking of this to his friend George Jones that 'if they will have such scraps instead of important pictures, they must pay for them'.[60] It is a revealing anecdote in one sense, but these prices were actually no higher than those for his other works of the same dimensions, which he maintained at these fixed rates for around thirty years.

The second of Munro's acquisitions, the celebrated *Juliet and her Nurse* (fig.61), represents a significant development in Turner's treatment of Venetian subject matter, introducing ravishing nocturnal effects that are striking but more understated than those in the two canvases of 1835 depicting the burning of the Houses of Parliament.[61] As is well known, however, the picture was attacked with stinging vitriol by the critic of *Blackwood's Magazine*, an assault which in turn unleashed Ruskin's righteous fury to defend Turner.[62] Yet the painting did, in fact, also receive reviews that were as complimentary as any of those lavished on the earlier Venetian

pictures. A measure of the painting's success with Turner's peers can be gleaned from the remarks of Constable, not always a charitable critic, who believed that Turner had excelled himself with his 1836 exhibits: 'he seems to paint with tinted steam, so evanescent, and so airy'. He was, nevertheless, also alert to the difficulties inherent in Turner's bold stylistic development, and noted insightfully: 'The publick thinks he is laughing at them, and so they laugh at him in return.'[63]

From the early 1830s Turner frequently prepared his exhibits as linked pairs, a tendency that affects most of his Venetian paintings. This practice has long traditions, but was rooted for Turner in the commissioned views he undertook in the 1790s of his aristocratic patrons' country houses, where he introduced contrasting atmospheric effects, or times of day, as a means of animating an otherwise lowly type of work.[64] In the mature paintings the connections are often quickly discernible from the title, or in terms of the shared subject matter (figs.197–8). Elsewhere the adoption of an identical format for images focusing on vaguely similar themes seems to have been Turner's way of making a connection. Where this was the case, he appears to have insisted on his pendants being exhibited in the same room at the Academy.[65] This provided the means of asserting a specific meaning in this public context. Practical financial imperatives, however, more often than not compelled him to break up the couplings he had devised in the studio, since few patrons would have wanted to take on groups of works unless they had been specifically commissioned to suit their particular circumstances (as was the series of four landscapes painted for the dining

9
Wreckers – Coast of Northumberland, with a Steam-Boat assisting a Ship off Shore
exhibited Royal Academy 1834
Oil on canvas, 91.4 x 121.9
Yale Center for British Art, New Haven
(B&J 357)

The contrast Turner deployed most often was the simple one of past and present, though this was not merely a means of suggesting disjunctions, as he was frequently concerned to suggest continuities. This is the ostensible link between the Shakespearian *Juliet and her Nurse* (*fig.61*) and the view of Rome he exhibited with it in 1836 (*fig.10*). Both were acquired by Munro, who is supposed to have commissioned the Roman subject specifically in order to have a modern view of the city.[68] The resulting elevated, sun-drenched depiction of the banks of the Tiber at noon is the perfect counterpart to the moonlit panorama of Venice, and introduces the yellow-blue, hot-cold opposition that is the staple ingredient of Turner's later pairs (long before he is supposed to have absorbed this principle from the 1840 translation of Goethe's *Fahrbenlehre*). Having established the images as opposing states, he created formal links through the strong verticals of tree and campanile. Similarly, the foregrounds of both works feature a young woman tended by an older figure, and each is linked to contemporary perceptions of the city in question that juxtapose the sacred and the profane: Rome, with religious conformism; Venice, with nocturnal romance.

Though this was the only time that Turner made a direct comparison between the legacies of the two great cities of the Italian peninsula, an offshoot of the confrontation was the ensuing series of canvases in which he further explored the continuing resonances of Rome's past.[69] Indeed, his renewed interest in Rome in the later 1830s was so complete that it temporarily eclipsed Venice as one of his favoured subjects, though not before he had painted his largest image of it in 1837 for the Academy's first exhibition in its new premises in Trafalgar Square (*fig.58*). This, too, is set in a version of the past drawn from Shakespeare, revealing that at this stage Turner remained content to engage primarily with the city at second-hand, as it had been conjured up in his imagination by his literary compatriots.

This steadfast connection with literature can be attributed to his involvement with the production of book illustrations during the 1830s, which may explain why it was also in this decade that he more regularly appended snatches of verse to the titles of his pictures in the Academy's catalogues. Since 1798 Turner had used poetic quotations to infuse his images with more profound meanings. As well as Milton and Byron, he often quoted from his own composition *The Fallacies of Hope*, which was never published other than in this fragmented form (see pp.63, 227). For the most part, these snippets are bleak, pessimistic utterances, heavily imbued with the eighteenth-century rhetorical devices Turner had absorbed from James Thomson, another of his favourite writers. Inevitably, the impenetrable obscurity of these poetic commentaries bewildered critics and admirers alike, and it seems that the Academy's officials, possibly acting for his good, were sometimes minded to suppress them (see p.243 and *fig.12*).[70]

room at Petworth House). Most collectors preferred to create their own couplings, buying a picture at one exhibition and commissioning a companion, which would appear at the next.

As far as Turner's paintings of Venice are concerned, the majority are of the first type of pairing, where the titles assert a basic contrast between morning and evening, something especially prevalent in his latest exhibits (*figs.264–8*). There are also pictures that are paired by subject or underlying theme (*figs.229, 248*). But, given the speculative nature of producing exhibits without a guaranteed sale, Turner may have avoided being overemphatic about suggesting a pairing, which in some cases makes these connections less certain. The 1834 painting *Venice*, for example, is most often understood as the pair to *Keelman heaving in Coals by Night* (*fig.105*), which McConnel commissioned a year later.[66] As linked pendants, they encourage the viewer to contrast the riches of Venice with the industrial might of contemporary Britain. The two works share a prevailing sense of calm that is heightened through the deliberate echo of an open expanse of untroubled water. Yet when it was first exhibited, the tranquil Venetian canvas would actually have been seen in conjunction with, and as the desired contrast to, the sublime *Wreckers – Coast of Northumberland* (*fig.9*), a coastal subject, also set in the north-east of England.[67] Despite the presence of a steamboat, a possible symbol of progress, the image is a stark reminder of the precarious nature of human ambitions. This meaning, in conjunction with the *Venice* picture, would surely have been even more compelling than that of the eventual pairing, where the viewer is not forced to consider the specifics of loss and destruction.

10
Rome from Mount Aventine
exhibited Royal Academy 1836
Oil on canvas, 91.6 x 124.6
National Galleries of Scotland,
Edinburgh (B&J 366)

As well as the five late Venetian canvases, which he intended should be enriched by extracts from *The Fallacies of Hope*, Turner made direct allusion to Byron's *Childe Harold's Pilgrimage* when exhibiting Venetian subjects in 1840 and 1844 *(figs.113, 263)*. If he had by this date shaken off the stylistic influence of Canaletto, it is evident that Byron's vision of Venice, splendid amid the evidence of its ruined mortality, continued to be a vital stimulus, even if the resulting images are invariably as much concerned with the living city as its shroud.

Venice in 1840

Turner's final visit to Venice took place during the late summer of 1840. A few months earlier his submissions to the Academy exhibition had included two views of the city, which anticipate the looser handling he was to achieve henceforth in his depictions of Venice. These were the distinctly Byronic *Venice, the Bridge of Sighs (fig.113)* and a bustling view of the Bacino *(fig.110)*, which was acquired by the wealthy collector John Sheepshanks, whose fortune derived from the cloth-making mills of his native Yorkshire. It is probable therefore that, as in 1833, Turner's decision to undertake a further visit to Venice arose in part from a renewed sense of the commercial possibilities of Venetian subject matter.[71]

It seems that, for much of his journey to Venice that year, he was accompanied by his cousin the solicitor Henry Harpur and his wife Eleanor (as suggested by Cecilia Powell on p.33).[72] According to the *Gazzetta Privilegiata*, he arrived in Venice on Thursday 20 August and remained there until Thursday 3 September, exactly two weeks later, when he set off for Trieste, making this his longest sojourn in the city.[73]

Once again he stayed at the Europa hotel, this time in a lofty room, high on the north-east side of the building *(fig.141)*, which effectively became a temporary studio, allowing him to make his remarkable series of watercolours *(figs.143–150)*. As well as the monuments, Turner's eye was captivated by the neighbouring balconies. These open, yet secluded spaces had traditionally provided Venetian women with an element of privacy, without precluding the possibilities for assignations. The presence of women in Turner's watercolours, some of them in a state of undress, is clearly an indication that the sixty-five-year-old had not lost his sexual appetite. Indeed, it appears that his travels provided him with an opportunity to gratify his desires, and that Venice, in particular, may have been a destination he associated with erotic possibility.[74] Once more this perception was evidently rooted in his appreciation of Byron's writings. Several of the watercolours from the 1840 trip are annotated with attempts at poetry, and though it is not always possible to transcribe these, the words 'Beppo' or 'Beppo Club' recur on a handful *(figs.142, 195, 249)*. This alludes to the title of Byron's playful evocation of the licentiousness of

Venetian carnival, and the custom by which women took a lover in the socially approved form of a *cavaliere servente*. Though the tale purported to be set in the past, when 'the sea-born city was in all her glory', Byron noted that 'They've pretty faces yet, those same Venetians, | Black eyes, arch'd brows, and sweet expressions still' – sentiments with which Turner apparently concurred.[75]

In spite of such distractions, he was as diligent as ever in pursuing his studies of the city, though those he made in pencil are frequently schematic, as if set down in a hasty personal shorthand. Ruskin and Finberg both despaired of making sense of his subjects and viewpoints, but the pencil sketches sometimes record the first ideas for the later oil paintings. They are also evidence of Turner's indefatigability in pursuing his observations. For, while other artists put their work aside as the afternoon came to a close, he carried on sketching determinedly until the absence of light made his job impossible. He was observed hard at work one evening by the watercolour artist William Callow, as the sun set behind San Giorgio Maggiore. The twenty-eight-year-old Callow was apparently a fellow guest at the Europa, where he and Turner 'sat opposite at meals and entered into conversation'.[76]

As on previous visits, Turner's sketches and watercolours reveal that he spent much of his time drifting across the waters of the Bacino, and passing up the palace-lined canyon of the Grand Canal *(fig.87)*. The chief novelty in his sketches this year was his concentration on the westerly reaches of the wide Giudecca canal *(fig.11)* and his renewed interest in the range of craft peculiar to Venice. But he also revisited many familiar places, such as the Frari and the adjacent Scuole Grande di San Rocco; and on the other side of the Grand Canal he went back again to Santi Giovanni e Paolo, discovering in addition the churches of Madonna dell'Orto and the Gesuiti in the Cannaregio district to the north. All in all, he used up a further two hundred or so pages of his sketchbooks during his two-week stay (see *fig.116*). This meant that the full extent of his compendium of Venetian topography amounted to some five hundred and fifty pages of pencil sketches from three visits; and because most sheets carry several notations, the total number of sketches made in Venice probably exceeds a thousand.

In addition to these mainly linear notations, he executed perhaps as many as one hundred and fifty watercolours, many of which are built up over preliminary observations made in pencil that were evidently begun on the spot. Certain of these may eventually prove to be related to the 1833 visit, as noted above. However, the majority must have been completed during or shortly after Turner's stay in 1840. In addition to the batches of loose sheets, some of which were toned rather than white, Turner filled two of his now standard 'roll' sketchbooks. Made up of sheets of Whatman paper, and bound in soft covers instead of the elegant but heavy leather-

backed books he had once selected, these considerably lightened his luggage and seem to have encouraged him to work directly from a motif more regularly in his final travels. The second of the Venetian roll sketchbooks contained a number of images, now widely dispersed, that were more fully developed than those in its companion. Though these have sometimes been considered 'finished' works, it seems that none was offered to collectors during Turner's lifetime and that no series of watercolour drawings, comparable with the late views of Switzerland, was ever produced.[77]

A large selection of the watercolours is illustrated and discussed in greater detail in the latter half of this book, but it should be observed, among these more general comments, that the sustained brilliance of this series has come to epitomise for many people the idea of 'late Turner'. These works are rich in colour, both evasive and elusive in their treatment of specific forms, and pervaded by layers of limpid wash that unite each image. Though such qualities are more accentuated because these are studies rather than finished works, none of these features is, of course, unique to Turner's Venetian watercolours: he brought much the same ingredients to his depictions of Britain in the 1830s, notably in grimy scenes of the industrial English Midlands, and afterwards to the Swiss lakes and passes. It is perhaps merely that these characteristics are so well suited to his subject, to the essentially mirage-like and vaporous character of Venice itself. And it is this sense of a dematerialised reality, combined with a physical sense of the air between objects, that is probably the most radical quality of the watercolours, though this too is common to much of the late work. In any event, all of this depends on Turner's fundamental engagement with colour rather than form, something that was recognised by Finberg, who noted its 'unearthly brilliance' in the Venetian watercolours: 'It is absolute colour chosen and used as a poetical medium. But though it is arbitrary the colour is not merely pretty. It is exquisite, and full of surprises, subtle variations and memories of things seen and loved; so that it creates its own atmosphere, an atmosphere of poetry, of love, and of infinite suggestion.'[78]

Marketing Atmosphere: the Paintings of the 1840s

A few years after this last visit to Venice, Turner was discussing his recent work with Ruskin, an occasion on which he apparently remarked that 'atmosphere is my style'.[79] This was in 1844, by which point his Venetian subjects had abandoned the detailed presentation of the cityscape in his earlier canvases, offering instead glorious prospects over expanses of water, on the peripheries of which shimmer the distant towers of the city (as parodied in *fig.*12). Turner's statement was consequently a very fitting description of his latest paintings, seeming to identify, unequivocally,

11 (cat.82)
Sketches on the Giudecca Canal near Santa Marta,
the Gesuati and Santi Biagio e Cataldo 1840
Pencil, 12.3 x 17.3 each
From the 'Venice and Bozen' sketchbook
Tate (TB CCCXIII ff.32v, 33; D31853, D31854)

the importance of the more transitory nuances of light and sensation to his artistic aims. Looked at another way, however, his words may have been a simple recognition of earlier and continuing criticisms of his work. As far back as 1816, for example, William Hazlitt had objected to Turner's tendency to produce 'abstractions of aerial perspective, and representations not so properly of the objects of nature as of the medium, through which they are seen … Some one said of his landscapes that they were *pictures of nothing, and very like*.'[80] But though Turner was clearly aware of these perceived shortcomings, his comment to Ruskin could also be understood as a profession of defiance. Indeed, within a year or so of this conversation he responded to a collector's reservations about the indistinctness of an 1832 canvas by declaring that 'indistinctness is my fault', a remark that is just as likely to be a humorous quip of self-justification as an acceptance of his failings (the final word was, moreover, for many years thought to have been 'forte').[81]

Thus, though there have been frequent suggestions that a deterioration in Turner's eyesight is the true reason for the increasing lack of precision in his later paintings,[82] he was clearly very conscious of the change others discerned in his handling and nevertheless obstinately continued with his looser, more indeterminate way of rendering the world in paint. A point that has often been made is that this major development takes place in Turner's watercolours before it occurs in his oil paintings. This is indeed the case with the Venetian subjects of 1840, where the colour studies he painted in the city are more pared down and insubstantial than the two oil paintings he had exhibited a couple of months earlier. But there was evidently a need for Turner to allow his public to adjust to this leap forward.

By the 1840s the Royal Academy audience was increasingly accustomed to pictures with a smooth finish that were rich in detail. Turner's paintings, by contrast, require that the viewer stand at a distance to allow the elements of the image to come together, and yet at the same time they insist on recognition of the physical properties of the painted surface itself. The critic of the *Athenaeum* noted this in response to Turner's Venetian exhibits of 1842 (figs.220, 257): 'As pieces of effect, too, these works are curious; close at hand, a splashed palette – an arm's length distant, a clear and delicate shadowing forth of a scene made up of crowded and minute objects!'[83] Similar sentiments about these hardly illegible images appeared in the *Literary Gazette*, which contended that they 'have a gorgeous *ensemble*, and [were] produced by wonderful art, but they mean nothing. They are produced as if by throwing handfuls of white, and blue, and red, at the canvas, letting what chanced to stick, stick; and then shadowing in some forms to make the appearance of a picture.'[84]

Such comments might suggest that the pictures Turner painted of Venice in the wake of the 1840 tour were as much derided as some of his

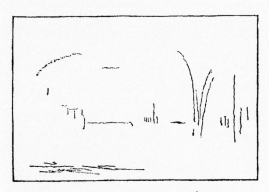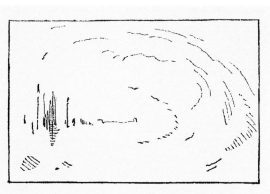

VENICE BY GASLIGHT—GOING TO THE BALL.
MS. Fallacies of Hope. (*An unpublished Poem.*)—TURNER.

VENICE BY DAYLIGHT—RETURNING FROM THE BALL.
MS. Fallacies of Hope. (*An unpublished Poem.*)—

more obviously challenging contemporary works. But, in fact, they initially tended to garner mostly favourable reviews. The *Art Union*, for example, wrote that 'Venice was surely built to be painted by Canaletto and Turner' and declared that 'The Venetian pictures are now among the best this artist paints.'[85] Further proof that the general opinion of these subjects was positive can be found in the fact that, of the eleven pictures Turner sold at the Academy between 1840 and 1844 (from a total of thirty-one exhibits), seven were of Venice.

All but one of the post-1840 Venetian canvases were of the same dimensions – roughly 62 by 92 cm – and were available at 200 guineas if specifically commissioned, or 250 guineas if bought from the walls of the exhibition.[86] Turner's shift to this smaller format as the standard for his paintings of Venice occurred immediately before the last visit, and was a response to market forces. Indeed, the more domestic proportions were probably specified by Sheepshanks when he commissioned his view of Venice in 1840.[87]

Given Turner's alleged frustration with his clients' preference for Venetian 'scraps' over his more ambitious paintings in the 1830s, one might interpret the adoption of smaller canvases for the later depictions of the city as a desire to play down this line of work, thereby encouraging the public to recognise the significance of the aspects of contemporary British life on which he focused in his larger subjects. Taking this point to its most extreme conclusion, a cynic might argue that the nineteen late Venetian canvases were essentially no more than a safety net that acted as a deliberate means of meeting public taste and ensuring income from the annual display at the Academy. With their sparkling colours and their

12
Caricatures of Turner's later Venetian paintings in *Punch*, June 1845

haunting stillness, these works could perhaps be seen as an effortless introduction to Turner's art. But to dismiss them in this way denies his profound personal engagement with the image and idea of Venice itself, and the considerable pleasure that pervades his work in watercolour, which is played out in the sequence of oil paintings. Moreover, Turner never truly sated his own appetite for Venetian subjects, and, despite his extensive knowledge of the city's topography, he was apparently considering yet another visit in the summer of 1845, though this was prevented by official duties and ill health.[88]

There is some truth, however, in the assertion that the Venetian pictures appealed to a type of patron who might otherwise not have acquired works from Turner at this stage in his career. Curiously, Munro of Novar bought none of the late Venetian exhibits. This left the field open to other steady patrons, such as Robert Vernon, who bought a picture in 1842 (fig.220), and B.G. Windus, who only became interested in the Venetian pictures in 1844 (figs.263–5). Another work was apparently 'painted expressly' for Turner's friend the sculptor Sir Francis Chantrey (fig.197).[89] Otherwise, those who were attracted to the Venetian subjects were mostly new Turner collectors: Elhanan Bicknell, Edwin Bullock, William Wethered, Frances McCracken, William John Broderip and Charles Birch. Once again these were primarily men who had made their money from industry, whether from iron, textiles or whale blubber.[90]

To this group should be added the more familiar names of the Ruskins (father and son), who were greatly impressed by the sequence of paintings produced between 1840 and 1843. Though they did not acquire a Venetian subject until 1847, when they bought The Grand Canal (fig.58) from a dealer for the vastly inflated price of £840, it is clear from an entry in Ruskin's diary for 1844 that they must have given the impression that they were interested in taking The Sun of Venice going to Sea (fig.248), though they had also enthused over St Benedetto, looking towards Fusina (fig.211).[91] The possibility that they might acquire one or the other would explain why Turner had not sold these appealing works during the twelve months since they were exhibited, and why they remained in his collection, unsold, at the time of his death.

One benefit to Turner of the new collectors was that several of them were civic-minded, keen to share the trophies they had acquired with the gallery-going public in their native cities. McConnel and Bullock, for example, lent their new purchases to exhibitions in Manchester and Birmingham respectively, in the same year that they had been shown in London, thereby rapidly bringing Turner's latest Venetian subjects to a wider audience (figs.104, 229).

Turner was deeply aware of the need to gain exposure for his work beyond metropolitan London, and his involvement in the engraving process had already brought affordable reproductions to thousands in Britain, continental Europe and America. But until the late 1830s the images circulating after his designs were primarily based on watercolours that had been made specifically with a view to their translation into black-and-white prints, and only a few of his oil paintings had been engraved. By this date, however, it was clear that there was a healthy market for large-scale prints of the most celebrated works in recent Academy exhibitions. In attempting to exploit this, Turner and his publishers selected two Venetian pictures among the dozen or so images that were published between 1838 and 1842. The first of the whole series was the 1835 view from the Salute steps (fig.109), which was engraved by William Miller as The Grand Canal (1838; R 648). Converting the finely nuanced effects in this and other late paintings was a laborious process that usually occupied an engraver for up to two years, a delay that meant a publisher's investment in what had seemed topical and fashionable was not always rewarded once the print was available. Publishers were also expected to pay Turner around £100 to cover the copyright, and he generally stipulated that he receive fifty proofs of each image, some of which had to be the finest early impressions.[92] Given the palpable risk of failure in such undertakings, one can understand the resentment that grew up towards Turner's hard-headed professionalism.

The difficulties of creating even a perfunctory reproduction of one of his paintings were self-evident to his contemporaries, though because of his close supervision of the process, some of the details that would otherwise be lost in a Turnerian haze were refined and more precisely delineated in the engravings. In spite of this, the engraver of one of the Venetian paintings was 'puzzled with the obscurer parts' and mistakenly 'turned some ships into houses'. This probably refers to George Hollis's engraving St Mark's Place, Venice (1842; R 654; based on fig.61), where the distant features of the Riva degli Schiavoni and the adjacent shipping merge. In his version of the anecdote, Thornbury concluded that, if Turner noticed this error he probably overlooked it, as the result 'did quite as well … The picture was not meant to be topographically correct, but to be a beautiful dream, true in the feeling it conveyed'.[93]

The success of the large engravings was perhaps a mixed blessing, for the clarity of these black-and-white translations of Turner's images served only to highlight his increasing adherence to the evocation of atmosphere in preference to a Canaletto-like descriptive realism. Even among his supporters this tendency was noted with some reservation, and by 1846 the critic of the Art Union was inclined to speculate that engravings of the two Venetian subjects Turner exhibited that year might be considerably more distinct, and hence 'more really agreeable', than the paintings themselves.[94]

If this progressive slackening of focus was not so firmly established as a feature of his work by the 1830s, one might be tempted to leap to the conclusion that Turner's handling became more diffused in the 1840s as a means of demonstrating the continuing vitality of painting in opposition to the inflexible reality presented in the new photographic technology of calotypes and daguerreotypes (i.e. *fig.93*). Yet caution is needed in this area, as the application of these innovations to the process of widespread image-making initially remained dependent on the intervention of traditional methods of reproduction, and so they did not represent quite the immediate threat to painting that is sometimes claimed. Likewise, it is questionable whether the beginnings of a photographic aesthetic gave an additional spur to the critical hostility towards Turner's late manner.

Though the Venetian paintings were not greeted with the sardonic bewilderment that peppered the reviews of pictures such as *Light and Colour* (*fig.53*), they also provoked some mystification in their first viewers. This became more marked in the responses to the later paintings of 1845 and 1846 (see *fig.12*), the last two years in which Turner exhibited Venetian scenes (*figs.209, 240, 264–8*). Writing of one of the 1846 pair, the critic of *The Times* was dismissive and declared that he would not 'expect that any but the ultra-Turnerites will admire the *Return from the Ball*' (*fig.268*).[95] Once again this sort of reaction was bound up in the matter of style, and such jibes continued for the rest of the decade (*fig.13*), despite the counter-attacks of Ruskin in the first volumes of *Modern Painters* (1843, 1846). Welcome though his advocacy may have been, his attempt to promote an idea of Turner forged in his own image was not universally accepted, and drew him within the sphere of the satirist:

There is not a picture by Turner,
That lord of poetical smear,
Whom R*****, of Poussin the spurner,
Declares is remarkably clear.[96]

Recent scholars have speculated about the significance of the lack of particularity in the later Venetian paintings, attributing this most often to the subject itself, rather than to the general tendency of Turner's mature style. In a stimulating essay, Margaret Plant reasoned that perhaps the gradual obscuring of the city, along with most traces of its great history, was actually 'the particular subject of Turner's paintings'.[97] She has since developed this point, suggesting that the later paintings 'seem rather to confirm the increasing recession of history, the redundancy of historical characters and the supremacy of the environment as a spectacle governed more by nature than by man'.[98]

A more apocalyptic view, which chimes with twentieth-century fears about the likely fate of Venice, was put forward by Max Schulz, who derived from Turner's pictures a sense of the city disappearing in front of the viewer's eyes, as if it were being reclaimed by the waters that gave it birth: 'the city has all but vanished, once awash in the morning light of Eden before it faded back among the ordinary days of man, now translated into

a haze of vapory light that is its final element. It is a city celebratory of death as much as of life. The accent is on the end of the day.'[99] Schulz seems almost to be suggesting that the paintings are a form of swansong to accompany the sunset of Turner's own declining years.

There is probably some validity to both these points, but the late pictures are not solely about retreat or withdrawal. As Lindsay Stainton has observed, the blurred form of Venice presented by Turner is just as likely to be emerging from the mists as dissolving into them. It is, in effect, 'a city in a state of "becoming" rather than "being"';[100] a city that is born anew in the wonder of unfamiliar eyes. Several of the paintings give emphasis to this interpretation, recreating the moment at which travellers advancing across the Lagoon are suddenly able to perceive the disposition of individual elements within the amorphous silhouette of Venice, and this process parallels the way viewers of the paintings make sense of the coagulated passages of Turner's brushwork.

With his love of complementary states, Turner paired his images of revellers arriving in the city at sunset with others in which they depart as the following day begins. Together these illustrate the process of a goal attained, while also suggesting the renewal inherent in the journey, which, for Turner the inveterate traveller, mirrored his own experience. Some commentators, however, have been inclined to interpret the journeys on a more symbolic level, linking them with the course of human existence (see p.227). Bizarrely, though movement is so often the ostensible subject of these pictures, with various 'comings' and 'goings' flagged up in their titles, there is surprisingly little evidence of discernible motion. This too harks back to the Byronic idea of the city preserved, or suspended in time, a notion that continues to appeal to visitors today.

One last observation about the paintings that post-date the 1840 visit is that so few of them are concerned with the celebrated sites known from the work of Canaletto. Invariably we are shown unfamiliar, peripheral areas: the back of the city; distant prospects; its cemetery; or churches that seem to have existed only in Turner's imagination (*figs.265–6*). This is coupled with a tendency in the later scenes to relegate the flanks of the city to the middle or far distance. Although these were original responses, Ruskin was not alone in complaining that Turner had wilfully selected the 'wrong' subjects in Venice.[101] But he may have missed the point, since it is likely that Turner deliberately sought such places as a means of avoiding the inevitable comparisons with Canaletto's views. In addition, Turner may have needed to lose himself in these obscurer settings, with their altered and confusing perspectives on familiar landmarks, in order to find his own distinctive vision of Venice.

For Venice presents very real challenges to artists. Despite the seemingly endless attention it has received, it somehow remains elusive, requiring from the greatest artists that they yield up something of themselves, instead of merely reflecting back the surface of its beauties. The fundamental problem was grasped by Dickens, who in his blunt, but perceptive way felt that, though Turner's paintings were 'very noble', neither they, nor the more factual images of Canaletto and Stanfield, approached the powerful impact of the city itself: 'Venice is above, beyond, out of all reach of coming near, the imagination of a man.'[102]

Notwithstanding Dickens's reservations, Turner's paintings and watercolours of Venice do address this dilemma and offer their own solution. In a way that goes beyond the responses of most other artists who have worked in Venice, Turner refashioned its topography in his imagination, painting it in his unique way, so that it is sometimes almost unrecognisable. His is a disorientating vision of the city lurking within the actual place. Try locating these images in Venice and you will find only stones and water. For what Turner created here was a profound fusion of reality with a deeply personal response, and in this lies his achievement.

Turner painting one of his pictures.

13
Caricature of Turner painting in
Almanack of the Month, June 1846

Approaches to Venice Cecilia Powell

When Turner exhibited *Approach to Venice (fig.263)* at the Royal Academy in 1844, he accompanied it with lines from Samuel Rogers's poem *Italy* beginning:

> The path lies o'er the sea invisible,
>
> And from the land we went
>
> As to a floating city, steering in ....

For most British travellers over the centuries, however, this magical, fondly remembered vision of Venice was the culmination of a tedious and gruelling journey. The English Channel had to be crossed, as did the Alps and sometimes parts of the Mediterranean. It usually took Turner five or six weeks but, as one of the most indefatigable and professional artist-travellers of his day, he embraced every challenge with fortitude and gusto. Each of his summer tours was unique and distinct, but his behaviour was consistent and he constantly refined his methods. He prepared for tours with diligent homework; he learned from his own experiences and those of colleagues; he revisited favourite places but also sought out new routes and fresh sights *(fig.14)*, especially ones that were topical. He always had a purpose as well as a goal; sometimes several disparate aims. This was particularly true with Venice, which he combined with such diverse destinations as Rome (1819), the Danube (1833) and Coburg, the home of Prince Albert, in the year of his marriage to Queen Victoria (1840).[1]

Turner never kept a journal and few of his letters refer to his travels. However, the thousands of on-the-spot sketches in the Turner Bequest provide abundant evidence of his routes (usually without any indication of day or year). Conversely, his movements are sometimes known precisely, on a day-to-day basis, thanks to the Europe-wide practice of registering the arrivals and departures of travellers, which were listed in local newspapers. By relating such references to the visual evidence of Turner's own drawings, it is gradually becoming possible to reconstruct more and more of his itineraries.

The 1819 journey to Rome was the longest of Turner's entire career, and the duration of the whole tour, six months to the day, reflected both the importance of Italy and his own frustration at being prevented from exploring it until his middle forties. He had made his first foreign tour in 1802, when the Peace of Amiens provided a respite after nine years' war with France, and this gave Turner his first view of Italy, albeit a brief one: he descended from the Alps into one of the beautiful, fertile and castle-crowned valleys of the north-west and reached the town of Aosta. Here he

doubled back but later realised his folly in not pushing further into Italy. Later that autumn the painter Joseph Farington recorded that Turner 'was within a days journey of Turin, – repents not having gone'.[2] In 1819 Turner made Turin his first major Italian stopping-point, drawing many sketches of its splendid buildings and prospects of the Alps.

Turner's itinerary was very different from one recently written out for him by a friend in a little notebook labelled 'Route to Rome' (TB CLXXI). For almost two years he had been working closely with the architect James Hakewill, preparing watercolours based on some of Hakewill's pencil sketches for engraving in *A Picturesque Tour of Italy (figs.29–33)*.[3] Not surprisingly, Hakewill suggested a tour based on his own travels of 1816–17. This began with the road over the Simplon Pass and, after Lake Maggiore and Lake Como, turned sharply down to Genoa, Tuscany and Rome. Venice and the north-east were scheduled for the final days of the tour. Turner ignored this advice, instead making a clockwise tour. He thus reached Venice by early September, rather than in the depths of winter, and enjoyed all the benefits of summer light. Had he followed Hakewill's plan, his experience of the city would have been very different; the winter of 1819–20 was exceptionally harsh. On 15 January his homeward-bound diligence was overturned in an Alpine snowstorm, a subject brilliantly evoked in the watercolour *Snowstorm, Mont Cenis* soon after he reached home.[4] Had he then been in Venice, which was so cold that the Lagoon was frozen over, he might have been walking and sketching on ice rather than floundering up to his knees in snow.[5]

His tour had begun on 1 August with a crossing from Dover to Calais which lasted from 10 in the morning until 3 in the afternoon. Turner mentions this in one of his few brief attempts at a diary, scribbled in a sketchbook later labelled 'Paris, France, Savoy 2' (TB CLXXIII). The next morning, he records, it began to rain as he was setting out in the diligence in the company of a Russian, two Frenchmen and two Englishmen. They discussed international affairs and the rain fell steadily all the way to Paris. Despite this, he managed to make quick sketches in several towns and in and around Paris itself.[6] Here he took the coach for the south, which bore him through Burgundy to the valley of the Saône. The road followed the river south to its junction with the Rhône at Lyon and he once again enjoyed the fertile countryside shown in his large Claude-inspired painting of 1803, *The Festival upon the Opening of the Vintage at Macon*.[7]

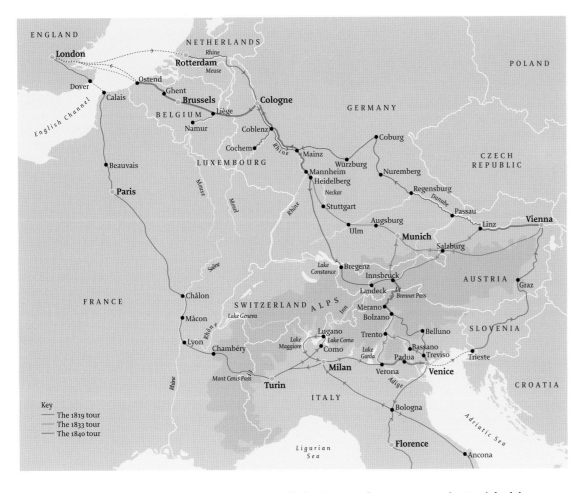

romantic scenery of Savoy and the towns of Chambéry, Modane and Lanslebourg to Mont Cenis.

Here, as so often on Turner's European travels, the road itself was a reminder of Napoleon, whose conquering armies had so recently built a carriageway over the pass. The hundreds of Grand Tourists who had used Turner's route through France and Savoy before the wars had been laboriously carried over the pass by servants while their carriages were dismantled and transported by mules.

The descent from Mont Cenis brought Turner to the town of Susa and thence along the valley of the Dora Riparia to Turin. Here he began a new sketchbook, which he later labelled 'Turin, Como, Lugarno [sic], Maggiore' (TB CLXXIV). This was the same size as 'Paris, France, Savoy 2' (11.1 x 18.6 cm) and he continued using books of this format throughout this tour. All were used exclusively for pencil sketches; it was only when he was settled, rather than constantly on the move, that he had the leisure to make larger sketches, which he would have coloured in his lodgings.

Turner did not go directly to Venice but made a long detour to enjoy the beauties of the lakes, walking miles along the water's edge. The sketches in 'Turin, Como, Lugarno, Maggiore' confirm that his progress matched the sequence of places in its title: from Turin to the town of Como; northwards up the lake to Menaggio; the short overland journey to Porlezza on the lake of Lugano; westwards on that lake to Ponte Tresa; and overland to Luino on Lake Maggiore. It was only after exploring all three lakes extensively, and even making a few larger records which he worked up in watercolour (fig.15), that he took himself off to Milan. Here he began using the 'Milan to Venice' sketchbook (TB CLXXV), but Milan inspired far fewer sketches than Turin and the long journey from Milan to Venice led to only a handful, despite the fact that it took him through Desenzano on Lake Garda and the historic town of Verona. He probably reached Venice on 8 September and remained there just a few days before leaving for Rome on 13 September;[9] he did not revisit it on his homeward journey.

It was fourteen years before Turner saw Venice again. In 1828 he made a second long trip to Italy but did not choose to include it.[10] By 1833, however, Venetian scenes by modern British artists had become much in vogue with the public and Turner recognised the potential of this new theme. His 1833 route was very different from that of 1819 but shared its characteristic blend of prudence and novelty: he initially used familiar routes and then made a long loop of a detour through new areas of celebrated scenery. His tour began with a crossing to Ostend and a journey through Bruges, Ghent and Brussels to Liège, where he revisited a stretch of the Meuse that he had explored in 1824. He then went east to Cologne and south up the Rhine valley to Mainz, through territory that was familiar from visits in 1817 and 1824.[11] After Mainz, however, he broke fresh ground by following the Rhine

Turner travelled to Lyon on the same route as in 1802; it had the advantages of being both familiar and direct. This was another city about which he had been filled with regrets in 1802. Farington records his comments: 'very fine matter' but 'place not settled enough' for sketching.[8] Turner would have been well aware that in 1793 the citizens of Lyon had suffered terribly for their attachment to the ancien régime, the city itself only avoiding complete demolition thanks to the fall of Robespierre the following year. In 1819 Turner continued eastwards, leaving France for Savoy, which was then part of the kingdom of Sardinia (a distinction observed in his title for his sketchbook). At Beauvoisin, travellers encountered the first of the many customs posts for which Italy was notorious in the days before unification; Turner characteristically used the delay to make sketches. His route then took him through the famously

14
Turner's routes to Venice in 1819, 1833 and 1840, depicted on a map of modern Europe

His outward journey must have taken well over a month, but he had embraced a range of stimulating new material, from the art collections of Munich to the drama of the Danube. He had filled four small sketchbooks with pencil sketches, buying two of them in Heidelberg and the last in Vienna.[15]

The date of Turner's departure from Venice is unknown, but he was back in Innsbruck on 23 September.[16] Much of his homeward route resembled his outward one, but he began by taking a different road northwards, following the Brenta from Bassano up to its junction with the Adige at Trento. The valley of the Adige between Trento and Merano was itself the subject of many quick sketches. Later he drew some meticulous views of Augsburg in a sketchbook he had been using in Venice. From Augsburg it would have been natural to head for the Rhine and a familiar route home and he was back in London before 15 October, when he appeared in a court case at the Mansion House, defending his reproduction rights over his own images.[17]

If Turner's route to Venice in 1819 reveals his debt to the Grand Tourists of the eighteenth century, that of 1840 marks him out as a true Victorian. After ascending the throne in 1837, the young queen had lost little time in acquiring a husband; she married her cousin Prince Albert of Saxe-Coburg-Gotha in February 1840. Turner, like several of his colleagues, sensed an opportunity. He may have had at least one order for a new painting of Venice, that for his friend Chantrey (fig.197), and a summer tour to that city could conveniently include some of Prince Albert's ancestral territory.

This year Turner took the unusual step (for him) of making a formal application to the Foreign Office for a passport. It was only the second time he had done this; the first was in 1802. Passports were not essential for Britons leaving the country but official permits were required to enter each and every territory in mainland Europe and travellers' documents were rigorously checked by police and customs officers. Turner may have acquired his pass in 1819 from the French Embassy in London; or he may have visited the British Embassy in Paris and obtained permission to enter Sardinian and Austrian territory from their respective minister or ambassador in that city.

In 1840 Turner acquired his passport on 14 July (for the price of £2 2s. 6d.) but he did not leave London for at least a fortnight, attending a meeting at the Royal Academy on 28 July and writing to his patron B.G. Windus the following day.[18] Early on 1 or 2 August he caught one of the steam packets which took passengers down the Thames from the heart of London (by the Tower of London or nearby Customs-House) and across the North Sea to Rotterdam. Here he bought a sketchbook and would thence have followed a familiar, and efficient, route up the Rhine; by this period it possessed an excellent steamer service. After pausing for a nostalgic detour on the Mosel he headed south, passing through Heidelberg and Bregenz on Lake

to Mannheim, travelling up the Neckar to Heidelberg, then driving as directly as he could to Stuttgart, Ulm, Augsburg, Munich and Salzburg.

In Salzburg he had a real break from travelling, exploring both the city and its environs at leisure, and it was here that he began his scenic detour, going north to Linz on the Danube. He proceeded to follow the dramatic course of the river downstream, past whirlpools and medieval ruins, capturing it all in hundreds of tiny sketches in his notebook, just as he had sketched the Rhine in 1817 and the Meuse and Mosel in 1824. He is recorded as reaching the imperial capital, Vienna, on 25 August and staying at the Golden Lamb in the Jewish quarter, the Leopoldstadt.[12] He then travelled swiftly back overland to Salzburg, reached Innsbruck on 3 September[13] and crossed the Alps using the Brenner Pass, the lowest and historically most frequented of all the main Alpine passes; the carriage road there had been built in the 1770s, a few years before his birth. After travelling through Bolzano, Trento, Verona and Padua, he arrived in Venice on 9 September.[14]

15
On Lake Como: from Menaggio, looking towards Bellagio 1819
Watercolour, 22.4 x 29
From the 'Como and Venice' sketchbook
Tate (TB CLXXXI 1; D15251)

Constance. From there he made briskly for Innsbruck, crossed the Alps over the Brenner Pass, revisited Bolzano (buying three further sketchbooks) and travelled along tortuous mountain roads and valleys through the Dolomites to Belluno.[19] He arrived in Venice on 20 August.[20]

For the early part of this journey Turner enjoyed the company of a married couple, from whom he parted at Bregenz on or around 10 August. The episode would be quite forgotten had not the husband written a long and informative letter to Turner in Venice once he himself reached Rome.[21] The letter itself, which was apparently signed with the initials 'E.H.', is now lost, but its content reveals an affectionate and easy relationship of long standing. It is tempting to suggest that Turner set out in the company of his cousin (and solicitor) Henry Harpur and his wife Eleanor; the entry in the passport register immediately above Turner's is for a Mr and Mrs Henry Harpur. On the only other occasion that he left London with a passport, he also had a travelling companion who was similarly well prepared.[22]

Turner left Venice for the last time on 3 September 1840 after the longest of all his sojourns: an entire fortnight.[23] He now took the steamer for Trieste, following the example of his friend David Wilkie, who had used this route in 1826 and praised 'the quietness, the comfort, and the celerity of this conveyance'.[24] He thus avoided having to retrace his steps across the Alps and was able to use the major trade route between Trieste and Vienna, stopping to explore the town of Graz on the way. On 7 September he reached Vienna, where he stayed at a more central hotel than in 1833, the Stadt Frankfurt, close to the Graben,[25] before making a week-long journey up the Danube as far as Regensburg. The first stretch of the Danube was familiar to him, but that from Linz up to Regensburg was a novel and exhilarating experience. Passau, beautifully situated at the confluence of the Danube with the Ilz and the Inn, inspired several sketches in colours, as did Regensburg itself (*fig.16*). These drawings are closely related in style to those recently made in Venice and, in many cases, are on similar or identical types of white, grey, brown or buff paper.

Turner's presence is recorded in the newspaper registers of visitors to Regensburg on 14 September, Bamberg on 15 and 17 September and Würzburg on 23 September.[26] He sketched enthusiastically in all these fine cities and nowhere more so than Prince Albert's home town, Coburg, on 17–20 September. Schloss Rosenau, the hunting lodge that had been Albert's birthplace on 26 August 1819 (when Turner himself had been approaching Venice for the first time), became the subject of a painting exhibited in 1841.[27] Having made this important detour, he followed a familiar route home: down the Rhine to Cologne and thence to Ostend. He was answering his letters within 'a few hours' of his return on 7 October.[28] Thanks to the power of steam, this deliberately extended

journey, with all its diversions and activities, had taken just five weeks.

Every day of a tour counted with Turner, not just those at the journey's end. The thousands of pencil sketches drawn between London and Venice in 1819, 1833 and 1840 provided the raw material for works ranging from a watercolour of the Roman amphitheatre at Verona to a huge oil painting celebrating the brand-new neoclassical temple of the Walhalla just outside Regensburg (the white dot in the distance of *fig.16*).[29] His painting of Schloss Rosenau failed to attract royal attention but countless viewers have marvelled at his ethereal colour sketches of the mountains, lakes and mighty rivers which delighted Turner on the long tours that took him to Venice.

16
Distant View of Regensburg from the Dreifaltigkeitsberg 1840
Pencil, watercolour and bodycolour on grey paper, 19.2 x 28.1
Tate (TB CCCLXIV 296; D36153)

Venice under the Austrians David Laven

When Turner first visited Venice, in 1819, the city had been under restored Austrian rule for five years. It was also in a state of degradation, a mere shadow of the powerful and prosperous imperial and commercial centre of the fifteenth and sixteenth centuries. In 1797, after a two-hundred-year trend of political marginalisation and economic decline, the ancient Venetian Republic abruptly lost its independence, a victim of the foreign policy of the revolutionary regime in France and, more specifically, of the unscrupulous aggression of the young Corsican commander of the Directory's Army of Italy, Napoleon Bonaparte. Previous centuries had often witnessed incursions and invasion of the Venetian mainland; but Venice itself had always remained inviolable: Huns, Longobards, Franks, Magyars, Saracens and Slavs, rival Italian states and the massed European powers of the League of Cambrai had all failed to overcome the city's watery defences. Yet, faced by Napoleon, the ruling patricians had meekly accepted his ultimatums, and, despite a brief, brave flurry of popular resistance, surrendered the city to French troops. For some contemporaries such craven capitulation on the part of the Doge and the Republic's Grand Council reflected the decadence of a once-great empire. Others, more charitable, recognised such conduct as the only intelligent response to a man who had already displayed his ruthless ability to crush those who dared to stand in the way of his overweening ambition.[1]

Occupied by Bonaparte's soldiers and shorn of its mainland territories, Venice briefly became a 'democratic municipality', a puppet regime run by bourgeois Venetian collaborators who were neither willing not able to resist the forced exactions, systematic looting and intermittent vandalism that accompanied French armies wherever they trespassed in the cause of Liberty, Equality and Fraternity (fig.17). Yet even as Venetian Jacobins erected 'liberty trees' in the Piazza San Marco, Bonaparte already planned to betray Venice's new revolutionary order. Under the Treaty of Campoformido of October 1797 he traded Venice and its mainland possessions to the east of the River Mincio to the Austrians; in exchange they accepted the extension of French hegemony in the Low Countries, on the Left Bank of the Rhine and in Lombardy. For the next twenty years Venice would be little more than a bargaining counter in international relations. A long, virtually uninterrupted period of foreign domination had begun.[2]

The Austrians did not enter Venice until January 1798. In the meantime the French plundered the city, often seeking to destroy what they could not carry away with them. It is little surprise that most Venetians welcomed the

arrival of Habsburg regiments and the establishment of an Austrian administration. However, the relatively benign first Austrian domination lasted only until January 1806. On 2 December 1805, exactly a year after Napoleon had placed the imperial crown on his own head in Notre Dame, the French emperor crushed an Austro-Russian army at Austerlitz. As part of the spoils of victory he seized the Austrians' remaining Italian territories, annexing Venice and Venetia to his recently established satellite Kingdom of Italy.[3]

The eight years which Venice spent under Napoleonic rule were among the saddest of its long history. Trade at Venice had been in decline for two centuries, but in the eighteenth century the port was still a significant if reduced centre for commerce; under Napoleonic rule, the ill-conceived economic warfare conducted against Britain, coupled with Napoleon's favouritism towards lands within the extended frontiers of metropolitan France, completely destroyed the Venetian economy. Meanwhile taxes grew heavier. While money was lavished on the court and bureaucracy in Milan, the Venetian provinces were treated with parsimony. Venetians were forced to serve in Napoleon's wars, dying in their thousands in Spain and Russia to satisfy his vainglorious lust for aggrandisement. No one could doubt the efficiency of the administration he had constructed, but its goal in Venetia was simply exploitation: the region was never more than a source of cash and conscripts. To make matters worse, within Napoleon's centralised system, the former seat of government of a once-mighty seaborne empire not only found itself reduced to the status of a mere departmental capital but also experienced the humiliation of subservience to its ancient Lombard rival, Milan.[4]

When the Austrians recaptured Venice in the spring of 1814, they were once again treated as liberators from Napoleonic oppression. By the Congress of Vienna both Venice and its mainland were incorporated into the Austrian Empire. Shortly afterwards they became one half of the Kingdom of Lombardy-Venetia, part once more of the vast, disparate and polyglot conglomeration of territories that formed the Habsburg dominions. Although elevated to the status of capital – on an equal level with Milan – Venice drew few immediate benefits from Austrian rule. The appalling economic legacy of the Napoleonic years could not be easily repaired, especially as the city had suffered from a drawn-out siege before the eventual capitulation of the French commander. With the mainland also suffering from the consequences of prolonged campaigning and a series of disastrous harvests in the second half of the 1810s, Venetians continued to live in poverty and hardship.[5]

The return of peace to Europe after 1815 enabled British travellers to visit Italy again for the first time in over a decade. At first relatively few included Venice in their itinerary. Those who did reach the city remarked on its sorry plight. Writing shortly after his arrival in November 1817 to fellow poet Thomas Moore, Byron pronounced himself pleased with its decay,[6] which, he would later suggest in Canto IV of *Childe Harold's Pilgrimage*, mirrored his own degradation.[7] Two days before Byron wrote to Moore, the British consul, John Hoppner, son of the eminent portraitist and a future friend of both Byron and Shelley, remarked at rather greater length on the sorry condition of Venice and its hinterland:

> This unfortunate country is in a truly deplorable state. The people are reduced to the greatest distress … and no [sic] one measure has been taken by the government to alleviate the general suffering. The people are no longer permitted to complain, nor draw a comparison between their present situation and that in which they were while under the French government, and the Austrians themselves seem to feel the justice of their general detestation in which they are held so strongly

as no longer to express any surprise at it. The little trade which was carried on here last year is now almost entirely at a stop … Venice indeed appears to be at her last gasps, and if something is not done to relieve and support her, must be soon buried again in the marshes from whence she originally sprang. Every trace of her former magnificence which still exists serves only to illustrate her present decay.
> (Hoppner to Hamilton, Venice, 15 November 1816, PRO, FO7, no.130)

Hoppner's attribution of Venetian distress to bad Austrian government was shared by many other British visitors to the city in the years immediately after Napoleon's defeat, who, witnessing Venice's suffering, drew the understandable, if mistaken, conclusion that the rule of Francis I of Austria was more damaging and unsympathetic than that of his now vanquished son-in-law. Thus Byron described the inhabitants of Lombardy-Venetia as 'perhaps the most oppressed in Europe'.[8] Lady Morgan, in her highly popular two-volume *Italy*, labelled the Austrian government in Venice as 'not only a pure and unmixed despotism, but a studied and designed aggregation of every abuse that can tend to desolate and oppress, to break the spirit of the species, to damp industry, and to quench hope'.[9] Catherine Govion Boglio Solari, the English wife of an Italian aristocrat, spoke of the Venetians as 'remorselessly consigned to the grasp of German rapacity'.[10] Less well-known commentators were equally damning: Henry Matthews wrote of the Austrians ruling 'with a rod of iron … as if they were to be turned out of possession to-morrow',[11] while Henry Coxe described the Venetians as living 'under perpetual restraint'.[12]

Such condemnation of Austrian government in Restoration Venice was unfair and ill warranted. With the possible exceptions of the Grand Duchy of Tuscany and the Duchy of Parma, ruled respectively by the Austrian emperor's brother and daughter, Restoration Lombardy-Venetia was the best-administered state in the peninsula, with fairer courts and less oppressive censorship than any other Italian state. This was reflected in the relative tranquillity of the kingdom. While almost every other Italian state experienced repeated conspiracy and open insurrection, Lombardy and more especially Venetia were marked by political stability in the Restoration years. Radicals and nationalists despaired of Venetia, which was perhaps the most politically quiescent region in the whole of Europe. This cannot be explained away in terms of a tradition of Venetian passivity: despite the capitulation of the government, the popular classes of both the mainland and Venice itself had shown courage and determination in resisting

Napoleon in 1797, and there had been significant anti-French insurrections in 1806 and 1809. Nor can Venetian passivity be attributed to heavy policing and the presence of a 'forest of bayonets', to use the phrase of Metternich, the great architect of Habsburg policy in the period 1815–48. After all, after 1820 Habsburg forces were repeatedly deployed across the rest of Italy to crush revolt, but quite failed to stifle the spirit of resistance in other Italian states. The principal reason for the tranquillity of political life in Venice and its mainland was the widespread recognition by its population, after the Congress of Vienna, of two simple facts: first, that the major powers would not restore the Venetian Republic; second, that Habsburg rule was vastly preferable to not only that of Napoleon but also that of the ruling houses of any of the other Italian states. While some British observers, including Byron and Lady Morgan, entertained an admiration for Napoleon, it would have been extremely hard to find any Venetian who shared their perverse nostalgia: Venetians knew the appalling reality of Napoleonic tyranny.[13]

It is significant that a common grievance among Venetians in the early years of Austrian rule was that the Austrians had retained far too much of the old Napoleonic structure of government and far too many former Napoleonic personnel – experienced and able government servants but men whose reputations were tarnished through association with the hated former regime. Moreover, these resilient remnants from the Kingdom of Italy were more often than not Lombards. Indeed, while many anglophone observers lamented the presence of German-speaking Austrians and Lombards – 'entirely ignorant of the language, manners and customs of the people', according to one such commentator[14] – the local people seem generally to have entertained more hostility towards fellow Italians from the west of the River Mincio. As the authorities carefully fostered Padua University (after almost a decade of Napoleonic neglect), its Faculty of Law began in the 1820s to produce a steady supply of graduates qualified to assume government posts. While the old patrician class of Venice rarely sought such a career, both the bourgeoisie of Venice and the mainland aristocracy started to play an ever greater role in the administration, even though the very highest posts tended to remain in the hands of outsiders.[15]

Genuine cause for antagonism towards Austrian rule certainly did exist. There is no doubt that both Venice and its mainland provinces contributed handsomely towards the Habsburg fisc: thus in 1819, the year of Turner's first visit, the government spent a figure in Venetia that amounted to only 47.2 per cent of total revenue for the region, the rest finding its way into central coffers, in large part destined to fund the army and to service the vast state debt. Yet while Venetians had good reason to grumble, and the poor especially suffered from consumption taxes and state monopolies on salt and tobacco, the situation compared extremely favourably with that under Napoleon. Not only was the fiscal burden notably lower under the Austrians, but they also proved much happier to spend than the French. Thus, in the first eight years of Habsburg rule, total expenditure almost doubled on roads and waterways, justice, education, religion and health, rising to a level similar to that enjoyed by the Lombard provinces, so disproportionately favoured by the previous regime.[16]

Besides fiscal policy, Venetians also had grounds for resentment with regard to military service. But yet again the situation after 1815 was a great improvement on that under Napoleon. Soldiers did have to spend longer in the colours after 1815, but the Austrian system conscripted far fewer men in total. Also, while there was some cross-deployment within the empire, most Venetian regiments tended to serve long periods within Italy, and were certainly never thrust into the sort of brutal and costly military adventures beloved of Napoleon. Young men from Venice and Chioggia also stood a good chance of serving in the navy, which meant better pay and conditions than in the infantry, and the likelihood of being officered by fellow Venetians.[17]

Contrary to the 'black myth' that surrounded Austrian rule of Venice, and which remains remarkably durable in some quarters, neither Francis I – himself a native Italian speaker who loved Venice – nor most of his counsellors viewed the lands of the former Republic in 'neo-colonial' terms. But if there was no conscious policy of exploitation, this did not mean that Habsburg policy always operated in the best interests of Venice and its mainland. Francis, after all, was responsible for a vast empire, with Venice the third biggest city within its frontiers; official figures put its population in 1820 at 101,628.[18] Even so, the number of Venice's inhabitants had declined dramatically since the last days of the Republic – in 1790 the population had been about 140,000[19] – and the city did not merit special treatment. Considerations of broader imperial policy held precedence in decision-making, and the imperial interest frequently ran counter to the wishes and aspirations of the Venetian population. At the same time the conflicting needs of different parts of so varied an empire, the ponderous nature of the Habsburg bureaucratic machine, and the emperor's own character – his instinctive conservatism, love of detail and tendency to procrastinate – combined to hamper reform. Although Francis I did genuinely care about his Venetian subjects – contrary to Hoppner's assertion, for example, he proved uncharacteristically energetic in addressing the economic crisis of the 1810s[20] – the period between 1815 and his death in 1835 saw few radical measures taken to confront the difficulties faced by Venice.

Certainly the majority of the difficulties faced by Venice were not originally the fault of the Austrians. Many were legacies of Napoleonic policy. Still more had their origins far earlier, in the rise of the Atlantic economy at the expense of Mediterranean trade. Yet historical explanations can have offered scant comfort to a city which suffered very real economic hardship. Trade was reduced to a trickle, in part the result of protective tariffs adopted by the Habsburgs to defend the remnants of traditional industries, a policy which Hoppner scathingly denounced as 'the encouragement of manufactures which exist only in the imagination' (Hoppner to Castlereagh, Venice, 18 October 1817, PRO, FO7, no.137). Hoppner exaggerated. Artisans and small factories did continue to manufacture goods, including textiles, beads and glassware, soap and candles, while dyeing, printing and metalworking continued to offer employment to a far from insignificant number of Venetians.[21] Yet Venetian goods faced stiff competition both from contraband and, following the abolition of internal customs barriers in 1825, from legitimate imports from elsewhere in the empire. This contributed to a situation in which up to a third of Venetians were directly dependent on charity for their survival. The one major reform, introduced in 1830, and trumpeted by the British consul, W.T. Money, as a 'measure of tardy justice, but sound policy', was the grant of free port status.[22] That such a concession had not been made sooner was not, as some British observers incorrectly suggested, to defend the position of Trieste, carefully fostered since the early eighteenth century as the Habsburgs' favoured Adriatic outlet.[23] On the contrary, the reluctance to open Venice to duty-free imports was premised on the authorities' fear that exposure to foreign competition might have a disastrous effect on Venetian manufactures and local agriculture. Indeed, when the free port was established it was accompanied not only by celebratory fireworks but also by a carefully designed package of measures to minimise any adverse effects an influx of foreign goods might have on Venetian producers.[24]

However, the free port failed to provide the hoped-for panacea for Venice's economic stagnation. Besides antagonising the landowners of the mainland (who feared to lose their Venetian market), it caused Venetian factory owners and artisans to suffer, swelling the ranks of the unemployed. Thus, a year before Turner's return to Venice, Money remarked on the 'almost mortal languor' of the city;[25] not long after Turner departed, a Habsburg official wrote to Metternich's great rival for power, Kolowrat, that 'Commerce still proceeds slowly in this city, and the same, alas, has to be said for industry.'[26]

The economic position of Venice had probably improved a little by the time of Turner's third and final visit to the city, in 1840. This was in spite of the problems experienced at the centre of power after the death of the old emperor in 1835. Francis had been succeeded by his amiable but intellectually feeble son, Ferdinand, scarcely capable of signing his own name, still less of running an empire. As the government collapsed into squabbling and immobilism, it might have been expected that the situation in Venice would deteriorate. Yet although the city was far from flourishing, the late 1830s and early 1840s saw signs of gradual economic improvement.[27] Trade began to revive, albeit slowly. A series of good harvests and the decision to build a railway from Venice to Milan also acted as stimuli for a gradual amelioration in conditions,[28] although the latter caused a level of speculation that would ultimately contribute to an economic crash. The construction of the causeway between Venice and the mainland which was begun in 1841 as part of the railway project also promised economic benefits, even though visitors to Venice sometimes objected to so unromantic an approach to the city.[29]

Unfortunately, the impact of these benefits was insufficient to maintain the loyalty of a population that was growing increasingly disillusioned with Habsburg rule. Within eight years of Turner's final visit, Venice erupted into revolt against its Austrian rulers.[30]

The 1848 revolution in Venice would certainly not have been predicted by British observers at the time of Turner's final visit. Venetians were simply considered too passive to pose any serious threat. As *The Times* would comment on 1 September 1849, at the very end of the Venetians' brave resistance to the Austrians:

> We know of no example in history of a State … which after so long a period of prostration, and as it were extinction of national spirit, has risen from its torpor with such good effect. Venice and its inhabitants had almost become a by-word in Italy for softness and effeminacy.

Indeed, while British visitors of liberal sympathies were often critical of Habsburg policy, few seem to have doubted that Venetians in some senses warranted foreign domination. Thus Byron's travelling companion, John Cam Hobhouse, denounced them for living in the past, thinking 'only on their vanished independence',[31] while the Austrophobe Catherine Govion Boglio Solari attributed the collapse of the Republic to not only Bonaparte's 'guile and ferocity' but also the shortcomings of the Venetians themselves: their failure to maintain a martial tradition, the 'supine abandonment of the ordinary resources of government' and their 'sluggishness and moral prostration'.[32] The same point was made succinctly by an unnamed author in dreadful doggerel:

> Their present grief may well deplore
> Their want of courage heretofore
> (*Rhymes from Italy in a series of letters to a friend in England*, p.3)

British visitors more indulgent to Austrian rule expressed similarly low opinions of Venetians as both idle and morally degenerate. Fanny Trollope, who considered Austrian government to be both mild and advantageous for Venice, found 'no good cause to mourn over the political changes which have befallen this once rich and powerful, but greedy and tyrannical republic', commenting that Venetians 'usually remain in bed … till about two o'clock in the afternoon … and even then, if report says true, their hours

are not spent in great activity'.[33] And Thomas Arnold announced himself 'delighted with Venice; most delighted ... to see German soldiers exercising authority in that place, which was once the very focus of degradation of the Italian race'.[34]

The low opinion in which modern Venetians were held – reinforced by liberal distaste for their political quiescence in the face of foreign domination – encouraged British visitors to dwell on the city's more glorious past. Yet the ever-present contrast between past grandeur and current ignominy only served to heighten a sense of decline, and to encourage commentators to put the blame for Venice's present condition on the Venetians themselves, who had allowed the Republic to sink to so

low a level. This perspective was further strengthened in Britain by the positive reception given to the works of two French historians, Léonard Sismonde de Sismondi's *Histoire des républiques italiennes du moyen âge* and Pierre Daru's *Histoire de la République de Venise*.[35] Both men had strong Bonapartist sympathies, and their vilification of the Venetian Republic as tyrannical and repressive was in large part motivated by a desire to legitimate its destruction at the hands of France, but this did not prevent their approach becoming a virtual orthodoxy, the historian Benjamin Webb, for example, remarking of Venice in his *Sketches of Continental Ecclesiology* that 'One cannot wisely regret ... the extinction of its wicked Republic.'[36] Such sentiments, however, generated unease in many English commentators –

18
Richard Parkes Bonington (1802–1828)
Santa Maria della Salute from the Piazzetta 1826
Pencil on grey-green paper, 36.2 x 26.4
National Gallery of Canada, Ottawa

19
Richard Parkes Bonington (1802–1828)
The Piazzetta, Venice exhibited British Institution 1828
Oil on canvas, 45.7 x 37.5
Tate (N00374)

and a certain sense of satisfaction in some French ones – given that there was a long history of drawing parallels between the Venetian Republic and Britain, as prosperous, commercial and maritime imperial powers with constitutional government.[37] Byron's warning in Canto IV of *Childe Harold's Pilgrimage* that:

> in the fall
Of Venice think of thine, despite thy watery wall!

struck a worrying chord that would be echoed repeatedly through the nineteenth century, perhaps most famously in the opening lines of Ruskin's *The Stones of Venice*.[38]

Yet if the sad state of contemporary Venice encouraged British artists and writers to seek refuge in its former glories, relatively few of Turner's contemporaries (bar the archivist and historian Rawdon Brown, who arrived in 1833 and would be resident in Venice for most of the next fifty years) actually engaged in a scholarly fashion with the city. Even Ruskin took extreme liberties with his interpretation of Venetian history, bizarrely locating its 'noblest achievements' in the twelfth and early thirteenth centuries, and perversely dating the origins of its decline to 1418, before it reached the height of its grandeur in the fifteenth and sixteenth centuries.[39] Ruskin's peculiar position was in large part conditioned by his love affair with the gothic, but, as in most cases of British misunderstanding of the city, his stance may also be attributed to the fact that he viewed Venice through the eyes of earlier artists and writers. This was obviously the case for Byron too, who famously wrote, in the fourth canto of *Childe Harold's Pilgrimage*:

> Otway, Radcliffe, Schiller, Shakespeare's art
> Had stamped her image on me.

The striking point of these lines is that Byron's idealised notion of Venice had been formed principally by writers who had never set foot there. In turn, it was the fictionalised, historical Venice of his *Marino Faliero* and *The Two Foscari*, not the decaying city of the 1810s in which he had actually resided, that shaped the imaginations of Turner, Ruskin and Dickens.[40] It is surely significant that the chapter that Dickens dedicated to Venice in his otherwise rather prosaic *Pictures from Italy* is entitled 'An Italian Dream'.[41] And it must not be overlooked that Turner, whose influence on the way Venice was perceived by the British was probably second only to that of Byron, perpetuated the latter's notion of it as a 'fairy city'.[42] Just as Richard Parkes Bonington felt more comfortable converting his lively sketches of contemporary Venice into major paintings set firmly in the glorious days of the Republican past (*figs.18–19*), Turner's oils of the city are populated either by almost ghostly figures or those from another age. Indeed, his very first oil painting of Venice, *Bridge of Sighs, Ducal Palace and Custom-House, Venice: Canaletti painting* (*fig.103*), which shows the eighteenth-century artist Canaletto improbably painting straight on to a gilt-framed canvas a view

that could not be seen from his supposed vantage point, in many ways characterises the way in which the British viewed Venice, distorting at will the reality of the post-Napoleonic city through the lens of past artists. Turner would thus play a major part himself in creating a mythologised image of Venice that bore scant resemblance to the reality of the city under the generally well-intentioned if ultimately doomed rule of the Austrian Habsburgs.

20
Ippolito Caffi (1809–1866)
Grand Canal with Snow and Ice 1849
Oil on canvas
Galleria Internazionale d'Arte Moderna
di Ca'Pesaro, Venice

Catalogue: Ian Warrell

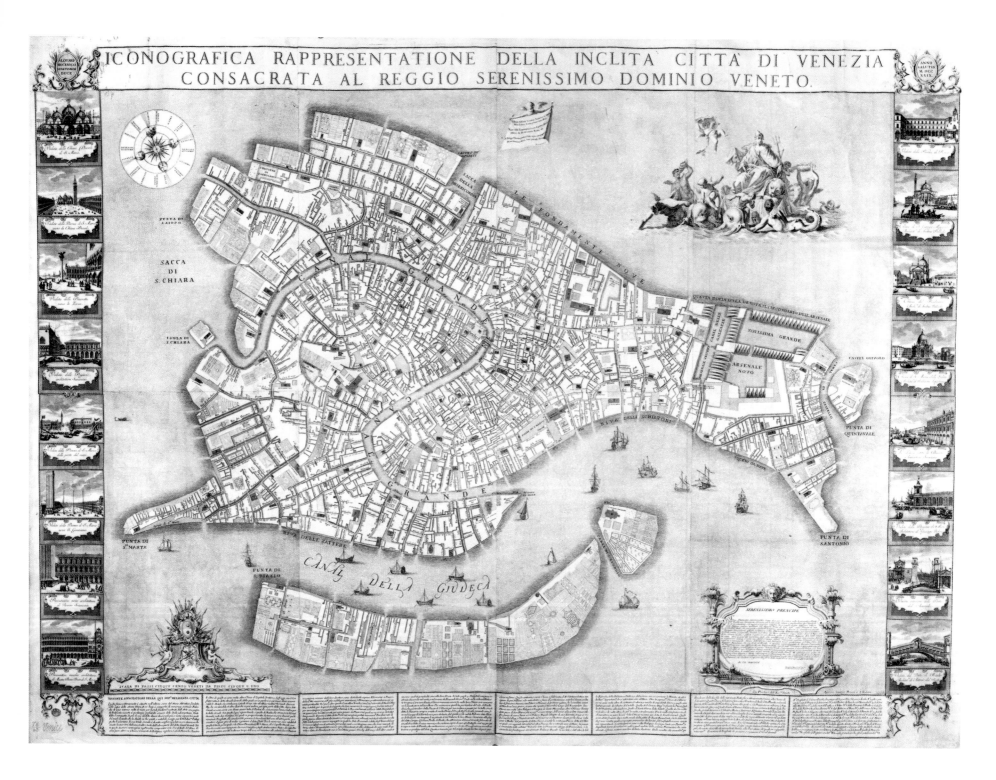

ICONOGRAFICA RAPPRESENTATIONE DELLA INCLITA CITTA DI VENEZIA CONSACRATA AL REGGIO SERENISSIMO DOMINIO VENETO.

Part One: 'No One Enters Venice as a Stranger'[1]

1 Beyond Canaletto's Venice

> To attempt to describe the city itself to you were superfluous if not impertinent; for Canaletti's pencil has been so much, and so ably employed in the illustration of it, as to have made every one more or less familiar with its leading beauties.[1]

These comments appeared in a London art journal in 1833, on the eve of Turner's second visit to Venice, but are typical of the way many British travellers reacted to the city even before the fall of the Republic in 1797. As early as 1789, for example, Dr Johnson's friend Mrs Piozzi remarked nonchalantly that she was able to recognise 'all the famous towers, steeples, &c before we reached them' because of her knowledge of Canaletto's views.[2] This dependence on Canaletto as a visual primer was intensified during the political upheavals of the final years of the eighteenth century, when his images were the most direct means the British had of visualising Venice. And the potency of his legacy was not diminished in the post-Waterloo era, when travel to Venice again became possible, even though some of the pictures were by then nearly a century old.

Given the nature of his training as a topographical artist, Turner cannot have escaped the profound influence of Canaletto. Among the generation immediately prior to his own, artists such as Samuel Scott and William Marlow had readily absorbed the principles of the crisp, structured and beautifully lit delineations that Canaletto produced while he resided in England (1746–55), and had infused their own scenes with these characteristics.[3] Accordingly, by the 1790s, when Turner was pursuing his apprenticeship, the influence of Canaletto's townscapes had become an established orthodoxy.

Direct knowledge of Canaletto's paintings, however, was to some extent limited to those who had access to the royal or aristocratic collections that contained them. The most substantial of these was the group of around fifty pictures belonging to George III, which was divided between the royal palaces. Gaining access would not have been easy for a young artist, however promising, without a formal introduction from senior officials at the Royal Academy.

Turner had a much better chance of seeing the twenty-four canvases by Canaletto in the collection of the Duke of Bedford, which hung in two rooms of the duke's Bloomsbury home until 1800.[4] The duke was the

cousin of Turner's important patron the Earl of Essex, a connection that may have gained him access to this marvellous series, afterwards installed at Woburn Abbey. An alternative entrée to Bedford House in the 1790s could have been through his associate Thomas Girtin, whose watercolours were admired by the duke. Girtin copied the view of the Rialto bridge in the Bedford group, but his sketch is more probably based on a print rather than the canvas itself *(fig.22)*.[5]

More certain is the opportunity that Turner and Girtin had of studying some of Canaletto's drawings. This came about through their involvement with Dr Thomas Monro, a physician specialising in mental illness, who was a notable collector of Old Master drawings and of watercolours by his contemporaries. Throughout the middle years of the 1790s they visited him regularly at his riverside home in the Adelphi, where they were employed to copy drawings by the brilliant but unstable J.R. Cozens. Both Monro and his neighbour John Henderson owned drawings by Canaletto, and these have often been claimed as a decisive influence on the cursive calligraphic draughtsmanship developed by the two young artists at this point in their careers.[6] But, like most of their generation, the principal means they had of gaining any sense of the range of Canaletto's work was through the set of thirty-eight engravings made by Antonio Visentini, first issued between

21 (cat.28)
Ludovico Ughi 18th century
Iconografica rappresentatione della Inclita Città di Venezia 1729
Engraving, 152 x 215
The British Library, London

22 (cat.12)
Thomas Girtin (1775–1802) after
Canaletto (1697–1768)
*The Rialto Bridge c.*1796–8
Pen and ink, 37.4 x 51.1
The British Museum, London

Regata dal Palazzo Balbi a Rialto.   3.   Regate depuis le Palais Balbi jusqu'à Rialto

La Piera del Bando. V

23 (cat.177)
Antonio Visentini (1688–1782) after
Canaletto (1697–1768)
A Regatta on the Grand Canal 1836
(plate 3 of *Trente Huit Vues Choisies
de la Ville de Venise...* published by
Joseph Battaggia 1836)
Etching, 38.7 x 54.7
The British Museum, London

24 (cat.6)
Giovanni Antonio Canaletto
(1697–1768)
La Piera del Bando. V[enice] c.1735–40
Etching, 14.2 x 20.9
The British Museum, London

1735 and 1742.[7] Many later editions of this set of prints appeared well into the nineteenth century (*fig.23*), and the compositions of some of Turner's images make plain his knowledge and dependence on this group as a source (*figs.61, 109, 151, 157–8, 173*). As an adolescent he may have copied the stiff outlines of Visentini's prints and worked them up as watercolours, much as Girtin did in the early years of their collaboration.[8]

The emphasis in Visentini's series falls chiefly on the Grand Canal, with other plates devoted to the churches and public spaces of Venice, and this focus was inevitably echoed in the earliest stages of Turner's response to the city.[9] A couple of the prints also attempted to evoke the animated vibrancy of regattas and the festive occasion on which the Bucintoro, the great ship of state, conveyed the Doge to the mouth of the Lagoon for the symbolic marriage of the city with the sea (*fig.65*).

It is thought that, in addition to these images of Venetian festivities, Turner was influenced by an important series of Canaletto's drawings at Stourhead, which belonged to his patron Sir Richard Colt Hoare. These comprised ten elaborate delineations of ceremonial duties conducted by the Doge, but just two or three of them feature the water-borne pageantry that found a place in Turner's later paintings.[10]

Because Turner was habitually attentive to printed imagery, there is the further possibility that he saw some of the thirty-one etchings produced by Canaletto himself. However, despite a receptive market for views of Venice throughout the eighteenth century, fine impressions of any of these are likely to have been much rarer in London.[11] That these exquisite images initially eluded him is suggested by one of the sketches he made during his 1833 visit to Venice. This is derived from the etching *La Piera del Bando. V* (*fig.24*), and its inclusion in his notebook, even as a rudimentary transcription, implies that Canaletto's design had previously been unfamiliar.[12]

From the later 1790s, as the young Turner's talents gained recognition, he was frequently away from London, undertaking work for new patrons, most often in the form of views of their country houses, a genre to which Canaletto had contributed during his time in Britain. These visits offered the chance to see the great picture collections, in some cases newly augmented through acquisitions bought at sales resulting from political turmoil in France. Of those that are known to have included genuine works by Canaletto, Turner was familiar with the collections of William Beckford and the Earl of Ashburnham (*fig.25*). The former acquired the marvellous panoramic canvas showing *The Riva degli Schiavoni looking West* painted before 1736 (Sir John Soane's Museum, London) from Charles-Alexandre Calonne, a former Finance Minister to Louis XVI.[13] Turner could thus have seen the picture as early as 1799, when he was preparing a group of watercolours of Beckford's new gothic abbey at Fonthill. It was one of the

25 (cat.7)
Giovanni Antonio Canaletto
(1697–1768) and assistants
Venice: the Bacino di San Marco c.1735–44
Oil on canvas, 71.3 x 187.7
Private collection

26 (cat.30)
London from Lambeth, with Westminster
Bridge c.1795–7
Pencil and watercolour, 31.8 x 45.1
Private collection

two paintings by Canaletto that he knew best, for it was afterwards bought by his friend the architect Sir John Soane and became a part of his museum. It remains a perfect introduction to the civic heart of Venice, with its wide expanse of water, skirted by the long sweep of quays, warehouses and church towers. It is surely no coincidence that during his visits Turner adopted a similar viewpoint for several of his sketches (figs.247, 249–51).

The other Canaletto canvas that was well known in artistic circles during the early nineteenth century was the famous *Stonemason's Yard c.*1727–8, now in the National Gallery, London (also known as *Venice: Campo San Vidal and Santa Maria della Carità*).[14] This was bought by Sir George Beaumont around 1808 and presented to the nation in the mid-1820s.[15] Turner is unlikely to have studied the picture closely until then because of the mutual hostility that arose between himself and the conservative Beaumont. But, at that point, he could not have failed to be impressed by Canaletto's dramatic use of light and shadow, and he may also have recognised an affinity with his own techniques in the occasional fuzziness, suggestive of rough textures, in the foreground details. Furthermore, he must have absorbed the fact that Canaletto could transform an apparently obscure part of the city into a subject alive with visual interest.

In contrast with the mastery of this painting, many of those Turner would have encountered as the work of Canaletto were, in fact, by other hands. Canaletto's pictures were widely copied in the eighteenth century by artists such as Antonio Joli and William James, and the attribution of such pictures was often deliberately misleading. Clearly such replicas tended to detract from a true sense of Canaletto's achievements (indeed Ruskin's 'determined depreciation' of Canaletto was largely based on pictures that are no longer accepted as genuine; see p.107). To complicate things still further, the name Canaletti, as he was frequently known, covered not only his own work but was also applied to the paintings of his nephew Bernardo Bellotto. A view of the Campidoglio area of Rome by the latter was in the collection of Lord Egremont, though it was only identified as Bellotto's work in the 1920s, having been displayed as a Canaletto throughout the time Turner was a frequent visitor to Petworth.[16]

There is evidence that Turner attempted to apply the lessons he had imbibed from his predecessor in some of the topographical watercolours of the mid-1790s. In a view of Westminster Abbey and Bridge from Lambeth, for instance, he seems to conflate his home-grown instinct for picturesque detail with Canaletto's flair for space and light (fig.26). The drawing echoes elements of a composition by Canaletto now in the National Gallery, Prague, of which there is also a formerly misattributed copy by Joli.[17] Turner may have seen a secondary version of another of Canaletto's London subjects in the collection of Sir Gregory Page-Turner, when engaged to paint the ruins of his home at Wricklemarsh, near Blackheath.[18]

Clearly, one way or another, the influence of Canaletto on British view-making was pervasive, and continued to be so even after the fall of the Republic. It has recently been proposed that it was this event in 1797 that stimulated William Marlow's *Capriccio: St Paul's Cathedral and the Grand Canal* (fig.27). By conflating the essence of one of Canaletto's views of the Grand Canal with the impressive façade and dome of London's greatest baroque building, it is possible that Marlow was reminding his countrymen of the similarities between the two commercial cities, with their shared belief in fundamental liberty.[19]

In the art of contemporary Venice, too, the city continued to be defined through the framework of Canaletto's legacy. Thus when it came to recording Napoleon's triumphal procession down the Grand Canal at the

27 (cat.18)
William Marlow (1740–1813)
*Capriccio: St Paul's Cathedral and the Grand Canal c.*1795–7
Oil on canvas, 129.5 x 104.1
Tate (N06213)

end of 1807, the local artist Giuseppe Borsato produced a vivid realisation of the spectacle staged to welcome the Emperor that consciously echoes the viewpoint of one of Canaletto's paintings (figs.28, 152). Significantly, when painting the image many years after the event, Borsato replaced his precursor's soft pearly light with a wintry sky in which darkening clouds appear to gather ominously. This may well be an accurate reflection of the weather, but it is difficult to resist interpreting it as a commentary on the fate of Venice, which in spite of the glittering surface it presented to its captors was despondent and oppressed.

Borsato was perhaps the most prominent artist in Venice at the time of Turner's visits. There is no evidence to confirm they met, but Turner made an attempt to set down the Venetian's name in one of the 1833 sketchbooks (fig.142), which might intimate that he had, at least, seen some of Borsato's pictures. When he returned in 1840, his stay coincided with the opening of an exhibition featuring three new views by Borsato, which was mentioned in the local newspaper, so there is every reason to believe he was acquainted with his contemporary's updated adaptation of Canaletto's vision.[20]

In spite of these manifold means by which Turner was able to assimilate Canaletto's art, it is worth considering whether there was a truly discernible impact on his own depictions of Venice. It is surely indisputable that he was indebted to Canaletto for his impressions of the appearance of the city before he got there in 1819, and that he continued to make use of some of Canaletto's images in his own compositions. Equally, the solutions Canaletto had arrived at in his presentation of the urban landscape were applicable to settings other than Venice. But, as with so many of the other influences on Turner's art, having absorbed the basic principles of his predecessor, he was more concerned to offer something different than to demonstrate a literal adherence to his model. Even in the first of his Venetian paintings (fig.103), which explicitly invokes Canaletto by placing him improbably at work en plein air, there is a sense in which Turner acknowledges his debt but is not constrained by a need to reproduce his precursor's individual stylistic manner.

In fact, though there are some residual similarities of approach in the handful of Venetian canvases of the 1830s (figs.104, 109), Turner had largely dispensed with the clear-eyed scrutiny of Canaletto's pictures by 1840, after which his application of delicate gauze-like layers of paint seems to be conceived in deliberate opposition to the earlier master. Though it is tempting to suggest that the greater liquidity of the later pictures was arrived at from an appreciation of the fluent brushwork of Francesco Guardi, such a conclusion is likely to prove unsound. Even if the pair of pictures attributed to Guardi that were owned by Turner's patron Munro of Novar were genuine, his pictures were not generally available or well known in Britain in the nineteenth century.[21]

Apart from Canaletto's, there were various other images of Venice that amplified Turner's knowledge of the city in the years before he set out on his first trip to Italy in 1819. Paradoxically the most significant were some modest pencil drawings by the minor artist James Hakewill (figs.29, 32). These are part of a batch of over 300 images compiled by Hakewill during his tour of Italy in 1816–17, apparently with the aid of a camera obscura, which he decided would serve as the basis for a series of illustrations to be published under the title A Picturesque Tour of Italy.[22] After enlisting the support of Byron's publisher, John Murray II, Hakewill hatched an ambitious plan intended to result in a volume of over seventy copperplate line engravings, though the published series was not so extensive. The aim was to tap the market that had suddenly arisen for images of the long-denied cities of Europe, which were once again accessible to the British traveller. Each of the engravings was to be based on a watercolour derived from Hakewill's on-the-spot sketches. However, a misunderstanding developed between Murray and Hakewill as to who would paint the watercolours, with the latter independently commissioning work from a team of eight artists, including Turner. This was forcefully challenged by Murray, who insisted on securing the services of Turner alone, for which he was prepared to pay the extravagant sum of twenty guineas for each of the designs (twice the price of the watercolours for Turner's contemporary series of Picturesque Views on the Southern Coast of England).[23]

Murray's reasoning went beyond the obvious celebrity that Turner would confer on the project, and was presumably as much motivated by his appreciation of the imaginative skills the artist brought to this line of work. In the preceding years Turner had demonstrated through his exhibits at the Royal Academy that there need be no loss of dignity for an artist of his stature working from the rudimentary material of gifted amateurs.[24] Moreover, his earliest training had instilled an inveterate proficiency in the reworking of other artists' designs that enabled him to invest comparatively slight efforts with his own powerful vision, and he continued to pursue this type of work throughout his career (see fig.66).[25] As it happens, the watercolours Turner produced for the Tour of Italy project are infinitely subtler and richer than those of any of the other artists who worked from Hakewill's outlines, despite the fact that he had still not experienced Italy for himself.

Significantly, Venice can be seen to be of only marginal interest to the traveller at this date, as the majority of subjects that were commissioned were located in the central region of the Italian peninsula, radiating out from a handful of views of Rome, together with details of the antiquities in its museums. This was also reflected in Hakewill's portfolios of field sketches, which incorporated a group of only thirteen views of Venice. Most are celebrated subjects, such as the Basilica of San Marco, the Piazza and

demonstrating that he was able to anticipate imaginatively the combination of light and water he would encounter when he got to Venice.

The view of the Rialto is based on one of two drawings that Hakewill made from the window of his hotel, the Albergo Leon Bianco (*fig.29*), looking obliquely across the façade of the Palazzo Farsetti, which differ only slightly in terms of what they encompass. That selected as the basis for Turner's watercolour is less conventional, moving the bridge away from the centre so the emphasis falls on a rank of gondolas and the receding line of palaces. Of the two, this drawing is much less resolved, the draughtsmanship less polished; these may have been decisive factors, offering Turner more scope to appropriate the scene as his own. His first step was to trace the outline of Hakewill's image on to a separate sheet of paper (*fig.30*), to which he then applied diluted washes of blue and yellow colour in order to create the basic tonal differentiation of his design.[27] This was a strategy he had developed comparatively recently in his watercolour practice. By setting down his colour in this seemingly abstract but highly structured way, he was better equipped to foresee how his image would come together.[28]

Unfortunately, the finished watercolour of the Rialto disappeared after it was last sold in 1916, so it is only possible to assess what Turner brought to his source material from John Pye's engraving of 1820 (*fig.31*).[29] In this the most striking embellishment is the sense of warm light playing across the surfaces of the palaces, which is already anticipated in the yellow washes of the colour study. A sense of the sun's brilliance is further heightened by the addition of a number of, presumably brightly coloured, canopies on the balconies.

Where Hakewill's foreground is peopled by just two faint figures, Turner adds a lively cast of elegant travellers, boatmen, merchants, vegetable sellers and children (as well as a dog), though it is not immediately obvious whether any of them wear contemporary costume. A female figure, wearing a feathered hat suggestive of an earlier period, can be seen through an invented window in the walled gateway to the Palazzo Loredan. This almost insignificant detail is, as John Gage has suggested, actually the seed of the painting *Jessica (fig.59)*,[30] which may imply that Turner also thought of the woman in this earlier scene as Shylock's daughter. The connection likewise makes plain the extent to which his perception of Venice was conditioned by Shakespeare's *Merchant of Venice*, in which the Rialto is the true hub of the city (see also *fig.58*).

In working up Hakewill's perfunctory outlines he made other changes to the architecture, devising his own windows and entrance for the Palazzo Bembo because they were obscured in his source material. But perhaps the most curious detail in the picture is the inclusion of a *capitello*, the covered tabernacle possibly containing an image of the Madonna and Child, in the

Campanile, the Doge's Palace, the Bridge of Sighs and the island of San Giorgio Maggiore, all of which lie on the tourist itinerary in the city's centre. There was also a more distant prospect taken from the far end of the Riva degli Schiavoni, as well as the classic view of the cluster of islands seen by the traveller setting out across the Lagoon from Fusina.[26]

The two views Hakewill selected for Turner to develop, however, are both situated on the Grand Canal: one showing the commercial heart of Venice around the Rialto bridge; the other focusing on the lower part of the canal where it is dominated by the looming dome of Santa Maria della Salute (*figs.29, 32*). Only the first of these was actually engraved, accompanied in its published form by a commentary explaining the bridge's history, which culminated in the recent attempts of the Venetians to defend their city from the French. Common to both designs are relatively open foregrounds created by the glassy surface of the canal waters. Turner took advantage of this emptiness to introduce shimmering reflections

28 (cat.3)
Giuseppe Borsato (1771–1849)
The Arrival of Napoleon in Venice 1847
Oil on canvas, 56 x 74
Pinacoteca Ambrosiana, Milan

lower right-hand corner, something entirely absent from either of Hakewill's views of the Rialto, though there does actually seem to have been one of these shrines in the equivalent place on the façade of the Palazzo Farsetti (*fig.4*). Presumably Turner learned of this from Hakewill.

The other Venetian subject prepared in watercolour for the Hakewill project is known to have been with an engraver, probably W.R. Smith, by 17 July 1818 (*fig.33*).[31] In this view of the lower Grand Canal Turner once more transformed the bare bones of Hakewill's arid pencil sketch into his own dazzling and full-bodied representation. No separate study is known of this composition, which may suggest that Turner simply painted the finished work over his traced outline. There are however occasional modifications to the architectural details, suggesting that he did not always adhere to his model slavishly, most notably where he mistook the trees behind the Palazzo Venier dei Leoni (now housing Peggy Guggenheim's collection) for the entablature of a classical façade. He was, as usual, quick to seize on the potential for contrast, and converted Hakewill's suggestions of billowing cloud into a thundery sky that throws the dome of the Salute into stark relief.

Another minor but revealing detail is the posture and punting motion of the gondoliers. Here again, it is necessary to remember that this is not derived from first-hand observation. Elsewhere, in the right-hand foreground, the eye is drawn to the figure of a man who supports his stylishly dressed young lady as she climbs into a gondola. A pair of figures rather like these two reappear in a number of Turner's Venetian images (*figs.67, 69, 109*), perhaps a leitmotif suggesting amorous Byronic adventures, a depiction of Jessica after her elopement with Lorenzo, or a personification of the city's marital bond with the sea.[32]

As already noted, the watercolour did not appear in the bound edition of the *Tour of Italy*, published in 1820, which proved to be a financial failure despite the quality of its contents. To recoup some of his losses Murray was forced to sell the twenty Italian watercolours by Turner in 1824, at a loss of five guineas for each work. Meanwhile some of Hakewill's prints were subsequently redeployed to form other published titles. Inevitably, in the long run Turner was the only one of those directly involved with the creation of these exquisite images to make a profit. But he would have been incensed by a later development which saw six of his designs, including the Rialto subject, re-engraved by Henry Adlard on a smaller scale, without his consent or involvement, for Josiah Conder's 1831 pocket guidebook to Italy. Similar examples of this kind of piracy occurred regularly in the early 1830s in spite of Turner's attempts to prevent them.[33] Despite the commercial failings of Murray's project, it was nevertheless a vital stimulant in nudging Turner towards a resolution to go to Italy for himself. When he eventually set off in July 1819, he would no longer be dependent on second-hand impressions.

29 (cat.13)
James Hakewill (1778–1843)
The Rialto 1817
Pencil, 14 x 21.5
The British School at Rome Library

30 (cat.61)
The Rialto, from the Albergo Leon Bianco, after a Drawing by James Hakewill c.1818
Pencil and watercolour, 18.2 x 26.6
Tate (TB CCCXVI 7; D32144; S 60)

31 (cat.178)
John Pye (1782–1874) after Turner
The Rialto 1820 (from James Hakewill's
Picturesque Tour of Italy 1818–20)
Engraving from Turner's own copy,
14.3 x 22 (image) on sheets 28.7 x 38.7
Private collection

32 (cat.14)
James Hakewill (1778–1843)
The Grand Canal, with the Salute 1817
Pencil, 14 x 21.5
The British School at Rome Library

33
The Grand Canal, with the Salute, Venice
c.1818–20
Watercolour, 14 x 21.5
Private collection

2 Turner and Venetian Painting

During the mid-1790s, when Turner was beginning his career, the London art world was gripped by a desire to understand the techniques that produced the saturated colours of sixteenth-century Venetian artists such as Giorgione and Titian. From the President of the Royal Academy down, it seemed that every painter in the establishment had succumbed to the wiles of an obscure young woman called Ann Provis, who claimed she possessed the 'Venetian Secret'.[1] This was allegedly preserved in a transcript from a lost manual that had revealed the materials and methods of these earlier masters, and which Miss Provis shared only with those prepared to subscribe to her demonstrations. From what is known of her disclosures, however, there was little that was revelatory, and her teaching stressed the well-known idea of painting in transparent colours on a dark, absorbent ground.

Nevertheless, by late 1797, the craze was so pervasive it warranted the satirical attentions of James Gillray's irreverent eye *(fig.34)*.[2] His densely packed etching is laden with well-informed mockery of the gullible Academicians, connoisseurs and critics, who sought to profit, one way or another, by the 're-discovered' methods. But amid its incidentals, almost obscured in the shadows on the left-hand side, is a detail that indicates that Turner was one of the few contemporary artists who stood apart from the prevailing vogue. Here Gillray exempted him and other doubters of the Provis 'Humbug' by placing their names on a portfolio that suffers the indignity of an attack from a spitefully incontinent monkey.

Ironically, Turner's aloofness from the Provis scam did not mean that he entirely refrained from experimentation in his own painting. But his materials, at least at this period, were generally sound.[3] It was only in the second half of his career, and especially in the 1840s, that he too was seduced by the potential for clear, deep glazes of colour of the kind Provis had been promoting; and the unstable materials he used sometimes resulted in disastrous changes to his canvases within a matter of years (see p.240).

Leaving to one side the issue of technique, Turner proved to be as passionate about the art of Titian as any of those ridiculed so pointedly in Gillray's caricature. Indeed, no other artist's work had such a profound and lasting influence on him, with the obvious exception of Claude Lorrain.[4]

In the absence of a national gallery, the earliest stages of Turner's infatuation were fed by pictures in the aristocratic collections for which his own works were commissioned. Many of these were considerably enriched by acquisitions from the major French and Italian collections, dispersed in the 1790s.

Undoubtedly the most significant group of pictures to arrive in England were those that had belonged to Louis-Philippe-Joseph, head of the subsidiary Orléans branch of the French royal family.[5] The majority of these were acquired by a consortium of three noblemen that included the Duke of Bridgewater, one of Turner's important early patrons.[6] To promote the works to other potential collectors, two exhibitions were staged at the end of 1798. The more impressive selection was displayed in the Lyceum, just off the Strand, not far from the Royal Academy and Turner's home in Covent Garden. Here the chief attraction was a spectacular group of works by members of the Venetian School, dominated by a fine assembly of Titian's mythological paintings.[7]

The broader handling of Titian's later works, with their lively scumbled surfaces and imprecise forms, may well have appealed to Turner, who was then seeking ways of making his own pictures more expressive. Though the bolder use of paint he aimed at was in tune with that of some of his more progressive colleagues at the Academy, who also looked to Titian as their model, it did not meet with universal approval. It was remarked during the run of the 1799 Academy exhibition, for example, in a phrase that anticipates the annual denigration of his mature canvases, that he was 'carrying breadth & indistinctness to an extreme'.[8]

Such objections might have knocked his burgeoning career off course had he not been fortunate in receiving early recognition from the Academy, winning associate and then full membership in record time. During these years, even as his art gained in assurance, he continued to apply his keen imitative skills to the great painters of the European tradition, assessing the efficacy of their techniques, and in the process absorbing their manner into his own. In this he followed the advice of the Academy's first President, Sir Joshua Reynolds, who had encouraged his students to scrutinise the past masters perennially, and to 'consider them as models which you are to imitate, and at the same time as rivals with whom you are to contend'.[9]

The greatest opportunity Turner had to further his knowledge of the art of the past came in 1802, during the Peace of Amiens, when a temporary pause in Anglo-French hostilities permitted him to travel to Paris to visit

34 (cat.11)
James Gillray (1757–1815)
Titianus Redivivus; or the Seven Wise-Men consulting the new Venetian Oracle, – a Scene in the Academic Grove 1797
Etching and watercolour, 54.9 x 42
The British Museum, London

the galleries of the Louvre, then incomparably enhanced by works of art looted from the vanquished parts of Europe. The paintings included many by Venetian artists, some of which had actually been taken from Venice itself. Indeed, on 16 May 1797, just two days after French troops invaded the city, it had been stipulated in the Treaty of Milan that a tribute had to be offered to Napoleon of two statues and eighteen pictures.[10] The most notable of these requisitions proved to be Veronese's vast canvas depicting the *Marriage at Cana* 1562–3 (Louvre, Paris), which had been painted specifically for the refectory of San Giorgio Maggiore, but other major works included Tintoretto's *Miracle of Saint Mark Freeing the Slave* 1548 (see *fig.48*), and Titian's *Death of St Peter Martyr* altarpiece (see *fig.40*).

A sense of the intense scrutiny Turner gave each painting is preserved in the small notebook he entitled 'Studies in the Louvre'. This is filled with commentaries on around forty pictures by perhaps sixteen artists.[11] Supreme among these was Titian, whose works were, with one exception, the only ones he took the trouble to copy fully in colour (*figs.35–9*).[12]

In concentrating so closely on Titian it was inevitably the technical realisation of colour that formed the focus of Turner's investigations, as well as the interaction between the prepared ground and the painted image. He ranked the *Entombment of the Dead Christ c.*1520–6 (*fig.35*) as 'among the first of Titian's pictures as to colour and pathos of effect', justifying this opinion through his observations on how the various coloured parts of the composition contribute to its impact.[13] He made a similar analysis of the picture, then thought to depict Titian and his mistress (*c.*1512–15; *fig.36*). These notes reveal the astute eye of a fellow practitioner, alert to technical shortcomings as well as strengths, and indicate his first-hand knowledge of Old Master collections in Britain, which enabled him to pass judgements as a connoisseur. A specific instance occurs in his comments on the celebrated *Concert Champêtre* (*fig.37*), which he felt suffered in comparison with other works by Titian in the gallery because of its sunken colours. In spite of this, he believed that 'the management of the whole is like but better [than] the pastoral subject of the Duke of B[ridgewater]' – the *Allegory of the Three Ages of Man c.*1512–13 (National Gallery of Scotland, Edinburgh) – qualifying this statement, however, by concluding that the colour of that picture surpassed the work in the Louvre.[14]

Of the paintings by Titian not normally in Paris, Turner paid particular attention to three works: the *St Peter Martyr* altarpiece; the earliest version of the *Crowning with Thorns* 1540–2, painted for the church of Santa Maria delle Grazie in Milan (*fig.38*); and a *Madonna and Child*, that seems then to have been attributed to Titian, but which is no longer known (*fig.39*).[15] These last two he copied in his notebook, amid remarks that dissect how Titian contrived drama from the interplay of light and shade.[16]

35 (above)
Copy of Titian's 'Entombment' 1802
Pencil and watercolour, 11.4 x 12.9
From the 'Studies in the Louvre' sketchbook
Tate (TB LXXII f.32; D04315)

36 (below left)
Copy of Titian's 'Alphonse de Ferrare and Laura de'Dianti' (formerly thought to show Titian with his Mistress) 1802
Pencil and watercolour, 12.9 x 11.4
From the 'Studies in the Louvre' sketchbook
Tate (TB LXXII f.25; D04301)

37 (below right)
Copy of part of the 'Concert Champêtre' (attributed variously to Titian or Giorgione) 1802
Pencil and watercolour, 12.9 x 11.4
From the 'Studies in the Louvre' sketchbook
Tate (TB LXXII f.56v; D04347)

His most reverent and critical comments, however, were reserved for the *St Peter Martyr* altarpiece, which he, like many of his colleagues, considered among the very finest of Napoleon's plunderings.[17] One of Titian's boldest paintings, this showed the devastating attack on a Dominican inquisitor, an unflinching opponent of heresy, who had been killed on the road between Milan and Como. Its most striking feature is the diagonal line of the central tree, which concentrates the eye on the violence of the assault. Turner was presumably already familiar with the basic composition from the engravings taken from the image, which he later utilised as a lecturer,[18] or he may well have seen a copy *(fig.40)*. It was, furthermore, one of the few pictures by Titian specifically discussed in Reynolds's *Discourses*, where the merits of its landscape were highlighted.[19] But none of these potential sources would have provided an adequate means of assessing the importance of Titian's colour to the image.

In fact, when they were confronted by the picture itself there was some controversy among the Academicians in Paris, with several, including Turner, believing that the blue sky was too forceful, detracting from the subtlety of the picture's collateral parts. In his notes in the 'Studies in the Louvre' sketchbook, Turner attributed this to an unsympathetic removal

38 (cat.73)
Copy after Titian's 'Crowning with Thorns'
1802
Pencil and watercolour, 12.9 x 11.4
From the 'Studies in the Louvre'
sketchbook
Tate (TB LXXII f.52; D04340)

39
Copy of a Madonna and Child, apparently attributed to Titian 1802
Pencil and watercolour, 12.9 x 11.4
From the 'Studies in the Louvre'
sketchbook
Tate (TB LXXII f.37; D04322)

40 (cat.29)
Unknown artist after Titian
(c.1490–1576)
The Death of St Peter Martyr 17th century
Oil on canvas, 141 x 94
Collection of the late Sir Brinsley Ford

41
*Interior of Santi Giovanni e Paolo, with
Titian's St Peter Martyr altarpiece* 1833
Pencil, 10.9 x 20.3 each
From the 'Venice' sketchbook
Tate (TB CCCXIV ff.34v, 35; D31992,
D31993)

42 (cat.74)
*Composition study for 'Venus mourning
the Dead Adonis'* c.1802–3
Pencil and chalk on blue paper,
43.3 x 27.2
From the 'Calais Pier' sketchbook
Tate (TB LXXXI f.52; D04954)

of glazes that might have unbalanced a harmonious effect.[20] Nevertheless, this was for Turner a painting with 'finely contrived' and 'wonderfully expressive' figures, posed in a landscape that 'tho' natural is heroic' – in other words one that plays a vital role beyond that of being only a setting. Most tellingly, he proposed that Titian's sublimity resided in the 'simplicity of the parts', because the need to replicate nature itself sometimes restricted the painter's dynamic range. This emphasis on naturalism challenged a point made by Reynolds, who had suggested that Titian tended to generalise in his details, individualising his foliage 'just as much as variety requires, and no more'.[21]

The altarpiece continued to preoccupy Turner once he got back to London, exerting a powerful hold on his imagination. A series of ideas for pictures in his 'Calais Pier' sketchbook are probably his earliest attempts to apply the strong vertical weight of Titian's trees to his own figure groupings (*fig.42*).[22] These were conducted through an exploration of the mythical subject of Venus and Adonis, which Turner also borrowed from Titian, in this case a painting recently acquired by the wealthy collector John Julius Angerstein.[23] In one of the studies, and in the oil painting he went on to develop from it (*fig.43*), Turner selected essentially the same moment as Titian, showing Venus trying to deter her lover from setting out on the hunt that will end in his gory death. It is possible to deduce from other preliminary studies that Turner also planned to paint a companion picture in which the goddess discovered Adonis's mutilated body.[24] Regrettably, the composition of both images is flawed by Turner's curious decision to obscure the faces of his protagonists, denying the viewer any engagement with their predicament, and it must be said that the finished oil is interesting chiefly for what it demonstrates of his synthesis of Titian's example.

A somewhat more successful exercise in Titianesque pastiche is the painting Turner exhibited at the Royal Academy in 1803 (*fig.45*). Here the underlying prototype was an early canvas by Titian of almost the same dimensions, which had been through the London salerooms in 1801 (*fig.44*), though the earliest studies for Turner's painting indicate that it too was begun as a variation on the *St Peter Martyr* altarpiece in an upright format.[25] The absence of blue in the immediate vicinity of the figures creates a warm intimacy around them that is contrasted by the intrusion of a chink of azure sky; Turner was evidently bringing to bear what he had learned from the *St Peter Martyr* picture.[26] In the event, the painting was a flop at the exhibition and did not sell, unlike its companion *Venus and Adonis* (*fig.43*) which entered a collection in south-east London.[27] The press were, indeed, unanimous in discouraging Turner from pursuing a career as a history painter, and even fellow artists were inclined to view the *Holy Family* as further evidence of his inattentiveness to a suitable 'finish' in his pictures. Henry Fuseli,

43
Venus and Adonis c.1803–5
Oil on canvas, 59 × 47
Private collection (B&J 150)

for example, was not averse to employing ragged and suggestive brushstrokes in his own paintings, but remarked that Turner's exhibit was 'like an embrio, or blot of a great master of colouring'.[28]

Possibly stung by these criticisms, Turner did not venture again into such overtly Titianesque material until the later 1820s. This did not mean that he abandoned Titian altogether as a model; merely that the influence is less blatant, and is discernible primarily in technical similarities. For example, he had consciously selected canvases prepared in the Venetian manner by the Italian colourman Sebastian Grandi since 1802,[29] and he used these in conjunction with the understanding he had gained from studying Titian's techniques. In paintings such as the *Fall of the Rhine at Schaffhausen* 1806 (Museum of Fine Arts, Boston), the earthy surface of the priming combines with his pigments to recall the sketchy finish of Titian's final works.[30]

The ensuing decade was the period in which Turner became closely involved with the Academy as its Professor of Perspective, which enabled him to propagate his views on landscape, and its potential, through a series of annual lectures beginning in 1811. Within these he made regular references to Titian's *St Peter Martyr* altarpiece, reinforcing the impression that it was his 'most constant inspiration among the Old Masters, both for its purely pictorial qualities, and for the drama of the action'.[31] Thus in the wide-ranging lecture in which he sought to make a distinction between landscape as a pure form and its subservient purpose as a background, Turner championed the painting as the 'highest honour that landscape has as yet', seeing the scenery as fully integrated and not secondary to Titian's purpose.[32] He pursued his point by focusing on the parallel role of architecture within history painting, turning for his examples to pictures by Veronese, such as the *Marriage at Cana* that he had seen in Paris, and the *Hermes, Herse and Aglauros* from the Orléans gallery *(fig.46)*. As in his remarks on Titian, it is clear that he respected Veronese above all as a colourist, but he went beyond this commonly held view in his attempts to elucidate the part played by light and shade in intensifying the formal relationships between colours.[33] The value of such personal observations is evident in the fact that Turner applied these acquired principles in paintings such as his own version of the meeting of *Mercury and Herse* 1811 (Private collection).[34]

Later, when preparing to deliver the perspective lectures in 1818, Turner completely revised the fifth in his series, devoted to colour and reflections, and in the process brought into play further insights about the great Venetian painters. Once again, the Titian altarpiece was foremost in shaping his thoughts, in this case about breadth of tone and its relationship to style; and he noted how when colour was applied 'in the union with lights and shadows' it could 'exalt' its subject. But he also looked to the example of Tintoretto in recommending the use of a monochrome palette as a means of engaging the viewer's imagination.[35]

44
Titian (c.1490–1576)
The Holy Family and a Shepherd c.1510
Oil on canvas, 99.1 x 139.1
National Gallery, London

45 (cat.31)
Holy Family exhibited Royal Academy 1803
Oil on canvas, 102.2 x 141.6
Tate (N00473; B&J 49)

By that date it was not far short of twenty years since he had first studied the great Venetian paintings in the Louvre, and it is probable that the factors contributing to his decision to travel to Italy in 1819 included a desire to see them yet again. In most cases, the looted pictures had been repatriated in the years after Waterloo, though Veronese's *Marriage at Cana* and Titian's *Crowning with Thorns* remained in Paris. But the return of the other major canvases meant that Venice had resumed its claim to be *the* place in which to study the work of its great colourists, a circumstance of as much importance to the generation of artists that flocked there in the 1820s as the parallel Byronic imperatives. In 1826, for example, David Wilkie was hastened on his way with the promise that seeing the works of Titian, Tintoretto and Veronese *in situ* would offer 'a treat such as you can find nowhere else, save in Venice'.[36]

Like some of the other paintings that had been to Paris, Tintoretto's *Miracle of Saint Mark Freeing the Slave* (see *fig.48*) was not returned to its original setting in the Scuola Grande di San Marco, but instead joined the group of pictures brought together at the Accademia as a result of the dissolution of many Venetian religious institutions after 1805. Begun as an adjunct to the state-run art school, the Accademia collection was by 1810 housed in the deconsecrated church and scuola of the Carità, not far from the entrance to the Grand Canal *(fig.173)*, and opened as a public gallery in 1817. During his visit Turner saw the Tintoretto painting in its main gallery, where it hung on the wall opposite Titian's newly restored *Assumption c.*1515–18 (see *fig.47*).[37] Though other British artists, such as Sir Thomas Lawrence, were inclined to prefer the Titian, Turner held fast in his admiration for Tintoretto's composition, with its vortex-like spiral of harmonious colour and light.[38] His veneration was presumably further enhanced by the athletic range of Tintoretto's skills manifest in the paintings at the Scuola Grande di San Rocco, some of which he transcribed in outline *(fig.49)*.[39]

There was another painting that Turner was eager to see while in Venice in 1819: Veronese's *Family of Darius before Alexander c.*1565 (National Gallery, London).[40] He had been encouraged to locate this highly rated picture in the Palazzo Pisani on behalf of Hakewill's wife, but his schematic record of the composition, with some generalised comments on the alternating cool and warm tones, seems an insufficient response to Hakewill's exhortation to 'observe particularly', making it possible that he made a fuller study on a separate sheet of paper. Elsewhere, his studies of Veronese's work were rewarded by a visit to the Doge's Palace, in which he evidently admired the series of painted Allegories set into the gilt ceiling of the Sala del Collegio.

Within a few weeks of this he was in Rome, where he made time to scrutinise Titian's *Sacred and Profane Love* 1514 at the Villa Borghese.[41] It has been suggested that he was drawn to this work after receiving a personal

46
Paolo Caliari, known as Veronese
(c.1528–1588)
Hermes, Herse and Aglauros 1576–84
Oil on canvas, 232.4 x 173
Fitzwilliam Museum, Cambridge

47
Giuseppe Borsato (1771–1849)
Leopoldo Cicognara giving the Funeral Oration before the Coffin of Canova in the Accademia di Venezia 1824
Oil on canvas, 61 x 78
Galleria Internazionale d'Arte Moderna di Ca'Pesaro, Venice

recommendation from the Scottish artist Hugh 'Grecian' Williams, who described it as a flawless 'piece of colouring',[42] though its renown hardly required such approval for him to seek it out. Significantly, the annotations he made to his pencil sketch reveal his interest in what he thought was a 'white ground', a preparation he had begun to introduce in his own work around 1805, and to which he was indebted for the greater luminosity of his pictures. But this comment alone does not explain Turner's fondness for the image, which induced him at some point to acquire the copy found among the contents of his studio after his death, one of several such replicas in his collection.[43] This may even have been his own work, as it was standard practice for artists to produce copies as a means of understanding the techniques of an admired master. Turner's colleague, William Etty, for example, spent much of his time in Venice in 1822–3 copying from pictures in the Accademia (fig.48).[44]

Rather than undertaking direct imitations of any of the Venetian painters he admired, in the wake of his first trip to Italy Turner chose to infuse his work with subtle allusions. This can be sensed in his Forum Romanum 1820 (Tate), which appears to borrow the pose of the central figure from Veronese's Preaching of St John the Baptist c.1562 (Villa Borghese, Rome), or in his Bay of Baiae 1823 (Tate), where a white rabbit is introduced in the foreground that brings to mind the pair in Titian's Sacred and Profane Love.[45]

During the second half of the 1820s Turner had further opportunities to study Italian art in the collection of Samuel Rogers (fig.63), with whom he collaborated on a book project immediately before he went back to Rome in 1828 (figs.64, 67). The poet shared the new interest in the previously overlooked painters of the fourteenth and fifteenth centuries, but had also recently added Titian's Noli me tangere c.1514 (National Gallery, London) to his collection.[46] While this work is more restrained than the St Peter Martyr altarpiece, it nevertheless possesses the same interaction between figures and their landscape, and Turner would inevitably have been reminded of the other painting by the downward thrust of its lone tree.[47] With this familiar image stirred up once again in his mind, soon after arriving in Rome he embarked on a large-scale painting (fig.50), which is built upon a similar structure to Titian's celebrated composition. Instead of sheltering

48 (cat.10)
Attributed to William Etty (1787–1849), after
Jacopo Robusti, known as Tintoretto
(1518–1594)
The Miracle of Saint Mark Freeing the Slave c.1823
Oil on paper mounted on canvas, 40.6 x 59.7
National Gallery, London. Bequeathed by
Lady Lindsey, 1912

a slaughtered martyr, Turner's sinister, dragon-haunted copse is the setting for the incantations of Medea, the spurned wife of Jason. Through auxiliary details Turner refers to both her past and future, revealing in some accompanying lines of his own poetry that her acute sense of Jason's betrayal prompts her to redress her grievances through the murder of their children.[48] In designing his picture he supplemented his knowledge of Ovid and Seneca's versions of the myth with particulars taken from a production of Johann Simon Mayr's opera *Medea in Corinto*, including the pose adopted by the great singer Giuditta Pasta in the title role.[49] There remains the further possibility that he augmented this topical reference with recollections of another of Titian's paintings, for Medea also bears comparison with the Virgin in the great *Assumption c.*1516–18 (Santa Maria Gloriosa dei Frari, Venice), who is similarly swathed in a billowing red gown. Furthermore, the putti floating up from the flames in the burning pot over which she casts her spell recall those in both the *Assumption* and the *Death of St Peter Martyr*. The connection with the latter is not coincidental. In fact Turner had seen its pair of winged infants as akin to the falling embers or sparks of the composition, which he had described as shooting upwards like a firework rocket.[50]

The *Vision of Medea* was exhibited with two other new works during Turner's stay in Rome, but this achieved little other than to extend the idea of his eccentricity far beyond the London art world.[51] Indeed, neither his subjects nor his style met with much comprehension. But it seems likely that Turner was using these dense and allusive works, with their deliberate echoes of Titian and Claude Lorrain, to demonstrate the continuing vitality of the classical tradition, at the same time asserting the potency of his own approach to history painting.[52] Ironically, by the 1820s most aspirations to succeed in this genre had largely been scotched by the difficulties of promoting such paintings as saleable commodities within the framework of the Royal Academy exhibitions. An instructive comment on the prevailing attitude comes in the diary of David Wilkie, two years before the *Vision of Medea* was painted. Standing in front of the *St Peter Martyr* altarpiece in 1826 Wilkie was conscious that, despite its greatness, it was essentially 'an example of all that is the object of an artist to avoid when painting' for the Academy.[53]

Though Turner could afford to persist in producing compositions that did not sell, he must surely have been aware of this change too. In any case, he pursued some of his tributes to Titian in a more private way. He had stopped in Florence on his way to Rome in 1828, and apparently saw the sensuous *Venus of Urbino* 1538 a second time in the Uffizi. The reclining figure of one of the three Fates in the *Vision of Medea* seems to resonate with the influence of Titian's famous painting. But a more personal meditation on the image of a naked woman, laid bare for the artist's eye, can be found in the so-called *Reclining Venus c.*1828 (Tate), one of three large unfinished

49 (cat.75)
Copies of 'The Crucifixion' and other pictures by
Tintoretto in the Scuola Grande di San Rocco
1819
Pencil, 8.7 x 11.7 each
From the 'Route to Rome' sketchbook
Tate (TB CLXXI ff.25v, 26; D13906, D13907)

academic studies that may have been begun in Italy.[54] He is known to have studied nude models at the Academy of St Luke and at the Venetian Academy of Painting in Rome in 1819 under the auspices of Antonio Canova, and though the sculptor had died in the meantime, it is presumably possible that he again had access to models that he was able to pose himself.[55] A page of his 'Rome to Rimini' sketchbook includes a sketch of a reclining figure that could also be a study from a model, though in this case the actual source may well prove to be Lambert Sustris's painting of *Venus* (Rijksmuseum, Amsterdam),[56] which was itself a deliberate attempt to rework Titian's *Venus of Urbino*.

Accordingly, though the 1828 tour did not include Venice, the art of its chief painter continued to exert a more significant influence on Turner than most of the pictures he found by local artists in Rome itself. Back in London his enthusiasm for the Venetian School was given additional impetus by the lectures of the Academy's Professor of Painting, his associate Thomas Phillips, who was also a fellow admirer of Tintoretto.[57] It was Tintoretto's bold chiaroscuro that seems to have provided the exemplar for the type of effects Turner set out to realise in the 1830s. In the series of canvases Turner had studied at San Rocco, Tintoretto managed to unite the vibrant colour of his earlier works with a compelling deployment of deep shadow, lending tremendous power to his narratives. It seems possible, therefore, that Turner had such works in mind when preparing *Pilate Washing his Hands* (fig.51), though this strange picture suffers from an overload of barely digested influences that probably also include paintings by Rembrandt, Wilkie and Delacroix.[58] While some or all of these may have contributed to the enclosed space illuminated by pools of light, the biblical subject was actually one treated by Tintoretto in the San Rocco sequence and had been noted by Turner in one of the fullest transcriptions he made there in 1819.[59] One further detail confirms it as a specific stimulus for Turner's painting: the diagonal smear of white paint above Pilate's head (he is the tiny figure in the upper left-hand side of the image). This and his twisted posture can both be found in Tintoretto's picture, though Turner has reversed them. It is also possible that the San Rocco context was responsible for the figure of Christ, since the upper halls contained a celebrated early canvas by Titian showing Jesus carrying his cross, as well as Tintoretto's own realisation of the subject. Such borrowings would seem to confirm Ruskin's contention that Tintoretto was 'the only man whom I could be certain Turner had studied with devotion'.[60] But these kinds of readily traceable links to Tintoretto's work are not common and, as with Titian, Turner's debt is most often located in inherited similarities of style or approach. Thus a sense of space reminiscent of Tintoretto can be discerned in *The Parting of Hero and Leander* 1837 (Tate, on loan from the National Gallery), where the brilliance of any one colour is held in check by a series of modulated neutral tones.[61]

50 (cat.32)
Vision of Medea exhibited Rome 1828,
Royal Academy 1831
Oil on canvas, 173.7 x 248.9
Tate (N00513; B&J 293)

A less obvious instance of the lurking influence of Tintoretto is Turner's pair of paintings devoted to Goethe's colour theories, and especially *Light and Colour (fig.53)*. These were exhibited three years after the last trip to Venice, during which Turner seems to have made a final visit to Tintoretto's series at San Rocco.[62] As contrasted effects of light, the two small canvases were intended to test and question Goethe's assertion that colour was produced through the commerce of light with shade and darkness. Ironically, they have frequently been seen as a tribute to the German poet, but Turner's reservations emerge more explicitly in the annotations he made to his own copy of a translation of Goethe's *Fahrbenlehre*, where he adhered to the Newtonian principle that colour results from light alone.[63] It should be apparent that the issues he was addressing here, about colour and its relationship to pictorial chiaroscuro, could not be more fundamental to an appreciation of Tintoretto's mature art. It is consequently not surprising to find that Turner introduced a reference to another of the San Rocco canvases in *Light and Colour*.

His composition is presented on one of the square canvases he had begun to use in 1840. These hark back to the Venetian paintings of the later sixteenth century, as featured in decorative or programmatic ceiling schemes.[64] As well as those of Veronese in the Palazzo Ducale, he had copied many of Tintoretto's pictures in the ceiling of the Upper Hall of the scuola in 1819, reserving his fullest study for the central panel, *The Brazen Serpent (fig.52)*. Here, as in his own picture, the figure of Moses commands the area above the centre of the image, and is seen alongside a coiled snake. In addition to this, the vertiginous riot of Tintoretto's soaring figures finds an echo in the swirling motion of Turner's crowd, as it rises through liquid into light. If Turner's title refers specifically to the Deluge, its apocalyptic overtones suggest that he could also have been thinking of the reference to Moses and the serpent later in the Bible, where eternal life is promised as a result of the new covenant between man and God.[65] His own outlook, as suggested by the poetic thoughts associated with the painting, was considerably less optimistic, denying the viability of hope as an option, in spite of the connotations of rebirth implicit in the morning light.

A belief in Art's power to transcend time, if nothing else, sustained Turner to his end, and fittingly he remained constant in his esteem for Titian, whose work continued to provoke idiosyncratic responses from him. His last overt reworking of an image by Titian appeared in an exhibit of 1840 *(fig.55)*. This borrowed the expressive but arrested postures of the celebrated *Bacchus and Ariadne*, by then an established highpoint of the National Gallery collection *(fig.54)*, and an image well known to Turner from the copy in his own collection.[66] From the late 1830s the Royal Academy shared half of the National Gallery's building in Trafalgar Square, and though this enabled students to engage directly with the great history of western painting, there

51 (cat.33)
Pilate Washing his Hands exhibited
Royal Academy 1830
Oil on canvas, 91.4 x 121.9
Tate (N00510; B&J 332)

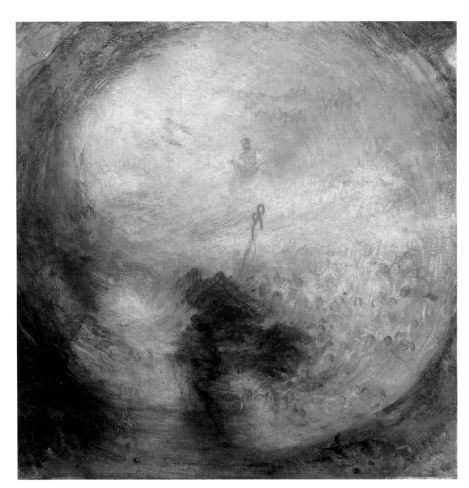

was a body of opinion that feared this proximity would result in art that fed exclusively on art, and which was not seasoned by the study of nature. These were, coincidentally, a resurgence of the objections Turner and others had expressed in the earliest decades of the century to the dominance of contemporary taste by certain connoisseurs, who favoured only the manner of the Old Masters.[67]

Such concerns make it likely that the 1840 picture evoked the Titian picture not only as a means of paying it homage, but also as a lesson to the Academy's students that, in imitating the Old Masters, they needed to refashion what they absorbed to their individual ends. Turner's picture does this by transporting Titian's figures to a classical landscape of the type he had made his own, and in doing so he effectively fused his respect for Titian with his analogous devotion to Claude. The result, with its doll-like

figures, may be comical in comparison with the majesty of Titian's authoritative image, but it suggests how these apparently disparate influences could coexist and overlap in Turner's imagination. Admittedly none of the works resulting from his admiration for Titian comes near the true splendour of what he assimilated from Claude,[68] but one can surmise that there was a considerable degree of personal identification with Titian and his position as the head of his particular school.

Turner's admiration for these two precursors was also conflated in one of the ten canvases that rework images from the group of mezzotints known as the *Liber Studiorum (fig.57)*. These seem to have been begun in the mid-1840s, when he was contemporaneously most intensely engaged with the image and art of Venice in his exhibited works. Clearly conceived as a series, the late *Liber* canvases perhaps recall the linked sequence of *poesie*

52
Jacopo Robusti, known as Tintoretto
(1518–1594)
The Brazen Serpent 1575–6
Oil on canvas, 840 x 520
Scuola Grande di San Rocco, Venice

53
Light and Colour (Goethe's Theory) –
The Morning after the Deluge – Moses
writing the Book of Genesis exhibited
Royal Academy 1843
Oil on canvas, 78.7 x 78.7
Tate (N00532; B&J 405)

54
Titian (c.1490–1576)
Bacchus and Ariadne 1518–25
Oil on canvas, 172.2 x 188.3
National Gallery, London

55 (cat.35)
Bacchus and Ariadne exhibited Royal Academy 1840
Oil on canvas, 78.7 x 78.7
Tate (N00525; B&J 382)
Reproduced here with the original frame of Turner's picture,
The Dawn of Christianity (Flight into Egypt) 1841 (Ulster Museum, Belfast; B&J 394),
to give an approximation of how the painting was first exhibited

Titian painted for Philip II, several of which had been in the Orléans gallery back in 1798. That depicting the *Rape of Europa (fig.56)* had so impressed Turner that he adapted the image as the frontispiece to the *Liber*.[69] Titian's painting was subsequently in the collection of Lord Darnley at Cobham Hall, just outside Rochester, and was presumably seen there by Turner when he made a group of sketches of the building in the early 1820s.[70] Failing this, he could also have seen it at the time he was embarking on the late *Liber* canvases, as he seems to have made frequent trips through this part of Kent in the mid-1840s, on his way to and from the coast at Margate.

As was his wont, in working from Titian's painting for his frontispiece Turner co-opted the figures to serve his own ends, so that the composition focuses on the receding image of Europa clinging to the disguised bovine form of Jupiter as he ploughs out to sea; in its source, however, the view looks back from the abducted Europa towards a distant shore.

It was essentially the same design that Turner repainted around 1845 in what is the most sumptuous of the late *Liber* images *(fig.57)*. This is built up with diluted glazes of colour similar to those Turner was applying in his Venetian exhibits, where even in the finished paintings forms are sometimes unintelligible. Allowing each layer to dry fully before the next was applied was a time-consuming process, but does not in itself explain why the ten *Liber* subjects were all left in much the same sketchy state. Turner was probably about seventy when he began them, and his health was already declining, which makes it possible that the series was a last ambitious gesture he was simply unable to complete for a public forum. Nevertheless, one is forced to consider that the group was in some sense 'finished' as far as Turner's own aesthetic was concerned. By this stage in his career the gap between his exhibited paintings and the colour structures, or beginnings, he had evolved in his work on paper was at its narrowest, and there is a sense in which the transformations he effected to his formless canvases on the Academy's Varnishing Days were really a process of bringing his personal vision into acceptable focus. In the case of the *Europa* subject, the ravishing colour reflects Turner's desire to emulate the vibrancy and richness of Titian's tones. Even when placed among the competing splendours of other brightly painted canvases from the 1840s, it must have glowed radiantly in his studio: a tribute from one master of colour to another.

56
Titian (c.1490–1576)
Europa (Rape of Europa) 1559–62
Oil on canvas, 185 x 205
Isabella Stewart Gardner
Museum, Boston

57
Europa and the Bull c.1845
Oil on canvas, 91.1 x 121.6
Taft Museum of Art, Cincinnati, Ohio,
Bequest of Charles Phelps and Anna
Sinton Taft (B&J 514)

3 From Shakespeare to Byron: Turner and the Literary Vision of Venice

The idea of Venice formed by Turner's generation was fundamentally derived from literary sources, which provided human dimensions to set against the image of the city inherited from Canaletto. Central to these impressions were the Venetian plays of Shakespeare, Thomas Otway's *Venice Preserv'd* and a range of Byron's poems and verse-dramas, but especially the fourth canto of *Childe Harold's Pilgrimage*.[1] The influence of these formerly classic texts was so entrenched by the end of the 1820s that the author of an English guidebook felt justified in making the absurdly patriotic claim that 'Venice and the Venetians, but for Shakespeare, Lord Byron, and a few eminent native painters would, long ere this, have been all but forgotten'.[2]

In subsequent years this core group was supplemented by Thomas Moore and Samuel Rogers, who featured Venice in their poems, but it was Shakespeare and Byron above all others whose works continued to provide the key triggers for British responses to Venice. Indeed, it was from Byron's group of evocative poems that the most enduring image of Venice emerges: an impotent city, haunted by shadows of its former glory, and threatened with the fate of sinking back into the element that gave it birth. It was a satisfying metaphor, quickly established, that Venice has since never quite managed (or chosen) to shake off. Turner was not aloof from these influences, and they inevitably permeate his paintings and watercolours, sometimes in isolation, but more often through an accumulation of interrelated ideas.

His exposure to Shakespeare probably began with his early interest in the London theatre.[3] Links between artists and the theatre were especially close from the 1790s onwards, as productions assimilated the verisimilitude of contemporary landscape painting, including the novelty of panoramic imagery.[4] Furthermore, the period was also that in which many aspiring history painters produced pictures for John Boydell's *Shakespeare Gallery,* which were engraved to form a bold if commercially unsuccessful series.[5]

Of the two plays by Shakespeare specifically set in Venice, there were frequent productions of *Othello* and *The Merchant of Venice* in the 1790s and afterwards. Heavily edited versions of the latter gave the character of Shylock greater prominence, to provide a vehicle for actors such as John Philip Kemble, later the manager of Covent Garden, whom Turner admired sufficiently to track down his grave above Lausanne some forty years later.[6] But perceptions of how Shylock should be acted were altered in a revolutionary way from 1814 onwards by the fervent performances of Edmund Kean. His interpretation exploited Shylock's tenderness for his daughter Jessica, and has been seen as having contributed to a perceptible change in the anti-Semitic prejudices surrounding the character. Indeed, Kean's electrifying reading of Shylock was an unmissable sensation, and there is consequently a strong possibility that Turner witnessed this celebrated rendition at some point.[7]

Whether as the result of a performance by Kean, Kemble or their contemporary William Macready, it is apparent that Turner was sufficiently familiar with the play for it to colour the way he thought of Venice. Moreover, since the most notable omission in his personal library was a copy of Shakespeare's complete works,[8] he would have been largely dependent on his recollections of an evening at the theatre for the basic information about any incident he chose to depict.

The area in Venice with the strongest resonances of Shakespeare's play was, of course, the Rialto. On seeing the legendary bridge, British visitors thought immediately of Shakespeare. Catherine Taylor, writing in 1841, spoke for many in conveying her sense of this symbiotic relationship: 'Who can behold the Rialto, or wander through the streets of Venice, made classical by the names of Shylock and Othello, of Portia and Desdemona, without a thrill of pleasure?'[9]

It has already been noted that Turner's earliest depiction of the Rialto includes a figure whom he may well have intended to be Jessica (*fig.31*). Such an identification would imply that the two figures at the adjacent portal are Shylock and his servant, Launcelot Gobbo. The incident seems to come from Act 2, scene 5, where Jessica is left on her own and instructed to seal herself within the house, though she has by then already planned her elopement with Lorenzo. The stooped figure, seen from behind in the action of closing the door, is the more likely of the two to be Shylock, and may recall the character as portrayed by Kean, whose charisma could not disguise his diminutive stature.

During the 1820s the Royal Academy exhibitions featured a number of Shakespearian subjects, and Turner would certainly have been aware of other attempts to illustrate *The Merchant of Venice*, such as that by Francis Danby in 1828, which showed Jessica and Lorenzo at Belmont after their

Scholars have devoted a great deal of time to the possible influences on Turner's composition, generally ignoring the relevance of the Hakewill print.[11] What is clear is that the origins of the painting stem from the easy-going milieu of Petworth House, the home of Lord Egremont, for whom Turner had recently completed a set of four landscapes.[12] Apart from Turner, most of the other habitués of the country house were genre or portrait painters, such as Charles Robert Leslie, Sir William Beechey or Thomas Phillips, which reflected the third earl's preference for such subjects as a collector.

According to a long-standing tradition, on one occasion the conversation among the assembled artists focused on Turner's dependence on a high-toned yellow palette, which had been much derided since the early 1820s.[13] One of those present suggested that, while yellow was perhaps permissible in landscapes, it would not work in figurative pictures. Turner needed no further inducement to take up the implicit challenge, although the anecdote proposes that he archly twisted his patron's arm, claiming that 'subject pictures are not my style, but I will undertake to paint a picture of a woman's head with a yellow background if Lord Egremont will give it a place in his gallery'.[14] This implies that *Jessica* became a commission of sorts, though the first reference to the picture's acquisition and arrival at Petworth was not until a year after its first exhibition.

The clutch of contemporary artists producing literary scenes included the American-trained Gilbert Stuart Newton, who was a close friend of Leslie, and therefore on the periphery of the Petworth circle. In 1829, when the preceding discussion must have taken place, he had just exhibited a painting showing a young woman at a window, which perhaps prompted Turner to go back to his earlier idea of Jessica looking out of her casement.[15] As Andrew Wilton has remarked, Turner did not need to consider Newton's picture an important source in itself for him to adopt elements of it in his own design, as his opportunistic nature would have recognised that it was 'typical of a currently popular mode'.[16] But, in fact, his deeply ingrained need to compete would have been further pricked by the news that Newton was preparing a painting of Shylock and Jessica for the 1830 exhibition *(fig.60)*.

Newton's painting confirms the expected associations, and inevitably includes a glimpse of the Rialto through the open door of Shylock's home. His Jessica wears a number of substantial pieces of jewellery befitting the sequestered wealth of her father. Turner went much further and decked his heroine out in extravagant finery, her costume studded with stones and pearls, offset by a shawl of sheer filigree lacework that spills over the balcony from which she is supposed to be withdrawing.[17] It has to be said that Turner's picture was an unqualified failure at the Royal Academy, being memorably, but unkindly, damned by the critic of the *Morning Chronicle* as a

escape.[10] But it is significant that when he did return to the play for his 1830 painting *Jessica (fig.59)*, it was to the very scene that appears to be the incidental subject of his 1818 drawing. This startling picture, unique in Turner's exhibited oeuvre for its focus on a single figure, appeared at the Academy with an improvised version of Shakespeare's text beneath its title: 'Shylock – "Jessica, shut the window, I say" – *Merchant of Venice*'. Why he provided only this summary of the scene, instead of a precise quotation, remains a mystery. Though he was not alone in conflating the original lines (see *fig.60*), this raw précis is typical of Turner's rather cavalier approach to Shakespeare's words and settings.

59 (cat.34)
Jessica exhibited Royal Academy 1830
Oil on canvas, 122 x 91.5
Accepted by H.M. Government in lieu
of tax and allocated to the Tate Gallery
1984; on deposit at Petworth House
(T03887; B&J 333)

depiction of a 'lady getting out of a large mustard-pot'.[18] Along with other mocking reviews, these comments reflect the ongoing opposition to Turner's work, anticipating the more widespread sense of befuddled amusement that greeted his next attempt at a Shakespearian subject set in Venice: *Juliet and her Nurse (fig.61)*.

The problem in 1836 was not so much the realisation of Venetian topography, which Turner had by then studied during two visits. It was rather his choice of Venice itself as the setting for *Romeo and Juliet*, which blithely ignored the statement in Shakespeare's prologue that the ensuing action takes place 'In fair Verona'. To explain this glaring anomaly, scholars have put forward a range of ingenious solutions, offering alternative sources of inspiration, such as the tale of the ill-fated 'Marcolini' in Samuel Rogers's *Italy*, which Turner had illustrated nearly a decade earlier *(fig.64)*.[19] Yet the way Juliet leans lightly on her cheek, as described by Romeo, and the fact that Turner changed the title of the image to a basic topographical description when it was engraved, to avoid further embarrassment, together indicate that he clearly meant the heroine to be Shakespeare's.

Prior to *Juliet and her Nurse*, his Venetian exhibits had been fundamentally straightforward views, with no specific literary references (other than the incidental presence of Canaletto in the 1833 canvas, *fig.103*). It is, therefore, quite possible that the painting was also begun as a descriptive subject, evoking the romance of hazy moonlight on the city. The composition adapts a view of the Piazza by Canaletto, but raises the vantage point dramatically so that it is comparable to, but some distance from, that which Turner enjoyed from the top of the Hotel Europa in 1833 and 1840 (see *figs.149–50*).[20] When improvising his design on canvas, without the benefit of any detailed sketches made on the spot, Turner used the strong receding lines of the Procuratie Nuove to lead the eye towards the Basilica of San Marco and the Doge's Palace, though this intrinsically resulted in an opposite thrust into the lower-right corner. He created much the same problem in the earlier *Rome from the Vatican* 1820 (Tate), where he had attempted to disguise the force of his outward perspective by introducing a cluttered table to enliven the area of the picture closest to the viewer. Juliet's balcony could, therefore, be a similar attempt to counter the perceived weakness of an empty foreground. Indeed, it is illuminating to compare the radical effect produced when Turner left this area open in another picture structured on much the same perspective model: *Rain, Steam and Speed* 1844 (National Gallery, London). But in the mid-1830s he still held fast to his preference for what Maurice Davies has called 'welcoming foregrounds', and the balcony consequently serves the same purpose as the invented parapet, bustling with onlookers, that he added to Westminster Bridge in his depiction for the previous year's exhibition of the burning of the Houses of Parliament.[21] In developing the idea

of a setting for Juliet, ironically constructed like a box at the theatre, he would have been able to draw on his recollections of the *altane*, the terraces built across the rooftops of Venice.

Of course all these considerations would also be applicable if Turner's original aim had been to provide a balcony for Juliet's romantic meditations. But there is actually little in the picture to confirm that it grew from a desire to create a historically appropriate evocation of the play. The fireworks were a regular feature of contemporary celebrations in Venice, and the ships resemble the brigs and schooners of the early nineteenth century. Likewise the golden light within the Piazza, seemingly erupting from a conflagration at Florian's café, probably replicates the gas lighting which had been introduced on Napoleon's orders. It is also significant that several of the promenading revellers below in the Piazza wear bicorn hats,

61
Juliet and her Nurse exhibited Royal
Academy 1836
Oil on canvas, 92 x 123
Sra Amalia Lacroze de Fortabat,
Argentina (B&J 365; S 97)

Whittingham has speculated that Turner's decision to fuse the two cities may actually have been influenced by the use of stock sets, including views of Venice, for a variety of different plays, often with completely inappropriate results.[25] But this tendency was already changing by the 1830s, as actor-managers like Macready insisted on a greater unity of effect in their productions, a factor that made those who first saw Turner's painting even more conscious of the incongruous setting.

Yet Turner himself plainly did not feel his relocation of the young lovers' tragedy was entirely inappropriate, even after he was savagely abused by the critics for his apparent oversight.[26] For him the woeful story of Juliet seems to have been in some way synonymous with the fate of Venice itself, as epitomised in Byron's metaphor. The latter encouraged the perception of a city denuded of its beauties, except in the remembrance of its past, and it was surely no coincidence that Turner borrowed (and altered) lines from Byron's *Childe Harold* to add this more contemporary dimension to his image when it was engraved in 1842, as if explaining his reasoning:

> ...but Beauty doth not die –
> Nor yet forget how Venice once was dear-
> The pleasant place of all festivity
> The revels of the earth, the Masque of Italy [27]

It is worth noting that Turner was not alone in making the seemingly quixotic connection between the customary Byronic vision and Shakespeare's play. In 1833, three years before the picture was exhibited, Hans Andersen described Venice as a place better appreciated by moonlight, when the 'queen of Adria, that in the day-time is a dead swan upon the muddy water, gets then life and beauty'. Disliking these sepulchral qualities, Andersen left Venice 'without regret, to go to another city of graves – that where the Scaligers repose, and where is the tomb of Romeo and Juliet – the city of Verona'.[28] While the relationship Andersen saw between the two cities may be partly fortuitous, it nonetheless demonstrates the associative links made by some of Turner's contemporaries, which as an imaginative artist he too toyed with and chose to exploit.

In 1837 Turner went back to the more conventional association of Shylock with Venice for his depiction of the Grand Canal below the Rialto bridge *(fig.58)*.[29] This was easily the largest of all his Venetian subjects. Measuring 148 x 110.5 cm, it dwarfs most of the preceding views, and was painted on a canvas effectively twice the size of the largest of the post-1840 pictures *(fig.205)*. This circumstance probably arises from the fact that it was prepared for the Royal Academy's first exhibition in its new home in the eastern wing of the National Gallery building (where it remained from

linking them more to Turner's time than to Shakespeare's. Consequently, rather than evoking the masqueraders at the ball from which Juliet retired before her tryst with Romeo, it is likely that Turner was actually recording the nightly carousing in the Piazza in the 1830s.[22]

As with *The Merchant of Venice*, Turner's experience of *Romeo and Juliet* was probably rooted in performances dating from the 1790s, though he is likely to have seen more recent productions too, as it was apparently a play for which he had a special affection. He is known to have acquired some of Thomas Stothard's illustrations to it in 1830.[23] Furthermore, his knowledge of Shakespeare's text is clear from the way he characterises Juliet, taking his cue from Act 2, scene 2, where Romeo claims she possesses a radiance to challenge the moon. Most tellingly, as already mentioned, the pose he gives Juliet originates in the text, though it is perhaps also reminiscent of that in an image of the actress Maria Ann Pope, who took the role at Covent Garden and Drury Lane before her early death *(fig.62)*.[24]

There remains a possibility that contemporary theatrical performances contributed to the switch of the setting from Verona to Venice. Selby

62
Martin Archer Shee (1769–1850)
Maria Ann Pope as Juliet exhibited Royal Academy 1803 and Queen's Bazaar, Oxford Street 1833
Oil on canvas, 92 x 76
Garrick Club, London

1837 until 1868). These new premises had three substantial galleries, as opposed to the single Great Room of Somerset House, and Turner was consequently forced to reinvent the strategies he had adopted for dominating the annual show.[30] However, he did not rely on size alone to attract attention: the picture forcefully asserts its presence through its wonderful luminosity, being the first of his exhibited Venetian paintings to create a true interaction between the nuances of aerial perspective in the wide expanse of sky and the way this effect is caught and reflected on the shimmering surface of the Grand Canal.

With the exception of the classic view of the Doge's Palace from the Bacino, the Rialto bridge was the most frequently painted subject in Venice. As well as its Shakespearian connotations, the scene had personal associations for Turner, in that he had stayed within sight of the bridge at the Leon Bianco, one of the buildings to the right of the orange sail. Rather than repeating the formula of his earlier works, he clearly felt the need to introduce some novelty to the 1837 painting, hence the upright format. This certainly permitted the greater emphasis on water and sky, but he seems to have encountered problems in adapting his horizontal sketches to the revised orientation. Thus, while the diagonal recessions towards the diminished bridge are essentially the same as in the related pencil sketch made in 1819 (see also *fig.*161),[31] the placing of the line of palaces across a narrower and deeper picture plane creates more pronounced vertical accents, most noticeably that of the brightly lit bulk of the Palazzo Grimani, which towers uneasily above everything else. Parallel to this, the bell tower of San Bartolomeo has been moved so that it lies on the central axis, its exaggerated white form drawing the eye into the image.[32] Although these modifications were intended to strengthen the composition, they actually create a sense of imbalance; this may have induced Turner to counter their weight by introducing the otherwise inexplicable cloth-draped platforms on the left, from which a monk seems to deliver a blessing. This brings us back to the subject of the picture.

In some versions of the Royal Academy's catalogue the title of the painting appeared as *Scene – a street in Venice*, rather like the stage directions in printed editions of Shakespeare's plays, which teasingly suggests that Turner did, after all, have his own copy of the Bard's works. On this occasion he clearly referred to the printed text to get an accurate quotation from Act 3, scene 3 of *The Merchant of Venice*, which supplemented his title:

Antonio: Hear me yet, good Shylock
Shylock: I'll have my bond

These lines come from the point in the play where Antonio's gaoler has brought him to Shylock to plea for clemency, though the moneylender remains dogged in his insistence on the terms of their agreement. As in *Juliet and her Nurse*, this incident, which forms the ostensible subject of the picture, is inexplicably squeezed into the lower-right corner: Shylock is the figure leaning out of a window, clutching in one hand the document recording the loan and in the other a knife and a pair of scales, with which he intends to take and weigh the contracted pound of Antonio's flesh. Below him, perched precariously on a landing-stage, stands Antonio, his arms stretched out imploringly. In this case, the costumes of the protagonists and the rest of the crowd are appropriate to the sixteenth-century setting. Clearly, however, the presence of Shylock is secondary to the evocation of one of Venice's great festivities, though the nature of the event itself remains problematic. The fur-edged splendour of one of the figures positioned alongside a brightly draped barque may well be intended to be a newly appointed Doge, perhaps Marino Grimani, who was elected in 1595, an interpretation that would serve to set Shylock's story against the greater drama of state affairs.[33] But another suggestion is that the picture illustrates Samuel Rogers's poem 'The Brides of Venice', as the bustling scene recalls the wedding morning described in the poem, and there is also a slight echo of Stothard's vignette for the 1830 edition in the group of nuns on the left.[34] Common to both of these interpretations are the attentive faces lining the balconies and the invented stairway on the right, which recall the mobs in Turner's images of the burning of the Houses of Parliament in 1835, though those ranked here fail to lend emphasis to the principal event depicted.

Because of his insignificant place in the overall design, Shylock has been seen as an afterthought, included as a taunt to the critics who had mocked the fanciful Shakespearian subject of the previous year.[35] The most savage of them, the Reverend John Eagles, duly fell into the prepared trap (specifically flagged as a danger in the painting) by describing Shylock as 'an undoubted portrait of Punch, the common street Punch; and there he is at the side of the picture as looking out of his box'.[36] One can perhaps speculate that Turner felt some instinctive sympathy for Shylock's plight as an outsider and a Jew, for on more than one occasion it is reported that his Punch-like physiognomy, his canny business acumen and his frugal way of living induced some contemporaries to assume that he must therefore be Jewish, as these qualities fitted the prevailing racist stereotype.[37]

Like the other two Shakespearian subjects with Venetian associations, the Grand Canal picture is very much Turner's own reading of his source, and a far from pure reading at that. The underlying influence of Byron and Rogers has already been remarked on, but before examining Turner's interest in these two poets, it is worth speculating whether he knew other

ruins, he probably could not have resisted the idea of a place that was supposedly crumbling before the poet's eyes. Yet, though Turner surely did imbibe Byron's elegiac vision at an early stage, it did not become palpably linked to his own publicly exhibited depictions of Venice until 1840 (figs.113, 263).

During the 1820s and 1830s, Turner became increasingly involved in the production of illustrations for lavish volumes of poetry. The first of these was the highly successful new edition of Samuel Rogers's verses, grouped under the title *Italy* (1830).[41] Known today more for his connection with Turner than as a poet in his own right, Rogers was then one of the most prominent figures in the literary world. The gatherings at his house in St James's Place brought together talented, famous and powerful people from different aspects of London life, though the implication, in a depiction of one of his convivial get-togethers, that Turner and Byron encountered each other in this setting is purely imaginary (fig.63).

Painted in 1826–7, Turner's watercolour designs for *Italy* condensed the experiences of his 1819 tour into palm-sized images bursting with vitality and light. In the context of so much skilful invention, the vignette he created of Venice is somewhat stiff, its architectural details inaccurate, despite a dependence on Canaletto's image of the Bucintoro returning to the Molo (figs.64–5). Presumably he was deflected from working up any of his own sketches of Venice by an assumption that the city could be seen only on Canaletto's terms. Nevertheless, the image illustrates effectively Rogers's invocation of Venice as a 'glorious City in the Sea'. Since these opening words became as well known and as widely quoted as those introducing the Italian section of *Childe Harold*, their association with Turner's illustration would have ensured it was one of the most familiar designs in the book.

Few would argue that Rogers's volume has the narrative sweep or the kind of philosophical intensity pursued by Byron, but it shares an interest in whimsy, a sensitivity to mood and a passion for historical anecdotes, such as that concerning the Foscari family, which attracted both writers (hence figs.70, 84, 87, 169). Another of Rogers's poems, 'The Gondola', is concerned with the city after dark, and describes how the palaces and churches appear to glitter in the moonlight, as if covered with a frost that melts away as day breaks, then become merely 'an emblem of themselves'. This conjunction of Venice with nocturnal imagery was becoming firmly established by the 1830s, though it was part of a broader taste for the romance of the moon, which was applied to other famous sites.[42] Rogers had anticipated this particular fascination in his poem 'Human Life' (1819), a work that was part of the anthology gathered in the 1834 edition of his *Poems*, also

literary evocations of Venice, such as Wordsworth's famous sonnet 'On the Extinction of the Venetian Empire'. This was written around 1802, but not published until 1807, at a time when Turner was experimenting with his own verse, some of which focused on issues of empire. Coincidentally, by 1810 he and Wordsworth shared a patron in the Earl of Lonsdale.[38]

Comparing Wordsworth's idea of Venice with Byron's is revealing, demonstrating how the idealism of the revolutionary 1790s gave way to world-weary romanticism. Wordsworth characterised the city as 'the eldest Child of Liberty', a sentiment that articulated what many felt about the crushed Republic prior to the publication of Daru's history (see p.38), even though its systems had been oligarchical rather than truly democratic. But, though the poem was widely known by the 1830s, none of Turner's images can be specifically traced back to it.[39]

In contrast, Turner had been quick to adapt lines from the third canto of Byron's great travel narrative, *Childe Harold's Pilgrimage*, for his *Field of Waterloo* 1818 (Tate),[40] and he was therefore receptive to the publication of the final section later that year. The poem converged with Turner's contemporaneous interests in the art, history and landscapes of Italy, and can be seen to have given a renewed impetus to his desire to go there himself. Furthermore, Byron's plaintive evocation of a ruined Venice at the start of the poem may have contributed to Turner's decision to stop there in the earliest stages of his travels in 1819–20: as an artist whose career was partly founded on depictions of picturesque

63 (cat.19)
Charles Mottram (1807–1876) after
John Doyle (1797–1868)
Samuel Rogers at his Breakfast Table c.1830–50
Engraving and mezzotint, 58 x 86.6
Turner is the second figure from the
right; Byron sits at the table, resting his
head upon his hand
Tate (T04907)

64 (cat.62)
Venice: The Ducal Palace, for Samuel Rogers's
*'Italy' c.*1826–7
Watercolour, 24 x 30.6
Tate (TB CCLXXX 193; D27710)

illustrated by Turner. In a roving travelogue, evidently influenced by Byron, he briefly lighted on Venice:

Now the scene shifts to Venice – to a square
Glittering with light, all nations masking there,
With light reflected on the tremulous tide,
Where gondolas in gay confusion glide,
Answering the jest, the song on every side;

Turner may actually have been thinking of these words when he embarked on *Juliet and her Nurse*. But the illustration he provided to accompany them was yet another depiction of the Rialto bridge, seen this time by moonlight and from its northern side *(fig.67)*.[43] In the shadow of the bridge he placed a young couple, who have either just left their gondola or are preparing to board it. A significant change was made in the course of engraving the design: in the watercolour the man wears a bicorn hat, so that he (like the masqueraders in the 1836 painting) is redolent of the present. But in William Miller's engraved version of the subject both figures are clothed in costumes from an earlier period, in accordance with the Romantic tendency to lend a greater enchantment through the distancing effect of time.

Even before preparations got underway for the illustrated edition of Rogers's *Poems*, the sales of its companion volume made it apparent to opportunistic publishers that Turner was as much of a draw as the poet himself, if not more so. He was consequently swamped with commissions for similar finely crafted illustrations throughout the next decade, among the first of which was a set of watercolour vignettes for a revised edition of *The Works of Lord Byron: with his Letters and Journals, and his Life*, by the Irish poet Thomas Moore, produced by John Murray.[44] The idea was to combine Byron's poems and biographical material with places described by or associated with him. Accordingly Turner was commissioned to make views of various places, some of which he had not visited for himself. His dependence on drawings by other artists for the unfamiliar sites was, remarkably, also extended to Venice *(fig.66)*. In view of the mass of material he had compiled in 1819, it is odd that he thought it necessary to model his watercolour on a design by T[homas?] Little, an apparently unknown amateur.[45] Presumably the reason lies in the subject – the Bridge of Sighs – which Turner had somehow omitted from his survey of Venetian landmarks. Little's sketch positioned him almost below the bridge, alongside the Doge's Palace, with the prisons to the left, and the dome and campanile of San Giorgio Maggiore glimpsed beyond the Ponte della Paglia.

The Bridge of Sighs image eventually appeared in November 1832, as the frontispiece to the eleventh volume in the sequence, featuring *Manfred* and *Beppo*. The latter was certainly a Venetian tale, and evidently one of Turner's

Bucentaurus et Nundinae Venetae in die Ascensionis.   XIV.

favourite works by Byron (see p.24). However, given the intrinsic emphasis on the bridge, the vignette might more aptly have served as an alluring introduction to *Childe Harold*, reminding the reader of the celebrated opening words of the fourth canto:

I stood in Venice, on the Bridge of Sighs;
A palace and a prison on each hand:

Already by this date, on encountering the bridge for the first time, these lines sprang unbidden to the front of most travellers' minds, as the literary equivalent of a Pavlovian reaction. In the 1830s, for example, though James Fenimore Cooper dismissed the passage as bad grammar, Frances, Lady Shelley experienced the more typical reaction, which she justified by claiming that 'Until I had read Byron's works actually on the spot, I had no idea of the Shakespearian force of his descriptions. To me, even Shakespeare's Rialto has become of secondary interest.'[46]

In fact, *Childe Harold* had already been illustrated in the Murray edition by views of Rome and Bacharach on the Rhine.[47] But the association of the design with *Beppo* was not such a bad second choice. Washed by moonlight,

65
Antonio Visentini (1688–1782) after
Canaletto (1697–1768)
*The Bucintoro returning to the Molo on
Ascension Day c.*1742
(from *Prospectus Magni Canalis Venetiarum*)
Engraving
Private collection

66 (cat.181)
Edward Finden (1791/2–1857) after a
watercolour by Turner (W 1225), based
on a sketch by T. Little
The Bridge of Sighs 1832
(from *Byron's Life and Works*, vol.XI, 1832)
Line engraving, published volume,
17.7 x 10.7
Dr Jan Piggott (R 421)

67 (cat.63)
*Venice (The Rialto – Moonlight), for Samuel
Rogers's 'Poems'* c.1830–2
Watercolour, 24.2 x 30.7
Tate (TB CCLXXX 196; D27713)

Turner's image chimes with Byron's account of unfettered nocturnal carnival. The figures may stem from the discussion of Venetian beauties, who, 'like so many Venuses of Titian's', lean enticingly from their balconies:

I said that like a picture by Giorgione
Venetian women were, and so they *are*
Particularly seen from a balcony
(For beauty's sometimes best set off afar)

It was no doubt these sentiments that prompted the popularity of paintings of young women seen at their windows, including Etty's *Window in Venice, during a Festa* 1831 (Tate) and Turner's own *Jessica (fig.59)*, who boldly engages the viewer in the flirtatious manner described by Byron. Yet, at the same time, the moonlit balcony scene inescapably also conjures up the way Romeo courts Juliet. It is probable, therefore, that Turner's involvement with the production of this design, as well as those for the Rogers's volumes, set in train the layering of ideas that resulted in *Juliet and her Nurse (fig.61)*. Indeed, one of the unfinished vignette studies seems to be an interim stage in the painting's development, bringing moonlight, an ambling crowd and a puppet show to the basic composition borrowed from Canaletto *(fig.68)*.

It is noticeable that for at least three of these four vignettes Turner was indebted to existing images, rather than his own sketches, confirming the suspicion that he was not yet ready to capitalise on the most revelatory aspects of the 1819 visit. This attitude was already changing in 1833, before he made his second trip, and informs his subsequent work. After returning that year he completed his set of designs for Sir Walter Scott's account of the *Life of Napoleon Buonaparte* with a group of watercolours that included his view of the Campanile of San Marco from the Bacino *(fig.69)*.[48] When published in 1835 this ornamented the title page of the third of the nine-volume edition, dealing with Napoleon's campaigns in Italy. In view of the momentous historic consequences of Napoleon's actions for Venice, Turner's image might seem a little frivolous in this context. However, as the historical costumes indicate, it recalls the harmonious, carefree decadence of an earlier century, before Venice was ruled by outsiders.[49]

Looking back from a twenty-first-century standpoint, it is perhaps difficult to comprehend why these sharply focused and somewhat fiddly vignettes satisfied Turner's audience more consistently than his contemporary oil paintings. But it was precisely their detail and their refined manipulation of familiar subjects that appealed most directly. As well as the elegant vignette form of these book illustrations, he joined others in producing landscape watercolours for popular annuals such as *The Literary Souvenir, The Amulet* and *The Keepsake*. Assured of the viability of

this format, editors calculated that there was sufficient interest among the increasingly mobile middle classes to warrant books devoted to specific countries or to extended journeys through Europe. For Turner, this resulted in three sets of drawings recording the banks of the Rivers Loire and Seine, which were accompanied in their engraved form by a letter-press written by Leitch Ritchie.[50] By the time these illustrations were being prepared Ritchie was one of the established names in this genre, writing anecdotal material for *Heath's Picturesque Annual* from 1832 onwards. His account of Venice that year during his tour of Italy, the Tyrol and the Rhine was illustrated by Clarkson Stanfield *(fig.71)*.

The other notable writer of these travel books was Thomas Roscoe, who described an imagined journey through Switzerland and Italy in the *Landscape Annual for 1830*. What makes his account especially interesting is that in the years before this, Roscoe had translated the writings of Ugo Foscolo, an exiled Venetian, who vehemently opposed Austrian rule and the imputation that Venice had been constitutionally corrupt before its fall.[51] The Venetian part of his narrative is accordingly rich in local insight, and the book's disproportionate emphasis on Venice is further underlined by the fact that four of the ten illustrations of Italy by Samuel Prout are views of the city *(fig.70)*. Hardly adventurous as a selection, the choice of subjects was probably based on the same factors that had induced Turner to refer to Shakespeare, Rogers and Byron in his literary subjects. This concentration on images of Venice is nevertheless one of the earliest indications that there was a real appetite for the city's picturesque qualities among a growing British audience. During the ensuing years it became possible to extend the range of this visual repertoire, so that even as early as 1832 Stanfield was able to include the cathedral church of San Pietro di Castello *(fig.71)* and the islands of Murano and Mazzorbo alongside more obvious subjects such as Santi Giovanni e Paolo or the Dogana *(fig.101)*.

Both Prout and Stanfield also contributed views of Venice to the various Byron publications, defining the city in a very literal way that seems at odds with the imaginative vigour and panoramic energy of the writer's thought. By contrast, Turner's own attempts to gild his designs and especially his paintings with a Byronic meaning were surely more successful, and it is not stretching the bounds of credibility to see an affinity between the poet's writings and the range of the painter's responses to Venice, a connection that was first propagated by Ruskin.[52] More recently, Lindsay Stainton has remarked that Byron's 'imagery is shifting, fluid', and resembles 'the way in which forms and light dissolve into their reflections in Turner's paintings'.[53] That such perceptions of a shared sensibility were so quickly established testifies that it was not simply a matter of Turner depicting the sights mentioned by Byron, or of him illustrating celebrated lines. As is plain from the discussion below of pictures such as *The Bridge of Sighs (fig.113)* or

68 (cat.64)
Study of the Piazza San Marco, Venice;
possibly for Samuel Rogers's 'Italy' or
'Poems' c.1826–32
Watercolour, 20.4 x 24.1
Tate (TB CCLXXX 2; D27519)

69 (cat.182)
William Miller (1796–1882) after a
watercolour by Turner (W 1105)
The Campanile 1835
(from *Scott's Prose Works*, vol.X, 1835)
Line engraving, published volume,
16.5 x 20.5
Dr Jan Piggott (R 528)

Approach to Venice (fig.263), Turner not only responded to the adapted words he associates with these paintings, but offered instead a richer embodiment of Byron's imagery that is evidently a deeply felt response to it. In other instances, he seems to allude to Byron's ideas without drawing the viewer's attention to a specific source – though these connections were possibly obvious to his well-read audience *(fig.229)*.

The nature of what Turner took directly from Byron is somewhat complicated by the fact that some of the other poetic sources he favoured delivered the essence of Byron's ideas at second-hand. For example, Shelley's *Lines Written Among the Euganean Hills* (1818), which is a discernible influence in the paintings of 1843 onwards (see p.227; *figs.209, 240, 248*), features a darkly portentous depiction of a decayed Venice that restates the sentiments Byron had already expressed.

Having noted this vital affiliation with Byron, it is nevertheless clear that Turner retained an independent outlook. Incidental details in some of the later paintings suggest that he did not wholly endorse the languid resignation of Byron's view of Venice, and that he also recognised the attempts of the city's inhabitants to make a new life for themselves within their externally imposed constraints.[54] It is consequently difficult to generalise about the extent to which Turner's Venice is the same as Byron's. What is indisputable is that there was a shift towards the poet's vision in the paintings postdating 1840 that corresponds with a similar adjustment in British attitudes to Venice. This did not efface the popularity of Shakespeare's Shylock, but it introduced a greater understanding of the city's history and its inimitable beauties. For Turner, this resulted in images that delight in purely sensory effects, where Venice is conjured up as an enticing illusion. Even so, perhaps the most significant way in which Byron informs Turner's views of Venice is through a lurking awareness that there is an uneasy darkness behind the brilliant façades; that a palace may conceal a prison.

70 (cat.179)
J. Tingle after Samuel Prout (1783–1852)
Palace of Foscari, looking south towards Accademia 1830
(plate 20 of the *Landscape Annual for 1830*; also known as *The Tourist in Switzerland and Italy* by Thomas Roscoe)
Engraving, published volume, 14 x 20.3
Private collection

71 (cat.180)
R. Wallis after Clarkson Stanfield (1793–1867)
Church of San Pietro di Castello 1832
(plate 13 of *Heath's Picturesque Annual for 1832*; also known as *Sketches in the North of Italy, the Tyrol, and on the Rhine* by Leitch Ritchie)
Engraving, published volume, 13.5 x 20.4
Private collection

Part Two: Discovering Venice 1819–40

4   Sketching the City

That Turner became in some sense addicted to Venice was readily apparent
to his contemporaries through the long series of twenty-five oil paintings
exhibited between 1833 and 1846. However, a much richer understanding of
his unquenchable appetite for the shifting patterns of the city's topography
emerged more fully after his death, once access was permitted to the
extensive body of Venetian sketches he had accumulated in his studio.
This amounts to many hundreds of pages, in ten sketchbooks, on which he
set down variation after variation on the well-known landmarks bordering
the great waterways at the heart of the city. Just as significant is the large
group of watercolours, arguably his most compelling engagement with
the physical and atmospheric character of any of the cities he visited in the
course of fifty years of travelling. This material is all the more remarkable
in that it demonstrates Turner's determination to overcome the specific
difficulties associated with sketching in Venice (fig.73).

By making repeated visits, Turner gradually expanded his knowledge
of Venetian topography, with each stay bringing new discoveries that drew
him steadily away from the area around San Marco. Since Turner's subject
itself underwent comparatively little change, it is fascinating to compare
the draughtsmanship of his earliest views with the increasingly spare and
summary studies he made on subsequent trips.[1] This not only provides
a predictably clear sense of his artistic development towards a leaner, less
exact approach in the mature work, but it also reveals how each mark and
line in these later studies is loaded with significance. Far from being pure
abstractions of the observed forms, his sketches are acute and concentrated
in what they reproduce.

Prior to the visit to Venice in 1819, he had already evolved a habit of
spreading his chosen view across the full width of a page opening, and he
repeatedly adopted this practice in the sketches of the 'Milan to Venice' and
the 'Venice to Ancona' books (figs.72, 76). He also occasionally extended the
extent of his panorama by curling his page up to allow him to continue the
view on the next sheet, so that one viewpoint covers two or three pages.[2]
His interest in encircling views may have been heightened by Baker and
Burford's panorama of the Piazza, which went on display just before Turner
left London.[3] His own grand sweeps of Venetian topography are in some
instances set down in serried ranks, with the water in one image becoming

72 (cat.76)
*The Cannaregio Canal, with the Palazzo
Labia and San Geremia on the Left, with
the Ghetto in the Distance, from the Grand
Canal; also a Group of Gondolas* 1819
Pencil, 11.2 x 18.5 each
From the 'Milan to Venice' sketchbook
Tate (TB CLXXV ff.87v, 88; D14482,
D14483)

73
Clarkson Stanfield (1793–1867)
*'Darn the Mosqueetos': Letter written from the
Albergo Leon Bianco relating the Hazards of
Sketching in Venice* 5 October 1830
Pen and ink
National Maritime Museum, Greenwich

74 (cat.84)
San Giorgio Maggiore – Early Morning 1819
Watercolour, 22.3 x 28.7
From the 'Como and Venice' sketchbook
Tate (TB CLXXXI 4; D15254)

75 (cat.85)
The Punta della Dogana, with the Zitelle
in the Distance 1819
Watercolour, 22.3 x 28.5
From the 'Como and Venice' sketchbook
Tate (TB CLXXXI 6; D15256)

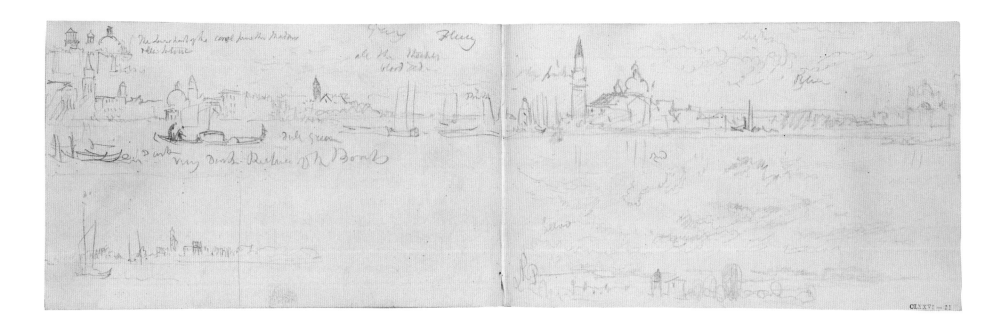

76 (cat.77)
*The Bacino looking East, with Sketches of the
Sky* 1819
Pencil, 11.1 x 18.4 each
From the 'Venice to Ancona'
sketchbook
Tate (TB CLXXVI ff.20v, 21; D14526,
D14527)

77 (cat.86)
*Venice: Looking East towards San Pietro
di Castello – Early Morning* 1819
Watercolour, 22.3 x 28.7
From the 'Como and Venice' sketchbook
Tate (TB CLXXXI 5; D15255)

the sky in the one below. Because the forms are defined against the white paper simply as pencil outlines, with little indication of mass, the effect resembles an oriental fantasy of floating palaces.

Colour is for the most part present merely in written comments: at this date Turner seldom sketched in colour on the spot. The reason he gave was that 'it would take up too much time to colour in the open air – he could make 15 or 16 pencil sketches to one coloured'.[4] In spite of this creed, the visit resulted in a handful of unforgettable watercolours that confront the challenge of rendering in paint the luminous sparkle of Venice's reflected sunlight. These occurred in a sketchbook that also contained ravishing studies of Lake Como (fig.15).[5] It is evident that some or all of these were painted directly in front of the motif, most obviously the two studies that show the view from the Palazzo Giustinian, subsequently the Hotel Europa (figs.74–5). Even Turner himself rarely surpassed the revelatory immediacy these works possess in their presentation of a moment defined by light. Lindsay Stainton has noted that this pair can be placed side by side to create an almost continuous panorama,[6] and this anticipates the subject, though not the effect, of the painting Turner exhibited in 1842 (fig.220). Clearly painted relatively quickly one after the other, the watercolours capture the brilliance of the sun an hour or two after it had risen. Both works are restrained, combining a deft use of the white paper with planes of blue-grey colour to suggest the blinding dazzle, making the objects seen against the light appear essentially flat. Away from this glare, Turner subtly introduced more colour. He also noted how the light on partly illuminated buildings, such as the church of the Zitelle on the Giudecca in fig.75, seems to dissolve and absorb the actual structure.

The left-hand side of the panoramic view recurs in a further study (fig.77), which may also have been painted en plein air, though its relationship to a study in the 'Venice to Ancona' sketchbook (fig.76) indicates how Turner played with the positioning of bell towers and domes to produce a greater sense of recession. These differences simultaneously indicate the constraints of the sketchbook format, which frequently resulted in compressions of actual space in order to create satisfying designs on the page. As in the paired watercolours, the day is just beginning and the presence of rosy clouds perhaps indicates a moment just before sunrise. This could be a directly observed phenomenon, but the pencil sketch is also annotated with remarks about the colours of the clouds, and is accompanied by a separate study of the sky that could have provided Turner with sufficient information to develop his watercolour some time later.[7]

Judging from the cluster of moored gondolas in the foreground, Turner's real or imagined vantage point was alongside a landing-stage, possibly that beside the Palazzo Giustinian, which would have permitted him to look eastwards towards the shadowy form of San Pietro di Castello.

Comparing the watercolour with the pencil sketch once more reveals that he omitted the campanile that should appear to the right of the cathedral, rising behind the Public Gardens, which can probably be identified as that of Sant'Isepo. A series of small flicks of the brush suggest the trees of the giardini, which had been created in the preceding years as a result of the suppression and demolition of a number of churches. More conspicuously, he left the right side of the composition open, without the island of San Giorgio Maggiore.

The last Venetian view in the 'Como and Venice' sketchbook, which depicts the Doge's Palace and the Campanile from the piazza of San Giorgio, is built up over a faint pencil outline that suggests it was recorded on the spot (fig.78).[8] None of the other studies bears any evidence of under-drawing, which in this instance may have helped resolve the complex interaction of architectural forms. Once again, the brilliance of the light is intensified by the underlying white ground which, as it shimmers through the yellow washes, perfectly replicates the effect of sunlight reflected on the buildings bordering the Molo. A more exaggerated version of the elements deployed here can be found in Turner's first Venetian oil painting (fig.103).[9]

Another study, now in Boston, is probably also intended to be a view of Venice, a conclusion first put forward by Barbara Reise (fig.79).[10] This design was engraved by Turner in the first half of the 1820s for an unpublished set of mezzotints generally known as the 'Little Liber'.[11] In the later states of the image Turner added an erupting volcano to the left-hand edge, which induced early collectors of the prints to think he had depicted Mount Etna, near Catania in Sicily. Apart from the fact that he never ventured so far south, there is an echo of this composition in one of the late oil paintings depicting the Giudecca canal, though that too is imprecise in its presentation of topography (fig.266). Turner's own list of the subjects he had completed for the 'Little Liber' group confirms a Venetian identification, because it includes a view entitled simply 'Venice', which must be this image.[12] The volcano, added in the course of refining the mezzotint is, in fact, far more likely to be Vesuvius, which he had also sketched in 1819. The watercolour thus represents a fascinating early instance of Turner making use of his Italian travels in an imaginative way, allowing his memory and his emotions to produce a dramatic scene that reveals something of what he felt about Venice, and complements his more 'purely visual' watercolours.[13]

All of these pencil sketches and watercolours were for Turner's own benefit, providing information he could cull, while advancing his technical prowess. It is difficult to think of any other artist who adopted such a voracious means of gathering material. Indeed, a comparison with the on-the-spot sketches of those British artists who came to Venice in search of picturesque subjects in the years after Turner's first visit highlights his

78 (cat.87)
*The Campanile of San Marco and the Doge's
Palace* 1819
Pencil and watercolour, 22.3 x 28.7
From the 'Como and Venice' sketchbook
Tate (TB CLXXXI 7; D15258)

unique approach. Foremost among these pioneers was Prout, who spent three weeks in Venice during September 1824 and probably returned there again in 1825 or 1826.[14] He exhibited his very detailed pictures at the Old Water Colour Society, where he made a name for himself from 1820 onwards with views resulting from his Continental travels (see *fig.98*). These were developed from incredibly meticulous pencil sketches, such as that of the Pilastri Acritani (*fig.81*). Unlike Turner, who was prepared to summarise and trust to memory far more often, Prout's method was laborious, bringing the whole image to a uniform degree of refinement.

Prout probably had the chance to share his sketches with Bonington in Paris on his way back to England.[15] It may have been this encounter that further encouraged the young Bonington to undertake his own Italian tour in 1826, a month of which was spent in Venice. The pencil sketches he made there are as precise as Prout's but were executed with a lighter, more expressive hand that also introduced a sense of bulk and the sculpting

of shadows. Bonington was similarly undaunted by intricate architectural subjects, which are fixed on his page with incredible assurance. The same miraculous ability to record minute detail is apparent in a small group of oil studies that also use broader touches of the brush to create soft, melting distances. Many of these were sold in London during the early 1830s, after Bonington's early death, and it is possible that the almost tangible freshness they possess captivated Turner at the moment when he was beginning his own painterly explorations of Venice.[16] He later had opportunities to study Bonington's pictures in the collections of his friends and patrons. For example, Sir James Willoughby Gordon and his wife acquired the oil study of a stretch of palace façades in July 1844 (*fig.80*; see also p.104).[17]

Despite his appreciation of the airy naturalism of Bonington's art, Turner remained dogged in his adherence to the practice of sketching in pencil from the motif during his stay in Venice in 1833, charting his explorations of the city in three small notebooks (*figs.8, 83, 112*). His draughtsmanship for the scenes he had previously missed is tighter than in the sketches of buildings he had observed before, but even so it is not nearly as fastidious as his handling in 1819. Then he had invariably selected his subject so that it filled his sheet, but in 1833 his approach was much more fragmentary, both in terms of its focus and also in the way he constructed the buildings he studied with restless, energetic lines.

As mentioned in the introductory essay (p.21), it is perhaps conceivable that some of the colour sketches on sheets of grey paper were made during this stay (see *figs.82, 111, 172, 180, 189, 190*). With their use of a limited tonal palette over pencil outlines, the impression they create is of observations recorded on the spot. As either personal memoranda or as preparatory studies for paintings, these watercolours, with their blurred blocks of colour representing the palaces and churches, could not be more different from the equivalent types of drawing by his contemporaries.

Just a year after Turner's second trip the precocious William James Müller passed through Venice with fellow artist George Fripp.[18] Unlike Turner's fleeting visits of a week or so, they stayed for nearly two months, and as in the case of Bonington's similarly protracted stay, this more leisurely pace explains why Müller was able to execute very fine drawings that pursue a highly rigorous and thorough scrutiny of complicated architectural surfaces. His precise but stiff depiction of the Palazzo Foscari (*fig.84*), for which Müller required the use of a pair of opera glasses to overcome his short-sightedness, exemplifies his approach. As his inscription on the sketch admitted, even with this aid it was incredibly taxing to attempt such unflinching precision. By 1834 the palace increasingly attracted the attention of artists and tourists (*fig.70*), chiefly because of Byron's account of the intrigues of the Foscari family, though Rogers had also devoted a section of his *Italy* to their saga.

79
A Recollection of Venice (also known as *Catania, Sicily*) c.1820
Watercolour, 23.1 x 28.1
Museum of Fine Arts, Boston (W 774)

80 (cat.2)
Richard Parkes Bonington (1802–1828)
Palazzi Manolesso-Ferro, Contarini-Fasan, and
Contarini on the Grand Canal c.1826
Oil on board, 36.8 x 47.6
Richard L. Feigen & Co, New York

Though other Byronic subjects were also drawn into the picturesque repertoire, the generation of travellers who came to Venice in the 1830s continued to favour the most celebrated landmarks. The able amateur Lady Susan Percy made a view of the Punta della Dogana from the balcony of the Doge's Palace which is typical of the kind of 'snapshot' imagery that was sought and created by tourists *(fig.85)*. At the same time artists such as Stanfield had already begun to mine the potential of more obscure corners of the city, proliferating images of outlying islands and backwaters in exhibited pictures or in publications *(fig.71)*. Another novel means of revealing a different character to Venice can be found in the sketches and finished paintings of James Holland, who was there in 1835 and again on three occasions after 1845.[19] Though they became formulaic through frequent repetition, his pictures were initially striking in focusing down a stretch of narrow canal, at the end of which he closed the vista with the façade of a famous palace or church, basking in brilliant sunlight. Many of these works are capriccios, bringing together unrelated groups of buildings to suit his designs.[20] His sketches likewise demonstrate an inherent fascination with the traditionally picturesque, as in the view of the rarely depicted Santa Maria dei Miracoli *(fig.86)*, where his eye was presumably caught by the contrast between the ramshackle scaffolding and the church's jewel-box exterior.[21]

After the crisply dispassionate way in which Holland transcribed the crumbling fabric of Venice, Turner's final sketches of 1840 inevitably seem much less particular in their snatched and ragged approximation of the features of the city. However, in turning the pages of the three sketchbooks containing these jottings, one is constantly amazed by the economy with which a few dashes of his pencil created not only instantly recognisable outlines of familiar sights, but how effectively they suggest the ornamental detail on buildings like the Doge's Palace *(fig.116)*. There is the same edgy compulsion to absorb the bare essence of the visible world that was evident in the earlier sketches, but, perhaps more noticeably than in those of 1833, Turner seems to have been endlessly driven to move on to the next subject, even as he rushed to define what lay in front of him. His vigorous line bounds between buildings in the many panoramic profiles he made of the city from the water, as he sought increasingly to summarise Venice as a silhouette, studied against the setting sun. And though he frequently selected subjects represented many times by others, such as the Palazzo Foscari *(fig.87)*, and less familiar ones, like the buildings bordering the wide Giudecca canal *(fig.11)*, he was driven by instinct to be inventive, to reject the commonplace.

Much the same attitude prevails in the watercolour studies associated with the 1840 visit, which were painted on various loose sheets of paper, and in two 'roll' sketchbooks (see Appendix p.258). The first of these, in the

82 (cat.68)
The Punta della Dogana, with San Giorgio
Maggiore beyond 1833 or 1840
Pencil, watercolour and bodycolour on
grey paper, 19.5 x 28.1
Tate (TB CCCXVII 22; D32207; S 35)

83 (cat.78)
Views of the Punta della Dogana and Santa
Maria della Salute from the Hotel Europa 1833
Pencil, 11.3 x 18.4 each
(From the 'Vienna up to Venice'
sketchbook)
Tate (TB CCCXI ff.80v, 81; D31573, D31574)

84
William James Müller (1812–1845)
*Looking towards the Palazzo Foscari, with the
Palazzi Nani and Giustinian, from the Grand
Canal* October 1834
Pencil, 27.6 x 42.9
Inscribed, 'When built no Window-Tax;
but *it's one on the artist.*'
Private collection

85 (cat.22)
Lady Susan Elizabeth Percy (1782–1847)
Venice, with the Salute 1834
Chalk and watercolour on blue paper,
18.7 x 27.5
Tate (T10699)

Turner Bequest, documents a journey through the centre of Venice, and then away to its unfamiliar western edges. Its twenty-two sheets are accordingly regrouped here as the 'Grand Canal and Giudecca' sketchbook, to differentiate them from the other 'Venice' sketchbooks in the collection. In addition to these, there are a further eighteen or nineteen Venetian subjects on sheets of Whatman paper in collections around the world, which it has sometimes been suggested were originally part of the same book. In fact, these watercolours more probably constitute a second roll sketchbook that was broken up by the dealer Thomas Griffith after Turner's death. Described here as the 'Storm' sketchbook, these non-Bequest sheets are most consistently defined by squally atmospheric effects that transform the city, offering a completely original way of representing Venice. Just occasionally these studies overlap with the Bequest works in the adoption of a similar viewpoint or in the use of the same palette range, and it seems possible that in some instances Turner worked on an image in both books simultaneously, allowing his colours to dry as he went back and forth between the two (*figs.243–4*).

Where the great body of work produced by Turner in 1840 does overlap with views made by other artists, it is instructive to note differences in his approach to composition, as well as more obvious technical disparities. A case in point is a sketch of the Grand Canal by William Callow (*fig.89*), a follower of Bonington, which was probably executed within days of the pair of watercolours that Turner made of the same view (*figs.88, 90*). Both artists would undoubtedly have been aware that the scene had been immortalised by Canaletto (*fig.23*), and may have been consciously pitting themselves against his achievement, though it should be said that the view of the Rialto from the Palazzo Foscari, situated along the outer curve of one of the tightest bends on the canal, is a natural point from which to survey the stately line of palaces leading up to the bridge. Significantly, Callow chose to omit the grand façade of the Palazzo Balbi on the left, and thereby placed greater emphasis on the palaces facing it. This decision was presumably influenced by the fact that one of the latter had been Byron's home in Venice. In place of the Palazzo Balbi, the near left foreground is closed by the low bulk of a *trabaccolo*, which is also evident, if only summarily, in Turner's study. It is also noticeable that Callow, like Canaletto, does not distort the scale of the distant bridge or the churches seen above the rooftops, in contrast with Turner, whose tendency was always to exaggerate such eye-catching landmarks.

Both of Turner's watercolours were sketched initially in pencil, but not in any detail – one in the Bequest roll sketchbook, the other on a loose sheet of pale buff wove paper. Whether he applied the watercolour in studies such as this actually on the spot or sometime later, back in his hotel room, is a matter of continuing debate (see *fig.91*). For he had trained himself as a

86 (cat.16)
James Holland (1799–1870)
The Church of Santa Maria dei Miracoli, Venice 30 September 1835
Pencil, watercolour and bodycolour, 35.7 x 23.9
Whitworth Art Gallery, University of Manchester. Gift of A.E. Anderson, 1918
(D.1918.3)

young man to be able to develop his simple outlines, sometimes many years after the event. From at least 1836, however, when he toured the Aosta valley, it is clear that Turner began to paint more regularly in watercolour during his travels.[22] In the present pair it is difficult to believe that the delicate touches of paint defining the windows, balconies and roof tiles were not informed by close study on location. Indeed, this is also the case for many of the other watercolour views of the Grand Canal (see p.150).

There are significant differences in the degree to which Turner developed the watercolours in his two 1840 roll sketchbooks, and yet the more 'finished' storm images possess a forceful sense of untrammelled immediacy and of Turner's direct involvement in the observed scene (figs.114, 186–8). Paradoxically, the imaginative potency of these studies required the controlled environment of his workroom for their realisation, demonstrating how effectively Turner was able to bridge the gap between site and studio. The true nature of the impressive alchemy by which rudimentary first-hand impressions were transformed into fully developed statements was not always apparent, even to Turner's most fervent admirer, Ruskin. For many years he convinced himself that Turner was utterly faithful to the objective fact of the visible world, even though the research he conducted, following in the artist's footsteps, threw up glaring discrepancies of scale, detail or colour.[23] During his own tour of Italy in 1840–1 he visited some of the places he knew from Turner's book illustrations, but the sketches he made are factual picturesque studies in the manner of Prout and David Roberts (fig.92); he did not arrive at his imitative Turnerian manner until a year or two later.

Unlike Turner, Ruskin's obsession was with detail, frequently at the expense of a more holistic approach, and his images invariably come into sharp focus in only one area, like vignettes. Thus it is not surprising that he subsequently welcomed the new development of photography, seeing its application as a means of seizing a precise and absolute record of any subject, but especially those containing intricate features that sometimes eluded the best artists. Writing with enthusiasm of some daguerreotypes he bought in 1845, Ruskin noted: 'It is very nearly the same thing as carrying off the palace itself – every chip of stone & stain is there – and of course, there is no mistake about *proportions*.'[24]

Turner's last trip to Venice coincided with the first wave of the international frenzy of excitement about the potential of photography. At this stage its practitioners primarily created daguerreotypes, with lengthy exposure times, which produced highly reflective images on silver-coated copper plates. Unlike Fox Talbot's contemporaneous paper negative method, each daguerreotype was unique, which meant that it had to be engraved exactly like a drawing if it was to be more widely propagated, although this process was aided by the fact that the images were generally

87 (cat.83)
Two Views of the Palazzo Foscari 1840
Pencil, 12.6 x 19.8 each
From the 'Venice: Passau to Würzburg'
sketchbook
Tate (TB CCCX ff.4v, 5; D31284, D31285)

88 (cat.104)
The Grand Canal, from the Palazzo Balbi and the Palazzo Mocenigo to the Rialto Bridge 1840
Pencil and watercolour, 22.3 x 32.8
From the 'Grand Canal and Giudecca' sketchbook
Tate (TB CCCXV 20; D32136; S 55)

89 (cat.5)
William Callow (1812–1908)
The Grand Canal 3 September 1840
Pencil and watercolour, 25.4 x 36.2
Private collection (courtesy of Agnew's)

90
Palazzo Balbi on the Grand Canal 1840
Pencil and watercolour, with coloured crayon, on pale buff paper, 20.6 x 29.9
National Galleries of Scotland, Edinburgh (W 1372)

91
Turner's portable watercolour palette.
Pigments identified include Mars
brown, vermilion, Prussian blue, Indian
yellow, reddish-brown ochre, Sienna,
Red Lake, orange-brown iron oxide,
with possibly rose madder and indigo.
Turner's medium was gum arabic with
some honey or sugar added.
Private collection

92 (cat.25)
John Ruskin (1819–1900)
Court of the Ducal Palace, Venice May 1841
Pencil, pen and ink, with wash, 34 x 46
Ashmolean Museum, Oxford. Ruskin
School Collection

captured in reverse. Inevitably, as Venice was increasingly a focus of tourist itineraries, it was among the first places recorded by the camera. In 1840–1 Alexander John Ellis made a set of daguerreotypes, which he tried unsuccessfully to develop as a printed publication (*fig.93*). Meanwhile, views of Venetian landmarks were engraved for Noël-Marie Paymal Lerebours's *Excursions Daguerriennes* (1841–2).[25]

Though it is well known that Turner was fascinated by the development of this new technology in the later 1840s, it is doubtful whether he saw any immediate advantages for his own methods of gathering information during his travels.[26] His sketching practice was by then finely honed to the wide-ranging approach described above precisely because he did not choose (or need) to encumber himself with the clutter of the professional artist. So there would have been little appeal in the bulky apparatus necessary to make daguerreotypes. And though photography offered a means of capturing all that fell within the camera's lens at a particular moment with an effortless, unblinking clarity, its procedure was then too slow and costly to be used like a sketchbook, where a variety of impressions and sensations could be set down, floating free of their original contexts, ripe for imaginative redevelopment. Such practical considerations are likely to have been of far more significance to Turner than the benefits of reliably factual images, and he continued his unwavering reliance on the act of sketching up to the end of his life. Moreover, contrary to apocryphal anecdotes, he was unlikely to have feared that photography would quickly supplant what was possible in painting, even if he had the foresight to appreciate that it represented a new direction of image-making.

93
Alexander John Ellis (1814–1890)
The Molo, with the Campanile, the Zecca and the Doge's Palace 1841
Daguerreotype
National Museum of Photography, Film and Television, Bradford

5 Contemporary Approaches to Venice in British Art

It was not until the later 1820s that any of Turner's contemporaries really began to exploit Venice as a subject in their exhibited and published work. Yet in 1837 the profusion of Venetian paintings and engravings caused Balzac to complain that these depictions by British artists had engendered a deplorable over-familiarity with the city's famous sights.[1] By 1850 the ceaseless tide of views caused Thackeray to grumble, 'I am weary of gondolas, striped awnings, sailors with red night (or rather day) caps, cobalt distances and posts in water. I have seen too many white palaces standing before dark purple skies, black towers with gamboge atmosphere behind them.'[2] With his concluding allusion to the yellow pigment that was invariably associated with Turner, it is clear that Thackeray saw the artist as partly responsible for this steady inundation. But though Turner's paintings of Venice were a conspicuous element of his last working decades, it is curious that it took him so long to make use of his vast store of sketches.

It was not until 1830, in fact, that the public was offered the Canalettoesque vignette in Rogers's *Italy* (fig.64) as the first tangible evidence that Turner actually knew Venice. Long before this, however, he had painted a couple of watercolour views for a more private forum, which represent his first real attempt to assimilate the experience of his first stay (figs.94–5). These were completed in 1821, a year or so after his return, for his close friend and patron Walter Fawkes, as part of a group of seven Italian drawings, priced at twenty-five guineas each.[3] The subjects were probably selected in discussion with Fawkes, who had himself travelled on the Continent in the 1780s. Significantly, the emphasis of the set initially fell on Rome, with those of Venice following a year afterwards.

Partly because it is now a less familiar subject, the more striking of the pair is the watercolour in which the spires and domes of the city are seen in the distance from the edge of the Lagoon (fig.94). Yet this was once a prospect that greeted all visitors, acting as a magical prologue to the experience of Venice itself, and was only superseded when the rail bridge was constructed from Mestre in the early 1840s (see fig.272). Turner had no sketches of his own to guide him when painting the watercolour,[4] and focused more generally on the unique nature of the approach to Venice by water, so that the drawing became another of the visual accounts of his own travels.[5] Conspicuous among the foreground staffage is an ostentatiously framed picture, alluding to the glorious legacy of Venetian painting.

There is a similar sense of vibrant bustle in the related watercolour of the Rialto bridge (fig.95), which, though similar to the earlier Hakewill view (fig.31), is based on sketches made near the Traghetto San Benedetto.[6] The greater distance from the bridge brings the elegant, obelisk-crowned façade of the Palazzo Coccina Tiepolo into view on the left, while the right-hand side of the canal is dominated by the towering mass of the Palazzo Grimani in a way that anticipates the oil painting of 1837 (fig.58). Working from his own sketches gave Turner a greater confidence to telescope and distort scale, one of the results being the raising of the height of the Fondaco dei Tedeschi beyond the bridge, where he corrected the inaccuracies he had introduced to his earlier depiction of the building.[7] As in the Fusina view, the surface of the water is enlivened with dashes and squiggles of the brush, and Turner evidently added highlights by scratching the paper.

A third watercolour, on Whatman paper and of the same dimensions as the other two, depicts the view down the southern stretch of the Grand Canal from under the Rialto bridge, but was abandoned unfinished (fig.96). Its early history is not known before it was sold in 1964, though it was probably also begun for the Fawkes group.[8] The idea of framing a city scene within the arch of a bridge comes from Canaletto, who had introduced this device in one of his London paintings.[9] In the early 1820s Turner also conceived an oil painting of the Rialto, again spanned by the bridge, but likewise inexplicably failed to finish it (fig.5).

The famous bridge was an immensely popular subject, since it was so well known from its Shakespearian context. Among Turner's contemporaries, Prout's earliest exhibits of Venice at the Old Water Colour Society in 1825 and 1827 were predominantly views of the Rialto, and these would have been seen by the young John Frederick Lewis, who made his own trip to Venice in October 1827. Two pages of his sketchbook are devoted to the bridge, the first of which Lewis later developed as a watercolour (fig.97), and this may be the work he exhibited in 1830.[10] As in his other Venetian subjects, the Grand Canal setting was essentially just a stage on which he grouped characteristic examples of the city's inhabitants, giving a foretaste of his sympathetic anthropological depictions of the Middle East. There is a greater sense of these figures as individuals than in the work of some of Lewis's contemporaries. Turner and Prout, for example, were inclined to use stock types in their finished pictures, which vary in the degree to which they convince as representations of human beings.

94 (cat.65)
*Venice from Fusina c.*1821
Watercolour, 28.6 x 40.6
Private collection (W 721)

95 (cat.66)
The Rialto, Venice c.1820
Watercolour and bodycolour on
off-white paper, 28.6 x 41.3
Indianapolis Museum of Art, Gift in
memory of Dr and Mrs Hugo O. Pantzer
by their Children (W 718)

96 (cat.67)
The Grand Canal, with the Palazzo Grimani,
from below the Rialto Bridge c.1820
Pencil and watercolour, 28.3 x 40.7
National Gallery of Ireland (W 725)

97 (cat.17)
John Frederick Lewis (1805–1876)
The Rialto Bridge 1827
Watercolour, bodycolour and gum
arabic, 21.5 x 34.4
Trustees of the Cecil Higgins Art
Gallery, Bedford

98 (cat.24)
Samuel Prout (1783–1852)
The Rialto Bridge Venice, from the North
possibly exhibited Old Water Colour
Society 1827
Watercolour, 74 x 114
Private collection

As well as contributing an annual batch of exhibits right up to the 1840s, Prout produced a stream of engraved designs. Many of these plates were simultaneously published in London and Paris, contributing, no doubt, to Balzac's disdain for the prevalence of Venetian images. Prout's painstaking watercolours may be factually accurate, but he customarily chose to render the buildings in a drab brown wash that rarely evokes the rich surfaces of sparkling marble or worn plaster. Occasionally, however, in the better-preserved examples, it is possible to see why his works were so sought after. The impressive large-scale view of the Rialto and the Fondaco dei Tedeschi (*fig.98*), for example, is tightly composed and teems with boatmen and traders on the busy canal, perhaps intended to recall the more prosperous merchants of an earlier century. The handling is quite bold, with a spirited use of a brighter palette, and though it has sometimes been dated later, it is possible that this was the large watercolour exhibited in 1827.[11]

Another view of Venice that made its debut that year was Bonington's oil painting of the Doge's Palace (*fig.99*), which was shown at the Salon in Paris from November, before moving on to London for the British

Institution exhibition in February 1828. Both French and British critics inevitably compared it favourably with Canaletto, in the absence of any more recent paintings of Venice on this scale. And while the English reviewers tended to suggest that its strength lay in its precision, Auguste Jal marvelled at its painterly range of 'Vivacity, firmness, effect, colour, breadth of touch'.[12]

Bonington's viewpoint coincides almost exactly with that in a watercolour produced by Prout for the *Landscape Annual* of 1830.[13] Whereas Prout peopled his quayside with idling sailors in exotic costumes, Bonington more explicitly evoked the past with a long procession of cowled monks of different orders. This was deliberate set-dressing, based on no obvious festive occasion or historical incident, and was of a piece with Bonington's predilection for the romance of the past, as manifest in his creation of many other costume subjects. Back in Paris, he completed another Venetian painting, which was also shown in London in the spring of 1828, among his first exhibits at the Royal Academy.[14] This depicted the Salute from near the Accademia, one of the most appealing views in Venice for its tapering line of palaces and its mixture of gothic and baroque architecture, perfectly offset by water and sky. It was a scene inevitably also painted by Turner (*figs.174–5*), but he is known to have been an especial admirer of Bonington's version when the picture was in the collection of Munro of Novar, apparently insisting that it should always be displayed in conjunction with his own canvases (*figs.61, 109*).[15]

In 1830 the image was made more widely available as a lithograph. This was engraved by James Duffield Harding, a former pupil of Prout, who was by then an established exhibitor at the Old Water Colour Society. A brilliant draughtsman, he subsequently became a respected drawing teacher and briefly nurtured Ruskin's talent. Harding made the first of several visits to Venice in 1831, producing afterwards a large watercolour, which is fundamentally only a reworking of the Bonington painting (*fig.100*). Nevertheless, a journalist recommended that Turner take note of its 'exquisitely fine' details when it hung in the same 1835 Academy exhibition as his painting of the lower Grand Canal (*fig.109*), which the critic condemned for its 'brilliant obscurity'.[16]

These pictures by Prout, Lewis, Bonington and Harding represent just a select sample of the earliest attempts to introduce Venice to British exhibition visitors at the end of the 1820s. With the exception of Lewis, in his depictions of stoical gondoliers and peasant women, none of these artists made a concerted effort to represent the widely reported listlessness of contemporary Venice, dressing it up instead in its former glories. But this predisposition to blur past and present was perfectly in tune with its age, and was the foundation on which tourist expectations of Venice have since been developed.

99 (cat.1)
Richard Parkes Bonington (1802–1828)
Venice: Ducal Palace with a Religious Procession exhibited Salon 1827, British Institution 1828
Oil on canvas, 114.3 x 162.6
Tate (N05789)

As the 1830s got under way, Venice became closely associated in the minds of some Londoners with Clarkson Stanfield. Originally trained as a painter of stage scenery, he did not start exhibiting until 1820, but had since then supplemented his success in the theatre with acclaim in the professional art world, which was in 1831 cemented with a commission from William IV (a favour that Turner's defenders felt should have been conferred on him). It was in that year that Stanfield created the apparently spectacular diorama of Venice, as viewed from the Bacino di San Marco, for the Drury Lane pantomime *Harlequin and Little Thumb*.[17] His timing could not have been more opportune, for December 1831 also saw the publication of his views of Venice in *Heath's Picturesque Annual (fig.71)*. The most impressive of the series is that of the entrance to the Grand Canal *(fig.101)*, where the Salute rises up against the blackening sky of an oncoming storm. The effect is inherently dramatic, if not especially original (see *fig.33*). As a painter of marines he seems to have intuitively recognised the visual similarities between the tip of the Dogana and the prow of a ship, and this was a motif that Turner also chose to isolate in his paintings *(figs.227–30)*.

Comparisons between the two artists' works were already being made before 1833, but Turner's decision to exhibit views of Venice that year for the first time unleashed the opprobrium of the critics, who accused him of deliberately attempting to upstage the younger man *(figs.6, 102–3)*.[18] The key point to recognise here is not so much the element of rivalry that was certainly a part of Turner's tactics in his choice of subject: far more noteworthy is the prevailing attitude that one artist could be felt to possess exclusive rights to the depiction of somewhere as rich in topographical material as Venice, which indicates that, despite the advances made in graphic representations of the city, Venetian scenes were still comparatively novel in the context of the Academy exhibitions. In fact, Stanfield's 1833 painting of the Punta della Dogana *(fig.102)* was only the second of his sequence of ten views of Venice to appear at the Royal Academy. It was widely known that it was part of a commission from Lord Lansdowne for a set of pictures that eventually decorated the dining room at Bowood, and which included two other views of Venice. This circumstance has led one scholar to suggest that Turner's principal Venetian picture this year *(fig.103)* was in part a satire on Lansdowne's desire to furnish himself with a room comparable with the Canaletto room at Woburn Abbey.[19] Yet Turner would surely have been encouraged to see a collector buying contemporary works of art in preference to Old Master paintings, even if the commission had not gone to him.

Neither of Turner's much smaller Venetian paintings was displayed in the same room as Stanfield's picture at the Academy. So the comparison between the paintings of the Dogana, though implicit because of a similarity of viewpoint, was not as immediate as the critics led their readers

100 (cat.15)
James Duffield Harding (1797/8–1863)
The Grand Canal, Venice exhibited Royal Academy 1835
Pencil, watercolour, bodycolour, pen and brown ink, with gum, on paper laid down on wood panel, 77.8 x 106
Yale Center for British Art, Paul Mellon Collection

to believe. *Arnold's Magazine*, for example, unjustly claimed that 'Mr Stanfield comes to rather awkward moorings when anchored alongside of Turner'.[20] But if the reviewers sought to rebuke Turner for appropriating Stanfield's subject matter, they were nevertheless unanimous in agreeing that he was the victor in the confrontation. William Henry Pyne proclaimed that:

> Unlike Canaletti, and Guardi, or Bonington, Turner has not made his Venetian view of the 'Bridge of Sighs' a mere vehicle of splendid handling, and hardly better than a dry transcript of the scene; but thrown over the picture of this once city of palaces that death-like stillness and calmness so soothing to the mind, and likewise so characteristic of Venice. Altogether it is a most poetic composition, and [a] brilliant example of the genius of the English artist.[21]

With typical audacity Turner deliberately courted comparisons not only with Stanfield but more explicitly with Canaletto, adding the Venetian's name to the title of his painting in order to explain the presence of an artist in the lower-left corner, working away at an easel like an Impressionist, directly in front of his subject. It has generally been overlooked that another of his 1833 exhibits was a picture in which Van Goyen is shown in the process of absorbing material for his work.[22] Considered together, the pair focus on the individual nature of these painters' responses to their particular settings.

A posthumous anecdote suggests that the intensely blue sky was a late addition, introduced as an attempt to out-dazzle an adjacent picture by George Jones,[23] and further evidence of Turner's combative attitude this year can be found in his second Venetian subject *(fig.6)*.[24] From the engraving made of it, this now lost work seems to jockey with Bonington, who had exhibited a similar study of the columns of the Piazzetta in 1828 *(fig.19)*. Like Bonington, Turner transformed a pencil sketch that included Austrian soldiers *(fig.3)* into a bland evocation of a timeless Venice, untouched by contemporary history.

Despite having renewed his acquaintance with the city during the summer of 1833, a similar dislocation between past and present was also to be found in Turner's first large-scale painting of Venice, shown at the Academy the following spring *(fig.104)*.[25] With its funnel-like perspective receding towards the island of San Giorgio Maggiore, this has a wide and deep foreground, over which Turner traces delicate reflections and shadows, their forms scarcely broken on the glassy surface. On either side of this expanse of water, figures gaze across at each other impassively. Once more, these are not from Turner's own era, and the richly laden boats in which they stand similarly conjure up the former wealth of Venice. This detail was very appropriate for a view of the Dogana di Mare, or Custom

101 (cat.26)
Clarkson Stanfield (1793–1867)
*The Dogana and the Church of Santa Maria della Salute c.*1830–1
Watercolour and bodycolour with scratching-out, 22 x 31.5
The British Museum, London (S 109)

House, where goods imported by sea were monitored and registered. Turner's depiction of the brick warehouses flanking the marble building is as flawed here as it was in the 1833 painting, probably because he had no detailed sketches. In this instance, he may have developed the composition from one of the colour studies *(fig.82)*.

Once again, most critics were prepared to concede that Turner's picture easily surpassed Stanfield's new view of the Piazza during a festival, but, of course, the comparison renewed allegations of malign intent, though these seem entirely unfounded this year. It may be, as mentioned above, that Turner sought to suggest a link between Venice and contemporary Britain, pairing the canvas with his painting *Wreckers (fig.9)*, and thereby juxtaposing plenitude with ruin (p.23). The message for his viewers was unequivocal, and profoundly Byronic:

> in the fall
> Of Venice think of thine, despite thy watery wall.[26]

That the essence of this meaning was understood is implicit in the fact that when Henry McConnel, the northern industrialist who first owned *Venice*, commissioned a pendant, he apparently selected a subject that made a similar, but less pessimistic point. This was *Keelmen heaving in Coals by Night (fig.105)*, which was based on an earlier mezzotint of *Shields, on the River Tyne* 1823.[27] The resulting picture is more in harmony with its intended companion, sharing the same underlying composition, though this perhaps diminishes the original sense of contrast that had invoked the consequences of empire. For *Keelmen heaving in Coals* inescapably illustrates how Britain's pre-eminence around the globe was rooted in its development of iron and steel, and in the process emphatically celebrates the industrial age.

Byron was the essential link between another pair of Turner's pictures at the Academy in 1835 – one of Ehrenbreitstein, the other of Venice *(fig.109)* – though Turner made an overt connection with *Childe Harold's Pilgrimage* only for the German scene.[28] His viewpoint in the Venetian painting is a little way further up the Grand Canal from that of the 1834 picture, alongside Longhena's great church, and the Hotel Europa would probably be among the buildings behind the masts on the left, if these were more precisely individualised. Finberg thought they looked 'more like English villas of the Gothic revival' than Byron's crumbling palaces.[29] The composition is set out in a very slight pencil sketch, but Turner may well have been dependent once again on a rudimentary colour study *(fig.180)*.[30] On the other hand, the viewpoint was one that had been majestically painted by Canaletto *(fig.106)*, so the habitual element of competition may also be at work. The comparison reveals that Turner refrained from

giving the full height of the Salute, and that he sought ways of balancing the overall design, deploying to advantage a soaring, attenuated version of the Campanile and the clustered masts with their decorated pennants.

The painting was bought by Munro of Novar and remained in his collection until 1860. At that point Ruskin's father hoped to generate support for the picture to be acquired for the Louvre, but in the event he was unable to enlist enough subscribers. His decision to propose this gift was, no doubt, chiefly motivated by a public-spirited desire to make Turner's art more widely available outside Britain. However, the viewpoint depicted is curiously almost the same as that in the Louvre's painting of the Salute by Michele Marieschi.[31] This would not be significant, except that, since its acquisition in 1818, the Marieschi had been attributed to Canaletto, and, as such, had contributed substantially to the younger Ruskin's reservations about the acclaimed Venetian view-painter.[32] As a result, one cannot but suspect that it would have entirely suited his purposes to have both pictures in the same building as a means of proving the supremacy of Turner – a modified version of the Turner–Claude pairing in the National Gallery.[33]

There were an increasing number of Venetian subjects by other artists at the spring exhibitions of the Royal Academy and the British Institution of 1835, including William Etty's *Bridge of Sighs (fig.132)*, various views by Prout, Thomas Hartley Cromek, Edward Pritchett and George Belton Moore, as well as historicist images by J.R. Herbert and James Stephanoff. By this date more and more Britons were travelling on the Continent, and this new breed of tourist customarily passed through Venice at some point in their itineraries, providing artists with a receptive audience for their evocations of the city's picturesque splendours. Competition for novel viewpoints was perhaps their greatest concern, which meant that the smaller islands, with their fishermen and craftsmen, were documented with a growing frequency. In 1836, for example, Turner's friend Augustus Wall Callcott exhibited his view of Murano *(fig.107)*. There is a clarity to Callcott's representation that inevitably recalls Canaletto, which must have appeared naturalistic seen in conjunction with the operatic moonlight of Turner's contemporary picture *Juliet and her Nurse (fig.61)*. Indeed, other paintings by both artists in the same exhibition were contrasted by the critic of *The Times*, who favoured Callcott's work because it seemed 'as cool and refreshing as iced champagne after [Turner's] mulligatawny'.[34]

Whether Turner was deterred from pursuing other pictures of Venice after 1837 by the kinds of critical response that met *Juliet and her Nurse* cannot be established. There is, however, an unfinished work that dates from this period, which was clearly intended to depict the departure of the Doge from the Piazzetta on Ascension Day *(fig.108)*. The climax of the Venetian year, this ancient ceremony in which the Doge 'married' the sea, was conducted

102 (cat.27)
Clarkson Stanfield (1793–1867)
Venice from the Dogana exhibited Royal
Academy 1833
Oil on canvas, 130 x 165.4
Lord Lansdowne, Bowood House

103 (cat.36)
Bridge of Sighs, Ducal Palace and Custom-House, Venice: Canaletti painting exhibited
Royal Academy 1833
Oil on canvas, 51.1 x 81.6
Tate (N00370; B&J 349; S 96)

104 (cat.37)
Venice (the Dogana and San Giorgio
Maggiore) exhibited Royal Academy 1834
Oil on canvas, 91.5 x 122
National Gallery of Art, Washington,
Widener Collection (1942.9.85; B&J 356)

105 (cat.38)
Keelmen heaving in Coals by Night
exhibited Royal Academy 1835
Oil on canvas, 92.3 x 122.8
National Gallery of Art, Washington,
Widener Collection (1942.9.86; B&J 360)

106
Giovanni Antonio Canaletto
(1697–1768)
Venice: The Grand Canal with Santa Maria della Salute looking towards the Bacino 1744
Oil on canvas, 33 x 22.5
Royal Collection

107 (cat.4)
Augustus Wall Callcott (1779–1844)
Murano ('The Old Part of Venice') exhibited
Royal Academy 1836
Oil on canvas, 74.9 x 109.9
Private collection (courtesy of Agnew's)

108 (cat.55)
Venice, the Piazzetta, with the Ceremony of the Doge Marrying the Sea c.1835
Oil on canvas, 91.4 x 121.9
Tate (N04446; B&J 501; S 98)

109 (cat.39)
*Venice from the Porch of Madonna della
Salute* exhibited Royal Academy 1835
Oil on canvas, 91.4 x 122.2
Metropolitan Museum of Art, New
York, Bequest of Cornelius Vanderbilt,
1899 (B&J 362)

110 (cat.41)
Venice, from the Canale della Giudecca,
Chiesa di S. Maria della Salute, &c
exhibited Royal Academy 1840
Oil on canvas, 61.2 x 91.8
Sheepshanks Bequest 1857,
Victoria and Albert Museum (B&J 384; S 100)

with great pomp and culminated in a gold ring being thrown into the sea. Canaletto had recorded the event in paintings and drawings, some of which Turner could have seen, but another, more immediate stimulus may have come from W.J. Müller's 8.2 metre canvas of the same subject, completed in 1835.[35] Turner does not include the great state barge, the Bucintoro, which had been burned on Napoleon's orders, but instead introduces the figure of the Doge on a floating platform on the left. His juddering brushwork conveys a sense of watching crowds, but otherwise there is little detail, and the buildings are simply blocked in, probably indicating that this was a work Turner intended to finish on the walls of the Academy. The brown smear across the upper level of the Doge's Palace serves no purpose in the design, and merely preserves the accidental traces of a brush.

When Turner resumed painting Venetian subjects in 1840, shortly before his last visit, he modified his format, adopting canvases of 62 x 92 cm, instead of the larger 92 x 122 cm (see p.26). Rather than reducing the power of his subsequent pictures, the smaller size gave them an intense intimacy, like powerful large-scale watercolours. Infused with the luminosity that arose from Turner's habitual use of white grounds, these works are also characterised by their rich colours, which adhere to the prepared surface in a way that barely conceals their material essence.

In the first pair of the series, Turner's focus returns to the impressive scenes known to all visitors to Venice. One picture illustrates the general prospect from the Giudecca canal, looking back towards the Doge's Palace *(fig.110)*, while the other depicts the link between the palace and its gaol, inevitably invoking Byron, though with a botched quotation *(fig.113)*:

> I stood upon a bridge, a palace and
> A prison on each hand.[36]

Given the choice of these two works, Sheepshanks selected the panoramic view, which was perhaps based on a simple colour study *(fig.111)*. The picture is dominated by the glistening domes and campaniles of the Salute, seen from behind, looking oddly stretched and out of proportion. Turner's brilliant white for this building alarmed one critic, who claimed it appeared 'as if built of snow by children in sport'.[37] Although the effect does not jar so noticeably today, it is still possible to recognise what he meant. This is because the painting is one of the few to have been well preserved since Turner's day, its condition stabilised in 1893 by being kept inside an airtight container that has prevented the deterioration of its colours. It joined the new museum collection in South Kensington in 1857, and thereafter became one of the most frequently copied of Turner's pictures (see *fig.274*).

Oddly, the *Bridge of Sighs* painting *(fig.113)*, which Sheepshanks had rejected, remained unsold at the Academy and afterwards. This was in spite

111
The Punta della Dogana and Bacino from the Giudecca Canal 1833 or 1840
Pencil, watercolour and bodycolour on grey paper, 19.4 x 28.4
Tate (TB CCCXVII 24; D32209)

of Turner's attempt to enlist the authority of Byron for his emphasis on the subject of Venetian justice. In an era in which accounts of imprisonment and torture in the prison were greatly exaggerated, the momentary shadows passing across its surface were perhaps too morbid and unsettling for potential purchasers. It was, in any case, a disappointing year for the sale of Turner's exhibits, and only two of his seven pictures found buyers. Matters were not helped by the press, and even the usually sympathetic *Spectator* lambasted the Venetian subjects, calling them 'mere freaks of chromomania'.[38] Yet the modulated and harmonious tones of the *Bridge of Sighs* picture scarcely merited such critical hysteria. By the standards of the period, Turner perhaps cropped his picture awkwardly, but its only other faults are less to do with its colour, which magnificently captures the play of light on the palace exterior, and more a result of its failure to represent the architecture of the edifice accurately.[39]

Unlike the earlier views of Venice, it is not evident if this painting (or its pair) is a historical scene. The costumes of the figures are too indeterminate, and as a result it seems as though the boatmen animating the channels and quaysides inhabit a city not quite bound by the contingencies of real time. It is interesting that Turner had evolved this imprecise state for these paintings which predate his final visit, for this was, in fact, largely the way he went on presenting Venice in the seventeen pictures that followed between 1841 and 1846.

112 (cat.79)
Two views of the Bridge of Sighs, with a study of the Doge's Palace 1833
Pencil, 10.9 x 20.3 each
From the 'Venice' sketchbook
Tate (TB CCCXIV ff.30v, 31; D31985, D31986)

113 (cat.42)
Venice, the Bridge of Sighs exhibited
Royal Academy 1840
Oil on canvas, 68.6 x 91.4
Tate (N00527; B&J 383; S 99)

Part Three: Locating Turner's Venice

6 Monumental Venice

Turner's images of the splendours of the Doge's Palace, the Campanile and the Basilica of San Marco may arise from his habitual desire to absorb and recreate the distinctive character of a city's topography, but resulted in extraordinary watercolours that bathe the architectural fabric in a softer, purely subjective vision. To some extent, this somewhat dreamlike condition may be accentuated by the unfinished nature of these works.

Four of the studies focus on the Doge's Palace, ranging in their handling from a summary impression to one of his most consummate statements (figs.114–15, 117–18). Like most visitors to Venice, he had dutifully toured the palace during his first visit, surreptitiously making studies of some of the glorious allegorical paintings decorating the great state rooms.[1] Progressing through this sequence of spaces is the best way of comprehending the building's diverse functions as city hall, courthouse and residence of the Doge – the largely powerless figurehead of the Venetian state. A visit to the adjoining prisons, via the infamous Bridge of Sighs, also permitted the curious nineteenth-century British tourist to feel a sense of righteous outrage at the supposed injustices perpetrated by the legendary Council of Ten, who sat in judgement on those accused of crimes against the state.

A general sense of how the building is situated immediately adjacent to the sheltered waters of the Bacino is evident in many of Turner's colour studies, including one of those painted on grey paper (fig.115). This is similar in its composition to the unfinished oil painting depicting the embarkation of the Doge (fig.108), though here the Campanile is stunted and the depth and width of the Piazzetta are slightly foreshortened and narrowed. Turner made little attempt to delineate the rich gothic details of the Doge's Palace, which later so obsessed Ruskin and induced him to see it as 'the central building of the world'.[2] From this study it is only just possible to determine that there is an arcade at ground level, above which sits a highly decorated gallery, with quatrefoil openings set into the spaces between ogee arches. The use of white paint, however, nicely differentiates the marble of these two levels from the warmer colour of the upper walls, where interspersed lozenges of white Istrian and red Verona marble are arranged to form diamond patterns.[3] This diaper facing is repeated in regular diagonal rhythms across the surface, irregularly punctuated by windows and the loggia of the Grand Council chamber. An arched pencil line reveals that Turner abandoned a hesitant attempt to place one of the windows in its correct position on the façade, but as in most of his other depictions of the palace his desire for accuracy was handicapped by the fact that he had only recorded the southern aspect of the building indistinctly from distant viewpoints prior to his 1840 visit. That year he made a more attentive study, which includes a note on the number of columns on the gallery.[4] Nevertheless, this closer inspection did not result in a better understanding of the asymmetrical placing of the two easterly windows, which are older and sit lower than those to their left. The other buildings that can be seen on the left-hand side of the view are the Libreria Marciana, the Zecca (or Mint), and beyond this the white dome of the Salute, bringing the angle of vision encompassed in the image to nearly 180 degrees.

Another feature worth noting is the sentry box below the south-west corner of the palace (see also fig.123). One of a pair positioned on either side of four canons, this was painted in Habsburg black and yellow stripes and was one of the most prominent assertions of the Austrian presence in Venice. Surprisingly, this resented furniture of occupation rarely appears in contemporary paintings (as opposed to sketches) and is also absent from Turner's most detailed representation of the Doge's Palace (fig.114). This is one of around ten watercolours on Whatman paper that evoke the passing of a violent thunderstorm, and which were previously part of the 'Storm' sketchbook. These studies develop imaginatively what was evidently a vivid real experience, offering something visionary that transcends the limitations of naturalistic documentation. It is apparent that in 1833, and again in 1840, Turner was subjected to the scirocco winds, which bring sudden and sustained inundations during the long summer days in Venice. In fact, his jottings in the later pages of the 'Venice and Bozen' sketchbook of the final visit are quite specific in documenting the unexpected arrival of lowering clouds and driving rain.[5]

Turner's viewpoint in this watercolour is from the seaward end of the Libreria Marciana, looking back to the Doge's Palace past the columns of the Piazzetta. The nearer column in Turner's drawing is topped by a marble sculpture, made up of fragments, representing St Theodore, a Greek warrior, who was Venice's first patron (now replaced by a replica). Its pair is graced by the bronze lion of St Mark, similarly transformed from an earlier existence by the addition of wings in order to serve the purposes of Venetian propaganda. This made it an obvious target for the French when

114
Lightning in the Piazzetta 1840
Watercolour and bodycolour, with
scratching-out and details added using
a pen dipped in watercolour, 22.1 x 32.1
From the 'Storm' sketchbook
National Galleries of Scotland,
Edinburgh (W 1352; S 88)

115 (cat.115)
The Piazzetta and the Doge's Palace from the
Bacino c.1840
Watercolour and bodycolour on grey
paper, 19.3 x 27.9
Tate (TB CCCXVII 1; D32180)

116 (cat.81)
The Porta della Carta of the Doge's Palace;
and various views of the Piazzetta 1840
Pencil, 14.9 x 8.9 each
From the 'Rotterdam to Venice'
sketchbook
Tate (TB CCCXX ff.87v, 88; D32434, D32435)

117 (cat.116)
The Giants' Staircase in the Doge's Palace
*c.*1840
Watercolour and bodycolour on grey
paper, 19.1 x 28
Tate (TB CCCXVII 2; D32181)

118 (cat.144)
*The Porta della Carta, Doge's Palace c.*1840
Pencil, watercolour and bodycolour on
pale buff paper, with some stopping-
out, 30.5 x 23.4
Tate (TB CCCXVIII 28; D32247; S 25)

CCCXVII – 19

they invaded in 1797. So, to the humiliation of the Venetians, the famous lion was taken down and included in the tribute exacted from Venice by Napoleon. In Paris it was displayed at the Invalides, with its tail quite literally between its legs. There was further ignominy when it was eventually returned in 1815, as it had been broken into many pieces and had to be skilfully recast in the foundries of the Arsenale.[6] Turner saw it first in 1819, just three years after it was returned to its vantage point, and sketched it on a page that juxtaposes its proud outline with his notes on the uniforms of the now-presiding Austrian soldiers (fig.3).

What is most extraordinary about this watercolour is the palpable flash of lightning in the confined space of the Piazzetta, produced by a purposeful scratching of the surface of the paper. Like an explosion, this bursts behind St Theodore and ripples worryingly in the direction of the palace, creating a ghostly light across the southern front of San Marco. Turner's admiration for Tintoretto is possibly at work here, for comparable elements can be found in that artist's dramatic depiction of *The Stealing of the Body of St Mark* (c.1562–6; then in the Scuola Grande di San Marco, now in the Accademia). Perhaps the most effective detail is the urgency of the two figures, who rush between the columns seeking the protection of the city.

The focus of the third watercolour of the palace is restricted to its magnificent entrance, the Porta della Carta, at the north-west corner, where its walls meet those of San Marco (fig.118). This sumptuous doorway, ornamented with emblematic statues and variegated stonework, had been constructed by Bartolomeo Bon between 1438 and 1442, and was originally enriched with blue and gold paint. The word 'Carta' is thought to refer to the paper of the Archives, which were housed inside, though other theories link it with the written decrees posted there. The gateway was the sort of architectural subject so often treated by Prout, but Turner's rendering is more acutely sensitive to the play of light, yielding a clear idea of the different visible textures. Much of this was attained with paint alone, but he indicated the window and its surrounding features with the use of a stopping-out agent or gum, protecting the areas where he wanted to retain highlights. The way in which the eye is compelled to dwell on certain details anticipates some of Ruskin's intricate studies of the palace, yet curiously the writer seems to have omitted this work from the group of Venetian watercolours he most prized.[7]

As in the sketch from which Turner probably developed the watercolour, there is an awkward blank space above the door (fig.116). This was originally occupied by a sculpture of Doge Francesco Foscari kneeling before the lion of St Mark, which had been removed after the fall of the Republic, not by the French but by their successors, the local Municipalists.[8] It was, however, restored and replaced in 1885. Through the open doorway it is possible to look beyond into the palace courtyard, where the Giants'

Staircase rises upwards. A closer assessment of this grand, ceremonial flight of steps, from the darkness of the Arco Foscari, occurs in Turner's final colour study of the Doge's Palace (fig.117), though he made various pencil sketches of the courtyard from other angles in both 1833 and 1840.[9] Topped by Sansovino's monumental statues of Mercury (or Mars) and Neptune, representing the maritime trading character of Venice, these stairs had provided the setting for the inaugurations of all later Doges after their completion around 1496. In Turner's time, however, they were mistakenly most closely associated with Doge Marin Falier, who was executed on an earlier staircase, probably leading up to the southern wall, for his traitorous attempt to seize more direct power as Prince of Venice.[10] His reprehensible life was dramatised in verse by Byron and staged (against the poet's wishes) at Drury Lane in 1821. The details of Falier's plot were afterwards familiar to most tourists, and by 1828 Byron's account had also stimulated a major painting by Delacroix (Wallace Collection). Turner's image is much more modest, but is wonderfully atmospheric, suggesting an abandoned palace, seen by moonlight.

Retreating to the Porta della Carta, he painted the view towards the Campanile, which, even in its compressed form on the page, towers above the surrounding buildings (fig.119). Where Prout had left its great bulk isolated in his depiction of this scene (fig.81), it is here cunningly integrated into the design with the aid of the framing façades of the Doge's Palace and San Marco. In a significant detail, the upper level of the Campanile is clad in scaffolding, which indicates the drawing must date from 1840, the only occasion when Turner's time in Venice coincided with major repair work: a smaller platform was in place in 1819, which is present in some of the sketches of that year.[11] Over the centuries the great bell tower, the highest in Venice at 97 metres, had suffered repeated damage and despite continued maintenance it eventually collapsed in 1902, whereupon it was quickly replaced by an exact replica.

The foreground of Turner's image features the Pilastri Acritani, another pair of trophies brought back to Venice from the east. The angle from which Turner depicted them was quite close and very low, and indicates that he must have been sitting near to the doorway to the palace. As the light on the Campanile is warming its eastern flanks, it is probable that the study was executed early one morning, before too many people arrived in the Piazzetta.

While early-nineteenth-century artists were usually fascinated by the Doge's Palace, comparatively few of them turned their attention to the neighbouring Basilica (recently upgraded from palace chapel to the status of cathedral of Venice by Napoleon). To most visitors, its fusion of Byzantine and Venetian styles of architecture was incomprehensible and absurdly fantastic. Thomas Moore described its effect bluntly as 'barbaric',

119 (cat.117)
The Campanile of San Marco, with the Pilastri Acritani, from the Porta della Carta 1840
Pencil, watercolour and bodycolour on grey paper, 28.2 x 19.1
Tate (TB CCCXVII 19; D32204; S 30)

120 (cat.136)
The Interior of San Marco: the Atrium,
looking North 1840
Watercolour and bodycolour on red-
brown paper, 24.3 x 30.4
Tate (TB CCCXVIII 22; D32241)

121 (cat.129)
The Interior of San Marco, looking into the
North Transept 1840
Watercolour and bodycolour on grey-
brown paper, 29.6 x 22.3
Tate (TB CCCXVIII 7; D32226; S 14)

while the travel writer Henry Sass was of the opinion that it was 'the most singular and curious building in every respect which I ever beheld'.[12] For his part, when Turner first saw the spectacular, heavily encrusted western façade in 1819, a few years after its four bronze horses had arrived back from Paris, he spent some time trying to digest its polychromatic rhythms and its subtle asymmetries, making studies of individual components as well as one of the whole ensemble.[13] During the subsequent visits of 1833 and 1840 he renewed his scrutiny, venturing inside to observe the cycle of mosaics high above the nave.

A couple of his pencil sketches are devoted to the atrium, located immediately after passing through the central door, where the large mosaic figure of St Mark is supposedly based on a design by Titian.[14] This also seems to be the space that Turner attempted to recall in a watercolour he painted on one of the assorted sheets of toned paper (*fig.120*). Its ruddy brown serves as the perfect neutral ground on which to build up the glistening surfaces of the darkened interior, while the predominantly gold and blue tesserae of the mosaics are suggested in a combination of watercolour and bodycolour (the opaque form of watercolour, also known as gouache).

At the southern end of the atrium is the funeral chapel of Cardinal Giovanni Battista Zen, which forms the subject of another of Turner's studies.[15] The centre of the chapel is dominated by a sarcophagus and bronze statue of the supine cardinal, and beyond this in Turner's sketch is an altar, on which stands the *Madonna della Scarpa*; both sculptures are by Lombardo.

Turner produced two further colour studies that depict the main nave of the Basilica in the same generalised way. The first is a comparatively slight sketch on a lighter brown paper than its predecessors, showing the view from the southern nave, looking across the central space and up towards the great angels beneath the Pentecost dome.[16] When treating the part of the nave beside the rood screen, or iconostasis, in front of the main altar (*fig.121*), Turner chose paper from a third batch, clearly experimenting with the different properties of each type, and noting its ability to deliver the results he wanted for these interior subjects (see Appendix p.258). Once again, his depiction is far from accurate, especially when compared with a rare interior view of the same scene by Canaletto (*fig.122*). Given the absence of any related pencil sketches, the inexactness of these interiors suggests that Turner created them solely from his general impressions.

Leaving San Marco behind, Turner made a number of colour sketches of the Piazza and the adjoining Piazzetta, some of them by moonlight. The larger square is one of the world's great public spaces, and has famously been described as the 'drawing-room of Europe' (although doubts have arisen as to whether it really was Napoleon who first described it as such).[17] For travellers from northern Europe in the 1830s it continued to exude the

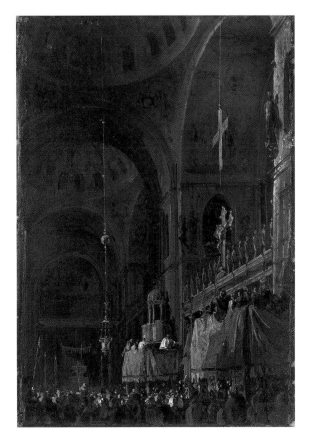

magic of the East: peopled by traders from around the Mediterranean, various entertainers, and the Venetians themselves, its long phalanxes of regular arcades climaxing in the glinting domes, tabernacles and statuary of the great Basilica. The effect of this heady mix is most effectively realised in Turner's picture *Juliet and her Nurse (fig.61)*, but his studies also capture its pulsating vitality.

A group of these was painted on two of the standard-sized pieces of buff-coloured paper, which Turner divided into four smaller sections (*figs.123–6*). With their progressively more intense blues, these appear to chart the shift from evening into night, making manifest how the Piazza vibrated with the animation of fickle crowds, oscillating between brightly illuminated puppet shows and the surrounding cafés. All but one of the sequence adopt roughly the same viewpoint, looking from the Piazza, past San Marco, into the Piazzetta, with the Doge's Palace beyond, and the island of San Giorgio in the distance. Perhaps significantly, this was a prospect that Turner knew Canaletto had favoured (see *fig.24*). The fourth study

122
Giovanni Antonio Canaletto
(1697–1768)
*The Interior of San Marco: the Crossing
and North Transept* 1730s
Oil on canvas, 33 x 22.5
Royal Collection

a charmingly picturesque study of the canal that passes under the apse of the great gothic church of Santo Stefano (*fig.129*). This is derived from a pencil sketch made during Turner's reconnoitres in 1840, a short walk from the Hotel Europa.[19] Comparing the watercolour with the spot it depicts reveals that some of its details are inaccurate. For a start the campanile is an embellishment that replaces the trumpet-shaped chimneys Turner had observed in his sketch. Nevertheless, the sense of airiness and bright Venetian sunlight is well recreated, sharpened, no doubt, by the contrast between the fiery red bricks of the church and the cool stonework below.

After the monuments surrounding the Piazza, the other sight that invariably attracted nineteenth-century travellers was the Arsenale at the eastern end of the city (*fig.130*). The immense scale of these naval yards was tangible evidence of the powerhouse on which the Venetian Empire had been founded. At its zenith during the fourteenth century it employed some 16,000 workers, who were able to complete the construction of an armed galley in a matter of hours. Its legendary name is derived from the Arabic 'Dar sina'a', meaning 'House of Construction', but this great ship-building tradition had been brutally interrupted and suspended by Napoleon's troops soon after their arrival in 1797. Later revived to prevent them becoming obsolete, the yards never again saw the industry they had been designed to accommodate. By the 1840s visitors found little work in progress. Dickens was struck forcefully by the silence of the Arsenale, by the absence of the banging of hammers. He was one of the many who saw in its decline a symbol of the wider plight of Venice.[20]

The presence of Austrian soldiers near the entrance to the Arsenale, and probably throughout the complex, may have discouraged Turner from making more than a couple of pencil sketches.[21] If this seems uncharacteristically faint-hearted, it is probable that he was wary of being apprehended as a spy as he sketched away furtively in his little notebooks in such close proximity to a strategic military site. The Arsenale's distinctive gateway, with its attendant pride of four lion sculptures, had, nevertheless, been depicted by many other artists, and Turner is also likely to have seen Bellotto's striking painting of the entrance when he stayed at Saltram in 1811.[22] Such images are quite different from Turner's watercolour, which is more of a visceral response to his subject, recalling the claustrophobic imagery of Piranesi. As Lindsay Stainton has eloquently written, 'it is as if he had started from the fact of the red brick, which then transformed itself in his imagination into the walls of a furnace symbolising the great armaments factory which the Arsenale had once been'.[23] Further indications of the purpose of the enclosed structure are present in the tops of masts glimpsed over the protecting walls. All of this is very evocative; yet the bridge and patrolled entrance that Turner depicts seem never to have existed. His view is imaginary, based on that looking up the Rio San

reverses the viewpoint, and is taken from near the columns of the Piazzetta, looking back to San Marco (*fig.123*). Here again, Turner introduces the menacing presence of an Austrian soldier beside his sentry box, his foreignness underlined by his isolation from the crowd opposite.

There are two more studies of the Piazza (*figs.127–8*). For these works Turner retreated to the fringes of the Piazza, to the arcades beneath the Procuratie Nuove, from there surveying the façade of San Marco and its Campanile. Looking through these arches makes plain the great height of the tower, the full extent of which cannot readily be contained by the frame the architecture provides. In both studies, the brilliance of the partly glimpsed Piazza is made all the more enticing by being seen from the confines of a darkened space. The effect is ultimately derived from Canaletto, who had used a similar device in some of his drawings and prints.[18]

Unlike Canaletto, however, Turner did not pursue a more sustained survey of the other great churches and *campi* around Venice. Even though he had steadily expanded his knowledge of peripheral areas of the city, there are, in fact, just two further watercolours that confront landmarks or buildings that cannot be seen from the main waterways. The first of these is

123 (cat.130)
The Piazzetta, with San Marco and its Campanile; Night 1840
Watercolour and bodycolour on grey-brown paper, 15 x 22.8
Tate (TB CCCXVIII 1; D32220; S 8)

Daniele, at the point where it meets the Rio della Tana, to the east of the Corderie, which has neither gateway nor crenellated walls on the right.[24] Instead of the more common focus on the main entrance, such an obscure corner perhaps allowed him greater scope to project his own ideas of Venetian history. He may, in fact, have developed the drawing over a rudimentary sketch made on the spot, for the back of the sheet has pencil studies of figures, horses and carts that were possibly jotted down while touring the Arsenale. It is one of the more obviously 'finished' works in the Venetian group, making it clear that Turner felt this was a subject as significant as the Doge's Palace in its power and meaning. After his death, it became the first of the Venetian watercolours in his bequest to be displayed publicly, subsequently retaining its spell over later generations.[25]

124 (cat.131)
San Marco and the Piazzetta 1840
Watercolour and bodycolour on grey-brown paper, 14.9 x 22.8
Tate (TB CCCXIX 8; D32256)

125 (cat.132)
The Piazzetta with the Campanile; Night 1840
Watercolour and bodycolour on grey-brown paper, 14.1 x 22.5
Tate (TB CCCXIX 10; D32258)

126 (cat.133)
San Marco and the Piazzetta, with San Giorgio Maggiore; Night 1840
Watercolour and bodycolour on grey-brown paper, 14.8 x 22.8
Tate (TB CCCXIX 2; D32250; S 9)

127 (cat.137)
The Campanile and San Marco, from the Atrio of the Palazzo Reale 1840
Watercolour and bodycolour on red-brown paper, 31.9 x 23.8
Tate (TB CCCXVIII 26; D32245; S 24)

128 (cat.118)
The Arcades of the Procuratie Nuove and the Palazzo Reale, with the Piazza beyond 1840
Watercolour and bodycolour on grey paper, 15.5 x 22.4
Tate (TB CCCXIX 7; D32255)

129 (cat.119)
The Church of Santo Stefano, from the Rio del Santissimo 1840
Pencil, watercolour and bodycolour on grey paper, 27.8 x 19.1
Tate (TB CCCXVII 32; D32217; S 41)

130 (cat.158)
Venice: An Imaginary View of the Arsenale c.1840
Watercolour and bodycolour, 24.3 x 30.8
Tate (TB CCCXVI 27; D32164; S 75)

7 Venice after Dark

The idea of Venice seen by romantic moonlight has become such a cliché for the modern tourist that it is hard to remember that in Turner's time this was a relatively novel way of depicting the city. Up until the early nineteenth century Venice was, in fact, most consistently celebrated for its sparkling sunlight, as extensively propagated in the images of Canaletto and his followers. Indeed, among the hundreds of pictures credited to him, Canaletto painted just a couple of nocturnal subjects (see *fig.267*).[1]

Perhaps the most important influence on the developing vogue for moonlight was the poetic sensibility that decried the state of contemporary Venice, with its dilapidated palaces and its canals choked with stinking weed, and which yearned for the more magical city revealed in the half-light, after dark. The foremost instance of this was Thomas Moore, whose widely known Venetian poems inspired both Mendelssohn and Schumann, but who was himself not impressed with Venice in 1819 until the moon deprived it 'of its deformities by the dimness of the light'.[2] Shortly afterwards, Samuel Rogers devoted several of his most vibrant passages to the evocation of the moonlit city (see pp.75–7), and others, too, thereafter became enamoured of its cooler nocturnal atmosphere.[3] It was, however, Byron's friend the Countess of Blessington who expressed most acutely the beneficial effects of moonlight for Venice: 'Moonlight is a great beautifier, and especially of all that has been touched by the finger of decay, from a palace to – a woman. It softens what is harsh, renders fairer what is fair, and disposes the mind to a tender melancholy in harmony with all around.'[4]

Only one of Turner's publicly exhibited paintings tapped into this ongoing exploration of nocturnal Venice (*fig.61*). It is, nevertheless, clear from the substantial group of studies made solely for his own purposes that he found the revelation of the transformed, night-time city a truly compelling subject. For nowhere else did he dwell so intensively, or in such a sustained sequence, on a nocturnal setting. Confronted with the power of these images, it is surprising to learn from his earliest biographer that 'Turner used to say that he found moonlights very difficult'.[5]

Now dated to 1840, the colour sketches on toned paper can be interpreted as the murky counterpart to the luminous watercolours also painted that year. It is evident that Turner developed many of these atmospheric images from raw impressions stored in his memory, much in the way that Whistler was to work when painting his set of Nocturnes on the River Thames in the early 1870s. Both artists trained themselves to remember the basic shapes of a view, along with distinctive details and the differences between tones.[6] It is more probably this fundamental correspondence of artistic practice, rather than a direct influence of one artist's work on the other, that explains the similarities between Turner's and Whistler's watercolours and pastels of Venice.[7] In fact, few of Turner's 'brown paper' series were considered worthy of being exhibited until comparatively recently.[8]

What the Countess of Blessington had deemed the 'tender melancholy' of moonlit Venice perhaps resided most profoundly in the image of the Bridge of Sighs. It was a highly charged subject, resonating with Byron's sense of it as a conduit between two states of fortune, but also carried sombre associations of injustice and ignominy. A picture of the bridge by Etty (*fig.132*) illustrated how the bodies of executed prisoners were disposed of after dark, the grisly details made more explicit in a note in the Royal Academy exhibition catalogue.[9] Words and image combined here to create a powerful impact on the viewer. Since one of Turner's pictures hung in immediate proximity to Etty's canvas, it is unlikely that he could have remained immune to its emotive directness.[10] It is, therefore, no coincidence that one of the studies he made on a piece of light-brown paper is a recollection of the painting (*fig.131*), with the same tight focus and a low perspective to give greater height to the bridge.

There were two other artists who were also chiefly known for their moonlight subjects: Henry Pether and Ippolito Caffi. The first of these exhibited regularly in London, and by the early 1840s included views of Venice among his rather hard-edged topographical images (*fig.133*). These could not be further from Turner's contemporary work, and lack any of the mystery he induces through his avoidance of a strident polish. The paintings of the native Venetian Caffi, on the other hand, are more sensitive to spectacle, and original in their presentation of rarely painted natural effects such as snow and fog (*fig.20*).[11] There is, however, no specific evidence that Turner knew his work.

Within the confines of his studio, Turner far outstripped both these men in his more radical means of representing the darkened city. In this he was greatly assisted by the earthy tones of the papers, which had proved so effective when depicting the interiors of San Marco. For these Turner diluted his colours so that they were tonally integrated and did not separate out

131 (cat.134)
The Bridge of Sighs; Night 1840
Watercolour and bodycolour on grey-brown paper, 22.8 x 15.2
Tate (TB CCCXIX 5; D32253; S27)

from the rest of the design. The effect of working from dark to light on a coloured ground was a retreat to the traditional methods with which he had begun his career, and which he had only practised intermittently after about 1810, most notably for the views of European rivers that he executed during the 1830s.

One group of studies depicts the view over the Grand Canal from the steps of the Hotel Europa, or from the nearby Traghetto del Ridotto (*figs.138–40*).[12] As in the 1842 oil painting, the other side of the Grand Canal is dominated by the low mass of the Dogana, with the Salute rising palely above it. Two of the studies include a lantern guarding the landing-stage to which the gondolas are tethered, but the only other direct source of light in the group comes from the effervescent trail of a rocket, exploding above the tower on the Dogana (*fig.140*). Venetians had a long and distinguished reputation as the 'masters of pyrotechnics', arising from their extravagant firework displays.[13] These were staged on saints' days and other festivities, but as none of Turner's visits coincided with the most significant of these celebrations, it is possible that he saw only an impromptu demonstration, or that he simply imagined how the abrupt burst of light would contrast with and ornament the retreating silhouettes in his scene.

During the nineteenth century, evenings in Venice were keenly anticipated by British visitors for the opportunities they provided to attend theatrical entertainments. The most celebrated theatre was then, as now, the Fenice. Originally inaugurated in 1792, it had burned down at the end of 1836 but was quickly rebuilt in barely a year, staging its first production in the new house on 26 December 1837 (sadly the Phoenix has not risen so swiftly from its more recent fire of 1996). In spite of its fame, the theatre was

132 (cat.9)
William Etty (1787–1849)
The Bridge of Sighs exhibited Royal
Academy 1835
Oil on canvas, 80 x 50.8
York City Art Gallery

133
Henry Pether (active 1828–1865)
*A Moonlight View on the Grand Canal, with
Santa Maria della Salute c.*1840s
Oil on canvas, 78 x 113
Private collection

only active during the winter 'season', and so was not available to Turner during any of his visits. Nevertheless, the hugely popular operas of Rossini, as well as a constantly changing repertoire of dramas, comedies and panoramic spectacles, were available at other venues throughout the city. Thus in 1819 Turner could have been entertained at the theatres of San Benedetto, the Vendramin at San Luca (both near his hotel) or the Arena Gallo, the first of which was hosting *Il Barbiere di Siviglia*.[14] His options in 1833 were mostly confined to the Teatro San Benedetto, although what was on the bill varied every night. Similarly, during his final visit in 1840, there were different programmes each evening at the three theatres competing for his attention: the San Samuele, the Apollo and the Malibran.

The interior of one of these was the subject of a study by Turner in which he deftly conveyed the intense sensation of being part of an audience in a darkened auditorium *(fig.134)*. On the stage are two figures, one of which is indicated with a downward flick of red colour that stands out sharply from the surrounding monochrome. The colour suggests something bloody, and it would be tempting to link this pair with the characters of Othello and Desdemona, who would have appeared in the production of *Otello*, presumably Rossini's rather than Shakespeare's, at the Teatro Malibran on 28 August. However, despite a similarity in the shape of its proscenium arch, the blurred details of the architecture in Turner's study also resemble those of the Teatro di San Samuele.[15] Only one performance is listed at the theatre during Turner's visit, a mixed bill including part of Donizetti's opera *Belisario*, on 29 August. This rarely heard piece had premièred in Venice a few years earlier, in 1836, and is an involved tale of treachery, suspicion, exile and murder which culminates in the eponymous hero's death, though not before he has been exonerated of accusations of infanticide. Clearly its tragic outcome would also match the gory impression created by the actor decked in red.

A more blistering version of this red occurs in a study that has also been identified as an evocation of a theatrical performance in Venice *(fig.135)*, though this seems not to be the interior of any of the gaily decorated theatres mentioned above: the stark lines of its 'proscenium' are more modern. If it does indeed record a staged spectacle, it is more likely to be an improvised production in the Public Gardens, of the sort witnessed by George Sand in 1833.[16] However, another possibly more plausible idea is that Turner depicted a workshop of some kind, perhaps one in which glass was being manufactured. This would explain the boxed-in area which may represent the white heat of a furnace. Furthermore, the intensity of the red flames would be alarming outside such a context. As a matter of fact, the arrangement of these elements prefigures a painting in which Turner depicted the furnace where a statue of Wellington was being cast: *The Hero of a Hundred Fights* 1847 (Tate).[17]

In a city already alive with Shakespearian associations, it was hardly surprising that every young woman who appeared at a window suggested Jessica to her onlookers *(fig.136)*.[18] Not all of these women were as chastely modest as Shylock's daughter, for Venice continued to live up to a less enviable reputation as a centre of sexual licence. Prostitution was more evident under the Restoration because the Austrians had closed the brothels sanctioned by previous regimes, leading churchmen to complain about the increase in the number of women walking the streets.[19] Byron's 'low amours and reckless associations' were widely reported, and it is probably not coincidental that part of the existing corpus of Turner's erotica can be associated with his journeys to and from Venice.[20]

A tantalising glimpse of the erotically charged fantasies Turner created for himself can be found in two studies *(figs.136–7)*. Though the first has commonly been associated with *The Merchant of Venice*, it actually has two

134 (cat.143)
Venice: The Interior of a Theatre 1840
Watercolour and bodycolour on a warm
buff paper, 22.4 x 29.3
Tate (TB CCCXVIII 18; D32237; S 20)

134

135 (cat.135)
A Study of Firelight 1840
Watercolour and bodycolour on grey-
brown paper, 22.6 x 29.4
Tate (TB CCCXVIII 4; D32223; S 11)

136 (cat.140)
Venice: Women at a Window 1840
Watercolour and bodycolour on red-
brown paper, 23.6 x 31.5
Tate (TB CCCXVIII 20; D32239; S 21)

137 (cat.128)
Reclining Nude on a Bed 1840
Watercolour and bodycolour on a
textured grey wove paper, 21.6 x 28.4
Tate (TB CCCXVIII 17; D32236)

138 (cat.138)
The Salute from the Traghetto del Ridotto 1840
Watercolour and bodycolour on
red-brown paper, 25 x 30.7
Tate (TB CCCXVIII 11; D32230)

139 (cat.120)
*The Punta della Dogana, with Santa Maria della
Salute, from the Traghetto del Ridotto* 1840
Watercolour and bodycolour, with ink wash
on grey paper, 22.3 x 30.4
Tate (TB CCCXVIII 13; D32232; S 17)

140 (cat.139)
Santa Maria della Salute, Night Scene
with Rockets 1840
Watercolour and bodycolour
on red-brown paper, 24 x 31.5
Tate (TB CCCXVIII 29; D32248; S 29)

women leaning from the window instead of one, the second of whom appears to be both buxom and topless. There is, moreover, a strong suggestion of flirtation in evidence that is at odds with the glowing statue of some saint in the niche to the right. Matters seem to have proceeded from this introduction, for the other work shows a reclining nude on white sheets, possibly sprawling in post-coital abandon. As so often with the surviving examples of this kind of material, it would be over-simplistic to accept the images in a literal sense as documents of Turner's behaviour. For even if they recall specific experiences, they were as much transmogrified by the act of painting as his less sensational impressions of Venetian topography. All the same, they do reveal a sexual side to Turner that remains difficult for many people to accept, which also shocked his Victorian contemporaries when first brought to light by his earliest biographer in the 1860s.[21]

A more concrete picture of where Turner slept in Venice occurs in the first of a group of watercolours he made actually in his room in the Hotel Europa (fig.141). At the top of this sheet of fake Whatman paper there is a small area where a fold has prevented the colour from settling. In the image itself the rigours of strict perspective are temporarily suspended, and the eye scans in quick succession the stuccoed ceiling, the patterned walls and the open windows, through which the bell towers of San Marco and San Giorgio beckon. On the right, bright yellow curtains enclose Turner's bed, perhaps also serving as netting to ward off mosquitoes. This is another of the watercolours in which there are faint indications of scaffolding on the Campanile, confirming the 1840 date. During this visit Turner seems to have used the room as a makeshift studio, though there is no evidence of this in the watercolour, presumably because he was actually sitting at his work table.

The Palazzo Giustinian, which housed the Europa from the 1820s until the early twentieth century, had three levels above its ground-floor entrance, and it is clear from the lofty elevation of Turner's watercolours that he must have been staying on the highest floor, towards the back of the palace, with the view to the east uninterrupted by neighbouring buildings. The sequence of watercolours that resulted from his contemplation of this vista was unprecedented because few other artists had produced pictures from the rooftops of Venice. Canaletto, admittedly, had drawn for himself a pair of charming studies of the houses and churches surrounding his home near San Lio.[22] There were also occasional panoramic surveys of the city from the Campanile, though these became rarer once access to the bell tower was restricted under the Austrians.[23] But other than these, Turner had discovered an original subject, and he might justifiably have claimed, as Whistler was to do later, that 'I have learned to know a Venice in Venice that the others seem never to have perceived'.[24]

Part of the attraction of the rooftop setting for him appears to have been the informal means it provided of watching the activities of people on neighbouring balconies. His idle voyeurism did not go unnoticed, however, and in some of the studies the faces of his subjects are turned in his direction. In one, a woman wearing a mob-cap has her back to the viewer as she engages the attention of a seated figure, who in turn glances over her shoulder to stare in Turner's direction (fig.143). Meanwhile, a third face peers above the rooftops. The back of the sheet is inscribed with a note that appears to read, 'This b[elongs] to the Beppo Club', as though Turner was commenting on the amorous follies of his neighbours. An atmospheric companion to this work is TB CCCXVI 5, which features washing hung up to dry between the chimney stacks.

Given that Turner was restlessly patrolling the city during daylight hours, most of his rooftop series were made at either end of the day, capturing effects of dawn or dusk. As well as further studies painted on the brown papers, there are eight smaller sheets of white paper measuring about 19.5 x 28.5 cm, that he used almost exclusively for this rooftop series (figs.144–8, 215, 222, 252; see Appendix p.259). The only striking exception is a moonlit study which was probably made after an excursion on the Lagoon one night (fig.252). In other respects, the group is unified by a spontaneity and directness in the way it replicates the early and late traces of the sun, which is most comparable with that of the colour sketches of 1819. Turner's circumstances in 1840 obviously permitted him to make most of these studies in his bedroom, either as he looked out directly on the scene below, or while his impressions of San Giorgio and the Salute to the south were still fresh in his mind.

Two of the watercolours were painted between dawn and sunrise, using the same soft yellow for the gathering light of the eastern sky (figs.144–5). Turner's almost childlike sense of wonder at his good fortune in being the temporary possessor of the view before him is acutely tangible in his remark on the back of the first of these, which reads, 'From my Bed Room | Venice' (a similar inscription appears on the back of fig.146).[25] He had made separate studies of the bell towers visible from the Europa in 1833 (fig.142), but here he combined the three most prominent of them in an unnaturally extended panorama that sweeps from a shored-up San Marco, on the right, past San Moise, to the distant Santo Stefano. Reference to his earlier sketch would have informed him that the smaller campanile of Sant'Angelo, which formerly stood immediately adjacent to the last of these, was no longer visible, having been demolished in 1837.[26]

The sun is about to appear in the second watercolour (fig.145), which turns from the northerly prospect to look east over the rooftops and the Giardino del Palazzo Reale, towards the Doge's Palace and the Riva degli Schiavoni. In contrast to the golden colours used for the sky, the lower half

141 (cat.145)
*Turner's Bedroom in the Palazzo Giustinian
(the Hotel Europa)* 1840
Watercolour and bodycolour on pale
buff paper, 23 x 30.2
Tate (TB CCCXVII 34; D32219; S 42)

of the design is loosely sketched in grey wash, as if emerging from a morning fog settled on the Bacino. On the right, barely visible through this mist, is the outline of the dome and campanile of San Giorgio. Much the same view appears in two further studies that were painted at a later point in the day, probably towards the end of the afternoon (*figs.146–7*). One of these records the specifics of the topography in a crisp mesh of pencil lines, and is supplemented by the same pink and blue colours that are the foundation of the second version of the scene. In making the more literal sketch, Turner's sharp eyes lighted on an open window in the building to the left, through which can be seen a reclining nude, stretched out like an odalisque (see also *fig.149*).

Continuing his survey from the Europa, he focused on the distinctive outline of the island of San Giorgio at twilight, recording how the church façade takes on an ashen glow amid the fading sunset colours (*fig.148*). This is the only sheet in the Europa group outside the Turner Bequest: how it got separated from the others remains a puzzle.[27] It was first recorded in the collection of newspaper magnate John Edward Taylor, who owned many watercolours by Turner. Sadly, its somewhat faded condition detracts from the way the layers of wash are built up, but its blues might once have been as rich as those in the moonlit Lagoon subject (*fig.252*). The backs of both of these works are annotated with Turner's largely illegible attempts at poetry. What can be deciphered hints at his sensory engagement with the way Venice was transformed by different transient effects.

A perfect illustration of these dramatic shifts from one mood to another is present in some of the other studies he made from the roof of the Europa, and most vividly in the contrast between tranquil moonlight and thunderstorm (*figs.149–50*).[28] In the more violent of these, the Campanile's silhouette is brought into sudden sharp relief by a flash of lightning that seems to pass right through it. As in the similarly electric view of the Piazzetta (*fig.114*), the sublimity of this force of nature is a powerful reminder that the city is not impregnable.

142
Campaniles and Chimneys seen from the Hotel Europa 1833
Pencil, 10.9 x 20.3
From the 'Venice' sketchbook
Tate (TB CCCXIV f.100v; D32116)

143 (cat.159)
Among the Chimney-pots above Venice;
the Roof of the Hotel Europa, with the
Campanile of San Marco 1840
Pencil, watercolour and bodycolour,
24.5 x 30.6
Tate (TB CCCXVI 36; D32173; S 74)

144 (cat.150)
*Looking north from the Hotel Europa, with
the Campaniles of San Marco, San Moise, and
Santo Stefano* 1840
Pencil and watercolour, 19.8 x 28.2
Tate (TB CCCXVI 3; D32140; S 56)

145 (cat.151)
*Venice at Sunrise from the Hotel Europa, with
the Campanile of San Marco* 1840
Watercolour, 19.8 x 28
Tate (TB CCCLXIV 106; D35949; S 85)

146 (cat.152)
*View over the rooftops towards the Giardini
Reale and the Campanile of San Marco 1840*
Pencil, watercolour and bodycolour,
19.3 x 28
Tate (TB CCCXVI 42; D32179)

147 (cat.153)
*Venice from the Hotel Europa; Looking East over
the Rooftops towards the Campanile, the Doge's
Palace and San Giorgio Maggiore 1840*
Watercolour, 18.8 x 28.4
Tate (TB CCCLXIV 43; D35882)

148 (cat.154)
San Giorgio Maggiore from the Hotel Europa,
at the Entrance to the Grand Canal 1840
Watercolour, 19.5 x 27.6
Whitworth Art Gallery, University of
Manchester. Gift of John Edward Taylor,
1892 (D.1892.114)

149 (cat.141)
*The Campanile of San Marco, from the Roof of
the Hotel Europa: Moonlight* 1840
Watercolour and bodycolour on red-
brown paper, 24.2 x 30.7
Tate (TB CCCXVIII 5; D32224; S 13)

150 (cat.142)
Lightning behind the Campanile of San Marco,
from the Roof of the Hotel Europa 1840
Watercolour and bodycolour on red-
brown paper, 15.8 x 23.2
Tate (TB CCCXIX 6; D32254; S 12)

8 The Grand Canal

The Grand Canal is Venice's main artery, combining in the course of its two and a half miles the functions of market place, high street and millionaire's row. It snakes through the city in the form of a reverse 's', and effectively bisects the principal islands of the Venetian archipelago. The serpentine shape of the canal ensures a succession of varying perspectives, each of which is augmented by the features of distinctive churches and palaces. These overlapping vistas had been frequently delineated, most notably by Canaletto and Visentini in the engravings of the *Prospectus Magni Canalis Venetiarum (fig.23)*.[1] It is perhaps a measure of the comprehensive scope of this set that many of Turner's watercolours of the Grand Canal correspond with its viewpoints. This was probably both a conscious attempt to face up to the unavoidable comparisons with Canaletto, and, more simply, an adoption of the choicest positions on the canal. Some of Turner's images were observed from the water, but the majority were made from the landing-stages of the ferry boats, or *traghetti*, which enable Venetians to overcome the canal's natural barrier. As a rule, the viewpoints are lower than in the comparable images by Canaletto.

Whereas the documentary nature of Canaletto's series required that he delineate the full length of the canal in a relatively even-handed fashion, the more private character of Turner's watercolours meant that he focused only on those subjects that especially appealed to him. This accounts for the concentration of images between the Rialto and the Dogana, closest to the hotels he stayed in and which he had consequently frequented most often. Despite this preference, it is apparent that during his stay in 1840 Turner purposefully set out to make a more representative survey of the entire thoroughfare within a roll sketchbook devoted specifically to the task. Identified here as the 'Grand Canal and Giudecca' sketchbook, this volume originally included at least twenty-two pages of Whatman paper, of which fourteen were painted with scenes on the Grand Canal. Unfortunately the original arrangement of the book was not recorded before its pages were dismembered by Ruskin, but it is possible that Turner did not progress logically from one subject to the next. Indeed, his numerous pencil sketches of the Grand Canal demonstrate that he frequently returned to its course after sketching other areas of the city, and that he contemplated the same groupings of buildings again and again. Rather than replicating this practice,

151 (cat.94)
The Upper End of the Grand Canal, with San Simeone Piccolo; Dusk 1840
Watercolour and bodycolour, with pen and ink, 21.9 x 32
From the 'Grand Canal and Giudecca' sketchbook
Tate (TB CCCXV 8; D32124; S 46)

152
Giovanni Antonio Canaletto
(1697–1768)
The Upper Reach of the Grand Canal with San Simeone Piccolo 1738
Oil on canvas, 124.5 x 204.6
National Gallery, London

153
The Grand Canal (perhaps looking to Ca'Grande) c.1840
Watercolour; re-photographed from a print by J. Hogarth, Jun., taken from the original sketch when in the possession of Louis Huth. The sheet was probably part of the 'Storm' sketchbook
Present whereabouts unknown

his watercolours are discussed here in the order that the sights they depict would be encountered passing down the canal from its north-western end.

Turner ignored the modest entrance to the canal, which was attended only by the largely unremarkable convent buildings of Santa Chiara and Corpus Domini.[2] His series begins instead with a view of the domed church of San Simeone Piccolo, looking beyond it to where the canal turns for the last time before meeting the open waters of the Lagoon *(fig.151)*. The scene was studied from alongside the church of the Scalzi, just where the modern stone bridge now spans the canal, but curiously the church's baroque façade, which should appear on the right, has been omitted. Turner was fully conversant with this topography, having made several sketches of the quayside between the Scalzi and its neighbouring church of Santa Lucia.[3] So it is probable that the watercolour was executed from memory. But it is also possible that, by excluding the Scalzi, Turner was seeking a way of avoiding an exact repetition of Canaletto's famous painting of the same view *(fig.152)*. As well as taking its place in the Visentini edition, the picture would have been newly familiar in 1840 as one of the National Gallery's latest acquisitions.[4] There is a further connection with Canaletto's painting in the decision to depict the scene at much the same time of day, as the sun fades away to the west. Compared with the undiminished brightness in his predecessor's painting, Turner's realisation of twilight is much more evocative, summoning up a vaporous haze through which the buildings are only half-seen. The effect epitomises the comment that 'it was Turner who first turned the palaces into cliffs of marble'.[5]

It was this more or less unbroken wall of palaces that characterised his response to the northern half of the canal, and which he charted in a group of five or six colour studies, perhaps including a now untraced watercolour *(fig.153)*.[6] Curiously, this sequence neglects a number of noteworthy subjects, even though Turner had transcribed their specifics several times in his notebooks. There is, for example, no watercolour of San Geremia and the Palazzo Labia at the opening to the Cannaregio canal *(fig.72)*; no study of the picturesquely ruined Fondaco dei Turchi and the Deposito dei Megio; and nothing of either San Stae or the Ca'd'Oro. His neglect of these outstanding buildings is all the more perverse in that the steady curve of the canal here tends towards an unrelieved, formulaic type of composition, which seemingly taxed even Canaletto's inventiveness.

Most of this small series of watercolours depict settings in close proximity to the Rialto and its markets. Two were made from, or near, the Traghetto di San Felise, to the north-west of the Ca'd'Oro, and can be aligned to offer a panoramic survey of the canal in either direction *(figs.154–5)*.[7] Both are painted in the same pallid greys and greens, which lend an insubstantiality to the architecture, as if seen in shimmering

154
The Grand Canal looking towards the Pescaria and the Fabbriche Nuove 1840
Pencil and watercolour, 22.1 x 32.1
From the 'Grand Canal and Giudecca' sketchbook
Tate (TB CCCXVI 41; D32178)

155 (cat.103)
The Grand Canal from the Traghetto di San Felise, with Ca'Corner della Regina and Ca'Pesaro on the left 1840
Pencil and watercolour, 22.2 x 32.4
From the 'Grand Canal and Giudecca' sketchbook
Tate (TB CCCXV 19; D32135)

morning sunlight. The same evaporating effect, this time incorporating a diluted ochre colour, is created in a study of the Pescaria, or fish market, framed by the Fabbriche Nuove (TB CCCXV 16), as well as for a view of the Rialto bridge (fig.156). These views can similarly be taken in from one viewpoint, probably from a mooring near the Ca'da Mosto. This would seem to imply that Turner worked on both pairs of images concurrently, maximising his time by alternating between them to allow his washes to dry.

Two more watercolours support the emerging pattern of Turner's method of painting direct from the motif in 1840 (figs.157–8). Again these share much the same palette, in this case a muted range of milky tones, and they are additionally linked in having been painted on sheets of the same slightly off-white paper. One is dominated by the eastern end of the Fabbriche Nuove, the long arcaded building created by Sansovino to house the Ministry of Trade. Rising above it is the brick campanile of San Giovanni Elemosinario, much as it does in Canaletto's raised prospect of the same scene.[8] Canaletto is inevitably also recalled in the view of the Rialto from the north, where the bridge is flanked on the right by the ingeniously plotted Palazzo dei Camerlenghi.[9] The white tower projecting above the crenellated rooftop of the Fondaco dei Tedeschi is the familiar onion dome-capped campanile of San Bartolomeo, more often seen in conjunction with the bridge in views from the south (see figs.31, 58, 95, 161).

After passing under the Rialto bridge Turner made another pair of watercolours, apparently from a boat moored alongside the Riva del Vin, near San Silvestro (figs.159, 160). In both of these there are details which initially seem random and generalised, but which prove to be derived from close inspection. The view of the bridge, for instance, contains the suggestion of the open arcade in the Palazzo Manin, while to its right there are a number of gothic arches to indicate the window openings on the first floor of the neighbouring Palazzo Bembo. Looking in the opposite direction, the complementary view examines the southern leg of the canal beyond the Palazzo Grimani, which, as always, is somewhat monolithic in Turner's rendition of it (fig.160). To its left, next to the building with a series of grey canopies, is the Albergo Leon Bianco. The right-hand side of the image is closed by the façade of the Palazzo Coccina Tiepolo.[10] However, the focus of the study falls on a couple of anchored vessels, one of which sports a painted sail reminiscent of that in The Sun of Venice (fig.248).

A couple of the studies Turner painted on loose sheets of paper record the view from a little further down the canal, glancing back in the direction of the Rialto bridge (fig.161).[11] The one on grey paper forms part of a small sequence dedicated to an exploration of the Palazzo Grimani and its immediate vicinity. If this was also made in 1840, it is likely that Turner was here re-evaluating a scene he had painted in oils for the Royal Academy exhibition just a few years earlier (fig.58). Before assessing the group, all

of which are newly identified here, it is possible to get an overview of the Grand Canal frontage of the palace in one of the roll sketchbook watercolours, taken midstream (fig.162). By showing it in harmonious conjunction with the adjacent Palazzo Corner-Contarini dei Cavalli, which is actually less imposing, Turner diminished the daunting proportions of the Grimani palace, but nevertheless retained his overriding idea of its commanding presence. Its unconventional and ostentatious design was the work of Michele Sanmicheli.[12] Girolamo Grimani, who commissioned the palace, served the Republic as Procurator of San Marco, while his son Marino subsequently became Doge between 1595 and 1605. Two centuries afterwards, as an indication of how far fortunes in Venice had fallen, Turner would have known the building as the city's main post office; it is now the Court of Appeal. In the watercolour, the angled south-western corner of the building catches the brilliant afternoon light, and this effect is strengthened by the tapered reflection of sky in the gap left for the tributary canal, the Rio San Luca, running between the palaces. Yet again, at the left edge of the sheet, he includes his former lodgings.

156 (cat.89)
The Rialto Bridge from the North 1840
Watercolour, 22.1 x 32
From the 'Grand Canal and Giudecca' sketchbook
Tate (TB CCCXV 3; D32119)

157
The Rialto Bridge from the North 1840
Pencil and watercolour on pale buff
paper, 22.7 x 30.2
National Galleries of Scotland,
Edinburgh (W 1369)

158 (cat.146)
On the Grand Canal near the Rialto, with the
Fabbriche Nuove and the Campanile of San
Giovanni Elemosinario 1840
Pencil and watercolour on pale buff
paper, 22.5 x 30
Tate (TB CCCXVI 12; D32149)

159
On the Grand Canal looking towards the
Rialto Bridge from the South 1840
Pencil and watercolour, 22 x 31.9
From the 'Grand Canal and Giudecca'
sketchbook
Tate (TB CCCXV 2; D32118; S 44)

160 (cat.105)
*The Grand Canal, looking towards the Palazzo
Grimani* 1840
Pencil and watercolour, 22.2 x 32
From the 'Grand Canal and Giudecca'
sketchbook
Tate (TB CCCXV 21; D32137; S 54)

The uncompromising focus on the two palace façades, studied head-on, is untypical of the rest of the series. There are, in fact, only a few other instances when Turner turned away from the main course of the Grand Canal to inspect particular buildings in this way *(figs.173, 176, 179)*. Otherwise, like most earlier artists, he had tended to depict stretches of the canal in which the retreating palaces are seen obliquely, in profile only. A possible influence on the more frontal views could perhaps have been Dionisio Moretti's exhaustive *Prospetto del Canal Grande di Venezia*, first published in the 1820s, which diligently transcribed every building on either side of the canal in an unfurling panorama *(figs.4, 237)*. These finely engraved images are built up from hundreds of individual studies in which each building was evidently observed from exactly the same distance, so that the perspective is unerringly uniform. That Turner did not adopt the frontal format often, or as rigidly as Moretti, attests to his habitual preference for compositions with greater depth. Indeed, few of the river scenes he had produced earlier in his career were as blunt in their construction as these watercolours of the Grand Canal, which anticipate the constricted emphasis on palace façades, and their reflections, in the work of Whistler and Monet.[13]

Turner's studies of the Palazzo Grimani continued just off the Grand Canal in the Rio San Luca, one of a chain of canals that cuts across the lower half of the city to emerge near San Moise, thereby connecting the two neighbourhoods in which Turner stayed. He had first noticed the back elevation of the palace in 1819, and had then recorded the complicated intersection of architectural planes produced by its landward gate and the adjoining buildings.[14] Returning to this setting twenty years later, he selected much the same viewpoint to make an elaborate pencil sketch on one of his pieces of grey paper *(fig.164)*. This looks down the narrow canal towards the Grand Canal, and was clearly sketched from a boat beside the church of San Luca, then newly restored. Visiting this spot, it is immediately apparent that Turner took considerable licence with perspective, and encompassed what amounts to two viewpoints by ingeniously extending the parameters of his image beyond what the human eye can take in. The result is dense and tightly composed, its deep recession recalling the formula for Venetian pictures that James Holland had concocted and begun to repeat steadfastly *(fig.86)*.

Intriguingly, the other side of the sheet on which Turner made the sketch was afterwards used for a highly worked watercolour of virtually the same scene *(fig.165)*. This seems to be the only occasion in 1840 when he developed a separate colour study from a sketch, instead of painting over it. To overcome the practical difficulty of making reference to one image while creating the other on its verso, he seems to have taken a second sheet of paper, this time a similar-sized piece of Bally, Ellen and Steart's blue

161 (cat.121)
The Rialto Bridge on the Grand Canal from near the Palazzo Grimani c.1840
Pencil, watercolour and bodycolour on grey paper, using a pen dipped in watercolour for details, 19.6 x 28.1
Tate (TB CCCXVII 27; D32212; S 36)

162 (cat.93)
The Palazzo Grimani and the Palazzo Corner-
Contarini dei Cavalli on the Grand Canal, with the
Rio San Luca 1840
Pencil and watercolour, 22.1 x 32.4
From the 'Grand Canal and Giudecca'
sketchbook
Tate (TB CCCXV 7; D32123)

drawing-paper, which he had also recently used for views of Bregenz on his way to Venice *(fig.163)*.[15] Working broadly in gouache, he reproduced the essence of his pencil sketch, animating it by differentiating the way he wanted the light to fall across the various surfaces. The only discordant feature is the façade of San Luca on the right, which has been twisted so that it appears to be directly in front of the viewer, rather than at ninety degrees. This rudimentary, but decidedly expressive study then served as the basis for the more finished drawing *(fig.165)*. Why he did not simply use another piece of his plentiful supply of grey paper for the watercolour is puzzling. Turner was, admittedly, never prone to wastefulness with his materials, but this occurrence may be related to a deeper need to let his ideas evolve through the process of reworking the basic design. The columned building that Turner introduced on the left may be intended to be the Teatro San Benedetto, though it is not visible in the sketch. Indeed, the final image departs in many details from the original rough draft and the actual setting, but yet contrives to convey a vivid idea of a journey through Venice's back canals. Perhaps the most effective addition is the arch at the top left, which frames the scene, as if the viewer has just passed under a bridge and been presented with this attractive prospect.

The entrance to the Rio San Luca from the Grand Canal is the subject of another colour study *(fig.166)*.[16] Turner's realisation of sunlight and shadows in this work is exceptional, and is greatly assisted by the tone of the paper. On the left, the faint pencil lines describing San Luca and the Palazzo Grimani are supplemented with white highlights to replicate the dazzle of marble and stucco, while the facing walls recede through a sequence of soft, earthy washes. As in some of the related studies on grey paper, an area of the sky was rubbed with blue and then balanced below by its reflection.

Back on the Grand Canal, Turner made the last of this group of studies among the gondolas at the Traghetto San Benedetto *(fig.167)*. Scanning the palaces on the opposite side of the canal, his attention was caught, as it had been before, by the most conspicuous of these petrified remains of Venetian wealth and ambition – the combined bulk of the gothic Palazzo Pisani-Moretta and the abutting Palazzo Barbarigo della Terrazza, with its terrace leading off the *piano nobile*.[17] The first still housed Veronese's great

163
San Luca and the back of the Palazzo Grimani, from the Rio San Luca 1840
Watercolour and bodycolour on blue paper, 19.4 x 28.2
Tate (TB CCCXVII 31; D32216; S 39)

164
San Luca and the Back of the Palazzo Grimani from the Rio San Luca 1840
Pencil with lead white highlights on grey paper, 19.4 x 27.9
Tate (TB CCCXVII 30v; D40159)

165 (cat.122)
The Church of San Luca and the Back of the
Palazzo Grimani from the Rio San Luca 1840
Pencil, watercolour and bodycolour on
grey paper, using a pen dipped in
watercolour for details, 19.4 x 27.9
Tate (TB CCCXVII 30; D32215; S 40)

166 (cat.123)
*The Rio San Luca alongside the Palazzo
Grimani, with the church of San Luca 1840*
Pencil, watercolour and bodycolour on
grey paper, using a pen dipped in
watercolour for details, 19.1 x 28.1
Tate (TB CCCXVII 29; D32214; S 37)

historical subject *The Family of Darius before Alexander c.*1565 (National Gallery, London) and other paintings, which Turner had seen and sketched in 1819 (see p.59). Strongly weighted on one side by buildings rearing up right next to him, the composition is counterbalanced by the much greater expanse of open water. Several of the later pencil sketches adopt this model, including one that he set down close to the Palazzo Mocenigo *(fig.87, lower sketch)*. Though rather cursory, this was possibly the basis for an unfinished oil painting that Turner seems to have prepared around 1844, when he was aware of Frances McCracken's interest in acquiring a Venetian subject *(figs.168, 178)*.[18] The Mocenigo palace, with its connection with Byron, would have been a good commercial choice, as various contemporary artists had made it a well-known subject. However, Turner's picture did not advance far beyond an intimation of the building on the left, with floating objects that appear to be the incipient stage of gondolas.

One of the least familiar pages of the 'Grand Canal and Giudecca' sketchbook manages to combine a view of the string of Mocenigo palaces, just before the tight bend to the south, with the Ca'Foscari on the other bank *(fig.169)*. Apparently never exhibited before, its restrained colouring

is closest to the freshness of Bonington's Venetian watercolours. As noted above, the impressive palace on the right, the Balbi, formed the immediate foreground of two of Turner's 1840s watercolours that depict the classic view back towards the Rialto *(figs.88, 90)*.

Passing on down the canal beyond the Ca'Rezzonico, Turner paused once more to create another pair of watercolours that record the view in both directions *(figs.170–1)*. It is possible to work out Turner's position fairly accurately from the annotations he made to the first of these, which suggest he was temporarily moored off the Palazzo 'Falier', by the Ca'del Duca, looking directly at the 'Balbi' palace.[19] The campanile of the Frari rises imperiously behind the latter, but at the top of the sheet Turner wrote 'C. St Rocco'. Rather than assuming this to be a misidentification, it is possible that he was signalling the location of the nearby church and scuola where he had been awestruck by Tintoretto's paintings, and which he evidently revisited at some point during his stay in 1840.[20]

Facing about, the next stretch of canal is ornamented by the pale dome of Santa Maria della Salute, glimpsed at the end of the vista for the first time *(fig.171)*. Its slightly elliptical form eluded many artists, including Turner,

167 (cat.124)
Looking down the Grand Canal towards the
Palazzo Pisani-Moretta and the Palazzo
Barbarigo, from near the Palazzo Grimani
1840
Pencil, watercolour and bodycolour on
grey paper, using a pen dipped in
watercolour for details, 19.1 x 28.1
Tate (TB CCCXVII 28; D32213; S 38)

168 (cat.56)
Scene in Venice, probably looking down the
Grand Canal from alongside the Palazzo
Mocenigo c.1844
Oil on canvas, 62.2 x 92.7
Tate (N05488; B&J 503)

169 (cat.88)
On the Grand Canal, looking towards the Palazzi
Mocenigo, with the Palazzo Foscari beyond 1840
Pencil and watercolour, 22.1 x 32
From the 'Grand Canal and Giudecca'
sketchbook
Tate (TB CCCXV 1; D32117)

who was here only satisfied with his second attempt at it, which improves on the version he painted back in 1818 (*fig.33*). As was often the case with subjects he had painted before seeing them for himself, he absorbed the actual setting through repeated observation, shifting his viewpoint subtly to ensure he understood how the various component parts fitted together. There is, for example, a study on grey paper which duplicates this view, while moving perceptibly towards the Campo San Vidal, so that the church's bell tower is visible between buildings (*fig.172*). By capturing the scene from the water, rather than from the campo next to the Accademia as Bonington and Harding had done, Turner retained the impression that both sides of the canal culminate in the Salute.

The Accademia itself was the focus of one of the colour studies that break off laterally from the more regular forward progress (*fig.173*). This is the first of a sequence of more fully resolved watercolours depicting the lower Grand Canal, which were formerly part of the second roll sketchbook. Turner's viewpoint is not greatly dissimilar from that in Canaletto's *Stone Mason's Yard c.1728* (National Gallery, London), although the important *traghetto* crossing shown by both artists has long since been replaced by a bridge – first by the English steel one of 1854, so loathed by Ruskin, and then by the existing wooden one of the 1930s. Similar changes to the urban infrastructure have also resulted in the filling in of the small canal, seen running behind the gallery towards one of the Gesuati's campaniles.

The exterior of the gallery has remained largely unchanged, however, highlighting the inaccuracies in Turner's representation. Part of the collection is housed in the red-brick shell of the former church of La Carità, but this is considerably longer than Turner indicates, with a rounded apse on the left, and has lancet windows only at its lowest level. By contrast, he made the neoclassical entrance to the gallery more significant, expanding its width yet faithfully delineating Antonio Giacarelli's crowning sculpture of *Minerva Seated upon the Adriatic Lion* 1830 (now moved to the Public Gardens). He had first visited the Accademia in 1819 and would have been interested to monitor on his later visits how the institution had expanded in the meantime.[21]

Instead of surveying the last stretch of the canal from either the Campo della Carità, or the Campo San Vio, as Canaletto had done, Turner made a cluster of watercolours a little way west of the *traghetto* running between San Maurizio and San Vio (*figs.174–6*). All are pervaded by a radiant afternoon sunlight, which catches the flanks of buildings and the domes of the Salute so powerfully that they become disembodied.[22] Watercolour is used not merely to describe form, but also to represent the shadows by which form is defined. In one luminous study his viewpoint was just beyond the Campo San Vio, which is the open space into which light floods on the right (*fig.174*). Looking further down this side of the canal is the low,

170
The Grand Canal looking towards the Palazzo Balbi and the Campanile of the Frari 1840
Pencil and watercolour, 22.2 x 32
From the 'Grand Canal and Giudecca' sketchbook
Tate (TB CCCXV 18; D32134)

171 (cat.101)
The Grand Canal from near the Accademia, with Santa Maria della Salute in the Distance 1840
Pencil and watercolour, 22.3 x 32.5
From the 'Grand Canal and Giudecca' sketchbook
Tate (TB CCCXV 15; D32131)

172 (cat.69)
Looking down the Grand Canal towards Santa Maria della Salute, from near the Accademia c.1833 or 1840
Pencil, watercolour and bodycolour on grey paper, 19.1 x 28.2
Tate (TB CCCXVII 25; D32210)

173 (cat.106)
The Accademia from the Grand Canal 1840
Pencil and watercolour, using a pen
dipped in watercolour for details,
with some scraping-out, 21.7 x 31.8
From the 'Storm' sketchbook
Ashmolean Museum, Oxford. Presented
by John Ruskin, 1861 (W 1366; S 91)

174 (cat.92)
*Looking down the Grand Canal to Palazzo Corner
della Ca'Grande and Santa Maria della Salute* 1840
Pencil and watercolour, 22.1 x 32.5
From the 'Grand Canal and Giudecca'
sketchbook
Tate (TB CCCXV 6; D32122; S 47)

175 (cat.160)
Santa Maria della Salute from near the
Traghetto San Maurizio 1840
Pencil and watercolour, 24.2 x 30.4
Tate (TB CCCXVI 1; D32138; S 58)

176
The Campo San Vio from the Grand Canal,
with the Palazzo Loredan-Balbi on the right
and the Palazzo Barbarigo on the left 1840
Pencil and watercolour, 24.6 x 30.7
Tate (TB CCCXVI 6; D32143)

unfinished façade of the Ca'Venier dei Leoni, and on the opposite side of the canal is the immense Palazzo Corner della Ca'Grande. At the left edge of the sheet Turner wrote the word 'BALBI', referring to the Palazzo Balbi Valier, besides which he was moored.

It was this part of the canal that he set out to commemorate in another of the unfinished oil studies begun around 1844 *(fig.178)*. Like its pair *(fig.168)*, this was not accessioned until the 1940s, when it was rediscovered as part of a cache of neglected canvases, their condition so deteriorated that they were very nearly mistakenly destroyed.[23] The painting was subsequently transformed by skilled conservation work, and it is now possible to gain a sense of the preliminary design that Turner could have developed had he been convinced that there was the possibility of selling the result to a collector like McCracken.[24] By the time he was working on these canvases he had moved away from the crisp definition he had initially borrowed from Canaletto, but in their existing state these works are more extreme than any of the paintings he exhibited of Venice, revealing how the atmospheric imprecision that his critics ridiculed was inherent to the process of their creation.

Drawing nearer the Salute brought Turner within sight of the Hotel Europa, and it was his proximity to this last sweep of the Grand Canal in 1840 that allowed him to produce so many watercolours of Longhena's majestic ensemble *(figs.177, 179–80, 182–3, 222)*. The church had been erected towards the end of the seventeenth century in gratitude to the Virgin Mary for halting the ravages of plague in Venice during 1630–1, when 82,000 people died.

Only one of Turner's watercolours examines the extravagant baroque rhythms of the Salute's architecture directly *(fig.179)*, but the factual delineation of pediments, pilasters and curlicues is overwhelmed by his dramatic evocation of shafts of sunlight, which pierce through the thundery rain clouds above the abbey of San Gregorio on the right. This study and all but a couple of the watercolours of the Salute come from the 'Storm' sketchbook, which he used almost exclusively on the waters close to his hotel. These works are frequently finished by a skein of red lines, applied with pen and brush, to represent the windows, balconies and chimneys of the palaces facing the Salute. The lively energy of these strokes of strong colour neatly contrasts with and amplifies the stillness of the water. In several of the group Turner deployed to great effect the black silhouette of a gondola, creating a sharp distinction between its inescapable solidity and the limpid washes of the surrounding reflections. Two of the watercolours resemble the composition of the oil painting Turner had exhibited in 1835 *(figs.180-1)*, though the study on grey paper could well be the basis for that picture, rather than another variation on a familiar theme. In contrast with the painting, the roll sketchbook

177 (cat.107)
The Grand Canal, with the Salute 1840
Pencil, watercolour and bodycolour, using a pen dipped in watercolour for details, 21.5 x 31.5
From the 'Storm' sketchbook
Ashmolean Museum, Oxford. Presented by John Ruskin, 1861 (W 1363; S 93)

178 (cat.57)
Venice with the Salute c.1844
Oil on canvas, 62.2 x 92.7
Tate (N05487; B&J 502)

179
*The North-Western Façade of Santa Maria
della Salute, seen from the Grand Canal* 1840
Watercolour and bodycolour, using a
pen dipped in watercolour for details,
21.9 x 32.1
From the 'Storm' sketchbook
National Galleries of Scotland,
Edinburgh (W 1370; S 92)

watercolour narrows the width of the canal, so that the view is closed by the Zecca and the Doge's Palace; another of Turner's minor shifts of emphasis was to raise the height of the Palazzo Giustinian, as if he was reminding himself where he was staying.

His elegiac image of the Salute just after sunset, in which its white stone shimmers dimly against the evening sky, in fact records the view from slightly closer to the Europa, looking back up the canal (*fig.183*; see also *fig.222*).[25] Here again, so much is achieved with comparatively little evidence of effort. Yet the apparent ease with which Turner was able to realise the details resulted from his recurring contemplation of the vista over a period of twenty years (see *fig.83*).[26]

The rest of the watercolours from the 'Storm' sketchbook chart the arrival of a late afternoon squall. These begin with a pair of studies that reduce the Dogana and the island of San Giorgio to grey shapes, as if seen through an oppressive miasma before the storm breaks (*figs.184–5*). Colour is restored once the rain starts, so that the buildings assume a flame-like redness, or are left stark white against the lurid blue sky (*figs.186–8*). In the study now in the British Museum, a gondolier seeks shelter in the Grand Canal from the tossing waters of the Bacino (*fig.188*). Whether fortuitously, or as a result of his observations, the opaque jade green that Turner uses in this work unerringly replicates what occurs when a storm aerates the Lagoon during a sudden downpour.[27] The more complete state of these final views of the Grand Canal might argue that Turner prepared them for the market. But, unlike the powerfully conceived view of the Piazzetta, these studies retain the feeling of having evolved on the page. It is as though, having returned to the Europa wet and dripping after being caught in the storm, he needed to work through the impressions that were still so vivid and fresh. What we witness in the sequence, therefore, is the translation of reality into something more potent and universal.

180 (cat.70)
The Mouth of the Grand Canal, with the Steps of
Santa Maria della Salute c.1833 or 1840
Pencil, watercolour and bodycolour on grey
paper, 18.4 x 27.8
Tate (TB CCCXVII 23; D32208; S 34)

181
*View down the Grand Canal towards the Dogana and
the Campanile of San Marco c.1840*
Pencil and watercolour, using a pen dipped in
watercolour for details, 22.1 x 32
From the 'Storm' sketchbook
The British Museum, London (R.W. Lloyd
Bequest; W 1359; S 73)

182 (cat.91)
*The Steps of Santa Maria della Salute, looking up
the Grand Canal* 1840
Pencil and watercolour, with details added
using a pen dipped in watercolour, 22.1 x 32.3
From the 'Grand Canal and Giudecca'
sketchbook
Tate (TB CCCXV 5; D32121; S 45)

183 (cat.112)
The Grand Canal, with Santa Maria della
Salute, from near the Hotel Europa 1840
Pencil, watercolour and bodycolour,
with some scraping-out, 22 x 31.8
From the 'Storm' sketchbook
Private collection (W 1368; S 94)

184 (cat.111)
The Mouth of the Grand Canal 1840
Watercolour, with details added using a
pen, 21.9 x 31.8
From the 'Storm' sketchbook
Yale Center for British Art, Paul Mellon
Collection (W 1360)

185
Venice from the Punta della Dogana 1840
Watercolour, with details added using a pen,
22 x 32
From the 'Storm' sketchbook
Private collection

186
Storm at the Mouth of the Grand Canal 1840
Pencil and watercolour, with details
added using a pen dipped in watercolour,
21.8 x 31.9
From the 'Storm' sketchbook
National Gallery of Ireland (W 1358; S 80)

187 (cat.113)
*Venice: looking towards the Dogana and San
Giorgio Maggiore, with a Storm Approaching*
1840
Watercolour, with details added using a
pen dipped in watercolour, 22 x 32
From the 'Storm' sketchbook
Private collection (courtesy of Richard
Green; W 1355)

188 (cat.109)
Storm at Venice 1840
Watercolour, with details added using a pen,
21.8 x 31.8
From the 'Storm' sketchbook
British Museum (Sale Bequest; W 1354; S 87)

CCCXVII — 2 ?

9 The Giudecca Canal

The southern flanks of the two main islands of Venice are protected by the long crescent of the Giudecca, which begins just beside the Isola di San Giorgio Maggiore and stretches westward in a lazy curve. The Giudecca had always been characterised as a place at a slight remove from the city itself, inhabited by Jews, exiles, monks and nuns.[1] By the time of Turner's visits, following the suppression of its religious institutions, the area was in flux and had begun to be developed for industry.

Separating the island from Venice itself is the wide channel of the Giudecca canal. Bordered by a cluster of churches designed by Palladio at its eastern end, this affords spectacular views back to the heart of the city, as well as unusual perspectives that bring familiar landmarks into unrecognisable conjunctions. Sadly, the view westwards is no longer as appealing as it was in Turner's day, dominated as it is by the ceaseless flare of the petrochemical works at Porto Marghera. Nevertheless, the chain of the Euganean hills, and to the north the peaks of the Dolomites, can still be admired on clear days from the far reaches of the canal.

It was not until his final visit that Turner really assimilated the area as one of direct relevance to his art. He had made his first tentative survey in 1819, but then ventured no further than the church of the Redentore.[2] By contrast, his more adventurous circuit of the western edges of the city in 1833 resulted in various dutiful sketches of campaniles and domes, including those of the island of San Giorgio in Alga, halfway to Fusina.[3] But it was only during his stay in 1840 and afterwards that he really began to see that this previously neglected quarter offered original ways of presenting Venice.[4] There were, in fact, few precedents to follow, for the Giudecca canal appears just occasionally in the work of Guardi and Canaletto. Perhaps inevitably, the only contemporary artist of any significance to have painted it before Turner embarked on his series of the 1840s was Clarkson Stanfield, who exhibited a Giudecca view at the British Institution in 1837.[5]

Ironically, when Turner and Stanfield had first overlapped in their choice of Venetian subjects in 1833, they had both selected views from the Giudecca side of the Dogana (figs.102–3). Turner located the precise spot he had been attempting to depict on one of his subsequent visits, and was presumably forced to recognise that his perspective in the painting was flawed. Indeed, the colour sketch he made on a sheet of grey paper gives

a much more accurate idea of how the architectural elements come together (fig.189). The study also makes apparent that the southern side of the Dogana was where boats arriving in Venice would moor while their cargoes were registered. In the bottom-left corner, his annotation to the sheet seems to read '8 V', which could be its number in a series of Venetian views (see also figs.111, 212, 233).[6]

Another view of the Punta della Dogana includes the entrance to the Grand Canal on the right, with the campanile of San Moise behind the Palazzo Giustinian (fig.190). Rising in the gap between the Dogana and the Seminario Patriarchale are two towers, the taller of which is that of Santo Stefano. Its lower companion could be either Sant'Angelo or San Maurizio; if the former, this would date the study to before 1837 when the tower was

189 (cat.71)
The Dogana, Campanile of San Marco and the Doge's Palace c.1833 or 1840
Pencil, watercolour and bodycolour on grey paper, 19.3 x 28.1
Tate (TB CCCXVII 20; D32205; S 32)

190 (cat.72)
Boats in front of the Dogana and Santa Maria della Salute c.1833 or 1840
Pencil, watercolour and bodycolour on grey paper, using a pen dipped in watercolour for details, 19 x 28.1
Tate (TB CCCXVII 21; D32206; S 33)

191
*The Punta della Dogana, with the Campanile
beyond, from the Giudecca Canal* 1840
Pencil and watercolour, 24.6 x 30.7
Tate (TB CCCXVI 10; D32147)

192
*Boats Moored in the Giudecca Canal, near the
Dogana, with the Back of the Salute* 1840
Pencil and watercolour, 24.4 x 30.7
Tate (TB CCCXVI 33; D32170)

demolished. This is one of several Venetian studies in which the experience of sketching from the water led Turner to abandon the standard placing of the horizon about a third of the way from the bottom of his composition. Here it is just below the mid-point of the paper, giving equal weight to sea and sky.

Turner's fondness for these moorings at the eastern end of the Giudecca canal is readily apparent from the number of watercolours he painted *(figs.191–5)*. These are some of his most delicate studies of Venice, faintly developed in thinly coloured washes to replicate the blinding glare of morning *(fig.193)* or the softer fading light of the late afternoon, as it caught the highest tips of the Salute *(fig.194)*. In the more developed of these *(fig.195)* the church is indistinctly shrouded above a sugary pink expanse representing the warehouse buildings, and these evanescent colours give greater vigour to the dark outline of a gondolier plying his craft.[7] On the back of the sheet Turner referred to the gondola in one of his erratic attempts at poetry, characterising it as a 'sloppy thing', at the same time evoking Byron with the word 'Beppo' at the end of his inscription.

Another pair of these economically descriptive studies provides a more general view of the junction of the Giudecca canal and the Bacino *(fig.196)*.[8] Though they are fundamentally similar in viewpoint, Turner seems to differentiate between them subtly by lighting one from the left, so that the western faces of the Salute and San Giorgio are illuminated by the setting sun, while in the one reproduced here the sun's rays come from the right. This is a minor but not inconsequential point, for when Turner developed an oil painting of this view for the 1841 exhibition *(fig.197)*, it was permeated by the dazzle of fresh morning sunshine, indicating that it was derived from the second of these watercolours.

The painting was one of three views of the Giudecca by Turner in that year's exhibition, which were the first fruits of his recent trip to Venice (see also *figs.198, 205*). Collectively, they testify to his new fascination with the wide span of the Giudecca's waters. Each radiates with the uplifting character of southern light, an achievement all the more remarkable in having been accomplished in Turner's London studio during the wintry months at the beginning of 1841. The picture now at Oberlin was first owned by the sculptor Sir Francis Chantrey, with whom Turner liked to spar over their respective abilities as anglers. Anecdotal accounts conflict as to whether Chantrey bought the picture at the Academy on the advice of a colleague, or whether it was, instead, 'painted expressly' for him.[9] Yet no evidence survives to suggest if this was a formal commission, nor is there a record of how much Chantrey paid. The picture could even have been Turner's gift to an ailing friend, recalling their shared time in Venice in 1819. For by April 1841 Chantrey was already suffering from the ill health that brought his death at the end of the year.

193 (cat.161)
Boats Moored alongside the Punta della
Dogana, with the Doge's Palace beyond 1840
Watercolour, 24.6 x 30.7
Tate (TB CCCXVI 35; D32172; S 82)

Turner's viewpoint was, in fact, not greatly different from that of the picture bought by Sheepshanks at the 1840 exhibition *(fig.110)*, though it features the island of San Giorgio on the right in preference to the luminous domes of the Salute, which should be visible on the left. Compared with the two exhibits of the previous year, there is a more expansive handling of paint, especially in the delineation of the reflective surfaces of the canal, which grows directly from Turner's watercolour processes. As in his more developed colour sketches, the buildings are noticeably fortified by the addition of red for the details, and the pervasively warm tone is extended in the peripheral parts of the picture by the use of the same ruddy colour for the caps and trousers of the gondoliers. Turner's desire to create tonal relationships led him to introduce a couple of dashes to the foreground, which puzzled its first viewers. Eventually explained away as a couple of floating oranges, it was nevertheless apparent that the colour was too useful to be dispensed with as a means of complementing the surrounding blue.[10]

With its pendant *(fig.198)*, the picture was greeted enthusiastically by contemporary critics, one of whom even described the pair as 'two beautiful masterpieces'.[11] A couple of weeks later the *Athenaeum* was also impressed, especially by the absence of the extravagant mannerisms for which it had previously berated Turner:

> In these Venetian pictures it would be hard to exceed the clearness of air and water – the latter taking every passing reflection with a pellucid softness beyond the reach of meaner pencil [i.e. 'brush'].
> The architecture, too, is more carefully made out than has lately been the case with Mr Turner, and both pictures are kept alive by groups of southern figures, which, seen from a certain remoteness, give a beauty and not a blemish to the scenes they animate.[12]

The second painting was bought from the Academy by Elhanan Bicknell, who also acquired another Venetian subject the following year *(fig.257)*. In some respects it is less distinct and more consciously atmospheric than its companion, particularly where Turner worked up the distant towers and domes in glutinous white paint against an almost white background. This was the first of Turner's views in oil that really stood back from the monumental city celebrated by most other artists, even though the spirit of Canaletto continued to linger. The great Campanile may be readily apparent, but it is oddly conflated with the Salute and must disorientate those not familiar with this back view. More confusingly, on the extreme right Turner mistakenly introduced one of the towers of the Redentore, which would only be seen if the façade itself was also in view. Both of these sleights of hand arise from the way he cropped the watercolour study that he utilised as the basis of his composition *(fig.199)*. This is a sheet from the

194 (cat.162)
Looking up the Giudecca Canal, with Santa Maria della Salute on the Right 1840
Pencil and watercolour, 24.5 x 30.5
Tate (TB CCCXVI 26; D32163)

195 (cat.163)
Santa Maria della Salute from the Bacino 1840
Pencil and watercolour, 24.4 x 30.7
Tate (TB CCCXVI 37; D32174)

roll sketchbook containing most of his studies of the Grand Canal, which was also used for a series of views of the Giudecca. To compensate for the fact that this watercolour ingeniously embraced an expansive field of vision, he created a more condensed approximation of space in the painting, thereby moving the Redentore to the right, beyond the frame of the image.

A group of three colour sketches (*figs.200–2*), painted over taut pencil lines, could have provided him with more precise information about the exact topography of the eastern half of the Giudecca, but he patently did not return to this reference material. One of the studies shows the squat exterior of the late-sixteenth-century Palladian church of the Zitelle, correctly placing the dome immediately behind the turrets that surmount its pedimented façade (*fig.200*). However, in the painting Turner invented an elongated nave between the two features, which is closer in form to the neighbouring Redentore.

A longer stretch of the Giudecca, akin to that in the painting, appears in a rather wan watercolour study that was painted beside the steps of the Redentore (*fig.201*). Palladio's imposing church, one of his final designs, was another of those constructed as a means of imploring divine protection from the ever-present threat of plague. At the right edge of the image Turner recorded the austere lines defining the entrance façade, supplementing the main sketch with additional details. An inscription in the midst of these reads 'Giaca...', but this is not an attempt to identify the sculpted saints on the façade. Until the Napoleonic era the Redentore was flanked by the church and monastery of Santa Maria Novella, which was popularly known as San Giacomo Apostolo, and which, after its demolition, continued to be recalled in the name of the *fondamenta* and the adjoining *campo*.

The names of towns and buildings had often presented difficulties for Turner during his travels, and occasionally, when he worked up sketches that had perhaps seemed of only passing interest at the time he made them, he was unable to remember their identities correctly.[13] In Venice, however, it seems that he greatly benefited from the readily shared local knowledge of affable gondoliers, since many pages of his sketchbooks are suitably annotated with the names of churches, convents or palaces. Despite this, there were a handful of subjects on the Giudecca that repeatedly flummoxed him. The most surprising of these, given its recurrence in the sketches resulting from his campaigns on the Giudecca, was the Redentore itself. In January 1841, less than four months after returning from Venice, he wrote to Harriet Moore, the daughter of one of his friends, to thank her for supplying the name of the church, which he was evidently already planning to depict in one of that year's exhibits (*fig.205*).[14] This is an intriguing episode, for Turner had, in fact, merely to consult another of his sketches to find his own memorandum (*fig.202*), which not only identified the

Redentore (at a second attempt), but which also noted that it belonged to the 'Capuchin' order, whose monks had been exiled under the French but returned to their enclosed life on the Giudecca in the 1820s. More mystifying is the accompanying reference to 'S. Domenico', which appears on the right, below the deft rendition of the Gesuati, though the inscription probably refers to this Dominican church, more correctly known as Santa Maria del Rosario, since the area has no church of San Domenico.[15]

The Redentore is seen in the annotated sketch from a point to the east of the bridge over the Rio della Croce, but Turner's major picture of 1841 was based instead on the essentially monochrome study he made on a sheet of grey paper from the other side of the church (*fig.203*). In contrast with the simplicity of this preliminary design, Turner's resulting painting is congested with pageantry, which inevitably calls to mind comparable images by Canaletto (*fig.205*). The picture was the most substantial of his exhibits in 1841, and proved to be the largest view of Venice he painted in the years after his final trip. Unlike the two accompanying pictures of the Giudecca canal, it had an ostensibly historical subject, purporting to record

196 (cat.164)
Santa Maria della Salute, the Campanile of San Marco, the Doge's Palace and San Giorgio Maggiore, from the Giudecca Canal 1840
Watercolour, 24.5 x 30.8
Tate (TB CCCXVI 8; D32145)

197 (cat.43)
Ducal Palace, Dogano, with Part of San Georgio,
Venice exhibited Royal Academy 1841
Oil on canvas, 63.5 x 93
Allen Memorial Art Museum, Oberlin
College, Ohio. Mrs F.F. Prentiss Bequest,
1944 (B&J 390)

198
*Giudecca, la Donna della Salute and San
Georgio* exhibited Royal Academy 1841
Oil on canvas, 61 x 91.5
Privately owned, New York (B&J 391)

199 (cat.97)
The Giudecca Canal, looking towards Santa Maria della Salute 1840
Watercolour, bodycolour and coloured crayons, with details added using a pen dipped in watercolour, 22.2 x 32.1
From the 'Grand Canal and Giudecca' sketchbook
Tate (TB CCCXV 11; D32127; S 49)

the ceremony attending the installation of three pictures by Giovanni Bellini in the Sacristy of the Redentore. The precise date of this fanciful event is not given, but the costumes imply the sixteenth century. It is similarly ambiguous in both the title and the image whether Bellini himself is meant to be present. The fact that Bellini died in 1516, over seventy years before the completion of the Redentore, would not have deterred Turner from pursuing his subject. He had perpetrated comparable architectural anachronisms in his earlier attempt to commemorate Raphael at work in the Vatican loggia.[16]

Nowadays the paintings in the Sacristy are no longer attributed to Bellini, though Turner was not alone in believing them to be his work. Of his contemporaries, both Lady Murray and Ruskin, for example, also accepted the connection with Bellini.[17] In fact, these devotional images are distant cousins to the fine examples by Bellini already in the Accademia by 1840. The best of the group is now ascribed to Alvise Vivarini *(fig.204)*, with the others given variously to Francesco Bissolo, Lazzaro Bastiani and Rocco Marconi.[18] There is, however, nothing to suggest a historical basis for Turner's idea that they were conveyed to the church in a splendidly staged ritual. He is most likely to have imagined the occasion and grafted it on to the traditional festivities of the church marked each July by the building of a floating processional route across the Giudecca canal.[19]

Turner's allusion to Bellini, however imperfect, is evidence of his familiarity with Venetian art before Titian, and the latest instance of him paying his respects to one of the painters he admired. Since exhibiting his portrait of Raphael in 1820, his personal pantheon had included representations of Ruisdael, Rembrandt, Poussin, Watteau, Canaletto and Van Goyen.[20] The choice of Bellini in 1841 was astute, revealing that he was in tune with the *zeitgeist*, which at that moment was marked by a growing esteem among connoisseurs for pre-Renaissance artists. In fact, Turner's picture was exhibited in the same year that Paul Delaroche included Bellini and various other late-fifteenth-century artists in his Hemicycle of great masters at the Ecole des Beaux-Arts in Paris.[21]

As London's National Gallery did not acquire anything by Bellini until 1844, and there were few genuine pictures by him in private hands, Turner's experience of this precursor was largely confined to the picture collections he encountered during his travels in Italy and Germany.[22] His appreciation was therefore based on a comparatively slight acquaintance, and seems to have been of relatively recent origin. Back in 1828, in Rome, he had been somewhat dismissive of Bellini's realisation of the *Feast of the Gods* 1514 (National Gallery of Art, Washington) originally created for Alfonso d'Este's Camerino, remarking that it was really just a background, presumably out of respect for the landscape that Titian had added to create a greater harmony with his own canvases.[23]

200
San Giorgio Maggiore and the Zitelle from the Giudecca Canal 1840
Pencil and watercolour, 24.5 x 31
Tate (TB CCCXVI 40; D32177; S 84)

201 (cat.165)
On the Giudecca Canal beside the Redentore, looking towards San Giorgio Maggiore 1840
Pencil and watercolour, 24.4 x 30.7
Tate (TB CCCXVI 4; D32141)

202
The Redentore and the Western Parts of the Giudecca Canal 1840
Pencil and watercolour, 24.4 x 31
Tate (TB CCCXVI 9; D32146; S 61)

the general points of the remembered scene were correct, some of the details might have been altered (see also *fig.151*). Within the parameters imposed by these considerations, the pair of watercolours in question could perhaps be accepted as views of the Dorsoduro side of the Giudecca.

The first of the pair focuses on the dusky russet sail of a *trabaccolo*, apparently weighed down with barrels, behind which the towers and domes of Venice glimmer dimly (*fig.206*). The principal tower may be intended to be the campanile of Santa Marta, though, if so, its height is greatly exaggerated. To its left is the pale suggestion of a building with a pitched roof, and beyond that the regular lines of a series of windows in a red-brick structure. These elements, slightly modified, recur in the canvas Turner exhibited in 1846 as a view of Santa Marta (*fig.268*). In the watercolour, the principal dome behind the sail would seem to be that of the Salute, and the others are perhaps those of the churches along the Giudecca canal. Turner indicates that this is the city's periphery by his inclusion of a group of posts, or *bricole*, on the left, which conceivably mark the route into Venice from Fusina.

The other watercolour possibly shows the same church from a slightly different angle, but could also be a depiction of San Nicolo dei Mendicoli (*fig.207*). As Clarkson Stanfield had demonstrated in his 1837 oil painting of

Turner's own picture fared reasonably well with its first critics, garnering a selection of mostly favourably reviews (the exception, true to form, being *Blackwood's Magazine*), as well as stimulating interest from potential buyers.[24] In answering an enquiry from a Mr Collard, Turner stated that it was priced at 350 guineas, but warned that this did not include the copyright or permission for the painting to be engraved. These terms were respected by its first owners, but after Turner's death the picture was studiously engraved by James Tibbetts Willmore, and it was doubtless from this version of the image that various copies were made.[25]

Moving on from the Redentore, the final stretches of the Giudecca canal, to its west, have been completely transformed since Turner's time by the replacement of churches with factories and dockyards, which has made the identification of some of the views he recorded there much more difficult. The two most significant losses are of the churches and convents of Santi Biagio e Cataldo, at the end of the Giudecca on the site now occupied by the Mulino Stucky, and of Santa Marta, at the western tip of Dorsoduro. Both of these were deconsecrated under French rule, and by 1816 the former had been converted into a typhoid hospital.[26] It was almost certainly these buildings that Turner depicted in four of the remaining watercolours of the 'Grand Canal and Giudecca' sketchbook (*figs.206–8, 210*). All are characterised by sunset or twilight effects that clothe the city in a misty iridescence further frustrating attempts to pinpoint the localities represented. Even Ruskin, who knew pre-industrial Venice so intimately, was unable to make out the subjects of two of these studies when he selected them for display (*figs.206–7*).[27] To compound the problem, it is very likely that Turner worked on these views away from the motif, so that while

203
The Redentore, with the Eastern Parts of the Giudecca Canal c.1840
Watercolour and bodycolour on grey paper, 19.3 x 27.9
Tate (TB CCCXVII 4; D32183)

204
Alvise Vivarini (1442/53–1503/5)
Madonna Adoring the Sleeping Child with Two Angels Playing Music c.1490
Oil on canvas
Sacristy of the church of Il Redentore, Venice

205
*Depositing of John Bellini's Three Pictures in
La Chiesa Redentore, Venice* exhibited
Royal Academy 1841
Oil on canvas, 73.6 x 115.5
Private collection (B&J 393)

206 (cat.95)
A Boat near Santa Marta 1840
Watercolour, 22.2 x 32.1
From the 'Grand Canal and Giudecca'
sketchbook
Tate (TB CCCXV 9; D32125; S 43)

207 (cat.96)
Venice by Moonlight 1840
Watercolour, 22 x 31.9
From the 'Grand Canal and Giudecca'
sketchbook
Tate (TB CCCXV 10; D32126; S 48)

the Giudecca, the campanile of San Nicolo was formerly a more distinctive landmark at the far end of the Zattere.[28] This identification would associate the island in the distance with San Giorgio in Alga, with the moon setting behind it. However, the more usual interpretation is that the moon is rising, seemingly lending support to the connection with Santa Marta, which might be viewed from the west in conjunction with the island convent of Santa Chiara.[29] Whatever its identity, this is one of the most atmospheric pages of the roll sketchbook, its restrained nocturnal colouring indicating once again Turner's appetite for the meditative quality of Venetian moonlight. The absolute stillness causes the water to act as a mirror, creating peculiar shapes in the truncated reflections of a gondola.

Another work that seems to record this generally overlooked corner of Venice is one of the oil paintings Turner exhibited in 1845 *(fig.209)*. It is usually linked with the title *Venice – Sunset, a Fisher* because of the boat, laden with fishing nets, in the foreground. However Turner's identification of his pictures in 1845 and 1846 was far from reliable, so it is not altogether impossible that the picture actually shows the *Noon* effect specified for its companion *(fig.240)*. As will be seen, these temporal factors are of some relevance in that they may help determine what Turner depicted. In this instance, in addition to his stylistic vagueness, matters are considerably hampered by the poor condition of the pictures: both were completely removed from their original canvases during the first quarter of the twentieth century, after they returned from long loans to regional museums. The restorers then attributed the darkened colouring of the sky to atmospheric pollution, but the unstable materials Turner used were more probably to blame (see below, p.240). Little is left in either image of the 'gorgeous visions of *Venice*, blazing with sunlight that floods sea and sky' that the *Spectator* recorded when they were first exhibited.[30]

As far as it is possible to read the image in the *Fisher* painting, Turner's view is taken from an expanse of open water, looking back on a church or convent with a Roman-style tower. This is separated from the adjacent island by a narrow bridge, to the right of which are two domes. The block of land then appears to be interrupted by a wide channel, on the surface of which the sun is reflected; the composition is finally closed on the right by the tower of another church. If this is a sunset view, as implied by its present title, it is difficult to equate the disposition of the painting's individual parts with an identifiable location in Venice without making considerable allowances for artistic licence.[31] Ingenuity is still required, though rather less, to interpret the image as a midday view of the Giudecca canal, seen from close to San Nicolo, with the domes of the Salute and the Gesuati rising above the city. The church on the far right can then be linked with one of those on the Giudecca (perhaps Santi Biagio e Cataldo or Sant'Eufemia). This too is hardly watertight as an identification, but Turner had clearly not

208 (cat.98)
The Western End of the Giudecca Canal, from near the Convent of Santi Biagio e Cataldo 1840
Watercolour, coloured crayon, and details added using a pen dipped in watercolour, 22.1 x 32.2
From the 'Grand Canal and Giudecca' sketchbook
Tate (TB CCCXV 12; D32128; S 50)

209
Venice – Sunset, a Fisher exhibited Royal Academy 1845
Oil on canvas, 61 x 92
Exhibited with the caption,
'MS. Fallacies of Hope'
Tate (N00542; B&J 419)

210 (cat.99)
*The Giudecca Canal, looking towards Fusina
at Sunset* 1840
Pencil, watercolour and bodycolour
with coloured crayons, 22 x 32.3
From the 'Grand Canal and Giudecca'
sketchbook
Tate (TB CCCXV 13; D32129; S 51)

set out to paint a precise piece of topography, and it is entirely possible that he was playing with motifs recorded in his sketchbooks and reassembling them in arrangements that suited his own fancy (see *fig.11*).

A similar divergence between Turner's informal graphic work and its public expression occurs in the final images of the Giudecca canal. These include the other two watercolours from the roll sketchbook, both of which feature the shell of the deconsecrated church of Santi Biagio e Cataldo, but from opposing directions (*figs.208, 210*). Warmed to a variety of bruised pinks by the departing sun, the colours of the west end of the church are marvellously contrasted in one of the studies with the deepening greens of the Lagoon (*fig.208*); above these tones, the softly translucent yellow of the sky was built up with flecked and stippled brushwork. Meanwhile, in the foreground, some fishermen cast their nets in the shallow waters where Sacca Fisola has since been reclaimed.

The second watercolour faces the sun as it sets over Fusina (*fig.210*). Its glaring light reduces the buildings along either side of the Giudecca canal to flattened silhouettes, at the same time gilding the improbably dramatic peaks of the Dolomites. A strip of unpainted white paper replicates the glare of the sun's reflection, its centrality in the composition harking back to the example of Claude Lorrain's Seaports, to which Turner remained devoted throughout his life. This forceful perspective is lent additional strength by the gondolas and other boats, which mark out the route to and from the mainland. As in its companion, the surface is deftly enlivened by a dragged brush, with touches of colour embedded in its textures.

The study is one of the most complete of those in the roll sketchbook, and it is therefore not entirely surprising that Turner subsequently chose to rework it in oils (*fig.211*). There are a number of slight variations between the two works, including the narrowing of the church on the left so that it looks like a tower, the introduction of a fine campanile at Santa Marta and the pair of apparently colliding gondolas, but the most puzzling change was the title Turner gave his painting: *St Benedetto, looking towards Fusina*. As should be plain by now, none of the churches within the view is, or was, known as San Benedetto. In fact, the only church of that name is to be found in the centre of the city, close to where Turner had stayed in 1819, but which is more popularly known as San Beneto.

An attractive, but undoubtedly over-imaginative solution might be that Turner was aware of the vision of the sun experienced by San Benedetto (St Benedict of Norcia) in the final stages of his life, and applied it to a Venetian setting.[32] Pursuing this idea, the observer is perhaps offered the saint's viewpoint as he contemplates the sunset, the ephemeral effect traditionally associated with mortality. In an earlier picture Turner had adopted a somewhat similar strategy as a means of engaging the viewer's sympathies with the Carthaginian general Regulus, whose awful fate was to be blinded by the sun (though our viewpoint and that of Regulus are not, in fact, synonymous, as has sometimes been thought).[33] It is, moreover, possibly significant that Turner could have become familiar with the details of St Benedict's life while he was in Venice. Had he visited San Giorgio Maggiore during his 1840 visit, he would have been able to see the entire scope of the saint's mission, including the episode of the vision, presented in the finely carved choir stalls, the work of Albert van der Brulle and Gasparo Galti. The theme of mortality, too, could be understood as one of personal interest to Turner, who, at sixty-eight, had outlived most of his peers.

Appealing though the symbolism of this speculation may be, a much simpler and more plausible explanation lies in Turner's recurring problems with the names of churches. As mentioned above, he somehow thought one of those in Dorsoduro was called 'San Domenico' (see *fig.202*), describing it by the name of the administering religious order. So, for want of a record of its rather complex name, he might have resorted to a similar tactic to identify the church of Santi Biagio e Cataldo, which was one of several Benedictine institutions facing the Giudecca canal.

Despite his bewilderment about Turner's title and its viewpoint, the painting was one of Ruskin's favourites, and it appears that he and his father came close to buying it.[34] Once it had become national property he continued to admire it, writing that although it was 'without one single accurate detail', it was 'the likest thing to what it is meant for … of all that I have ever seen'. Despite the equally bold claims he made for other works, he stated that, 'Take it all in all, I think this is the best Venetian picture of Turner's which he has left to us.'[35] This statement was first issued in an unofficial catalogue, but may have affected subsequent evaluations of the Venetian pictures in the bequest. Indeed, the picture was one of the few retained at the National Gallery after the 1880s, where it seems to have had an influence on the many young artists who aspired to absorb something of Turner's talents by copying his best-known paintings. Certainly the picture, then known less controversially as 'The Approach to Venice', was the third most frequently copied of his works in the collection in the late nineteenth century, only surpassed in popularity by *The Fighting Temeraire* 1839 (National Gallery, London) and *Chichester Canal c.1828* (Tate).[36]

211 (cat.46)
St Benedetto, looking towards Fusina
exhibited Royal Academy 1843
Oil on canvas, 62.2 x 92.7
Tate (N00534; B&J 406)

10 The Island of San Giorgio Maggiore

The island of San Giorgio Maggiore presides over many of Turner's views of central Venice. Whether viewing it from the water or from the piazzas and canals of the city, Turner repeatedly placed its campanile and dome in such a way that the eye is inevitably drawn to these features, using them to close off much wider perspectives across the water. This is, of course, an effect the island itself imposes, situated as it is at the eastern end of the Giudecca and directly opposite the Doge's Palace and the long, curving waterfront of the Riva degli Schiavoni. But in a small group of watercolours Turner seems to engage directly with the island's form, experimenting with the play of light across its contrasted brick and marble surfaces. He seems also to have enjoyed the way the rigidly symmetrical elements of Palladio's great church are broken down and destabilised as the viewer drifts around the island.

Doge Tribuno Memmo had granted the island to a Benedictine order in 982, who founded its earliest monastery. The main buildings as they exist today, however, were largely conceived by Palladio during the mid-sixteenth century. Most conspicuous of these is the church of San Giorgio, designated 'Maggiore' to differentiate it from the smaller island church of San Giorgio in Alga to the west.

Among the other conspicuous buildings visible in Turner's watercolours are the apartments of the abbots to the right of the church façade, which were designed in the seventeenth century by Longhena. The long expanses of brick walls in which this accommodation is situated are punctuated by deeply inset windows surrounded by white marble, and the same stone is used to frame the wide arch of the boathouse close to the small piazza in front of the church. But the most memorable feature of the island is undoubtedly its campanile, which rises to 63 metres. Its apparent height is perhaps accentuated by its open setting, for it is actually only the fourth-highest steeple in the city. The present structure was rebuilt in 1791 after an earlier campanile collapsed in 1774.

After they resumed control of Venice in 1797, the French suppressed the monastery and appropriated the island for military purposes, building the harbour, guarded by two neoclassical lighthouses, on its northern side. In 1806 the island was designated a free port, but by 1829 continuing protests from the Venetians about their crushed economy finally persuaded the Austrians to permit an expansion of the port status to the whole city;

tax was, of course, still payable to Vienna. To circumvent this for their own produce, the Austrians introduced further legislation in the early 1830s to make the island a tax-free entrepôt.[1]

All this should account for the features that recur in each of Turner's views of the island, while perhaps also offering an explanation for why there is no evidence that he actually visited the inside of the church. For it is clear that he was habitually wary of sketching near places with any military function, as his imagined, rather than documentary, view of the Arsenale also testifies (fig.130). Better by far, as Lorenzetti suggests, to enjoy the island as 'a balanced rhythm of masses and lines almost like a marble stage setting put there on purpose to catch the last rays of the setting sun'.[2]

It was indeed the fading light at the end of the day that Turner sought to capture in nearly all his representations, choosing the moment when the bricks acquire a pink radiance, like the inside of a conch shell. This 'suffusion of rosiness', exaggerated by the glow of sun on stone, was seized on some forty years later by Henry James as perhaps the most pleasing characteristic of the San Giorgio Maggiore ensemble. He went further and professed that this rosy hue was, in fact, the key to the aesthetic experience of Venice. James was acutely sensitive to visual matters, and his ensuing evocation of Venetian pink seems almost a description of what the artist achieved in his views of the island (see figs.215–17): 'It is a faint, shimmering, airy, watery pink; the bright sea-light seems to flush with it and the pale whiteish-green of lagoon and canal to drink it in.'[3] Turner's views of San Giorgio stand at the head of a stream of images in which the island is seen in conjunction with a sunset effect, culminating in the eight canvases painted by Monet during his visit of 1908.[4]

We know that Turner worked especially hard to absorb the details of San Giorgio at sunset during his third stay in Venice from the only contemporary account of this visit. In his autobiography, the watercolour painter William Callow recalled an evening late in August 1840: 'whilst I was enjoying a cigar in a gondola I saw Turner in another one sketching San Giorgio, brilliantly lit up by the setting sun. I felt quite ashamed of myself idling away my time whilst he was hard at work so late.'[5] It has sometimes been conjectured from these comments that Turner was working in watercolour, direct from the motif. However, the sketches Callow witnessed him making are more likely to have been a sequence of pencil jottings in the 'Venice and Bozen' sketchbook, many of which include a circular outline denoting the sun, which from page to page sinks steadily lower towards the west.[6]

212
San Giorgio Maggiore and the Zitelle from the
*Giudecca Canal c.*1833 or 1840
Pencil, watercolour and bodycolour on
grey paper, 18.4 x 27.3
Private collection (W 1367)

One subject that does seem to contain the rudiments of an on-the-spot sketch is a study of San Giorgio and the Zitelle from a little way along the Giudecca canal (*fig.212*).[7] Making use of one of the standard size sheets of grey paper, like others in that series, it seems that the essence of the design was first set down in pencil. Turner then used bodycolour to create the highlights, where the sun catches the tips and sides of buildings. The more general colours are painted in thin washes of watercolour. This is one of the sketches in which Turner's position seems to imply that the campanile of San Giorgio has been moved from its correct place to the left of the façade, though this is entirely a trick of perspective.

The campanile is also distorted in a pair of studies made on pieces of imitation Whatman paper (*figs.213–14*). Both share the same palette, most notably for the diluted green of the Lagoon, and they were evidently painted during the same session. The one now at Cambridge was part of Ruskin's 1861 gift to the University Museum.[8]

As the group of views Turner made from his windows over the city have already demonstrated, the panorama he possessed actually embraced San Giorgio (*figs.141, 147–8*). It is therefore hardly surprising that the angle of the viewpoint in several of his other watercolours indicates that they were clearly painted from the Hotel Europa. The study, *fig.214*, for example, looks across the Bacino from much the same viewpoint. There is in this work an almost wanton attitude to the specifics of topography, so that the man-made constructions of the island and its church float as the intermediate zone in three bands of colour. This rudimentary suggestion is given scarcely any further substance by the addition of some slight touches of colour, though these begin the process of delineating architectural reality. The process was for some reason interrupted, and the study remains incomplete, a circumstance that has hitherto prevented the correct identification of the scene.[9]

Another view of San Giorgio from the Europa introduces the rosy light described so poignantly by James many years later (*fig.215*). This sketch was, in fact, one of those included in the didactic displays constructed by Ruskin from the Turner Bequest, and so could perhaps have been seen by the novelist, who was a professed admirer of the artist.[10] As in the images painted from his bedroom, Turner's observation of light here is extraordinarily subtle, confirming that the watercolour was painted direct from nature. Most marvellous of all are the violet shadows, which intensify the vibrancy of the colour used for the brick campanile. Looking back to his watercolours of 1819 (*figs.74–5*), there is in this later work the same jubilant wonder at the transformative effects of light, but the mature Turner brings with him an acute knowledge of how effects can be created through the simplest of means. One would not perhaps be able to undertake an empirical survey of the architecture from this study, but the vertical pencil marks are

213
Between the Giudecca and the Isola di San Giorgio,
with the Bacino di San Marco c.1840
Pencil, watercolour and bodycolour on pale
buff paper, with details added using a pen
dipped in watercolour, 23 x 30.5
Fitzwilliam Museum, Cambridge (W 1362)

sufficient to fix the idea of Palladio's façade in the mind's eye. The long reflection, exaggerated because of the impossibility of deciding where it begins, lightens the gravitational weight of the island so that it seems to be floating. Though this effect is most closely associated with Venice in Turner's work, he also achieved it in some of his late Swiss watercolours.[11]

Turner painted a more finished watercolour similar in mood to the small study, but in doing so he adopted a different viewpoint, slightly to the right of that available from the Europa, quite possibly from the Dogana (fig.216).[12] The Whatman sheet on which it was painted comes from the dispersed 'Storm' sketchbook. Again, it seems most likely that Turner initially only set down an outline in pencil, augmenting this later with colour. Grounds for this conclusion come from the mistake he makes in placing the campanile in front of the transept instead of behind it, something he would have been more likely to do if working his sketch up away from the motif. There are slight reworkings on the right side, too, in his placing of the refectory roof, which he has moved somewhat closer to the centre of the image. The almost insignificant detail of the boat on the right edge of the sheet is positioned as if it has just passed through the Canale della Grazia. Another watercolour, which shows the channel between the Giudecca and San Giorgio, also features a *bragozzo* just here (fig.254), so that one might conclude he was thinking of the same boat. Indeed, Ruskin found evidence that Turner frequently created simple connections of this kind between his designs.[13]

San Giorgio seems to be the subject of two further studies in which Turner's treatment of its distinctive architecture is again pared down to the most rudimentary forms by which the church can be recognised (figs.217–18). The second of these pays only the most cursory reference to San Giorgio as a motif, and was surely undertaken as a recollection of an effect rather than an attempt at topographical exactitude. Here Turner seems to imagine himself on the Lagoon side of the island, looking west at sunset. The distance between the campanile and the domed building has raised doubts that this is San Giorgio, rather than another church on one of the other islands. But the very basic under-drawing is reminiscent of the way Turner made notations of the island in his 1840 sketches, many of which show the sun moving westwards towards the horizon.[14]

The identity of the other schematic study has also been the subject of some conjecture (fig.217). This truly atmospheric study shows the moon rising in the east, with the burning embers of the sunset still alive on the brick walls of a church and its campanile. Ruskin initially associated the building with the cemetery church of San Michele, presumably believing there was a link between it and the oil painting of that island exhibited by Turner in 1842 (fig.257). Some years later, however, he revised his opinion to list it correctly as a San Giorgio subject.[15] More recently it has been

214 (cat.147)
Isola di San Giorgio Maggiore 1840
Watercolour on pale buff paper, with details added using a pen dipped in watercolour, 23 x 30
Tate (TB CCCXVI 11; D32148)

215 (cat.155)
San Giorgio Maggiore at Sunset, from the
Hotel Europa 1840
Pencil, watercolour and bodycolour,
19.3 x 28.1
Tate (TB CCCXVI 28; D32165; S 78)

216 (cat.114)
*San Giorgio Maggiore at Sunset c.*1840
Pencil, watercolour and bodycolour,
with details added using a pen dipped
in watercolour, 22 x 32
From the 'Storm' sketchbook
Private collection

217 (cat.166)
San Giorgio Maggiore at Sunset, from the
Riva degli Schiavoni 1840
Watercolour, 24.4 x 30.6
Tate (TB CCCXVI 24; D32161; S 77)

218
San Giorgio Maggiore at Sunset c.1840
Pencil and watercolour, 22.5 x 29
National Gallery of Ireland
(W 1357; S 76)

suggested that the island is viewed from the Hotel Europa.[16] But in fact the view is based on Turner's observations of the island from the north, a little to the east of the Pietà church, and just as likely from the Riva degli Schiavoni as from the water.[17] From this vantage point the campanile is situated to the left of the dome of the church, with other chapels to the left of the tower. A vertical accent of a lighter colour slightly further to the left is intended to represent one of the island's lighthouses. Technically this has much in common with *fig.215*, especially in its passages of lifted colour for the long reflections. But the green water also links it with the more developed view of San Giorgio, suggesting that all three works come from the same painting session.

Another study of the island from slightly further east provides a more precise idea of the setting, its details thrown into sharp relief in the crisply defining light of morning (*fig.219*). Though different in its handling from the preceding works, there is a similar restraint in its presentation of the scene. Instead of relying on washes of colour, the basic facts of the design are built up through an economical use of red line, which offers an indication of what Turner might have achieved in *fig.214* if it were more complete. As a result of the near-absence of watercolour across the lower half of the image there is a hollow stillness at its centre, which allows the brilliance of the white paper to suggest the shimmering dazzle of the water.

219
*Calm at Sunrise (looking towards San Giorgio and the Salute) c.*1840
Pencil and watercolour, with details added
using a pen dipped in watercolour, 22.2 x 32.5
From the 'Storm' sketchbook
Fitzwilliam Museum, Cambridge (W 1361; S 68)

11 The Bacino and the Riva degli Schiavoni

The deep waters of the Bacino di San Marco not only offer spectacular views of the magnificent public face of Venice, but have also been the site of the city's commercial pulse. In the anchorage alongside the old Custom House, the Dogana di Mare, seafarers from all nations were temporarily jumbled together, their vessels creating endlessly fluctuating compositions alongside the fixed points of the great Venetian landmarks. The vibrancy of this great expanse of water in the eighteenth century is especially evident in the paintings of Canaletto and his contemporaries *(fig.221)*, which are dotted with numerous different types of craft. By comparison, Turner's later paintings and watercolours of the Bacino offer a much more subdued image of Venice as a port. Though he does occasionally include the schooners and brigs which brought cargo from foreign countries, Turner generally gave greater prominence to the distinctive outlines of gondolas, or the brightly coloured sails of the local fishing boats, the *bragozzi*. The inclusion of very few large ships is a fair reflection of what he had found during his 1840 trip. An indication of those he could have seen can be gleaned from the *Gazzetta Privilegiata di Venezia*, which recorded, during the two weeks or so that Turner was in Venice, a mere thirty-seven vessels, a figure that hardly suggests a city with healthy commercial links.[1]

Confronted so forcefully by the problems arising from the loss of Venice's historic identity, many mid-nineteenth-century visitors ruminated on the significance of its diminished trading prowess. Dickens, for example, noted wistfully that 'the greatness of the city was no more … Indeed, it seemed a very wreck found drifting on the sea; a strange flag hoisted in its honourable stations, and strangers standing at its helm.'[2]

The waters lapping the Dogana formed the subject of a painting Turner exhibited in 1842 *(fig.220)*. As the title indicates, the picture is essentially a view from the Hotel Europa, at the point at which the Grand Canal meets the Bacino. For this he is thought to have utilised the sketches he had made back in 1819.[3] Despite his dependency on the more diligent observations of his earliest visit, there are various architectural shortcomings, and it is surprising that he did not make use of his more up-to-date pencil jottings, especially as he must have noted when making these that the building had recently undergone a series of repairs.[4] A less immediately obvious discrepancy occurs in the way Turner reduces the scale of some elements in the image in order to exaggerate others. For instance, the figure plying his tiny gondola towards the Bacino, in its compressed form, contributes to a sense of the width of the opening to the Grand Canal. The positioning of the gondola is, however, crucial to the recession across the glassy surface towards San Giorgio Maggiore, and continues a diagonal perspective line that starts in the lower-right corner, where the viewer is given a solid platform from which to enter the scene. From these imagined 'Steps of the Europa' two dogs indicate where to look. They are placed alongside a pair of pots – one orange, the other a piece of blue and white porcelain – which have been seen as an allusion to the vanished splendours of Venetian history, though it is possible Turner simply wanted some brightly coloured objects at this point in his composition.[5] This last consideration may also explain the contrasted black and white dogs, which are a common feature of his images, seemingly providing a scale of the extremes of chiaroscuro.

One of the watercolours that contributed to the realisation of the soft, departing light in the picture looks across to the Punta della Dogana at sunset, with grey shadows welling up beside the great mass of the Salute *(fig.222)*. Even closer to the mood of the painting is a slightly larger study that restricts its focus to the easterly end of the Dogana, with the new moon

220 (cat.44)
The Dogana, San Giorgio, Citella, from the Steps of the Europa exhibited Royal Academy 1842
Oil on canvas, 61.6 x 92.7
Tate (N00372; B&J 396; S 101)

221
Francesco Guardi (1712–1793)
*Venice: The Dogana with the Giudecca c.*1760–6
Oil on canvas, 68.2 x 91.3
By kind permission of the Trustees of the Wallace Collection

222 (cat.156)
*The Punta della Dogana, and Santa Maria
della Salute at Twilight, from the Hotel
Europa* 1840
Pencil and watercolour, with pen,
19.4 x 28
Tate (TB CCCXVI 29; D32166)

223
*The New Moon (the Punta della Dogana,
with the Zitelle beyond)* c.1840
Watercolour, 23.8 x 30.3
Private collection (W 1365)

rising above faintly glowing clouds just where it does in the oil painting (*fig.*223). There is here an awkward transition between the perspective on the right, which apparently looks down on to the building, so that the arches along its side are substantially reduced in height, and a lower perspective on the left that looks across to the shipping at water level.

In the 1842 exhibition the *Europa* painting was paired with a view of the newly expanded cemetery island to the north of the city (*fig.*257). One might conclude from this that the pictures offer opposing ideas of Venice, rather as Turner had contrasted modern Rome with its ancient splendour in the later 1830s.[6] This deduction would mean the Europa subject should be understood as Venice in its former glory, but in fact the image itself does not support this interpretation: it seems to evoke the dreamlike, enervated Venice of the nineteenth century, not the buoyant vitality of the era celebrated by the great *vedute* painters. This becomes clear by comparing the picture with the same setting as painted by Guardi (*fig.*221). What shipping there is in Turner's image is static and languid, apparently packed up for the night, and the representation of the last rays of sunset itself symbolically underscores the idea of temporality.

In spite of some qualms about Turner's increasingly unresolved handling of paint, which was felt to be unintelligible except from a distance, the picture was admired in contemporary reviews. That in the *Athenaeum* believed that 'Fairer dreams never floated past poet's eye'.[7] The painting was acquired by Robert Vernon, and just a few years later was among the first of Turner's works to enter the national collections.

The Dogana and the Salute occur as a conflated mass in a series of studies on Italian paper, which, with one exception, were not considered worth exhibiting until well into the twentieth century (*figs.*224–6; see Appendix p.259). As a linked sequence, these deftly recreate the graduated nuances of the failing light, using the landmarks nearest the Bacino to chart the onset of twilight, passing from a washed-out pink to a sombre lilac and finally becoming a more solid blue. It is perhaps surprising that one of these remarkably slight studies was selected for exhibition by Ruskin in 1878, at exactly the time he was facing prosecution for castigating Whistler's Nocturnes (*fig.*225),[8] though he was not so much interested in the image itself as in the fact that it revealed how Turner would make good use of accidents in his materials, such as the fold in the lower-right corner of the page.

Two pages of the 'Grand Canal and Giudecca' sketchbook that also treat the pyramidal bulk of the Dogana and the Salute as a combined motif are suffused with a zesty lemon sunlight (*figs.*227–8). In these Turner perfectly captures the eye's inability to pick out detail when looking at objects against the light. That adopting the more distant view reduces the buildings to a single plane of grey colour, though this flat area of paint does

224 (cat.148)
The Punta della Dogana and the Campanile, from the Giudecca Canal 1840
Watercolour on pale grey-white paper,
22.2 x 29.9
Tate (TB CCCXVI 14; D32151)

225
*Indistinct Impression of the Salute from the Bacino c.*1840
Annotated by Ruskin, 'Preserve this drawing exactly as it is, as evidence of the way he worked; the turned edge of paper painted upon'
Watercolour on pale grey-white paper,
22.9 x 30.5
Tate (TB CCCXVI 15; D32152)

226
*Distant View of the Entrance to the Grand Canal from the Bacino c.*1840
Watercolour on pale grey-white paper, 23 x 30.5
Tate (TB CCCXVI 13; D32150; S 57)

227 (cat.100)
Sunset over Santa Maria della Salute
and the Dogana 1840
Watercolour, 22.1 x 32.1
From the 'Grand Canal and Giudecca'
sketchbook
Tate (TB CCCXV 14; D32130; S 52)

228 (cat.102)
The Punta della Dogana at Sunset, with the
Domes of Santa Maria della Salute 1840
Watercolour, 22.1 x 32.2
From the 'Grand Canal and Giudecca'
sketchbook
Tate (TB CCCXV 17; D32133; S 53)

229
The Dogana and Madonna della Salute,
Venice exhibited Royal Academy 1843
Oil on canvas, 63 x 93
National Gallery of Art, Washington.
Given in Memory of Governor Alvan
T.G. Fuller 1961 (B&J 403)

230 (cat.48)
Venice – Maria della Salute exhibited Royal
Academy 1844
Oil on canvas, 61.3 x 92.1
Tate (N00539; B&J 411)

not destroy the illusion of depth within the image. Few of Turner's earlier images have the intense radiance he created in the close-up view of the Dogana, where it seems he has painted the light through which we see the objects, sacrificing clarity for effect. The muted purple shadows here are complementary to the yellow, but at the same time they seem to anticipate the approach to local colours adopted by Monet and his associates many years afterwards.[9] Turner's sketch is dominated by the looming tower of the Dogana, which seems metamorphosed into the prow of an otherworldly boat, bearing down on the viewer through the hazy sunlight, a conceit that is more fully developed in the oil paintings exhibited in 1843 and 1844 (figs.229–30).

The first of these, now in Washington, was one of three Venetian subjects that Turner exhibited in 1843 when he paired it with *The Sun of Venice going to Sea* (fig.248). By creating this coupling Turner was apparently suggesting a link between the sea-bound fishing vessel and the shiplike form of the Dogana and the Salute. As we will see shortly, in the first of these a boat sets sail at dawn, its crew unaware that they sail towards their doom. The Dogana picture forms the natural counterpart to this, offering a sunset to balance the sunrise. It is, moreover, an image that evokes the languid Venice of the present, still and inhabited by shadowy figures, returning us to Dickens's image of Venice as a becalmed wreck. But as this was actually a well-established comparison, also made by Hans Andersen in 1833, it is perhaps not fanciful to assume that the same idea underpins Turner's painting.[10] Throughout his career he had regularly featured ships in his paintings as metaphors for the state and its predicament.[11] While not wishing to overstate this point, it is quite likely that the pair complement each other as versions of the present, the sickly yellows and greens in *The Sun of Venice going to Sea* intensifying its more ominous mood.

Specific evidence that the Dogana picture, at least, records Venice as Turner had seen it in 1840 lies in the strange floating structure on the left, painted a vibrant red and orange. This can be identified as the bathing establishment run by a Dr Rima, which had been moored in the Bacino since 1833.[12] Prior to the development of Lido as a resort later in the nineteenth century, contemporary belief in the benefits derived from seawater bathing induced many people to make use of floating bath-houses, despite concerns about the quality of the Lagoon water.

In contrast with this detail, the prominent feature of the landing-stage in the foreground is entirely Turner's own invention. It is certainly useful to the composition, though the 1844 view of the same scene demonstrates that it was not strictly necessary as a means of bringing to life the expanse of water alongside the Riva degli Schiavoni. Nevertheless, the device invites the viewer into the space, recalling the design of one of Turner's vignettes from the 1830 edition of Samuel Rogers's *Italy*.[13] But it is the other great poet

231 (cat.125)
The Dogana and the Salute, with the Entrance to the Grand Canal, at Twilight 1840
Pencil, watercolour and bodycolour on grey paper, 18.8 x 27.9
Tate (TB CCCXVII 16; D32201)

of Venice – Byron – that Turner seems to be invoking here, for the balustrade on the left is littered with musical instruments that are surely an allusion to lines in *Childe Harold*:

> In Venice Tasso's echoes are no more,
> And silent rows the songless gondolier;
> Her palaces are crumbling to the shore,
> And music meets not always now the ear:
> Those days are gone – but Beauty still is here.[14]

At the Royal Academy in 1843 those who first saw the painting judged that, despite Turner's habitual preference for effect, it was actually a good representation of its subject. *The Times* noted: 'This is a splendid picture. It is divested of all absurdities, and shows the great power of the artist when he is content to copy nature as she is.'[15]

The picture was bought from the Academy exhibition by the Midlands ironmaster Edwin Bullock, but was the only one of Turner's six exhibits to sell. This may have been a factor in his decision to repeat essentially the same subject for the following year's exhibition (*fig.230*). The subsequent version of the conflated Dogana/Salute motif was again a realisation of a sunset effect, and contained essentially the same features, including Dr Rima's bathing platform (on the right). However, the viewpoint is further to the left of that in the Washington picture, which brings the campanili of San Moise and Santo Stefano into view on the far right, while making the central group of buildings more isolated and shiplike. In the foreground there are a couple of *topi*, the smaller Venetian fishing boats, with their nets strung up within the vessels.[16] Above everything Turner hangs the sliver of a pallid new moon. This serves as the link with its pendant, *Approach to Venice (fig.263)*, though in that picture the moon is full and rounded, and just beginning its ascent. The contrast inevitably suggests the idea of diminished, waning moonlight in the Dogana image, resulting in a cooler palette in opposition to the kaleidoscopic range of its companion.

A similarly controlled use of colour occurs in two studies on grey paper (*figs.231–2*), which combine the economy of Turner's graphic shorthand with broadly applied pastel washes.[17] Though his colour here is incredibly distilled, it is possible to recognise the orange tone in *fig.231* as a watered-down version of the more lurid colour in *fig.256*. The reductive quality of the draughtsmanship in the second of these Bacino sketches means that the architectural features of the Doge's Palace are barely individualised, and yet there is somehow enough for the eye familiar with the original to make sense of Turner's squiggles and dashes. He may also have experimented here with the use of a red chalk or crayon to build up some of his detail (see also *fig.210*).

232 (cat.126)
The Entrance to the Grand Canal, with the Campanile and the Doge's Palace 1840
Pencil, watercolour and bodycolour on grey paper, 18.8 x 28
Tate (TB CCCXVII 5; D32184; S 31)

Turner paid greater attention to the Doge's Palace in another study on grey paper, though again the forms were only given greater substance once they had been summarily implied in wash *(fig.233)*. Clearly related to the group in the Turner Bequest, this work was somehow separated from them but its early history remains obscure.[18] The viewpoint repeats that of the vignette for Rogers's *Italy (fig.64)*, but in this later version the Zecca, to the left of the Doge's Palace, is more accurately delineated, including its cupola.

Turner made a more luminous version of the same scene in one of the two roll sketchbooks he used in 1840 *(fig.234)*.[19] Of all his views of this part of Venice, this watercolour gives perhaps the most accurate impression of the way the dazzling southern light plays off the huge reflective surface of the Bacino to illuminate the façade of the Doge's Palace.[20] The general effect is hazy and impressionistic, but on closer examination it becomes apparent that details, such as the lozenge patterns across the upper levels of the palace, have been built up skilfully with a pen dipped in red watercolour. Turner also scratched the surface of the paper to create a flash of more brilliant western light on the upper level of the Campanile.

Turner's survey of the Palazzo from the Bacino is continued in two further studies *(figs.235–6)*, the first of which is among his most finished watercolours of Venice. As in the watercolour of the tip of the Dogana *(fig.228)*, our ability to see the buildings is inhibited by the brightness of the setting sun, so that we see light, not substance. The sun's glare prevents the eye from collecting clear information about the Doge's Palace, which sits near at hand. But beyond its rays, over on the left, the Zecca comes into much sharper focus. A thrilling detail is the way the sun just clips the top of the palace at its south-west corner, its white intensity seeming to eat into the structure. Turner had achieved a similar effect in his 1827 picture of a summer's evening beside the Thames at Mortlake (National Gallery of Art, Washington).[21]

When composing the image Turner deliberately chose to compress what can actually be found beyond the Zecca in order to include the domes of the Salute on the far left. He pursued a similar strategy in the related view *(fig.236)*, which shows the view to the east from the palace, stretching along the Riva degli Schiavoni to the church of the Pietà, his panorama ending with the campanile of San Antonino. Like its companion, this watercolour is ablaze with the golden light of late afternoon, with shadows already obscuring the lower levels of the buildings as the sun catches only their highest western flanks. On the bottom edge of the sheet Turner made a note to himself that the waters of the Lagoon needed to be 'green', an observation shared by other nineteenth-century visitors, though generally in a more disdainful tone.

In the 1840s few of the buildings along the waterfront between the Danieli and the Pietà rose above three storeys, which meant that the

233
The Doge's Palace from the Bacino c.1833/40
Pencil, watercolour and bodycolour on grey paper, 18.4 x 27
Inscribed on verso, '5v', together with a pencil sketch of the Giudecca canal
Private collection, USA

234 (cat.110)
The Doge's Palace from the Bacino 1840
Pencil and watercolour, with scratching-out
and details added using a pen dipped in
watercolour, 22.2 x 32.3
From the 'Storm' sketchbook
Walker Art Gallery, Liverpool. Board of
Trustees of the National Museums and
Galleries on Merseyside (W 1373)

235
The Doge's Palace and the Piazzetta c.1840
Watercolour, with details added using a
pen dipped in watercolour, 24 x 30.4
National Gallery of Ireland (W 1356; S 90)

236 (cat.167)
The Doge's Palace and the Riva degli
Schiavoni, from the Bacino 1840
Pencil, watercolour and bodycolour,
with details added using a pen dipped
in watercolour, 24.3 x 30.4
Tate (TB CCCXVI 17; D32154; S 63)

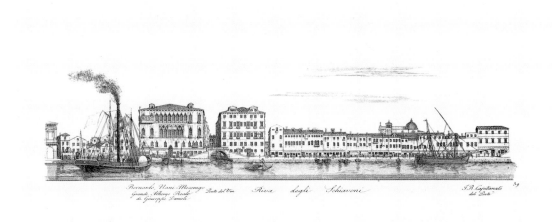

237
Dionisio Moretti (1790–?1834)
The Riva degli Schiavoni, with a Steamer
1828 (plate 39 from *Il Canal Grande di
Venezia, Descritto da Antonio Quadri*)
Engraving

238 (cat.50)
Venice Quay, Ducal Palace exhibited Royal
Academy 1844
Oil on canvas, 62.2 x 92.7
Tate (N00540; B&J 413)

239 (cat.108)
Venice: The Riva degli Schiavoni 1840
Watercolour, with some scratching-out,
and details added using a pen dipped in
watercolour, 21.7 x 31.8
From the 'Storm' sketchbook
Ashmolean Museum, Oxford. Presented
by John Ruskin, 1861 (W 1364; S 69)

campanile and dome of San Zaccaria could readily be seen from the water *(fig.237)*. It appears as a ghostly presence in an otherwise limpid watercolour once owned by Ruskin *(fig.239)*.[22] Behind the brick shell of the Pietà, with its unfinished marble façade, Turner left his paper blank to develop the campanile of San Giorgio dei Greci. The essential details of the composition were very likely set down in pencil on the spot, but the fine network of coloured lines, which darkens tonally from right to left, was more probably added back in the studio. Turner focuses here on the Venetian fishing fleet anchored along the Riva's long quayside, depicting specific local craft, such as the *bragozzi* with their painted sails, as well as other types of boats that may be the larger *rusconi* and *trabaccoli*. This juxtaposition of commerce with the soaring physical manifestations of spirituality recalls Turner's 1809 image of his native city, *London* (Tate).[23] As well as highlighting Turner's ambiguous thoughts on the maritime empire of which he was a citizen, this comparison is instructive in indicating how insubstantial the Venetian fleet must have seemed to a visitor from the thriving world city of the early 1840s.

Clearly a subject worthy of fuller treatment, Turner reworked the view for the 1844 Academy exhibition *(fig.238)*. In the process he substantially increased the number of boats, and consequently relegated the Doge's Palace and the campanile of San Marco to the far distance. But the idea of Venice as an earlier victim of a fate that perhaps awaited maritime Britain is not made explicitly, though the sunset may be a means of intimating the twilight of the once-great power. Refuse floats on the water, as it does in Turner's other images of Venice, but if he is explicitly presenting a fallen state, he also suggests that it continues to live in its own alluring way.

The picture did not find a buyer at the Academy, and this was, in fact, the last year in which Turner managed to sell a view of Venice from the annual exhibition. But a small group of new collectors continued to express interest in securing Venetian subjects, with the result that Turner set out various compositions that he clearly intended to develop more fully, had a guaranteed commission come his way. A pair of these, of unique dimensions, depict the buildings bordering the Bacino *(figs.241–2)*, though the viewer has to scan the surface of the canvas closely, piecing together the work of brush and palette knife before the particularities of the scene coalesce.[24] Even in these rudimentary designs it is possible to ascertain that both canvases are characterised by boats heavily laden with parties of revellers. As far as it is possible to see, many of the figures appear to be female, and Turner may here be recalling Rogers's poem 'The Brides of Venice', which describes the origins of festivities marking the capture and subsequent rescue of twelve Venetian virgins. But Turner may also have been looking back to the great fêtes on the waters in front of the Doge's Palace, as depicted by Canaletto.

240
Venice – Noon exhibited Royal Academy 1845
Oil on canvas, 61 x 91.8
Exhibited with the caption,
'*MS. Fallacies of Hope*'
Tate (N00541; B&J 418)

241
Venetian Festival: View over the Bacino, with
the Dogana on the left c.1843–5
Oil on canvas, 72.4 x 113.3
Tate (N04659; B&J 508)

242 (cat.58)
Riva degli Schiavoni, Venice: Water Fete
c.1843–5
Oil on canvas, 72.4 x 113
Tate (N04661; B&J 507)

243 (cat.90)
Shipping in the Bacino, with the Entrance to
the Grand Canal 1840
Watercolour, 22.1 x 32.1
From the 'Grand Canal and Giudecca'
sketchbook
Tate (TB CCCXV 4; D32120)

244
The Sun of Venice: Bragozzi moored
off the Riva degli Schiavoni c.1840
Watercolour, with details added using a
pen dipped in watercolour, 21.9 x 32
From the 'Storm' sketchbook
National Galleries of Scotland,
Edinburgh (W 1374; S 95)

One of the pictures Turner exhibited in 1845 seems to have been developed from this pool of ready-worked canvases, but regrettably its final glories were worked up in a type of paint that rapidly deteriorated (fig.240; see also figs.209, 264–5). The view is again taken from the Bacino, with the Campanile about a third of the way in from the right, and San Zaccaria at the edge of the image. As we have seen, it was paired in the Academy exhibition with the canvas apparently depicting the Giudecca (fig.209), though the 'Sunset' described in that work's title might be more applicable to this scene. Sadly, the painting's present condition obscures its original appeal, but the *Athenaeum* offers an idea of its initial impact: 'beheld from one particular point, [it] is a beautiful dream, full of Italy, and poetry, and summer'.[25]

The sultry stillness of summer is much better preserved in two atmospheric watercolours which, though similar in subject and colour, were painted in different sketchbooks (figs.243–4).[26] That in the Bequest is generalised and indistinct, made up of suggestive brushstrokes and forms that are implied rather than stated: the vertical smear of red paint on the upper right, for example, is probably the Campanile, but there is insufficient information to make sense of this unless viewers are able to supply it from their own experience.

A fixed reference point in both studies is the outline of the Salute, on the left, though it is fascinating to note how Turner uses essentially the same tone of watercolour in completely different ways to create this detail in each work. In the watercolour at Edinburgh (fig.244) the dusky silhouette contributes depth to the shimmering, mirage-like effect of the drawing, which is only brought into sharp focus through the fine detailing at its centre, used to delineate the group of *bragozzi* preparing for a fishing trip.

Turner made numerous memoranda of these characteristic Venetian fishing boats during his three visits, but this is the only watercolour in which they are his principal subject. Though the image perhaps lacks the

245
Edward William Cooke (1811–1880)
Bragozzi, the fishing craft of Venice
exhibited Royal Academy 1851
Oil on canvas, 91.4 x 127
Private collection

246
Anonymous
Model of Bragozzo, 19th/20th century
Wood, 110 x 110 x 20
Museo Storico Navale, Venice

close attention of one of E.W. Cooke's renderings (*fig.245*), Turner captures the craft's dynamics very effectively. As well as the radiating sun, he decorates the sails of the boat on the left with the crescent shape of the moon. Since he was especially fond of the combination of these opposing light sources in his paintings, sometimes when it was apparently impossible in nature, it is probable that the pattern was of his own devising. Even so, images from later in the nineteenth century reveal that the sails of some *bragozzi* carried a circular emblem intended to be the sun, as well as a range of other imagery.[27]

A decorated *bragozzo* sail forms the focal point of the oil painting *The Sun of Venice going to Sea* (*fig.248*). Effortlessly coasting on what appears to be a lively westerly breeze, the boat departs under a rosy dawn with all its sails billowing majestically. Its jaunty aspect is further strengthened by its visual amalgamation with the sails of a second boat in its wake. The glorious backdrop for this stirring embarkation is Venice itself, laid out between the towers of San Giorgio and San Marco on the left and those of San Antonino and San Francesco della Vigna on the right.

Turner had recorded the city from this spot in one of the most popular Venetian watercolours in the Bequest sequence (*fig.247*).[28] In that work he positions a group of fishermen on a sandbank, pulling in their nets, a reminder that even the principal channel of the Canale di San Marco possessed dangerous shallows for those unfamiliar with its hazards.

The oil painting carries a similar message of lurking menace, though this quality is really only evident to those who read the lines from Turner's *Fallacies of Hope* appended to his title in the Royal Academy's catalogue:

Fair shines the morn, and soft the zephyrs blow,
Venezia's fisher spreads his painted sail so gay,
Nor heeds the demon in grim repose
Expects his evening prey.[29]

The first two lines carry echoes of Thomas Gray's famous poem 'The Bard', but the idea of a doomed fishing boat may well have been borrowed from Shelley's *Lines Written Among the Euganean Hills*. An extract from this had been published as 'Venice' in an 1838 miscellany of poems and pictures, to which Turner had been an earlier contributor.[30] The contrasted states of *Noon* and *Sunset* in the paintings of 1845 may also reflect his knowledge of Shelley's poem, where they are evoked so precisely in the text (*figs.209, 240*). Turner's magpie-like tendency to appropriate from others whatever seemed useful to his art was noted in relation to the 1843 painting by the *Athenaeum*'s critic, who commented, 'his style of dealing with quotations is as unscrupulous as his style of treating nature and her attributes of form and colour.'[31]

Another review questioned whether Turner's pretensions to poetry 'may have had some deleterious influence on the painter's mind', and judged that the extravagance of the picture must be condemned by 'all sensible people'. Rejecting what he identified as Turner's avant-garde style, the same critic concluded by saying, 'nor "is the winter of *our* discontent / Made glorious summer by this 'Sun of Venice'.".'[32] This Shakespearian paraphrase was an easy gibe, but the critic must have seen that Turner was also playing with the relationship between word and image. The boat of the title is named specifically on its sail, but that expanse of canvas also includes an image of vessels clustered around a glowing sun, almost as a reduced version of a Turner picture (*fig.211*).

Given Turner's addiction to puns, some might also see a link between the word 'Sun' (or 'son') and the associations of motherhood in the related picture, for which Turner used the phrase '*Madonna della Salute*' (*fig.229*). This might validate one historian's suggestion that these late paintings tap into ideas of the city as a mother, with its waterways as amniotic fluids to be passed through.[33] Without going that far, there is in the pessimistic tone of Turner's accompanying poem an echo of Byron's warning to Albion of the need for Britain as a younger, seafaring empire to avoid the fate of its ancestor.

Leaving aside these conjectures, the picture is among the most successful of the later paintings of Venice, though it is true that its colour is now more even and generally subdued than when it was first exhibited. Indeed, Ruskin bemoaned that it was already duller in 1856. This was something he was able to verify because he had made diligent transcriptions and written commentaries about its colour while it hung at the Academy in 1843.[34] Ruskin was also able to testify to the general accuracy of Turner's depiction of the *bragozzo*, claiming that 'it is impossible that any *model* could be more rigidly exact than the painting, even to the height of the sail above the deck' (*fig.246*).[35]

The remote eastern end of the city that forms the backdrop to *The Sun of Venice* was the subject of several more watercolours (*figs.249–51*).[36] In each of these the brilliant sunlight refracted by the surface of the Bacino seems to dissolve the cityscape and, as Finberg noted, the emphasis is sensory rather than descriptive.[37] Turner's attempt to give one of them greater substance, through the addition of coloured outlines, seems to work against the subtle effect he sought to recreate, which perhaps explains why in this instance he took his draughtsmanship no further (*fig.250*). The design was conceived around the narrowing funnel of light on the left, which he intensified with several flashes of bright, unpainted white paper to suggest the flicker of momentary pools of light on the undulating water.[38]

The broad quayside and bridges of the Riva degli Schiavoni extend all the way to the new Public Gardens, which had only been completed

247 (cat.168)
Looking back on Venice from the Canale di
San Marco to the East 1840
Watercolour, with details added using a
pen dipped in watercolour, 24.5 x 30.6
Tate (TB CCCXVI 18; D32155; S 64)

248 (cat.47)
The Sun of Venice going to Sea exhibited Royal
Academy 1843
Oil on canvas, 61.6 x 92.1
Exhibited with the lines quoted on p.227
Tate (N00535; B&J 402; S 103)

comparatively recently. The Giardini Pubblici exemplified the Napoleonic principle that the populace needed somewhere green in which to relax, but by 1838 the composer Franz Liszt remarked that they were already little visited as the Piazza continued to exert a stronger spell on the Venetian temperament.[39] Turner's sequence suggests a promenade towards the gardens, and he constructs his compositions in such a way that the viewer is able to look back from a more distant prospect on the previous scene. For example, the canopy in *fig.250* recurs in *fig.251*. The first of these is another of the sheets on which Turner inscribed the words 'Beppo Club' (see p.24), and it may well be possible to detect the licentious behaviour of Byron's protagonist in the pair of figures seated beneath the awning.

The final view in this series *(fig.251)*, from near the Ponte della Veneta Marina (over the Rio della Tana), is a model of painterly restraint that consummately distils the essence as well as the facts of the scene, thereby recalling the watercolours of 1819. The composition is remarkably open, empty even, and is grounded only by the inclusion of the cropped prow of a gondola which serves to lead the eye towards the distant Campanile. Very few artists have expressed so vividly the saturated brilliance of Venetian light.

249 (cat.169)
Shipping off the Riva degli Schiavoni, from near the Ponte dell'Arsenale 1840
Watercolour, 24.3 x 30.6
Tate (TB CCCXVI 20; D32157; S 67)

250 (cat.170)
Looking across the Bacino di San Marco at Sunset, from near San Biagio 1840
Watercolour, with details added using a pen dipped in watercolour, 24.4 x 30.4
Tate (TB CCCXVI 21; D32158; S 65)

251 (cat.171)
Looking along the Riva degli Schiavoni, from near
the Rio dell'Arsenale 1840
Pencil and watercolour, 24.6 x 30.4
Tate (TB CCCXVI 22; D32159)

CCCLXIV — 334 1476

12 Away from the City

Rising magically from the waters of the Lagoon, the defiantly isolated setting of Venice is a motif that surprisingly few artists have sought to capture, though it increasingly became a feature of Turner's final images of the city. Among nineteenth-century artists the abiding preference for the great set-piece views to be found in the civic centre, established by Canaletto, was coupled with a partiality for picturesque scenes illustrating distinctive Venetian activities. Consequently Turner seems to have been alone in seeing the potential of the city as a glittering silhouette, its spires lit by the opposing effects of dawn or sunset.

Ironically, while Turner developed a fascination for the city's profile as seen from the broad expanses of adjacent water, it is apparent from his sketches that he did not venture far on the Lagoon. Though the outlines of San Michele, Murano, la Grazia, San Giorgio in Alga, Lido, San Servolo or San Lazzaro degli Armeni occasionally appear in his jottings, there is nothing to indicate that he visited any of them. Perhaps his most notable omission is the last of these islands, the Armenian convent, which by the 1830s was firmly established on the itinerary of those tourists seeking the places connected with Byron's Venetian sojourn. Turner would have been familiar with its appearance from a painting by Andrea Locatelli in the collection at Petworth.[1]

But even when restricting himself to the islands closest to the Bacino, Turner discovered vantage points that allowed him to frame the city in novel ways. Two of his watercolours adopt a viewpoint from the southern side of the Giudecca (figs.253–4). In both Turner looks back towards San Marco through the Canale della Grazia, but he exaggerates the width of the canal in relation to the other elements he has depicted in order to call attention to the familiar landmarks of the city beyond.[2]

As well as the domes of the Zitelle and the more distant Salute on the left, which are common to both works, the Bequest study (fig.254) introduces the church of San Giorgio Maggiore and a greater expanse of the monastery's walls. Its foreground is made up of an area of exposed ground: here Turner gathers what seems to be a group of fishermen or traders, surrounded by barrels and other packages. As human activity plays such a small role in Turner's Venetian watercolours, it is worth considering why he should give so much prominence to this group. One could conclude that they were introduced purely for compositional reasons: the single figure at the centre certainly strengthens the vertical accent of the Campanile. But the peculiarity of the location suggests he had other motives, possibly connected to the fact that the island had been the only part of the city designated a free-trade port when he first visited it in 1819. This piece of Napoleonic legislation had been dropped by 1829, when the Habsburg administration extended the terms of the agreement to cover the whole city, but perhaps Turner's figures are a recollection from his earliest visit of attempts to circumvent the officially approved trading methods. David Laven has noted that the free-trade status of San Giorgio during that period 'brought few tangible benefits, except perhaps to smugglers'.[3] Turner's inclusion of such an incident would be consistent with his habit of depicting smugglers in many of his watercolour views of the south coast of England, where the inhabitants set out to thwart the import duty to be paid on a range of goods, including tobacco and alcohol.[4]

The bragozzo passing through the canal is rendered with a masterly economy, its furled sail bound tightly to its mast, a detail seized on by Ruskin as further evidence of Turner's assured draughtsmanship.[5] In the companion drawing (fig.253) a summer storm sweeps in from the west, and its bragozzo's sail stretches taut with the pressure of the driving wind. The water, too, is driven and churned up, so that crests form on the tops of its waves as they wash towards the island.

On another sheet Turner depicted the storm at its most intense, bearing down on the Lagoon with such menace that it seems to threaten the safety of a steamboat (fig.255). Other than the characteristically Venetian bricole, the clustered piles marking the safe channel through the shallow waters, there is nothing to indicate that the subject is Venice. The forms on the horizon are, in fact, so indistinct that it is not even apparent whether we are looking towards the city or away from it to another part of the Lagoon. It is very striking that this is the only Venetian subject in which Turner shows a steamer, no longer a new form of transport, since steamboats had been introduced in the 1820s. The drawing possibly records the arrival of the Trieste steamer, which was Turner's means of leaving the city in 1840.[6] Over the preceding fifteen years he had repeatedly depicted steam technology, relishing the chance to emphasise the sometimes uneasy alignment of past and present, most memorably in The Fighting Temeraire 1839 (National Gallery, London).[7] This makes it all the more remarkable that he made so little of steamboats in the Venetian context.

Another image of contemporary Venice focuses on the recently expanded cemetery island (or Campo Santo) of San Michele, lying a little way off the northern side of the city, on the way to Murano *(fig.257)*. This area had been comparatively neglected by earlier artists, though Canaletto and Guardi had both produced images from the Fondamente Nove that included San Michele and the smaller island of San Cristoforo della Pace.[8] The latter had been remodelled as the principal city cemetery on Napoleonic principles in 1813, and subsequently subsumed as part of the more northerly island in the later 1830s, so was a topical subject, much as Père-Lachaise had fascinated visitors to Paris in the 1820s and 1830s.

Like Guardi, Turner chose to depict the cemetery from the east, looking inland to the undulating line of the Dolomites rising beyond the edge of the Lagoon. This viewpoint meant that the most interesting feature of the island, the beautiful church designed by Mauro Coducci, is almost obscured by the long, blank walls surrounding the burial ground. Over on the left-hand side, rising above the houses on the waterfront, is the square campanile of the church of the Gesuiti (then in use as a barracks), and beyond that the cupola-tipped spire of Madonna dell'Orto. But these topographical markers are really of only secondary importance to the much greater emphasis Turner places on the evocation of light and atmosphere. Crucial to his success is a great expanse of infinitely deep-blue sky, which is in the process of being effaced by banks of cirrus clouds blowing in from the north-west.[9] The same wind animates the twin sails of the boat that becomes the focal point of the composition. Placed almost exactly a third from the left edge, and on a perspective axis line running from the gondola on the left to a smaller vessel with sails in the distance, the positioning of the boat could not be stronger. Though this has sometimes been described as a *felucca*, it is most likely to be another *bragozzo*, or one of the slightly larger *trabaccolo*, the two most common types of Venetian craft. Both of these vessels had double masts with lateen sails, though Turner provided only a vague impression of how the boat is actually rigged.[10] As an image, however, the paired sails are a masterstroke, given extra potency by the magical reflections glistening on the still waters.

Conscious that Turner probably intended the image to be seen in relation to the 1842 view of the Dogana, scholars have attempted to locate symbolic elements that would be appropriate to the idea of a decayed civilisation, floating on the backwash of its moment of glory. Lindsay Stainton's observations are perhaps the most sympathetic to this viewpoint, especially her memorably phrased suggestion that the juxtaposition of the cemetery with the boat makes the 'white sails seem like an angel's wings, or the soul of a dead person come to haunt the Lagoon'.[11] While admitting the pertinence of this plangent conceit, especially as Turner used this motif again in another picture recording

253
Storm at Sunset 1840
Watercolour and bodycolour, with scratching-out, 22.2 x 32
From the 'Storm' sketchbook
Fitzwilliam Museum, Cambridge
(W 1353; S 86)

254 (cat.172)
The Zitelle, Santa Maria della Salute, the Campanile and San Giorgio Maggiore, from the Canale della Grazia 1840
Pencil and watercolour, with details added using a pen dipped in watercolour, 24.3 x 30.5
Tate (TB CCCXVI 19; D32156; S 62)

this area *(fig.265)*, it should be noted that the sails are not, in fact, completely white, as that on the left is painted with a sun, as in the 1843 painting *(fig.248)*. More tangible in the image is a sense of the polluted state of the waters of the Lagoon, which is made manifest in the detritus floating across the foreground (see also *fig.197*). The colours in the picture are still remarkably strong and clear, calling into question Ruskin's inclination to consider them irrevocably and detrimentally altered by the 1860s. In spite of this, he was prepared to concede that it was still among the greatest of Turner's views of Venice. At one point it was 'the most perfect', but on other occasions it did not meet the enthusiasm he felt for another distant view of the city *(fig.263)*.[12]

Most nineteenth-century visitors were captivated by the light of the Lagoon, noting how its purity brought into sharp focus the distant mountains, making them seem near at hand. Even in the 1870s, when industrialisation had become established in some areas, Henry James was still able to write:

> The light here is in fact a mighty magician and, with all respect to Titian, Veronese and Tintoret, the greatest artist of them all … Sea and sky seem to meet half-way, to blend their tones into a soft iridescence, a lustrous compound of wave and cloud and a hundred nameless local reflections, and then to fling the clear tissue against every object of vision[13]

Something of what James describes can be appreciated in the studies Turner made of the wider expanses of the Lagoon *(figs.252, 256, 258–61)*. Discussing one of them, Stainton has noted that Turner was the first artist 'to make sunset over the lagoon the subject of an entire picture' *(fig.259)*.[14] Most of these colour sketches are on white paper, but one is on the grey paper used for studies of the Bacino *(fig.256; see also figs.231–3)*. There is much greater force to this depiction of the sun hovering above the horizon, though it clearly shares the same tones as those works. However, the concentrated intensity achieved by the scalding vermilion, the fiery orange and a rather vaporous lilac are rarely met with in Turner's sketches, though such combinations occur repeatedly in late exhibited works such as *Slavers throwing overboard the Dead and Dying* 1840 (Museum of Fine Arts, Boston) and *War. The Exile and the Rock Limpet* 1842 (Tate).[15] Sometimes considered expressionistic or symbolic, this heightened use of colour is more often viewed as an eccentric shortcoming by those expecting art to offer an empirical truth to nature. Some have even attempted to explain Turner's dramatic colours by questioning whether his vision suffered an imbalance in later years.[16] Yet it seems that as far as the light of the Venetian Lagoon was concerned, he may not have been exaggerating.

A group of four related Lagoon studies are reunited here *(figs.258–61)*. These were evidently painted during one working session, so that it is possible to locate the same range of colours throughout the batch, as if watching Turner move from sheet to sheet. The movement in the series from warm golden sunlight to cool blue moonlight perhaps also reflects something of his interest in colour theory at this date. For it was in 1840 that Turner read and annotated the English translation of Goethe's treatise on colour.[17] These notes reveal that Turner questioned many of Goethe's ideas (see *fig.53*). There were, however, various points upon which the two agreed, including the idea of there being established visual polarities, such as warm and cool, light and dark, which converge with ideas of proximity and distance, or conceptions of strength and weakness. It would be perfectly natural for Turner to experiment with these in private sketches, where he could adumbrate the potential of colour contrasts.

In the lighter works of the group, Turner builds up his image in horizontal bands of colour. The predominantly yellow study is little more

255
A Steamer seen across the Lagoon c.1840
Watercolour, with scratching-out,
22.2 x 32.1
From the 'Storm' sketchbook
National Galleries of Scotland,
Edinburgh (W 1371; S 89)

than a suggestion of forms floating against a brilliantly illuminated sky (*fig.258*). The subtle rosy tints on the right side of the image are taken up in *figs.259* and *260*, but in each of these works almost the whole lower half is painted with the briny jade colour Turner habitually adopted for the waters around Venice.

Fig.259 is the most developed of the group, with its receding lines of *bricole* leading the eye deep into the picture space so that we attempt to make sense of the forms on the horizon, though there is actually nothing there. This did not deter Ruskin, who perhaps projected his own experiences on to the image in claiming that it was a 'reminiscence of a return from Torcello to Venice',[18] though none of Turner's sketchbooks confirms that he ventured so far north in the Lagoon. Finberg's more tenable suggestion was that it scans the Lagoon from near Fusina, a conclusion that was presumably as much influenced by the way the brush-strokes on the left assume the forms of clustered mountain peaks, as by the fact that this was the main route to the city and the one explored by Turner in other images.[19] This rather logical deduction is supported by the nearly illegible attempts at poetry on the verso of the sheet in which Turner refers to towers illuminated by the last gleams of a setting sun as a long evening begins, presumably musing on the fate of Venice.[20] Confirmation that this was an observed phenomenon, recalling a particular place, and not entirely a studio exercise, comes in the form of the band of orange colour that rises above the horizon from right to left. This sloping diagonal is repeated as a more subdued area of pink on the next sheet in the series (*fig.260*), suggesting the same setting seen under altered conditions.

A related but much more brooding image concludes this small series (*fig.261*). Here night has at last arrived, accompanied by saturated, inky clouds. As in *fig.188*, these were painted when the paper was still wet so that the marks Turner made diffused into the design. There is perhaps a suggestion of a dome and a campanile on the extreme left of the sheet, but it is unnecessary to speculate on its identity, as Turner's subject is less the specifics of place than a contemplation of the nocturnal Lagoon. Far from seeming oppressive and threatening, the subdued light opens out to the infinite. It was exactly this mood that caught the imagination of so many other visitors to Venice during the nineteenth century (perhaps it still does).

But, as so often with Turner, the Sublime runs hand in hand with a more prosaic reality, and it is evident that he was drawn to the activities of fishermen on the Lagoon. Another watercolour sketch (*fig.252*) shows some figures in a boat drawing up alongside one of the makeshift platforms used by fishermen and the hunters of the Lagoon's wildfowl. Both were activities that Turner enjoyed when he was able to get away from London. In his image, the central figure holds what could be either a rod or a gun, though both seem at odds with the absolute stillness of the scene. On the back of

the sheet Turner pursued the idea of serene moonlight in a draft of poetry, which includes the lines

… as the Moon descends yet Venice gleams of many winking lights
and lights [or 'like'] the darkening sails when she wanes

But it was to two texts by much more celebrated poets that he turned for inspiration when painting his 1844 exhibit *Approach to Venice* (*fig.263*). The title of the picture was accompanied in the catalogue by the following passages:

The path lies o'er the sea invisible,
And from the land we went
As to a floating city, steering in,
And gliding up her streets as in a dream,
So smoothly, silently. – *Rogers' Italy*

256 (cat.127)
Orange Sunset over the Lagoon 1840
Bodycolour on grey paper, 18.5 x 28
Tate (TB CCCXVII 18; D32203)

257 (cat.45)
Campo Santo, Venice exhibited Royal
Academy 1842
Oil on canvas, 61.2 x 91.2
Toledo Museum of Art; Gift of Edward
Drummond Libbey (B&J 397; S 102)

The moon is up, and yet it is not night,
The sun as yet disputes the day with her – *Byron*

The first of these is essentially a fair transcription of Rogers's poem 'Venice', though the word 'Invisible' should start the second line. However, in selecting his lines from Byron's *Childe Harold's Pilgrimage*, Turner changed the published text, introducing a suggestion of primeval conflict. In fact, what Byron actually wrote should read: 'Sunset divides the sky with her...'.[21] Turner's painting is nevertheless imbued with Byronic sentiment.[22]

Even after all the changes to the western side of the city, it is still possible to recognise the profile Turner depicts as that seen by the traveller crossing from the mainland near Mestre. It is even possible to pick out some of the landmarks, such as the Campanile, the domes of Santi Giovanni e Paolo and the Salute, though these are much more readily discernible in the large engraving of the painting undertaken by Robert Wallis, which was not published until 1859.[23]

It was exactly this gap between the beauty of Turner's effects and his sometimes unintelligible presentation of topography that continued to be a problem for the critics, though this picture (like most of the Venetian pictures) fared rather better in this respect than his other contemporary subjects. *The Times*, for example, noted rather grudgingly that it would 'present a beautiful and fantastic play of colours to the spectator, who will take his station amid the benches in the middle room, and be content with the general impression'. The critic of the *Spectator* believed that 'beautiful as it is in colour, [it] is but a vision of enchantment'.[24]

The same emphasis on the picture's colour prevailed with Ruskin, who recalled it four years after it had been exhibited: 'it was, I think, when I first saw it, the most perfectly *beautiful* piece of colour of all that I have seen produced by human hands, by any means, or at any period'.[25] By 1856, however, he stated that though he had previously considered it 'beyond all comparison the best' of Turner's Venetian paintings, it was 'now a miserable wreck of dead colours'.[26] In spite of these reservations, the picture is still ravishing to behold: the surface of the water, for example, is alive with the glittering phosphorescence derived from the twin light sources.

Turner had set out his composition in a watercolour study during, or shortly after, his 1840 trip (*fig.262*). In this the channel across the Lagoon is

258 (cat.173)
*Boats on the Lagoon, near Venice c.*1840
Watercolour, 24.6 x 30.6
Tate (TB CCCLXIV 137; D35980)

259 (cat.174)
*Looking across the Lagoon at Sunset c.*1840
Watercolour, 24.4 x 30.4
Tate (TB CCCXVI 25; D32162; S 83)

marked with evenly spaced posts, though these were dropped in the exhibited painting, in accordance, no doubt, with Rogers's phrase, 'The path lies o'er the sea | Invisible'. Finberg considered the sketch 'one of the finest' of the sequence in the Turner Bequest, noting that, 'It sets a standard of imaginative intensity which the majority of the drawings fail to reach.'[27] He was surely right to emphasise the vigour of Turner's imagination here, for not only does the study relate to the *Approach to Venice*, but it can also be seen as the seed of a second painting (*fig.265*) which was exhibited a year later, where the elegant boat with paired sails on the left is redeployed to play an important role in anchoring the design.

That work is one of a pair of paintings Turner exhibited in 1845, in which he continued his exploration of the theme of water-borne journeying to and from the city, so central to the character of the later Venetian images (*figs.264–8*). There has been an immense amount of confusion about the identities and histories of the pictures he showed in 1845 and 1846 because of the similarity of their titles and the tangled negotiations with the collectors for whom they were intended. Moreover,

as a rather exasperated Evelyn Joll confessed when cataloguing these works, the available documentation for them poses 'almost as many problems as [it] solves'.[28] What follows here is indebted to Joll's painstaking efforts to untangle this distinctively Turnerian muddle, but in fact overturns the titles and dates currently assigned to four of the canvases exhibited in these years.

The 1845 exhibition included two sets of Venetian subjects: *Venice, Evening, going to the Ball (fig.264)* with *Morning, returning from the Ball, St Martino (fig.265)* in the East Room; and *Venice – Noon (fig.240)* with *Venice – Sunset, a Fisher (fig.209)* in the Middle Room.[29] Though these were displayed as pairs in separate galleries, an attentive viewer could see them as a connected series, evoking the passage of four times of day. Indeed, the *Spectator* made exactly this point, but could not resist questioning the veracity of Turner's depictions: 'there may have been times when these different periods assimilated in nature as closely as they do in these pictures: only such must be exceptional cases!'.[30] Turner was aware that mistakes were habitually made by his initial audience in interpreting the effects he had depicted, and confided to one acquaintance that 'People talk

260 (cat.175)
An Open Expanse of Water on the Lagoon, near Venice c.1840
Watercolour, 24.8 x 30.7
Tate (TB CCCLXIV 332; D36190)

261 (cat.176)
Venice: Moonlight on the Lagoon 1840
Watercolour and bodycolour,
24.5 x 30.4
Tate (TB CCCXVI 39; D32176; S 81)

a great deal about *sunsets*, but when you are all fast asleep, I am watching the effects of *sunrise* far more beautiful.'[31]

A similar confusion has obscured the correct identity of the works shown in 1845. Of the four, it is much easier to identify the second pair, which take noon and sunset as their subjects *(figs.209, 240)*. As noted above, both works suffered from changes to their appearance, though this took place quite soon after they were first exhibited.[32] The fault for this seems to have been the novelty of untried materials, though Turner himself was inclined to risk such experiments since, as he put it, 'no one could tell if a method would answer, as he would be dead before it could be proved'.[33] But the factor that contributed substantially to the changes to the paintings of 1845 was Turner's partiality for megilps. These were a form of thixotropic paint made by combining mastic spirit varnish with a linseed drying oil that had earlier been cooked with a lead compound.[34] They were widely used as a means of building up layers of transparent glazes, to intensify colour effects and for areas of raised impasto. For Turner the use of glazes harked back to his admiration for the techniques of Venetian painters such as Titian, though it is ironic that as a young man he had avoided the general obsession with such practices (see *fig.34*). The downside of nineteenth-century megilps was that they tended to crack when varnished, and the delicate layers darkened and sank into the canvas very quickly. Turner's idiosyncratic methods were further compounded by a use of watercolour paint when preparing his canvases for exhibition, though his addiction to this medium was challenged by some collectors, who feared that it might prove fugitive.[35]

In the *Noon* and *Sunset* subjects the skies have suffered most dramatically as a result of the changes to the megilps. The clouds are reduced to flat expanses of grey paint, so that there is little or no sense of the aerial perspective Turner must have intended them to have. Similar changes can be observed in the two whaling pictures that Turner exhibited in 1845, though fortunately his use of the unstable megilps was less marked in either work.[36] It is significant, however, that these problems do not occur in the two works previously associated with the 1845 *Ball* paintings *(figs.266, 268)*, though they do in the pair that have until now been linked with the exhibits of the following year *(figs.264–5)*.

Further clues as to the identity of the 1845 *Ball* pictures can be found in the reviews of that year's exhibition. Of these, the most specific description came in the *Morning Chronicle*, which described *Venice, Evening, going to the Ball* as follows:

> the rising moon … with its long gleam of light coming across the waters, is really a curiosity worthy of study. Stuck on with the palette knife, or the thumb, who would think it would give the soft cool light it does? …

> Regretting his apparently incurable mannerism, we cannot but admit that in the present instance he has somewhat cured it of its extravagance[37]

Only one of the six Venetian pictures exhibited in 1845 and 1846 can readily be identified as a depiction of a rising moon trailing its reflection in the water *(fig.264)*.[38] This picture relates to the 1844 *Approach to Venice*, in showing the progress of several boatloads of revellers making their way across the Lagoon in the direction of Venice. The viewer looks east at dusk to where the moon begins its ascent. On the left is the Campo Santo, seen from the opposite direction to the 1842 picture *(fig.257)*. This also helps to resolve the issue of the locality of the ball to which the travellers are going, for Turner is surely thinking of the venue as Venice itself in carnival mode, rather than one of the many festivals that took place on the adjacent islands. All of which means that we are watching the party-goers from the mainland making their way across the water, allowing the viewer to empathise with this moment of anticipation.

262 (cat.149)
The Approach to Venice 1840
Watercolour and bodycolour on pale
grey-white paper, 23 x 32.2
Tate (TB CCCXVI 16; D32153; S 70)

263 (cat.49)
Approach to Venice exhibited Royal
Academy 1844
Oil on canvas, 62 x 94
Exhibited with the lines quoted on
pp.236–8
National Gallery of Art, Washington,
Andrew W. Mellon Collection
(1937.1.110; B&J 412)

264 (cat.51)
Venice, Evening, going to the Ball exhibited
Royal Academy 1845 (formerly listed
as 'Going to the Ball (San Martino)
RA 1846')
Oil on canvas, 61 x 91.4
Exhibited with the caption,
'M.S. *Fallacies of Hope*'
Private collection (B&J 416/421)

Confirmation that this inference is correct comes from Turner himself in a letter to the Irish cotton-spinner Frances McCracken, who commissioned the companion picture (fig.265) from Belfast, but was unable to attend the Royal Academy show and clearly wished to have an account of it. In his reply Turner outlined the pair as follows:

The Subject [of your picture] is returning from the Ball – the dawn of day when the Moon withdraws her light and rosy Morn begins – the company Pause. Going to the Ball – sun setting and the moon rising – over Venice [is] painted for a gentleman of King's Lyne: the Campo Santo with Boats and masqueraders proceeding towards the City – Yours returning to St Martino, an Island in the Adriatic.[39]

The gentleman from the Norfolk town of King's Lynn was William Wethered, a tailor and woollen draper, who had already acquired the *Approach to Venice (fig.263)* from the previous year's exhibition. Whether that work was a commission or not remains unclear. However, by October 1844 he had written to Turner seeking 'another approach to Venice'. In accepting to undertake this, the artist had demurred slightly: 'I beg to thank you for allowing me to make some change [from the designated subject] – tho I suppose you wish me to keep somewhat to the like effect.' He intended to have it ready for the 1845 show, and stated that as a commissioned work the price would be only two hundred guineas, fifty less than the pictures bought from the exhibition.[40] Yet in taking on this commission Turner was immediately faced with a problem. For if he was to paint the westward approach to the city, he was bound to repeat elements of his earlier composition. This explains the wider panorama of the 1845 canvas and its greater involvement with the details of the skyline from this point of the compass. But as this picture evolved as a companion to the *St Martino* image, there was always likely to be the possibility that Turner would not satisfy the requirements of his patron for a painting that would complement the one he already possessed.

There were similar risks at stake with McCracken, who was new to the process of collecting. Like Wethered, he had engaged Turner to paint a Venice subject in the autumn of 1844, though he seems also to have been interested in a view from the Swiss tourist peak the Rigi Kulm.[41] A week or two before the end of 1844 Turner told him that he was proceeding with the Venice subject: 'and if you do like it when done I shall feel happy in your approval – before the end of the first week's Exhibition of 1845 – after which the Picture to be mine exclusively if not taken by you'.[42] As already seen, this bold declaration of the terms by which McCracken could claim the picture as his own, at the agreed discounted rate, was frustrated by his inability to come to London at the time of the exhibition. However, it seems

that he was initially appeased by Turner's description of the picture and agreed to acquire it without actually seeing it. Certainly by the end of July he had written to Ruskin for his thoughts on the picture, a practice other collectors adopted when contemplating Turner purchases in the years after the publication of *Modern Painters* (1843). Ruskin was himself away travelling and had not seen the exhibition, but his father forwarded McCracken's letter, referring to the Irishman as 'the buyer of one of the Lovely Dreams Turner No.162 in Rl Academy'.[43]

Exhibit no.162 was indeed the *St Martino* picture, but the title presents further problems. This is because, as earlier commentators have noted, there is no island in the Lagoon with this name. There is a church dedicated to San Martino in the eastern *sestiere* of Castello in Venice itself, and there is another on Burano, but clearly neither of these is relevant to the island in Turner's description. We have seen already in relation to his view of the Redentore that he had problems recalling the correct names of some of the buildings he had sketched, perhaps a sign that age was taking its toll. So it is possible that a similar memory lapse affected the titling of his 1845 and 1846 exhibits. Despite this potential solecism, it is possible to establish from the letter to McCracken that he intended the image to be understood as a view with the moon setting and the sun rising – a matins scene. Furthermore, the deliberate pairing of the pictures required a subject that would offer the opposing scene to that in *fig.264*. Hence the scumbles of white paint on the left in *fig.265* should be perceived as the cool rays of the departing moon, and the viewer is clearly meant to be looking away from the city to the west. This would mean that Turner's island is probably based on San Giorgio in Alga, which lies directly on the way to Fusina, though this only ever had one campanile, as his own sketches would have attested. It is possible that he added the second tower as a means of giving a subtle echo to the paired sails of the *bragozzo*.

What must originally have been a wonderful arching vortex of cloud near the top of the canvas is another detail that helps to confirm that this was one of the pictures exhibited in 1845, for the same feature appears in one of two caricatures of Turner's exhibits that appeared in the popular, low-brow journal *Punch (fig.12)*. These were drolly described as *Venice by Daylight* and *Venice by Gaslight*, and the unknown satirist remarked further that 'Whether he calls his picture *Whalers*, or *Venice*, or *Morning*, or *Noon*, or *Night*, it is all the same; for it is quite as easy to fancy it one thing as another.'[44] Turner's habit of including extracts from his personal poem *The Fallacies of Hope* gave additional grounds for humour at his expense. Inexplicably, the titles of all four Venetian subjects made reference to the poem, but in each case failed to quote anything from its text. Whether this was simply because Turner had himself not delivered the copy in time, or because the catalogue typesetters had chosen to ignore (or suppress) it,

265 (cat.52)
Morning, returning from the Ball, St Martino
exhibited Royal Academy 1845
(formerly listed as 'Returning from the
Ball (St Martha), RA 1846')
Oil on canvas, 61 x 91.4
Exhibited with the caption,
'*M.S. Fallacies of Hope*'
Private collection (B&J 417/422)

remains unknown. Another possibility is that Turner intended the mere allusion to his pessimistic poem to undercut the festive mood. Whatever the actual cause, it was an opportunity *Punch* could not resist, and so, considering Turner 'too modest' to quote anything himself, it supplied the following exegesis on his behalf:

> Oh! What a scene! – Can this be Venice? No.
> And yet methinks it is – because I see
> Amid the lumps of yellow, red, and blue,
> Something which looks like a Venetian spire.
> That dash of orange in the back-ground there
> Bespeaks 'tis Morning! And that little boat
> (Almost the colour of Tomata sauce,)
> Proclaims them now returning from the ball!
> This is my picture, I would fain convey,
> I hope I do. Alas! *What* FALLACY!

This mocking tone was, however, counterbalanced by more reverent consideration in *The Times*, which described the *Ball* subjects as made up of 'a play of brilliant colours, sparkling as they vanish above smooth waters'.[45] And the critic of the *Spectator*, a frequent supporter of Turner's later works, noted that the paintings possessed 'magical effects of light and colour: the watery floor and aërial sky meet at the horizon in a gorgeous mass of orange and golden tints ... the intervening space being filled with the glowing atmosphere'.[46]

But the memorable wounds inflicted by *Punch* may have caused lasting damage, especially with new middle-class patrons such as Wethered and McCracken, who would not want their expensive outlay on pictures to be the subject of such widespread derision. By the end of July, as we have seen, McCracken was seeking reassurance that he had made a wise purchase. Wethered, too, seems to have dithered about claiming the picture he had ordered. This is apparent from a letter Turner wrote to him on the 31st, in which he seeks to salvage a situation that is rapidly slipping out of his control. In testing Wethered's commitment, he offers to return a down payment of £160, and says he will not draw the remaining £115 he is owed (including the costs of the frame and packing) until he hears from him. As an incentive to drive the sale home, he intimates that Wethered's purchase would be a bargain, as he plans to raise the price of Venetian works not sold to 300 guineas. As a final twist there was – inevitably – supposedly another potential buyer waiting in the wings, a 'Mr P' from Sheffield, ready to acquire whatever Wethered discarded.[47]

There is currently no further documentation recording the fate of the paintings in 1845. Nevertheless, as will become apparent, both collectors

rejected and returned the pictures undertaken for them. They remained in Turner's gallery until they were bought later in the 1840s by B.G. Windus, once he resumed his interest in Turner's work.[48] No doubt exasperated by this double volte-face, Turner surprisingly (for an artist of his wealth and independent temperament) remained courteous in his correspondence with both men at the time of the following Royal Academy exhibition. For it transpires that, having failed to answer their expectations in his 1845 exhibits, the commissions were renewed for yet another pair of Venetian views.

On 14 June 1846 Turner was writing to the patrons to clarify, once again, which work was intended for which patron.[49] He had, in fact, written to them both a week or so earlier, but had then put the letter for Wethered in the envelope for McCracken, and vice versa. This embarrassing muddle was made even more confusing by Turner's inability to remember the exact titles of his own exhibits, which he got only partly right in his letter to McCracken on the 14th. The actual titles of his two Venetian pictures this year were *Going to the Ball (San Martino)* and *Returning from the Ball (St Martha)*, but his letter exchanged the names of the two saints.

According to Thomas Sidney Cooper, the once-celebrated painter of bovine portraits, Turner's 1846 exhibits arrived at the Academy essentially unfinished, awaiting transformation: 'some of his work was, as usual, only rubbed in, and it was common practice of his, when he saw how his pictures were placed, to paint first a little on one, then on another, and so on till all were finished to his satisfaction'.[50] There were six paintings this year, constituting three pairs. It was the exhibits of 1846 that prompted Richard Doyle in the *Almanack of the Month* to lampoon Turner's preference for yellow, which he is shown administering to a canvas with a floor mop *(fig.13)*. As so often with good caricature, the jest is founded on acute observation. For the unifying characteristic of pictures like *'Hurrah! for the Whaler Erebus! another Fish!'* (Tate) and the *Angel standing in the Sun* (Tate), both exhibited that year, is a golden tone that could have been enhanced during the final stages of Turner's work on each canvas.[51] It is, therefore, significant that a similar quality can be found in the two Venetian pictures formerly dated to 1845, and especially to the first of these *(figs.266, 268)*. Moreover, the contemporary reviews of the pictures also remark on the honeyed tone as a feature of the evening subject: 'One of a pair of Venetian scenes, where an expanse of sky and water is flooded with golden atmosphere, called *Going to the Ball*, is in a blaze of sunshine that dazzles the sight; the pendant picture, *Returning from the Ball*, serving as a foil to the beaming brilliancy of its companion.'[52]

As in 1845, the subjects themselves puzzled Turner's viewers; this was not the landmark Venice they were familiar with from Canaletto, Guardi, Bonington or Prout. The *Art Union* protested, 'it is really much to be lamented that an artist possessing the powers of Mr. Turner should not exert them on some subject worthy of them'. But in writing of the evening subject, the same critic professed his opinion that 'There is here less of the utter absence of definition, which has of late years distinguished these works; the forms are more distinct, and it is probable that an engraving of the work would be more really agreeable than the picture itself.'[53]

Both of these comments can be more readily applied to the picture identified here as *Going to the Ball (San Martino) (fig.266)*, which does indeed give a topographical element a much greater prominence and clarity than any of the Venice subjects of the past two years. But what is the subject? Where are we in the city? If San Martino was a perplexing and apparently invented 'Island in the Adriatic' in 1845, why use this name again? The image itself only partly resolves some of these questions, as it is not by any means an accurate transcription of the part of Venice it seems to be depicting. This seems to be the western end of the Giudecca, an area Turner had represented in both 1843 and 1845 *(figs.209, 211)*. Such an identification would mean that the church with two towers could possibly be the Angelo Raffaele, with the soaring campanile of the Frari and the more stunted one of San Nicolo dei Mendicoli to its left. A slightly preferable alternative might be that the view shown is further down the canal, and that the principal church is the Gesuiti (though Turner has omitted its dome and pedimented façade), with the small campanile of San Trovaso and the more distant one of Santo Stefano.[54] The various buildings on the right would then need to be understood as part of the convent of Santi Biagio e Cataldo (as in *fig.208*), with Sant'Eufemia, the campanile of Santi Cosma e Damiano and the dome of the Redentore beyond. Turner had sketched all of these features individually, but it seems he had some trouble bringing them together as a recognisable scene, even though he had tried something similar after his first visit *(fig.79)*. This identification would mean that the intensity of the sunset has been moved impossibly from the viewer's right to the middle of the Giudecca canal, obscuring the Zitelle and the island of San Giorgio Maggiore. It is admittedly an imperfect solution, offering no clarification of the San Martino factor,[55] but, as there would not be a way of working around the existing campanile of San Martino to make the other elements fit, it will have to suffice until other evidence comes to light.

Furthermore, it works well in conjunction with the other 1846 image, which actually does show the church of Santa Marta *(fig.268)* on the opposite side of the Giudecca canal, at the furthest western tip of the city, though the remaining hull of the original building is now marooned amid dockyards. This Benedictine church formerly stood on an exposed peninsula known as the Arzere di Santa Marta, which extended towards the mainland. It was suppressed by the French, after which parts of its fabric, such as the bas relief over the porch, were removed to Sant'Eufemia on the Giudecca. Its campanile, however was not demolished until 1910 (it is seen here with what appears to be that of San Nicolo behind).

Turner made other sketches of the building and its vicinity *(figs.11, 206)*; it was, after all, one of the first churches that travellers arriving from Fusina would have seen, though few commented on it. He was perhaps also attracted to its district by his interest in all things related to fishing, as this is where many Venetian fishermen lived. But its most notable fascination, clearly relevant in an image concerned with revelry, was the famous festival held on the eve of the Festa di Santa Marta (29 July). This involved the roasting on the beach of freshly caught sole, and attracted Venetians of all classes, who converged on the neighbourhood in boats decorated with lanterns. Though none of Turner's visits actually coincided with the fête, he could very easily have learned of it from the locals he encountered, from other travellers or from a recent publication chronicling traditional Venetian festivities.[56] Another potential source may well have been an engraved version of Canaletto's image of the feast, based on the painting now in Berlin *(fig.267)*.[57] But Turner's painting does not make direct reference to any of this, other than in the parties of pleasure-seekers, their motion temporarily arrested; they seem to be neither coming nor going. The picture's evocation of the beginning of a new day is surely an apt image for St Martha, who has been traditionally associated with the active life, unlike her more contemplative sister, Mary.[58]

There were taunts this year about the *Ball* pictures in the magazine *The Man in the Moon*, which offered the following mystified recollection of a picture it entitled 'Getting Tired of the Ball':

> The azure moon, that through the verdant clouds
> Bathes the vermilion waves with floods of blue,
> Sees nought but yon gondola of pink haze,
> And red-hot dots of men![59]

Whether such high jinks reached Turner's intended clients for the paintings is unknown. But among those who admired his work there were indeed fears that he was no longer in his prime. Ruskin, who was once again out of the country for the Academy show, wrote to William Boxall (a future Director of the National Gallery) fretting:

> I hear very contradictory reports about Turner this year: I wish you had told me something. I don't know what I shall do when he fails altogether. I have been in the habit of feeding on him ever since I was fourteen, and already from what I saw of last year's work there seems to me a great blank in the world which nothing can ever supply.[60]

Just a couple of weeks after this, on 29 August, Turner packed up the canvas for Wethered and sent it to Norfolk. There is, however, no existing

266 (cat.53)
Going to the Ball (San Martino) exhibited
Royal Academy 1846 (formerly listed as
'Morning, returning from the Ball, St
Martino, RA 1845')
Oil on canvas, 61.6 x 92.4
Tate (N00544; B&J 417/421)

correspondence with McCracken after the letter of 14 June, in which Turner asked if he should order a frame for the painting. But the eventual presence of these two paintings in Turner's collection when he died indicates that both collectors reneged on their agreement and cancelled the commissions this year also. Perhaps it was simply that Turner's late style was unintelligible to them. Or perhaps they came to understand that the works had been conceived as pairs, and were drained of some of their potency in isolation.

What is astounding in these circumstances is that Wethered remained undeterred in his desire to get a 'Turner' for his collection. By October he had rather gauchely written asking for a 3 x 4 ft (91.4 x 121.9 cm) canvas of an English landscape. His letter evidently exhausted Turner's patience, and in a tart (but amusing) reply he appeared to agree to the request, at the same time raising his prices to such an extent that it would be very unlikely that Wethered would again waste his time: 'The Subject must be fixed (for I have faild twice in my choice in the Venice commission therefore I tremble about it and the price will be five Hundred Guineas.'[61] There was apparently no further correspondence on the matter.

Rejected for their intended homes, these and several other Venetian pictures remained in Turner's gallery. They were among the works seen propped up against the walls in George Jones's painted recollections of the gallery at the end of Turner's life. In the mid-1850s, shortly after this vast residue of material – some unsold, some unsaleable – was removed to the National Gallery, it appears that someone marked the *San Martino* and *St Martha* pair as the works exhibited in 1846. Yet this correct identification has until now been almost entirely ignored.[62] Subsequent attempts to connect the subjects of the two images were, in any case, undermined by the National Gallery's policy of farming out to the regions pictures by Turner that it could not itself display, with the result that for many years one of the pictures was away in Manchester. Reunited with their original titles at last, and now correctly placed as the climax to the sequence of Turner's Venetian paintings, these works demonstrate the artist's determination in his final years to seek new perspectives with which to challenge and enchant the viewer. Rather than ending in an increasingly vaporous haze, as has so often been thought, his last images of Venice are, in fact, more full-bodied, festive and, above all, fiery.

267
Giovanni Antonio Canaletto
(1697–1768)
Festival on the Eve of St Martha c.1755
Oil on canvas, 119 x 185
Gemäldegalerie, Berlin

268 (cat.54)
Returning from the Ball (St Martha)
exhibited Royal Academy 1846
(formerly listed as 'Venice, Evening,
going to the Ball, RA 1845')
Oil on canvas, 61.6 x 92.4
Tate (N00543; B&J 416/422; S 104)

Epilogue: The Legacy of Turner's Venice

Writing in 1930, A.J. Finberg observed that Turner's sequence of Venetian paintings and watercolours was 'more generally liked and admired at the present time than any other group of his works'; to which he added wryly: 'Critics who as a rule cannot "abear" Turner frequently burst into disconcerting raptures over the slightest of his Venetian sketches.' In attempting to explain the causes of this popularity, he questioned whether the issue was one of style or subject: 'The attraction may be the subject-matter; but I think it is also the way Turner treats it, for he so often succeeds in doing what the modern artists seem to want to do but fail in.'[1] Finberg was here being unduly harsh on those who wanted to claim Turner as a proto-Impressionist, yet at the same time he unwittingly highlighted the challenge implicit in so much of Turner's later work, which continues to provoke responses more than 150 years after his death. Set against the last century of endlessly fluctuating artistic aims, his views of Venice still appear radical and innovative, retaining the immediacy of their appeal.

Ironically, at the time Finberg was pondering over the dilemma of their allure, access to Turner's Venetian paintings was inhibited because they were widely dispersed around the country. Though this obviously enhanced their reputation, it must at the same time have diluted the impact of this element of the display at the National Gallery of British Art, as the Tate was then known. Indeed, Finberg's remark was made as some of these pictures were beginning to return after an absence from London of more than forty years, which had begun because of a shortage of hanging space for British pictures at the National Gallery before the Tate opened. Most had been included in the earlier, densely hung displays overseen by the National Gallery from 1856, when Turner's Bequest became national property. But after 1884 only four of the Venetian paintings were left behind: the so-called 'Approach to Venice' (*St Benedetto, looking towards Fusina; fig.211*), *The Sun of Venice (fig.248)*, *Returning from the Ball (fig.266)*, and the Vernon Bequest painting of 1833 *(fig.103)*. Nevertheless, these served as a vital touchstone to countless young painters, who understood them as examples of the way in which Turner was supposed to have anticipated French Impressionism.

Another significant factor, but one that Finberg was inclined to pass over when considering the celebrity of Turner's Venetian work, was Ruskin, who had regularly expressed his enthusiasm for these late pictures. Himself an owner of one of the views of Venice *(fig.58)*, Ruskin had peppered the earlier volumes of *Modern Painters* with his praise of Turner's idiosyncratic way of presenting the city, championing the apparently faultless representation of water in some of the paintings.[2] Thereafter, his widely available writings on Turner provided the dominant idea of the artist throughout the later nineteenth century, and his catalogues of the watercolours shaped the way the public approached the vast holdings of the Bequest.[3]

Ruskin was already familiar with Venice before 1840, when he began to become acquainted with Turner, but from then he developed a sense of mission that linked the two inextricably. This grew from his conviction that the Venetian paintings were the finest of Turner's most recent canvases, and he consequently made his way to Venice in 1845 in order to get 'authority for all that Turner has done of her'.[4] His attempts to study and absorb these paintings when they were first shown at the Royal Academy are alleged to have resulted in his being evicted from the exhibition, where copying was not permitted. Undaunted, he furthered his observations of those pictures that did not sell when they were restored to Turner's gallery.[5] As a result of Ruskin's repeated visits, he claimed to have observed that the vibrancy of the original colours sometimes dimmed comparatively quickly, and though this is borne out in the sad appearance of the four painted in 1845, the extent to which these dramatic alterations actually took place may be slightly exaggerated in his accounts.[6]

Ruskin's own response to Venice was initially greatly conditioned by contemporary influences, so that he viewed it largely at second-hand, with Turner as one of several intermediaries. When in the city, he noted in his diary and in letters home the uniquely Venetian features that he recognised from Turner's paintings, stressing (as usual) the artist's accuracy.[7] During the tours of 1841, 1845, 1846 and 1849–50 his drawings were often suffused with his desire to draw in a Turnerian manner. However, as Ruskin became increasingly obsessed with the city's decaying fabric, he abandoned Turner's generalised approach in favour of a more objective type of factual record.[8] It was the act of making these closely observed studies of architectural surfaces that set in train his research for *The Stones of Venice*, the first volume of which he presented to Turner shortly after its publication in March 1851.[9]

This proved to be the last year of Turner's life. When the fatal news reached Ruskin, who was coincidentally actually in Venice, he was moved to find 'every thing in sunshine and the sky so talks of him. Their Great witness lost.'[10] In order to press on with the ensuing volumes of the *Stones*, he quickly renounced his role as executor and only became truly entangled

269
Edward William Cooke (1811–1880)
*Evening sky looking West out of the
Canale della Giudecca* exhibited Royal
Academy 1864
Oil on canvas, 28 x 43
Private collection

in the great problem of how to make the contents of Turner's studio accessible once it joined the National Gallery collection. He was then dogged in believing the works on paper were just as important as the oil paintings, and was eventually permitted to select a representative survey of sketches and watercolours, which remained accessible in his groupings until the early twentieth century.[11] In fact about fifty of the watercolours reproduced in the preceding pages were included in this miscellany: the best-preserved ones were framed and stored in mahogany cabinets that were available to students, who evidently relished the challenge of pitting themselves against Turner by replicating his designs. Presenting sketches in this way was comparatively novel, but Ruskin made a clear distinction between their preliminary nature and what he felt to be acceptable in truly public works of art.

The principle of using Turner's works as exempla to instruct the inexperienced was one that Ruskin munificently extended to the museums at Oxford and Cambridge in 1861, dividing between the two institutions a group of more than seventy works from his own collection.[12] This included six Venetian colour sketches, which had somehow joined his fine group of

more conventional watercolours at an unknown point in the preceding five years (figs.173, 177, 213, 219, 239, 253). Although the Ruskin family accounts are not specific, these almost certainly came from Turner's agent, Thomas Griffith, who seems to have had access to material that was technically 'unfinished'.[13] The three studies that Ruskin gave to Oxford all came from the 'Storm' sketchbook, while Cambridge got two more of its pages, plus a sketch on a piece of buff paper.

Subsequently, in the late 1870s, Ruskin selected additional works from the Turner Bequest to be shown alongside the group at Oxford, and it may have been about that time that he made a copy of the funereal gondola in Turner's sketch of the lower Grand Canal (figs.177, 270). Copying, as he always advocated, was the best method of understanding another artist, especially in an age before artworks were endlessly reproduced. Indeed, all of his writings about Turner had been accompanied by engraved details from his own copies, included to stress a particular idea, such as the section of sky from the *Campo Santo* painting (fig.257), which appeared in the final volume of *Modern Painters* as a means of illustrating Turner's convincing rendering of cloud.[14]

It should by now be apparent that Ruskin greatly facilitated access to Turner's art in many ways and in many arenas. But even before Turner died, younger artists had begun to imbibe his Venetian work, digesting it perhaps more readily than some of the other themes he tackled late in his career. At this date the subject itself was of primary interest, though one or two artists were prepared to hazard a flirtation with Turner's notoriously wayward style. The most persistent of these was James Baker Pyne, who made a speciality of images of Venice, in some of which he dabbled with sun-drenched effects that are palpably derived from Turner (fig.271). The most remarkable of his pastiches, however, is a view of the rail bridge that had been constructed to span the Lagoon between 1841 and 1845, and which was inaugurated the following year (fig.272).[15] In this painting Pyne boldly appropriated the composition of Turner's *Rain, Steam and Speed* 1844 (National Gallery, London), fusing the artist's modern outlook with a potentially new and dynamic Venice, capable of miraculous feats of engineering on a scale to equal its past glories, and now linked to the mainland by one of the earliest stretches of track in Italy. Inevitably, despite the convenience it brought, the bridge was despised by those who wanted to preserve a timeless Venice, including Ruskin.

One of the artists that Ruskin admired and encouraged during his stay in Venice in 1851 was E.W. Cooke, the son and nephew of two of Turner's engravers.[16] Cooke was, in fact, steeped in Turner's art, and had quite probably been stimulated to go to Venice by his knowledge of the canvases of the 1840s. Essentially a marine painter, he focused expressly on the great variety of craft unique to the shallow waters of the Lagoon, bringing to his

270
John Ruskin (1819–1900)
Copy of the Gondola and the Punta della Dogana from Turner's watercolour 'The Grand Canal, with the Salute' ?1870s
Pencil on grey-green paper, 24 x 34
Ruskin Foundation, University of Lancaster

images the photographic exactitude that Turner avoided. A stylistic shift occurred in the later 1850s, coinciding with the point when Turner's paintings became available in displays from his Bequest, and Cooke's Venetian pictures then became more expansive and extravagantly coloured. Several of those he painted in 1863 explore the Giudecca canal, which had dominated Turner's final canvases, and it is evident from the coincidence of viewpoints and the representation of blazing sunsets that Cooke was sometimes consciously reworking these compositions in his own style (*fig.269*; compare with *fig.211*).

Other contemporary artists were evidently content merely to copy Turner's compositions, with the result that numerous versions exist of the most popular works, though sadly few of them are signed or dated. This practice affected even established painters such as David Roberts and Edward Pritchett, who produced dutiful replicas of the Bequest paintings (*fig.273*).[17] Both visited Venice themselves, so that its scenes also featured extensively in their own work.

But it was not only British artists who were attracted by the Venetian pictures. Another consequence of Ruskin's far-reaching influence was that many North Americans came to London to see for themselves the works of the master he had described so passionately. The list of distinguished visitors included Whistler, Nathaniel Hawthorne and Henry James. But perhaps the most ardent American follower of Turner and Ruskin was Thomas Moran, who made visits to London in the early 1860s specifically to see the paintings he had admired from afar.[18] During these trips he went to several of the places depicted by Turner, from which he deduced that the prevailing Ruskinian emphasis on 'truth to Nature' was generally inapplicable:

> All that [Turner] asked of a scene was simply how good a medium it
> was for making a picture; he cared nothing for the scene itself. Literally
> speaking, his landscapes are false; but they contain his impressions
> of Nature, and so many natural characteristics as were necessary
> adequately to convey that impression to others.[19]

These perceptions coloured Moran's own attempts to paint views of Venice, which he visited in 1886 and 1890. Several of his pictures are as much meditations on Turner's images as delineations of the actual place, and it is also evident from the sketches he made on the spot that Turner was frequently in his thoughts.[20]

The Frenchman Felix Ziem was another late-nineteenth-century painter who found the spectre of Turner in Venice inescapable, just as the artists at the other end of the century had been haunted by Canaletto.[21] Though he is not known to have visited London to study the paintings in the National

271
James Baker Pyne (1800–1870)
Moonrise at Venice 1849
Oil on canvas, 50.8 x 73.7
Private collection

Gallery until 1892, Ziem could have seen prints of them before this, and he may also have known the replicas which found their way into otherwise distinguished Parisian collections. One of these had been put together by Camille Groult, who was, however, aware that not all of his pictures were what they seemed. Among those who went into raptures about a Venetian picture attributed to Turner that was clearly not genuine were Gustave Moreau and the Goncourt brothers. In 1891 one of the Goncourts described it as 'liquid gold, and within it an infusion of purple', professing that 'For me it has the air of a painting done by a Rembrandt born in India.'[22]

During the 1890s the condensed display of the Turner Bequest at the National Gallery continued to attract French artists. One of the most significant of these was Paul Signac, who has been seen as the vital 'bridge between Turner and the modern period'.[23] In 1898, during a 'pilgrimage' to London, he was amazed by the later paintings, which he felt broke free of the naturalism he had been expecting from Ruskin's writings about them. He marvelled in particular at the use of 'colour for colour's sake', noting how Turner induced it to vibrate: 'the pictures are composed, the colours organised. It is complete and meditated control.'[24] Finding this kinship with his own work gave authority for the direction he was already pursuing, and he was accordingly grateful. At some point he transcribed Turner's 1840 painting of the Salute, seen from the Giudecca canal (fig.110), and annotated it with the words, 'This poor little prayer to our God Turner' (fig.274). This could have been in 1909, when he returned to London, though Signac's modest watercolour may perhaps have been based on the widely available engraving in the *Turner Gallery*, as the colours are quite different from Turner's.[25] A further echo of Turner can be discerned in Signac's own views of Venice, where his concentration on the patterned sails of the local fishing boats recalls the painting *The Sun of Venice going to Sea* (fig.248).[26]

Signac's second visit to Venice was in 1908, the year that Monet at last got there for the first time.[27] The latter stayed at the Grand Hotel Britannia, which, confusingly, is now the Hotel Europa, though not the same building as that in which Turner had stayed in 1833 and 1840. Although Monet's youthful enthusiasm for Turner had more recently been dissipated by a nationalistic desire to insist on the purely French origins of impressionism, he had spent periods of time in London between 1898 and 1901, which would have renewed his knowledge of Turner's art. One of the few Venetian canvases he could have seen then was *St Benedetto, looking towards Fusina* (fig.211), which is pervaded by a burnished yellow tone that obliterates all local colour except the black of the gondolas. Monet perhaps recalled the intensity of this effect in the golden colouring of some of his views of the Doge's Palace and San Giorgio Maggiore.[28]

Just a couple of years earlier, the abstract nature of Turner's preparatory work had become apparent for the first time, when a group of previously

272
James Baker Pyne (1800–1870)
The Rail at Venice c.1860s
Oil on canvas, 28 x 40.5
Private collection

273
Edward Pritchett (fl.1828–1864/79)
On the Lagoon, Venice; a variation on Turner's 1842 view from the Steps of the Europa Hotel
Oil on canvas, 28.5 x 46
Private collection (courtesy of Sotheby's)

unexhibited studies went on display at the Tate Gallery. One of these was the picture that has come to be known as 'Procession of Boats, with Distant Smoke, Venice' *(fig.277)*, but which was originally called 'The Burning of the Ships'. Though eclipsed at the time by the incredible revelatory quality of *Norham Castle, Sunrise c.*1845 (Tate) or the *Evening Star c.*1835–45 (National Gallery, London), this work nevertheless contributed to the reappraisal of Turner's later style in the early twentieth century. It was not linked specifically with Venice until 1966, when it was shown with its pair *(fig.276)* in Lawrence Gowing's celebrated exhibition at the Museum of Modern Art in New York. The second painting was part of a cache of around seventy canvases that Kenneth Clark unearthed in the National Gallery's basement during the Second World War, which until then had not even been accessioned.[29] Other Venetian pictures in this group included *figs.*168 and 241–2, as well as *fig.*178, with its magically ghostly image of the Salute. The presence of identifiable topographical features in these last four works gives good reason for identifying them as Venetian subjects. Yet for the two larger paintings, a link with Venice, while plausible, possibly says more about the myths that continue to envelop the floating city and Gowing's desire to enshrine Turner as the prophet of abstraction. Since 1966 his interpretation of the pictures has hitherto gone unchallenged, and has, in fact, been bolstered by recent writers.[30] However, many of the details do not readily sustain the current connection.

First, the size of the canvas is substantially larger than that used for the nineteen small Venetian pictures that Turner exhibited between 1840 and 1846. This is an important point, for he imposed fairly rigid limitations on himself with regard to his materials when working in series. In fact, the dimensions are the same as those of his standard mid-scale exhibition pictures, and, as the pair seems to date from the mid-1840s, they are closest in spirit and handling to the four canvases exploring the activities of whaling fleets.[31] In contrast with the grey tonality of that group, the two 'Venetian' pictures are much warmer, and were enhanced by the application of red outlines to suggest the presence of numerous figures. Looking closely at the pictures it is apparent that there is no architectural element, as if the eye scans a seaward horizon from the shore. Nevertheless, the presence of so many festive crowds indicates that the quayside is not far away. Indeed, in one of them a line of soldiers in red uniform stands patiently to attention, while in the boats below people point eagerly towards the distant smoke. These English troops are clearly an anomaly in a Venetian subject, but would not be so in one closer to home.

A more appropriate identification of the pictures could, therefore, be the arrival of the French king, Louis-Philippe, at Portsmouth on 8 October 1844 *(fig.275)*. One of Turner's own letters confirms that he was present on the occasion, and a group of studies have been related to the event.[32]

274
Paul Signac (1863–1935)
Venice, the Salute ?1909
Pencil and watercolour, 15.8 x 19.8
Inscribed, 'à Ch.Cherfils / P.S. / cette pauvre
petite prière à notre Dieu Turner'
Arkansas Arts Center Foundation Collection, Gift
of James T. Dyke 1999

He had known Louis-Philippe many years earlier, when the Duc d'Orléans's son lived in exile at Twickenham, but more recently, in 1838, the king had awarded him a diamond-studded, gold snuff-box in return for a copy of his *Picturesque Views in England and Wales*.[33] In the autumn of 1844 Louis-Philippe was attempting to consolidate the alliance with Queen Victoria, which had begun the previous year with her visit to his château in Picardy. His arrival in Portsmouth in his paddle steamer, the *Gomer*, was one of several carefully staged pieces of pageantry that were widely reported in the newspapers over the following week. To welcome him the Queen's guns were repeatedly fired, causing smoke to build up on the anchorage, and, according to the *Illustrated London News*, 'the whole population thronged the beach', watching as with every 'moment this scene increased in interest'.[34] One of the noteworthy features reported in the press was the presence of troops, 'disposed in two lines, each three deep', which stretched 'from the Royal Dock yard to the railroad terminus', which was presumably the same display of military decorum that impressed Turner. Though the steamer itself does not appear in his paintings, he shows the flotilla of smaller vessels containing local dignitaries that went out to greet Louis-Philippe. Moreover, the centrally placed boat in the *Procession* picture may, in fact, be intended to be that from which the king disembarked.

This is all a long way from the interpretation of these pictures as the wraith-like mists of Venice, with parties of revellers drifting to and from the city across the Lagoon. But it demonstrates the way in which Turner's vision of Venice relies less on the specifics of place, and far more on what he brought to the scene. Whether he was painting Venice or the Solent, he remained obsessed with the elusive qualities of light and colour, and it is his restless exploration of these characteristics that continues to captivate.

275
Thomas Sewell Robins (1814–1880)
Louis-Philippe's Visit to Queen Victoria, October 1844, passing the Flag in Portsmouth Harbour c.1880
Oil on canvas, 19.9 x 49
National Maritime Museum, Greenwich

276 (cat.59)
The Arrival of Louis-Philippe at Portsmouth, 8 October 1844 c.1844–5 (formerly listed as 'Festive Lagoon Scene, Venice' c.1845')
Oil on canvas, 90.8 x 121.3
Tate (No4660; B&J 506)

277 (cat.60)
The Disembarkation of Louis-Philippe at
Portsmouth, 8 October 1844 c.1844–5
(formerly listed as 'Procession of Boats,
with Distant Smoke, Venice c.1845')
Oil on canvas, 90.2 x 120.6
Tate (No2068; B&J 505; S 105)

Appendix: The papers used for Turner's Venetian Watercolours

Compiled by Ian Warrell with assistance from Peter Bower

1819 Tour

Sketchbooks

All acquired in London before setting out for Italy (see Bower 1990, pp.113–16)

'Route to Rome' sketchbook (TB CLXXI). Watermarked: 'ALLEE / 1813'

'Milan to Venice' sketchbook (TB CLXXV). Watermarked: 'ALLEE / 1813'

'Como and Venice' sketchbook (TB CLXXXI). Watermarked: 'J WHATMAN / 1816' (*see figs.15, 74–5, 77–8*)

'Venice to Ancona' sketchbook (TB CLXXVI). Watermarked: '[SMITH] & ALLNUTT / [18]18'

Fawkes Watercolours, *c.1820*

The watercolour at Dublin (*fig.96*) is on paper with the following watermark: 'J WHATMAN / 1818 / TURKEY MILL'. Other Italian subjects from this series seen by Peter Bower are on the same type of paper

1833 Tour

Sketchbooks

'Vienna up to Venice' sketchbook (TB CCCXI). Acquired in Vienna (see Powell 1995, p.115)

'Venice' sketchbook (TB CCCXIV). Watermarked with initials and crescent-moon motif; endpapers watermarked with crowned double-eagle motif. Both made by the Galvani mills at Pordenone (see Bower 1999, no.29). Probably acquired in Vienna, or Venice

'Venice up to Trento' sketchbook (TB CCCXII). As above for TB CCCXIV

Loose Sheets

Grey paper produced by Bally, Ellen and Steart (see Bower 1999, no.59). Turner was using sheets from at least four different batches of the same paper, possibly acquired in bulk after the firm wound up its business, on the retirement of Steart, in 1832. Powell (1995, p.44) has demonstrated that Turner used this paper on the way back from Venice in 1833 (as well as in 1840), so it is possible that the following items could have been made on this visit: TB CCCXVII 20 (*fig.189*), 21 (*fig.190*), 22 (*fig.82*), 23 (*fig.180*), 24 (*fig.111*), 25 (*fig.172*). See also under 1840

1840 Tour

Sketchbooks

'Rotterdam to Venice' sketchbook (TB CCCXX). Watermarked: 'JH&C'. Made by Jan Honig & Co, at De Wever mill, at Koog an der Zaan. Bought in Rotterdam

'Venice and Bozen' sketchbook (TB CCCXIII). Watermarked: 'J WHATMAN'. A fake Whatman paper, made and sold in Austria (see Bower 1999, no.35)

'Venice: Passau to Würzburg' sketchbook (TB CCCX). Watermarked: 'J WHATMAN'. As above

'Grand Canal and Giudecca Canal' sketchbook (TB CCCXV 1–21, plus TB CCCXVI 41 [*fig.154*]; with the exception of f.16, all of these watercolours are reproduced here). Sheets measure approximately 22 x 32 cm, and about half have the watermark: 'J WHATMAN 1834'. Both this and its companion below travelled with Turner from London

'Storm' sketchbook. Now widely dispersed. Sheets from this book are of the same dimensions as the disbound book in the Turner Bequest, and many are similarly imbued with the 1834 Whatman watermark. It has sometimes wrongly been suggested that these leaves were also part of TB CCCXV. However, few of Turner's late roll sketchbooks contained more than twenty-four sheets, which argues strongly for a second sketchbook; as does the fact that these sheets became separated from the main group of Venetian studies in the Bequest. Perhaps the volume was left with Turner's agent, Thomas Griffith, who offered them for sale after the artist's death. The nineteen sheets at the following locations were probably originally part of this book: Fitzwilliam Museum, Cambridge (W 1353, *fig.253*; W 1361, *fig.219*), National Gallery of Ireland, Dublin (W 1358, *fig.186*), National Gallery of Scotland, Edinburgh (W 1352, *fig.114*; W 1370, *fig.179*; W 1371, *fig.255*; W 1374, *fig.244*), Walker Art Gallery, Liverpool (W 1373; *fig.234*), British Museum, London (W 1354, *fig.188*; W 1359, *fig.181*), Yale Center for British Art, New Haven (W 1360, *fig.184*), Ashmolean Museum, Oxford (W 1363, *fig.177*; W 1364, *fig.239*; W 1366 *fig.173*), private collections (W 1355, *fig.187*; W 1368, *fig.183*; *San Giorgio Maggiore at Sunset*, *fig.216*; *Venice from the Punta della Dogana*, *fig.185*), whereabouts unknown (*Grand Canal*, *fig.153*)

Loose sheets

1) Seven watercolours on sheets of white paper probably made by Charles Ansell. These measure approximately 19.8 x 28.4 cm (indicating that they were folded and torn into eight pieces from an Imperial sheet): TB CCCXVI 3 (*fig.144*), TB CCCXVI 28 (*fig.215*), TB CCCXVI 42 (*fig.146*), TB CCCLXIV 43 (*fig.147*), TB CCCLXIV 106 (*fig.145*), TB CCCLXIV 334 (*fig.252*), plus the watercolour now at Manchester (*fig.148*). An eighth sheet (TB CCCXVI 29; *fig.222*) seems to relate to this group, both technically and in terms of its size, but this has been identified by Peter Bower as paper produced by Bally, Ellen and Steart

2) Sheets of white paper produced by Charles Ansell, each measuring around 24 x 30 cm, several watermarked with the date '1828': TB CCCXVI 1 (*fig.175*), 2 (Stainton 1985, pl.59), 4 (*fig.201*), 5, 6 (*fig.176*), 8 (*fig.196*), 9 (*fig.202*), 10 (*fig.191*), 17 (*fig.236*), 18 (*fig.247*), 19 (*fig.254*), 20 (*fig.249*), 21 (*fig.250*), 22 (*fig.251*), 23 (Stainton 1985, pl.72), 24 (*fig.217*), 25 (*fig.259*), 26 (*fig.194*), 30 (Stainton 1985, pl.71), 31 (Stainton 1985, pl.79), 33 (*fig.192*), 34 (Stainton 1985, pl.66), 35 (*fig.193*), 36 (*fig.143*), 37 (*fig.195*), 38, 39 (*fig.261*), 40 (*fig.200*); TB CCCLXIV 137 (*fig.258*), 332 (*fig.260*). Some non-Bequest watercolours may belong to this group (i.e. W 1356, *fig.235*; W 1365, *fig.223*)

3) White paper produced by an unknown source, resembling the Whatman papers made by William Balston & Co at Maidstone. It is similar in appearance to the Ansell batch, which may mean that some of those listed above will be found to be from this source once a full examination of all the sheets has taken place. For the moment, Bower has identified only the famous view of the Arsenale as an example of this type of paper: TB CCCXVI 27 (*fig.130*; see Bower 1999, no.36)

4) Pale buff wove, produced by an unknown maker, with the watermark: 'J W'. It has been suggested that this type of paper was a deliberate forgery of Whatman paper and was possibly produced in Austria (Bower 1999, no.63). Its inferior quality has resulted in visible changes to the paper, which is especially prone to fading: TB CCCXVI 11 (*fig.214*), 12 (*fig.158*), 32; TB CCCXVII 26, 34 (*fig.141*); TB CCCXVIII 28 (*fig.118*). Outside the Bequest, the following works are also painted on this paper: Fitzwilliam Museum, Cambridge (W 1362, *fig.213*); National Gallery of Scotland, Edinburgh (W 1369, *fig.157*; W 1372, *fig.90*)

5) Lightweight buff-grey paper from an unknown source, possibly English, with the watermark: 'W'. See TB CCCXVII 13, 14. These sheets were discussed in Bower (1999, no.66), but mistakenly linked with TB CCCXVIII 13 and 14

6) Greyish paper of the same type, but from a different source: TB CCCXVIII 6, 13 (*fig.139*)

7) Pale grey-white wove, watermarked: 'C S', followed by laurel leaves, and mould numbers. An Italian paper, probably made in the Brescia region (see Bower 1999, no.67): TB CCCXVI 13 (*fig.226*), 14 (*fig.224*), 15 (*fig.225*), 16 (*fig.262*)

8) Bally, Ellen and Steart grey paper. As mentioned under 1833, the dating of some these sheets is uncertain, though it is clear the material was in use on both tours. Those that seem to arise from the later visit are as follows: TB CCCXVII 1 (*fig.115*), 2 (*fig.117*), 4 (*fig.203*), 5 (*fig.232*), 15, 16 (*fig.231*), 18 (*fig.256*), 19 (*fig.119*), 27 (*fig.161*), 28 (*fig.167*), 29 (*fig.166*), 30 (*fig.165*), 32 (*fig.129*). There are a few sheets of this paper outside the Bequest: private collections (W 1367, *fig.212*; *The Doge's Palace from the Bacino*, *fig.233*). For half-size sheets of this paper used in Venice, see TB CCCXLI 183 and W 1037

9) Red-brown paper made at Cartieri Pietro Milani Mill, Fabriano, with a watermark showing the letter 'M' accompanied by laurel leaves (as described in Bower 1999, no.64). This material seems to be quite absorbent, so that the colours penetrate through to the back of the sheet: TB CCCXVIII 5 (*fig.149*), 8 (Stainton 1985, pl.15), 11 (*fig.138*), 19 (Stainton 1985, pl.16), 20 (*fig.136*), 21 (Stainton 1985, pl.23), 22 (*fig.120*), 26 (*fig.127*), 27 (Stainton 1985, pl.26), 29 (*fig.140*); TB CCCXIX 3, 6 (*fig.150*)

10) Warm buff paper, possibly made at the mills at Fabriano, but a different colour: TB CCCXVIII 18 (*fig.134*)

11) Grey-brown paper produced by an unknown maker (possibly also a batch made at Fabriano). These sheets are torn into two sizes: nine smaller pieces measuring around 14.8 x 23.2 cm; and seven pieces of approximately 23.1 x 29.5 cm. The first group is as follows: TB CCCXVIII 1 (*fig.123*); TB CCCXIX 1 (formerly attached at bottom edge to TB CCXCII 60), 2 (*fig.126*), 4 (formerly attached at top edge to TB CCCXIX 10), 5 (*fig.131*), 7 (*fig.128*), 8 (*fig.124*; formerly attached on right edge to right edge of TB CCCXIX 9), 9, 10 (*fig.125*). The larger sheets are: TB CCCXVIII 4 (*fig.135*), 7 (*fig.121*), 9 (Stainton 1985, pl.19), 10 (Stainton 1985, pl.28), 12, 14 (Stainton 1985, pl.18), 23 (Stainton 1985, pl.22)

12) Grey wove, with a textured surface, produced by an unknown maker. Sheets mostly measure about 21.8 x 28.5 cm: TB CCCXVIII 3 (Stainton 1985, pl.10), 15, 16, 17 (*fig.137*), 24, 25

Notes

Turner and Venice Ian Warrell

1 Turner exhibited seventy-five paintings between 1833 and 1846, of which twenty-five were views of Venice; see entries in B&J for further details.

2 This can be compared with the thirty-seven canvases begun by Monet during his two months in Venice in 1908.

3 C.R. Leslie, quoted in Ruskin *Works*, vol.XXXV, p.571.

4 See Liversidge and Farington 1993.

5 Hills 1999, p.9.

6 Ruskin *Diaries*, vol.I, p.186 (12 May 1841).

7 Dickens *Letters*, pp.217–18 (12 Nov 1844).

8 Byron, *The Two Foscari*, Appendix.

9 Sass 1818, p.281.

10 Cunningham 1843, vol.II, p.311.

11 Ruskin *Works*, vol.VII, pp.374–88.

12 Howard 2000.

13 Cooper 1838, pp.307–8, 315.

14 Finberg 1930, p.111.

15 Finberg 1930, pp.19, 78–9, 86–7, 119ff.

16 Bell MSS notes to Finberg 1930; Hill (2000, p.261) suggests a visit to Venice in 1838, but there is no record of Turner's presence there in the local paper.

17 George 1970; Powell 1995.

18 *GPdiV*; the entry for 17 September, p.4, conflates the arrivals for both the 8th and 9th, but as Turner's name was fourth from the top of this list, it is possible to assume that he arrived on the earlier day. When he departed on the 13th, he was again near the top of the list (recorded on the 20th). He was classified then as '*possidente*', meaning a landowner.

19 Dickens 1846, p.363; Shelley 1913, vol.II, p.240.

20 TB CLXXI f.24. See Powell 1987, p.18.

21 Blessington 1840, pp.119–20.

22 Bower 1990, pp.113–16.

23 TB CLXXI ff.24, 25.

24 TB CLXXV f.40v.

25 TB CLXXVI f.86.

26 Moore 1853–6, vol.VII, p.149.

27 *GPdiV*, 21 September 1819.

28 *GPdiV*, 20 September 1819.

29 See Powell 1987; Finberg 1930, pp.23–4.

30 B&J 228, 230 and 233, all Tate.

31 *Oxford Companion*, pp.194–5.

32 Thornbury 1862, vol.I, p.229; Hill 2000.

33 Thornbury 1862, vol.I, p.232; 1877, p.105. It has generally been assumed that Munro did not receive a finished watercolour. However, Thornbury's listing of Munro's collection includes a drawing described simply as 'Venice (Not engraved) (?)' (1862, vol.II, p.396).

34 See W 726–31. This may suggest that Munro was already in possession of his version of the view of Florence by this date (W 728) and was seeking the Venetian subject as a pendant.

35 Heath 1993, pp.23–48.

36 *Oxford Companion*, pp.354–8; Solkin 2001, pp.145–55.

37 Warrell 1999, pp.71–2.

38 Turner's anticipated involvement in the Cadell edition of Scott's Waverley novels led Hardy George (1970) to link a letter that appeared on p.501 of the September edition of *Arnold's Magazine of the Fine Arts* with Turner. This was written by an anonymous painter, newly arrived in Venice, who encouraged an unnamed fellow artist, still based in London, to make the journey to Italy. He professes to be bemused by his colleague's decision to stay 'behind to paint for the Waverley novels', when he ought to feel compelled to 'see that which, in these days, everybody else makes a point of seeing'. Attempts to establish the identity of the author from the *GPdiV* have provided no conclusive evidence to support George's contention.

39 11 May 1833, p.299.

40 *GPdiV*, 21 August 1833, p.759. TB CCCXII f.17. He would have needed to leave Venice by the 18th or 19th to arrive back in Bozen on the 22nd.

41 *Morning Chronicle*, 7 May 1833.

42 For instance 1836, Aosta valley; 1839, Spa, Belgium; 1841–4, Switzerland; 1845, Normandy coast.

43 Note the 'Cosmorana' advertised in the *GPdiV*, 2 September 1840, p.798.

44 Chateaubriand *c.*1840, pp.167–207; Whittingham 1985.

45 TB CCCXIV ff.17, 41v–42, 55, 55v–56.

46 TB CCCXIV ff.36v, 50, 59v, 71v.

47 TB CCCXIV ff.51v, 52v–53, 53v–54, 54v, 92, 92v.

48 TB CCCXIV f.15v.

49 TB CCCXIV f.58v, possibly based on a version of Queen Henrietta Maria. For Turner and Van Dyck, see Petworth 2002.

50 Powell 1995, p.44.

51 Finberg 1930, p.93; George 1970, p.317 n.23; Stainton 1985, pp.24–6. (However, see London 1974, pp.154–5, and Wilton 1975, p.134.)

52 Bower 1999, pp.110–13. Note that Bower's comments in no.66 should be applied to D32196–D32199 and not D32233.

53 Stainton 1985, pp.49–50; Lyles 1992, pp.67–9.

54 Powell 1995, p.161.

55 London 1974, pp.154–5.

56 Powell 1995, p.44.

57 B&J 356.

58 Plant 1996, p.157.

59 Treuherz 1986, p.37; *Oxford Companion*, pp.239–40.

60 Gage 1980, p.5.

61 B&J 359 (Philadelphia Museum of Art), 364 (Cleveland Museum of Art).

62 Finberg 1930, pp.93–101.

63 Beckett 1967, pp.32–3 (12 May 1836).

64 Petworth 2002, pp.42–63.

65 For instance B&J 338, 340 (1831); 374, 375 (1838); 394, 395 (1841).

66 B&J 360.

67 B&J 357.

68 B&J 366; Powell 1987, p.160.

69 B&J 374, 375 (1838); 378, 379 (1839).

70 B&J 355, 402, 416–19.

71 Though one of the 1841 paintings is known to have been completed for Turner's friend Chantrey, there is no documentation to confirm whether his request for the picture came before or after the 1840 tour. Note also the sale at the end of 1840 of a watercolour, attributed to Turner, of San Giorgio and the Dogana (Christie's, 9 December 1840, lot 156; bt Dyson 18s.).

72 Finberg published the now untraced letter from 'EH' (1930, pp.119ff.), speculating that this might be a member of the Hakewill family. For further references to Harpur, who was one of the chief mourners at Turner's funeral, see Gage 1980, pp.112, 192, 212; Guiterman 1989, p.7; and *Oxford Companion*, pp.193–4.

73 *GPdiV*, 21 August 1840, p.759; 4 September 1840, p.808.

74 Powell 1995, pp.37, 44; Warrell 2003.

75 Stanzas X–XI.

76 Cundall 1908, pp.66–7. The admittedly incomplete listing in the *GPdiV* on 28 August could imply that Callow's intended residence in Venice was the Leon Bianco. He stayed until 9 September. Another arrival during this period was a 'Brockedon', who may be the author of the guidebooks to Alpine passes used by Turner in 1836 and 1844, and with whom he was acquainted.

77 Thornbury 1862, vol.II, pp.284–5, misleadingly claims that 'Mr Ruskin had given Turner, on one of his late tours, a commission for a drawing of Venice, but it was so unfinished that it did not please him', which is impossible as there is no evidence that Ruskin commissioned anything until at least 1842.

78 Finberg 1930, p.135.

79 Ruskin *Diaries*, vol.I, p.273 (29 April 1844).

80 *Examiner*, 18 February 1816, p.109.

81 Holcomb 1972; C.R. Leslie's letter of 4 November 1845, reporting Turner's remark, is quoted in B&J 347.

82 These occur from at least as early as 1831 (Whitley Papers, vol.6, p.213); *Blackwood's Magazine*, September 1837, p.335; see also Liebreich 1872 and Trevor-Roper 1970, pp.92–3, pl.X.

83 *Athenaeum*, 7 May 1842, p.409.

84 *Literary Gazette*, 14 May 1842, p.33.

85 *Art Union*, 1 June 1842.

86 Gage 1980, pp.192–3.

87 Ibid., p.175.

88 Bicknell and Guiterman 1987, p.40 (24 June 1845).

89 B&J 390.

90 See entries in Macleod 1996 and *Oxford Companion*.

91 Account Book, 27 April 1847 (Ruskin Library, Lancaster: MS 29). See *Diaries*, vol.I, p.273 (29 April 1844). Some years later Ruskin seems to refer to this in a letter outlining his bitter regret at opportunities he had missed to gain major paintings (Bradley 1955, p.127; Warrell 1995, p.152).

92 Herrmann 1990, p.224; Gage 1980, p.162.

93 Thornbury 1862, vol.I, pp.407–8. See R 668 and R 679.

94 June 1846.

95 6 May 1846, p.5.

96 *The Man in the Moon*, 1847; undated cutting in A.J. Finberg's papers (Tate Prints and Drawings Room).

97 Plant 1996, p.145.

98 Plant 2003, p.97 n.129.

99 Schulz 1980, p.416. Schulz bases his evidence on the 'Venetian' paintings that are identified here as views of the Solent (*figs.*276–7).

100 Stainton 1985, p.28; Melville 1964.

101 Ruskin *Works*, vol.V, p.392.

102 Dickens *Letters*, p.217 (12 November 1844).

Approaches to Venice Cecilia Powell

1 For details of these tours, see Powell 1987 and Powell 1995.

2 Farington *Diary*, vol.V, p.1936 (22 November 1802).

3 See Powell 1982, pp.408–25.

4 W 402, 1820, Birmingham Museum and Art Gallery.

5 Alfredo Comandini, *L'Italia nei cento anni del secolo XIX, giorno per giorno illustrata*, 1801–1825, Milan 1900–1, p.1051.

6 See *Turner en France*, Paris 1981, pp.105–13; Warrell 1999, pp.18–19.

7 B&J 47, 1803, City Art Galleries, Sheffield.

8 Farington *Diary*, vol.V, p.1936 (22 November 1802).

9 *GPdiV*: 'Turner William, gent. inglese'; see Stainton 1985, p.13; and p. 16 above.

10 Powell 1987, pp.137–65.

11 For the 1817 and 1824 tours, see Powell 1995.

12 *Wiener Zeitung*, 28 August 1833: 'Hr. Turner, Mitglied der königl. Akademie zu London'.

13 *Intelligenz-Blatt zum KK. priv. Bothen von und für Tirol und Vorarlberg*, 9 September 1833: 'Hr. Turner-Mallord, Privat aus England und Mitglied der Akademie in London'.

14 *GPdiV*: 'Turner, gent. inglese'; see George 1971, p.84.

15 These sketchbooks were TB CCXCVI, CCXCVIII, CCC, CCCXI.

16 *Intelligenz-Blatt...*, 26 September 1833: 'Hr. Turner, Rentier und Mitglied der Akademie der Wissenschaften in London'. Parts of the journey are recorded in TB CCCXII.

17 Finley 1980, pp.229–31.

18 Public Record Office, FO 610/2, no.6232. Royal Academy, Minutes Book IV (1826–41), p.354. Whittingham 1993, p.95.

19 The sketchbooks were TB CCCXX (outward journey), CCCXIII (Venice), CCXCIX and CCCX (return journey).

20 *GPdiV*; George 1971, p.87.

21 Finberg 1930, pp.119–21. Since the letter from the couple is obviously written by the husband, it is necessary, with this argument, to postulate that Eleanor, despite being unwell, wrote her initials at the end; alternatively, that Finberg misread 'H.H.' as 'E.H.'.

22 Cecilia Powell, 'Turner's Travelling Companion of 1802: A Mystery Resolved?', *Turner Society News*, no.54, February 1990, pp.12–15.

23 *GPdiV*: 'Turner J. M., inglese'; George 1971, p.86.

24 Cunningham 1843, vol.II, p.367.

25 *Wiener Zeitung*, 10 September 1840: 'Hr. Joseph Mallard, und Hr. William Turner, Englische Edelleute'. Turner's last visit to Venice transformed him into two aristocrats!

26 *Regensburger Zeitung*, 14 September 1840; *Tagblatt der Stadt Bamberg*, 15 and 17 September 1840: 'Sir Jurner, Rentier von London'; *Neue Würzburger Zeitung*, 23 September 1840: 'Turner, Rent. von London'.

27 B&J 392, 1841, Sudley House, Liverpool.

28 Gage 1980, p.180.

29 *Verona*, W 1107, c.1833, private collection; *The Opening of the Wallhalla*, 1842, B&J 401, 1843, Tate.

Venice under the Austrians David Laven

1 The best account of the collapse of the Venetian Republic is G. Scarabello, 'Il Settecento' in G. Cozzi, M. Knapton and G. Scarabello, *La Repubblica di Venezia nell'età moderna. Dal 1517 alla fine della Repubblica*, revised ed., Turin 1992, pp.650–76.

2 Laven 2002, pp.40–2.

3 On the first Austrian domination, see M. Gottardi, *L'Austria a Venezia. Società e istituzioni nella prima dominazione austriaca 1798–1806*, Milan 1993.

4 Laven 2002, pp.46–51.

5 For the period of transition to Austrian rule, see R.J. Rath, *The Provisional Austrian Regime in Lombardy-Venetia, 1814–1815*, Austin, Texas 1969; and Laven 2002, pp.54–74.

6 Byron to Thomas Moore, Venice, 17 November 1816. Marchand 1976, vol.5, p.129.

7 For a discussion of Byron's attitude to the decay of Venice, see Tanner 1992, pp.28–9.

8 Byron to Thomas Moore, Venice, 19 September 1818. Marchand 1976, vol.6, p.66.

9 Lady Morgan, *Italy*, 2 vols., London, 1821, vol.II, p.74.

10 Solari 1824, vol.I, p.3.

11 Henry Matthews, *The Diary of an Invalid, being the journal of a tour in pursuit of health in Portugal Italy Switzerland and France in the years 1817 1818 and 1819*, London 1820, p.291.

12 Henry Coxe, *Picture of Italy being a guide to the antiquities and curiosities of that classical and interesting country: containing sketches of manners, society and customs: and an itinerary of distances in posts and English miles, best inns, &c. With a minute description of Rome, Florence, Naples, & Venice and their Environs. To which are prefixed directions to travellers; and Dialogues in English, French and Italian*, London 1815, p.445.

13 On the passivity of Venice and its mainland in comparison with other parts of Italy, see Laven 2002, pp.149–212; 'Law and order in Habsburg Venetia 1814–1835', *Historical Journal*, vol.39, 1996, pp.383–403. For Austrian intervention elsewhere in Italy, see Laven, 'Austria's Italian Policy Reconsidered: Revolution and Reform in Restoration Italy', *Modern Italy*, vol.3, 1997, pp.3–33.

14 Solari 1824, p.37.

15 On the composition of the Venetian bureaucracy, see M. Meriggi, *Amministrazione e classi sociali nel Lombardo-Veneto (1814–1848)*, Bologna 1983, *passim*. For the fate of Padua University, see Laven, 'Liberals or Libertines? Staff, Students, and Government Policy at the University of Padua, 1814–1835', *History of Universities*, vol.11, 1992, pp.135–55.

16 Laven 2002, pp.104–19.

17 Laven 2002, pp.120–46.

18 *Almanacco per le province soggette all'i.r. Governo di Venezia*, Venice 1821, p.533.

19 G. Zalin, *Aspetti e problemi dell'economia veneta dalla caduta della repubblica all'annessione*, Vicenza 1969, p.18.

20 'The Habsburgs and the Great Depression in Lombardy-Venetia, 1814–18', *Journal of Modern History*, vol.13, 1941, pp.305–20.

21 See, for example, 'Tabella dimostrativa l'odierno andamento, e stato delle varie manifatture, Provincia di Venezia, Dicembre 1818', enclosed with 'Über Künste, und Manufacturen in den Venezianischen Provinzen', Goess, Venice, 31 January 1819, Haus-, Hof- und Staatsarchiv, Kaiser Franz Akten 71.

22 W.T. Money, *An exposition of the good effects which have resulted from the measure of tardy justice but sound policy*, Venice, 15 May 1832, PRO FO7, no.237.

23 For a typical example of the mistaken British position, see J.D. Sinclair, *An autumn in Italy, being a personal narrative of a tour of the Austrian, Tuscan, Roman and Sardinian states in 1827*, Edinburgh 1829, p.88.

24 For the debate surrounding the free port, see Laven 2002, pp.95–102.

25 W.T. Money, Venice, 15 May 1832, PRO FO7, no.237.

26 Cattanei, *Bolletino politico-amministrativo* for December 1833, Venice, 16 January 1834, Haus-, Hof-, und Staatsarchiv, Minister Kolowrat Akten (1834) 622.

27 K.R. Greenfield, 'Commerce and New Enterprise at Venice, 1830–48', *Journal of Modern History*, vol.11, 1939, pp.313–33; Laven, 'Punti di vista britannici sull'economia veneziana, 1814–1848' in M. Costantini (ed.), *Venezia nell'Ottocento*, Mantua 1991, pp.93–114.

28 A. Bernardello, *La prima ferrovia fra Venezia e Milano. Storia dell'imperiale regia privilegiata strada ferrata Ferdinandea Lombardo-Veneta*, Venice 1996.

29 Ruskin wrote on 10 September 1845 of his horror at the construction of the bridge, 'cutting off the whole open sea and half the city, which now looks as nearly as possible like Liverpool at the end of the dockyard wall'. Cited in T. Hilton, *John Ruskin. The early years 1819–1859*, New Haven and London 1985, p.93. Fanny Trollope was also anxious that the railway would spoil Venice's charm. *A Visit to Italy*, 2 vols., London 1842, vol.II, p.145.

30 The best account of the insurrection of 1848–9 is P. Ginsborg, *Daniele Manin and the Venetian Revolution of 1848–49*, Cambridge 1979.

31 Hobhouse 1859, vol.I, p.122.

32 Solari 1824, pp.15–17.

33 Trollope, *A Visit to Italy*, vol.I, p.120 and p.94.

34 Thomas Arnold to George Cornish, 24 August 1830. Cited in E.C. Batho, *The Later Wordsworth*, Cambridge 1933, p.141.

35 J.C.L. Sismonde de Sismondi, *Histoire des républiques italiennes du moyen âge*, 16 vols., Paris 1809–1819; Daru 1817/19.

36 B. Webb, *Sketches of Continental Ecclesiology*, London 1848, p.299. Cited in Pemble 1999, p.116.

37 One of the best examples of the tradition of using the supposed similarities between Venice and Britain was Thomas Otway's *Venice Preserv'd*, written in 1681–2, in which the Tory playwright accomplished the interesting feat of attacking Lord Shaftesbury and his Whig supporters by associating them with both a corrupt and tyrannical Venice and the characters in the play who rebel against the established order.

38 For an illuminating discussion of British and French comparisons of Venice and Britain, see Pemble 1999, pp.87–108.

39 J. Ruskin, *The Stones of Venice*, vol.1: *The Foundations* in *Works*, vol.IX, pp.20–1.

40 Writing in the 1880s of his early trips to Venice, Ruskin remarked that 'My Venice, like Turner's, had been chiefly created for us by Byron'. *Works*, vol.XXXV, p.295.

41 Dickens 1846.

42 On Byron's perception of Venice as a 'fairy city', see Tanner 1992, pp.19–20.

CATALOGUE

PART ONE: 'NO ONE ENTERS VENICE AS A STRANGER'

1 Palgrave 1842, p.342.

1. Beyond Canaletto's Venice

1 *Arnold's Magazine*, September 1833, p.501. For the author and intended recipient of this letter, see p.260 n.38 above.
2 Quoted in Liversidge and Farington 1993, p.114; see also Sass 1818, p.279; *Athenaeum*, 14 May 1836, p.280.
3 Liversidge and Farington 1993, pp.104–17.
4 Constable and Links 1976, pp.188–9.
5 See the series of twelve prints by Joseph Baudin, 1739: the Rialto is no.7. I am grateful to Greg Smith for this information.
6 Liversidge and Farington 1993, p.108.
7 See Links 1971.
8 Smith 2002, p.130.
9 George 1970, p.10.
10 Gage 1974, pp.83–4; Constable and Links 1976, revised ed. 1989, nos.630ff.
11 See Alexander in Liversidge and Farington 1993, pp.38–45.
12 TB CCCXIV f.15v.
13 Soane Museum; Constable and Links 1976, no.122.
14 Constable and Links 1976, no.199.
15 Engraved in March 1832 by Henry Le Keux, one of Turner's printmakers.
16 Constable and Links 1976, no.398.
17 Ibid., no.426; Liversidge and Farington 1993, p.103.
18 Constable and Links 1976, no.437d. Turner's watercolour is in the Leicester Museum and Art Gallery; it resembles the capriccios that Joli painted, based on Canaletto's prototypes.
19 Liversidge and Farington 1993, pp.146–7.
20 *GPdiV*, 28 August 1840, p.781.
21 Frost and Reeve 1865; see Haskell 1960 and 1967 and Morassi 1973.
22 Powell 1982; Cubberley, Herrmann and Scott 1992.
23 Powell 1982, pp.412, 423 n.26; *Oxford Companion*, pp.239–40.
24 See B&J 132, 134.
25 E.g. B&J 234, W 1210–13, W 1236–63, W 1291–7.
26 Cubberley, Herrmann and Scott 1992, nos.6.26–6.38.

27 Stainton (1985, pp.57–8) mistakenly suggests this is a tracing of the finished watercolour.
28 See Shanes 1997.
29 W 700; R 144.
30 Gage 1987, p.52.
31 Powell 1982, p.414; Finberg 1930, p.72, pl.XII; Christie's, 11 November 1999.
32 Piggott 1993, p.58.
33 Warrell 1997, pp.196; Warrell 1999, pp.71–2.

2. Turner and Venetian Painting

1 Gage 1999, pp.153–61.
2 Godfrey 2001, pp.86–8.
3 Townsend 1993.
4 See *Oxford Companion*, pp.338–9 (Titian), pp.48–9 (Claude); Kitson in Warrell 2002.
5 See Haskell 1976, pp.39–44; Haskell 2000, pp.22–9.
6 *Oxford Companion*, p.30; B&J 14.
7 Haskell 2000, pp.25–6.
8 Farington *Diary*, vol.IV, p.1236 (9 June 1799).
9 Reynolds's *Discourses*, VI, p.113.
10 Habert and Volle 1992, p.91.
11 Finberg 1909, pp.181–94; *Oxford Companion*, pp.214–15.
12 Farington *Diary*, vol.V, p.1907 (7 October 1802).
13 TB LXXII ff.29v–31v.
14 See TB LXXII ff.56v–57v for Turner's copy of the Louvre painting, which Farington observed him making (*Diary*, vol.V, p.1901 [5 October 1802]). By the time Turner died this picture was more commonly attributed to Giorgione, and it is probable, therefore, that the copy of a work by this other great Venetian colourist listed in the contents of Turner's home was a version of the *Concert Champêtre* (Turner Bequest Schedule 1854, no.315). See also Haskell 1987, pp.141–53. Note also that the painting has recently been attributed to Domenico Mancini by Charles Hope (see Jaffé 2003, p.14).
15 It has been discovered at the time of going to press by Dr David Brown that *fig.39* is based on Guercino's painting of the Madonna and Child in the museum at Cento.
16 TB LXXII ff.36v, 51–51v.
17 Humfrey 1993, pp.314–17.
18 Gage 1980, p.72.
19 Reynolds's *Discourses*, XI, pp.199–200.

20 TB LXXII ff.27v–28v; see Farington *Diary*, vol.V, p.1929 (5 November 1802).
21 Reynolds's *Discourses*, XI, p.200. See Finberg 1930, p.56–8; Shanes 1990, pp.139ff.
22 TB LXXXI ff.48, 50, 52, 63.
23 National Gallery (no.34: Studio of Titian). On Angerstein, see *Oxford Companion*, p.7; Kitson in Warrell 2002, pp.23–4.
24 Gage 1969, p.141; Wilton and Turner 1990, p.116; Nicholson 1990, p.63.
25 See TB LXXXI f.63 (and ff.44, 47, 60, 62); TB LXXXIV f.20.
26 For a personal interpretation of the picture, see Hamilton 1997, p.81.
27 B&J 49, 150.
28 Farington *Diary*, vol.VI, pp.2022–3 (2 May 1803).
29 Gage 1987, pp.80–1; see also Townsend 1993, pp.18ff.
30 B&J 61; see also B&J 172.
31 Gage 1969, p.140.
32 Ziff 1963, pp.135, 140; Gage 1969, p.203.
33 Ziff 1963, p.138; Gage 1969, p.89.
34 B&J 114; see Gage 1969, p.90.
35 Gage 1969, pp.202–9, and see also p.117.
36 Sir George Beaumont, quoted in Cunningham 1843, vol.II, p.298.
37 In 1845 Ruskin described the *Assumption* as 'a complete Turner, only forty feet high'; see Shapiro 1972, p.210.
38 Gage 1969, p.91; George 1996.
39 See note on the series in Sass 1818, pp.277–8; and Thomas Phillips's lecture (1833, p.99).
40 National Gallery no.294. Turner's transcription is TB CLXXI f.24v.
41 TB CXCIII f.4; Powell 1987, p.66.
42 Gage 1987, p.60.
43 Gage 1969, p.243 n.94.
44 Farr 1958, pp.39–40, 182–3; for those in Munro of Novar's collection, see Frost and Reeve 1865.
45 Powell 1987, p.70.
46 National Gallery no.270.
47 The composition perhaps served as the basis for Turner's picture *The Loretto Necklace* (B&J 331).
48 Nicholson 1990, pp.274–6.
49 Powell 1987, pp.151–6.
50 Gage 1969, pp.141, 203.
51 Quoted Powell 1987, p.142.
52 Ziff 1982.
53 Cunningham 1843, vol.II, p.300. Note that in the 1830s, Cooper (1838, p.311) expressed reservations about Titian's altarpiece. See also Haydon, who measured Turner's critical success

against reactions to Titian (*Diary*, vol.III, pp.370–2 [3–16 June 1829]).
54 B&J 296, 297, 298. See Butlin, Luther and Warrell 1989, pp.53–5; Brown in Petworth 2002, p.73; Warrell 2003, pp.22–3.
55 Powell 1987, pp.70–1; Gage 1987, pp.32–3; Ziff 1963, pp.135–6.
56 See Martineau and Hope 1983, p.211.
57 Phillips 1833, pp.99–102. An admirer of Titian, he had, like Turner, produced a version of *Venus and Adonis*, which he gave to the Academy as his Diploma picture.
58 Gage 1969, p.91; Kitson 1988; Warrell 1999, pp.41–2; Brown in Petworth 2002, p.76.
59 TB CLXXI f.24v.
60 Shapiro 1972, p.223.
61 B&J 370.
62 TB CCCXIII ff.36v–37 show the Frari and the Scuola Grande di San Rocco.
63 *Oxford Companion*, pp.127–8.
64 Wilton (1979, p.216) considers the influence more Baroque.
65 John (3:14–15).
66 Turner Bequest Schedule 1854, no.314.
67 See Wilton and Turner 1990, pp.132–3; Nicholson 1980.
68 See Petworth 2002, pp.62–3 for B&J 439, which was stimulated by Titian's *Death of Actaeon*. This seems to have been produced for the collector Munro of Novar, who owned versions of many works by Titian, including *Diana and Actaeon* and *Diana and Calisto*.
69 Forrester 1996, pp.45–7.
70 TB CXCVIII ff.82v, 83, 84. Turner makes casual reference to Darnley among the guests at Cowes in 1827 (TB CCXXVI f.80v).

3. From Shakespeare to Byron: Turner and the Literary Vision of Venice

1 Byron identified these influences in stanzas IV and V.
2 Hollier 1831, p.143.
3 See *The Pantheon, Oxford Street, the Morning after the Fire* 1792 (Tate; TB IX A). Curtis Price's suggestion that Turner worked as a scene-painter at the Pantheon has recently been refuted by Judith Milhous (see Price 1987, and Milhous 1999).
4 Hyde and Wilcox 1988.

5 Winifred H. Friedman, *Boydell's Shakespeare Gallery*, PhD dissertation, Harvard University 1974, New York 1976; and Iain Mackintosh and Geoffrey Ashton, *The Georgian Playhouse: Actors, Artists, Audiences and Architecture 1730–1830*, exh. cat., Hayward Gallery, London 1975.
6 See Gross 1992, pp.102ff.; Warrell 1995, pp.142–3.
7 Bonington's sketches, see Noon 1991, pp.296–7.
8 Wilton 1987, pp.246–7. Alfrey (2000) suspected a copy lurked in the studio.
9 Taylor 1841, vol.II, p.190; Cunningham 1843, vol.II, p.305.
10 Greenacre 1988, pp.103–4.
11 Kitson 1988, pp.12–13; Butlin, Luther and Warrell 1989, p.55; Wilton 1989. See George Jones's rough transcription of the painting (Tate; A00333).
12 Petworth 2002.
13 Gage 1980, pp.99–100.
14 Letter from the great-grand-daughter of Lord Egremont to *The Times*, 9 December 1959, partly quoted in B&J, p.186.
15 Tate (N00354). My suggestion that the painting was connected with *Jessica* was taken up in Wilton 1990. Turner was at Petworth in the autumn of 1829, just after a visit to Paris. Newton too is known to have visited Paris that autumn, though it is not known if the visits overlapped, nor whether the artists met then (Leslie 1860, vol.II, p.205).
16 Wilton 1990, p.57.
17 Pointon 2000.
18 *Morning Chronicle*, 3 May 1830.
19 B&J 365.
20 Recognition of Turner's dependence on Canaletto is implicit in the review of the *Morning Herald* on 2 May 1836. See *fig.68*, which is also derived from Canaletto's image.
21 B&J 359; see Davies 1992, pp.77–81.
22 Dickens 1846, p.369, which is derived from Turner's imagery.
23 Sotheby's, 4–12 May 1830, lot 895; noted by Gage in Paris 1983, pp.129–30.
24 The painting was engraved by William Ward in 1804 and exhibited in 1833; see Ashton 1997, p.359.
25 Whittingham 1985.
26 B&J 365; Finberg 1930, p.102.

27 The actual lines are: 'but Beauty still is here. | States fall, arts fade – but Nature doth not die, | Nor yet forget how Venice once was dear…'.

28 Quoted in Sutton 1972, p.25. Turner too combined Venice and Verona on his 1833 tour.

29 B&J 368. See also Wark 1971; Asleson and Bennett 2001, pp.458–63.

30 Two of the other three paintings that year were among his largest formats: B&J 369, 370.

31 TB CLXXV ff.73–4.

32 For the pictorial advantages of white see B&J 340.

33 Asleson and Bennett 2001, p.460.

34 Ziff 1980.

35 Finberg 1930, p.102.

36 *Blackwood's Magazine*, September 1837, p.335.

37 Thornbury 1862, vol.I, p.407.

38 Wilton and Turner 1990. For Lonsdale, see *Oxford Companion*, p.178 and Warrell in Petworth 2002, pp.49–52. See the link Ruskin made between Wordsworth and Turner (*Works*, vol.III, pp.307, 347, 353, 363, 405; *Apollo*, vol.85, [1967], p.42).

39 Thomas Roscoe in the *Landscape Annual for 1830*, (p.202): 'No one can leave Venice without acknowledging the beauty and feeling of Mr Wordsworth's Sonnet'.

40 B&J 138. See Brown 1992; Piggott 1993.

41 Powell 1983.

42 Oxford 1990.

43 Based on TB CLXXV ff.77v, 82v; see also the study TB CCLXXX 108.

44 For this publication's complicated history, see Brown 1992, pp.43ff.

45 W 1225. Turner was paid £26.5s. for the watercolour, while Edward Finden received £37.5s.6d for engraving it.

46 Cooper 1838, p.319; Shelley 1913, vol.II, p.241.

47 W 1222–3.

48 W 1105; see Warrell 1999, pp.82–5.

49 Piggott 1993, p.58.

50 Warrell 1997, pp.193ff.; Warrell 1999, p.90.

51 Plant 2003, pp.88–90. Roscoe also translated a history of Italian painting, published in 1828. However, see Lockett 1985, pp.79 and 90 n.8, which reveals that Roscoe's tour was imaginary.

52 Ruskin *Works*, vol.XIII, p.143; vol.XXXV, pp.294–5.

53 Stainton 1985, p.9.

54 See George 1970, p.205.

PART TWO: DISCOVERING VENICE 1819–40

4. Sketching the City

1 E.g. TB CLXXV f.54v (1819); TB CCCXIV f.47 (1833); TB CCCXIII f.20v (1840).

2 E.g. TB CLXXV ff.61–60v–59v; or 56v–57v–58v; or 52v–51v.

3 See Hyde and Wilcox 1988, p.74, no.47.

4 Finberg 1961, p.262.

5 For the 'Como and Venice' sketchbook and the development of Turner's preparatory watercolours, see Shanes 1997, pp.36–7.

6 Stainton 1985, p.42. However, see TB CLXXV ff.40, 66v, which coincide with the watercolours, while a further sketch on f.54v completes the panorama to the right.

7 TB CLXXVI ff.11, 20.

8 TB CLXXV f.63v does not have sufficient detail for it to have been the source of the watercolour. A faint pencil sketch of boats on the verso of TB CLXXXI f.6 may have been opposite the view of the Doge's Palace in the original sequence, and could perhaps have been recorded during the same sketching session at San Giorgio.

9 Finberg 1930, p.23.

10 In Staley 1968, no.118.

11 Dupret 1989.

12 TB CCXXXIX, inside cover.

13 For Finberg's noteworthy reservations, see 1930, p.24.

14 Lockett 1985, pp.11, 54.

15 Noon 1991, pp.11, 203–16.

16 *Oxford Companion*, p.27.

17 Noon 1991, p.213; Warrell 1997, pp.181ff.

18 Greenacre and Stoddard 1991.

19 Bond 1990.

20 E.g. Sotheby's, 11 July 1990, lot 87.

21 See, however, the sketch of the chapel of San Dominic in Santi Giovanni e Paolo (Sotheby's, 24 November 1977, lot 186).

22 Hill 2000; Powell 1995, pp.122–4.

23 E.g. Ruskin *Works*, vol.XXXVI, p.33; Shapiro 1972, pp.172–7; and Ruskin *Diaries*, vol.II, p.465.

24 Shapiro 1972, pp.220, 233; Scharf 1968, pp.95–100.

25 Ritter 1994, pp.26–7, 199.

26 Scharf 1968, pp.100–2, 338; Gage 1969, pp.120–2, 184, 253; Hamber 1996, p.193; *Oxford Companion*, pp.185, 228.

5. Contemporary Approaches to Venice in British Art

1 Paraphrased in George 1970.

2 Quoted in Sutton 1972, p.13.

3 See TB CCXI f.10; the full group is W 718–24.

4 However, see Hakewill's unused sketch (Cubberley, Herrmann and Scott 1992, p.390, no.6.26).

5 E.g. W 402, 405 and B&J 236.

6 TB CLXXV ff.73, 74; Finberg 1930, pp.46, 71, 75.

7 The Hakewill engraving has only five chimneys instead of seven. For Turner's 'unpardonable offences against the Goddess of Architecture', see Finberg 1930, p.71.

8 Sotheby's, 15 July 1964, lot 50; not mentioned in W 725 or Dawson 1988, pp.104–5. The watercolour is loosely based on TB CLXXV ff.80v–81.

9 Liversidge and Farington 1993, pp.41, 64–5, 123, 172–3.

10 Fitzwilliam Museum, Cambridge: no.1054, ff.67, 68, dated 26 and 27 October. See also Wilcox 1990, pp.41–2.

11 This work is the strongest contender for the Premium Picture of 1827, sold to Countess de Grey. It is roughly the same size as the view of the Doge's Palace of 1830, which was also priced at 60 guineas (see Wilton and Lyles 1993, pl.292). Other years in which the watercolour could have been exhibited are 1838 (222) or 1843 (15), but the prices paid for those works seem too low for a work on this scale. The watercolour is based on a pencil sketch in the Fitzwilliam Museum, Cambridge (no.1418).

12 Noon 1991, pp.72, 74, 258.

13 For the watercolour see Halsby 1990; the Witt Library has a photograph of Prout's pencil sketch.

14 Noon 1991, p.211 (and p.73, fig.61).

15 Noon 1991, p.211.

16 *Fraser's Magazine*, vol.XII, no.LXVII, 1835, pp.52–5.

17 Van der Merwe 1979, pp.91–2.

18 Ibid. pp.111–12; B&J, pp.200–1.

19 Barbara Reise's notes, Tate Archive, pp.9–10; Gage 1987, pp.133–5.

20 *Arnold's Magazine*, July 1833.

21 *Arnold's Magazine*, August 1833, p.319; fully transcribed in Ziff 1986.

22 B&J 350.

23 B&J, pp.200–1.

24 B&J 352. The picture seems to have been owned by Henry Rice, appearing at his sale on 24 April 1845 (lot 889). It may then have been acquired by Windus.

25 B&J 356; Hayes 1992, pp.274–7.

26 *Childe Harold's Pilgrimage*, Canto IV, stanza XVII, lines 6–9.

27 R 752; TB CCVIII V.

28 B&J 361; Powell 1991, p.126.

29 B&J 362; Finberg 1930, p.85.

30 TB CCCXIV f.27v.

31 Constable and Links 1976, no.169.

32 Ruskin *Works*, vol.XII, p.468; vol.XIII, p.498; Shapiro 1972, p.209.

33 For Ruskin's appreciation of Turner's painting, see Hewison, Warrell and Wildman 2000, p.54.

34 *The Times*, 11 May 1836, quoted in Brown 1981, p.45.

35 Wilcox 1990, p.46.

36 B&J 383.

37 *Blackwood's Magazine*, September 1840, p.374.

38 *Spectator*, 16 May 1840, p.476.

39 Compare Hewison, Warrell and Wildman 2000, p.95. The picture draws on the following sketches: TB CCCXIV ff.5v, 24v, 29, 30v.

PART THREE: LOCATING TURNER'S VENICE

6. Monumental Venice

1 TB CLXXI f.29.

2 Ruskin *Works*, vol.IX, p.38.

3 Hills 1999, pp.65–7.

4 TB CCCXIII f.4.

5 TB CCCXIII ff.60, 61.

6 Plant 2003, pp.37, 82.

7 First selected for display by Ralph Wornum in 1868. For Ruskin's own sketches of the Doge's Palace, see Hewison 1978.

8 Lorenzetti 1926, pp.243–4; Plant 2003, p.27.

9 TB CCCXIV f.43; TB CCCXIII f.2v.

10 Norwich 1982, pp.223–9.

11 London 1974, p.155; Stainton 1985, p.50.

12 Moore 1860, p.226; Sass 1818, p.273.

13 TB CLXXV ff.41v, 43, 45.

14 TB CCCXIV ff.51v, 52v, 53; see Vio 1999, p.84.

15 TB CCCXVIII 8 (Stainton 1985, pl.15).

16 TB CCCXIX 4. This sheet was originally linked to a view in Germany, sketched during the return leg of the 1840 tour (see Powell 1995, p.161). The ragged top edge of the sheet matches up with that on TB CCCXIX 10 (*fig.125*).

17 Plant 2003, pp.65–6.

18 Constable and Links 1976, nos.19, 20–1, 47, 525–7. TB CCCXIV f.44 anticipates the view depicted in *figs.127–8*. Framing arches also appear in TB CCCXVIII 27 (Stainton 1985, pl.26) and CCCXIX 9.

19 TB CCCXX f.91v.

20 Dickens 1846, p.367; see also Cooper 1838, p.313.

21 TB CLXXV f.55; TB CCCXIV f.73.

22 Kowalczyk 2001, pp.70–2.

23 Stainton 1985, p.26.

24 Admiral Lorenzo Sferra, of the Museo Storico Navale, has kindly confirmed my suggestion.

25 Warrell 1995, p.148. In 1975 it was one of two watercolours reproduced as stamps to commemorate the bicentenary of Turner's birth.

7. Venice after Dark

1 Constable and Links 1976, nos.359–60.
2 Moore 1860, p.227.
3 For Disraeli in 1826, see Norwich 1990, p.47.
4 Blessington 1840, p.126.
5 Thornbury 1862, vol.II, p.340. For Turner's moonlight subjects, see Taft and Loukes 1998.
6 Dorment and MacDonald 1994, pp.120–2.
7 Grieve 2000; MacDonald 2001.
8 See, however, TB CCCXVIII 1 (fig.123), 3 (Stainton 1985, pl.10), 26 (fig.127), 27 (Stainton 1985, pl.26), 29 (fig.140), which featured in the regional loan collections from 1869.
9 Royal Academy 1835, no.235; see Stainton 1985, p.49.
10 B&J 363 (Royal Academy 1835, no.234).
11 Venice 1979.
12 See TB CCCXVIII 19 (Stainton 1985, pl.16) and TB CCCXIX 1.
13 Hills 1999, p.224.
14 GPdiV, 9–20 September 1819.
15 Ritter 1994, p.189; Busetto 1995, nos.92, 99.
16 Sand 1966, vol.II, p.264.
17 B&J 427; note forms dotted across foreground like 'cabbages'.
18 Stainton 1985, p.47.
19 I am grateful to David Laven for sharing his research on this aspect of Venetian history.
20 Blessington 1840, pp.146–7; see Warrell 2003, pp.24–7.
21 Thornbury 1862, vol.II, pp.168ff.
22 Links 1994, pp.110–11.
23 Links 1966, cover; Wilcox 1990, p.57.
24 Dorment and MacDonald 1994, p.179.
25 Numbered by Turner consecutively 35 and 36. Though TB CCCXVIII 5 is annotated as 38, it is not possible to reconstruct a full sequence.
26 Stainton 1985, no.56. See Sammartini and Resini 2002, p.213.
27 Armstrong 1902, p.282, not accepted by Wilton 1979, nor Hartley 1984. However, see Nugent and Croal 1997–8, p.104.
28 TB CCCXVIII 10 (Stainton 1985, pl.28).

8. The Grand Canal

1 Links 1971.
2 TB CCCXIV f.78v.
3 TB CLXXV ff.83v, 85; TB CCCXIV ff.79v, 81v.
4 National Gallery no.163, acquired in 1838.
5 Plant 1996, p.145.
6 Not included in Wilton's 1979 catalogue, but listed by Armstrong (1902, p.282) and Finberg (1930, p.161). It formerly belonged to J.E. Taylor, and measured around 22.2 x 31.7 cm. It was last documented when sold for £3,780 at Christie's in July 1912.
7 See TB CLXXV f.76v; TB CCCXIV ff.59, 77v, 82v; TB CCCX f.14.
8 Links 1971, Part 1, no.VIII.
9 Links 1971, Part 1, no.VII.
10 See also TB CCCXVI 32.
11 See also TB CCCXVII 26.
12 Ruskin Works, vol.XI, pp.43ff. (Quill 2000, p.168).
13 This idea will be discussed more fully in Toronto 2004.
14 TB CLXXV f.89v; the following watercolours have previously been identified as views of the Palazzo Tasca-Papafava (Stainton 1985, pls.37, 39–40).
15 Powell 1995, p.155; Bower 1999, pp.88ff.
16 TB CCCXIII f.57v.
17 TB CLXXV f.72v; TB CCCXIV f.84v.
18 Gage 1980, p.201; Warrell 1999.
19 See TB CCCXIV ff.86–86v; TB CCCXIII f.64v.
20 TB CCCXIII ff.36v–37.
21 See Nepi Scirè 1998; Farr 1958, p.40.
22 Warrell 1995, p.107.
23 Clark 1974, pp.276–7.
24 See n.18 above.
25 W 1368. This could well be the watercolour that Finberg described as 'Sunset: Venice. 8 3/4 x 12 1/2 [i.e. 22.2 x 31.7 cm]. On the Grand Canal, with gondolas and figures; S. Giorgio [sic – Salute] on the left. J.E. Taylor, sale 1912, £1365' (1930, p.161).
26 TB CLXXV f.54[v]; TB CCCXI f.81; TB CCCXIV f.80; TB CCCXX f.17v; TB CCCXIII ff.20v, 58.
27 Hills 1999, p.9.

9. The Giudecca Canal

1 See Giordani 2002, pp.617ff.; M. Laven 2002.
2 TB CLXXVI f.18v–19.
3 TB CCCXIV ff.19v–23v, 38v–40v.
4 See TB CCCX ff.6v–9, and TB CCCXIII ff.17, 30v–33.
5 Tate (N00407).
6 The 'V' could also stand for 'vessels'.
7 The same pink appears in TB CCCXV 38.
8 See also TB CCCXVI 2 (Stainton 1985, pl.59).
9 See B&J 390. For another picture with a possible connection with Chantrey, see Warrell 2002, p.154.
10 Once a Week, 1 February 1862, p.164. For other paintings with floating debris, see B&J 139, 286.
11 Literary Gazette, 8 May 1841.
12 Athenaeum, 5 June 1841, p.443.
13 Warrell 1997, p.81.
14 Gage 1980, p.182, where the letter is dated to 20 April, though a 'Wednesday 20th' fell only in January 1841.
15 Giordani 2002, p.601.
16 B&J 228.
17 Murray 1835, vol.V, p.155; Ruskin Works, vol.X, p.443 and vol.XI, p.399.
18 Gallo and Spadavecchia 1994, pp.28–33; see also B&J, p.242.
19 Constable and Links 1976 n.644.
20 See B&J 237–8, 340, 349–50 and W 1006.
21 Haskell 1976, p.8ff. Other pictures of Venetian artists from this period include those of Titian by R.T. Bone, W. Simson, J. Stephanoff and W. Dyce (respectively, BI 1828, RA 1840, RA 1844, and RA 1857), while Giorgione was portrayed by T. Von Holst, A. Geddes and J. Reed (RA 1832, RA 1841, and RA 1850).
22 Gage 1969, p.96; in 1844 the National Gallery bought Beckford's Doge Leonardo Loredan; the collection at Harewood included a Madonna and Child; while Munro of Novar owned a picture described as 'Virgin holding Child by the Right Foot, 12 1/2 x 9 3/4'.
23 Gage 1969, p.243 n.91. See Jaffé 2003, pp.101–11.
24 B&J 393.
25 R 668/677a; copies were with Spink in 1921 and Knoedler in 1944.
26 Musolino 1962, p.48.
27 Warrell 1995, pp.110–11.
28 See n.5 above.

29 A third possibility is that the church is intended to be the Gesuiti, with the island of San Michele to the north, though this would remove Turner some distance from the vicinity in which the rest of his studies were made in this roll sketchbook.
30 10 May 1845, p.451.
31 See B&J 419 for the original, though less plausible, identification.
32 The fullest account of St Benedict's life is Book II of Gregory's Dialogues.
33 B&J 294.
34 Ruskin seems to have copied it in oil (Diaries, vol.I, p.263 [8 February 1844; not 1841 as in Finberg 1930, p.147]).
35 Ruskin Works, vol.XIII, pp.164–6.
36 Extracted from National Gallery Reports. Note a concentration of interest in the picture around 1876–7, and then again in 1888–92.

10. The Island of San Giorgio Maggiore

1 Laven 2002, pp.100–2.
2 Lorenzetti 1926, p.787.
3 James 1882, p.16.
4 See Munday 1996, p.186; Wildenstein 1997, nos. 1745–9, 1768–9.
5 Cundall 1908, pp.66–7.
6 TB CCCXIII ff.16v, 22, 22v, 25v, 29, 32, 41v.
7 W 1367. Armstrong listed another watercolour of San Giorgio Maggiore on grey paper, exhibited at the Guildhall in 1899, when in the collection of the Revd Stopford Brooke, who also owned fig.187. It was apparently a 'Hasty memorandum of last flush of sunset', measuring around 12.7 x 22.2 cm. These dimensions do not correspond with any other Venetian subject on grey paper, though the sheet may have been trimmed (Armstrong 1902, p.282). No further record of it is known after 1930 (Finberg 1930, p.160), though it was presumably also in the Brooke family collection until the 1980s when its companion was sold.
8 Ruskin Works, vol.XIII, p.558.
9 E.g. Wilton 1975, no.251, as 'Campanile of St Mark's and the Doge's Palace'.
10 Ruskin Works, vol.XIII, p.296; Powell 1989.
11 E.g. TB CCCLXIV 311.

12 The documented history of this work starts with the T.S. Kennedy sale, 18 May 1895 (lot 89), when the drawing was bought by Agnew, and then sold to J.F. Schwann. However, Finberg and Armstrong both speculated that the original source for the drawing was Thomas Griffith. After Schwann, the watercolour was owned by L.J. Friedlander, who passed it to Dagnall G. Ells some time before 1930. It then remained in the Ells family until 1982, when it was sold at Christie's, 15 June 1982 (Armstrong 1902, p.282; Finberg 1930, pp.145,161, pl.XXVIII).
13 Ruskin Works, vol.XIII, pp.53–4, 74–5.
14 Stainton expressed reservations about the identity of the church (1985, no.76); see also Dawson 1988, p.110. If not a Venetian subject, it may be a scene on one of the Italian lakes from a year or two later.
15 Warrell 1995, pp.104–5.
16 Stainton 1985, no.77.
17 TB CCCXIII f.21v.

11. The Bacino and the Riva degli Schiavoni

1 Compiled from the GPdiV between 22 August and 5 September.
2 Dickens 1846, pp.364, 367.
3 TB CLXXV f.40. See Finberg 1930, pp.24–7; Stainton 1985, pp.33–4. For the view of San Giorgio Maggiore, Turner may have referred to TB CCCXIV f.27, as its page is marked with blue colour.
4 Lorenzetti 1926, p.538.
5 Paris 1983, pp.136–7 and Gage 1999, p.163.
6 See B&J 396.
7 7 May 1842, p.409.
8 Ruskin Works, vol.XIII, pp.560–8.
9 Neither watercolour was included in the displays at the National Gallery until after 1890.
10 Quoted in Sutton 1972, p.25.
11 See Egerton 1995; Warrell 2002, p.83.
12 Plant 2002, pp.125–6.
13 TB CCLXXX 150.
14 Canto IV, stanza III.
15 9 May 1843, p.6; see also Finberg 1930, p.148.
16 Compare Munday 1996, p.157.
17 See also TB CCCXVII 15.
18 See From Gainsborough to Turner, exh. cat., Andrew Wyld, London 1984, no.57.
19 W 1373; Milner 1990, no.31
20 Hills 1999, pp.67–8.

21 B&J 239.

22 W 1364.

23 B&J 97.

24 B&J 507 depicts essentially the same subject as TB CCCXVI 34 (Stainton 1985, pl.66); B&J 508 is like CCCXVI 14 (fig.224).

25 17 May 1845, p.496.

26 W 1374; Campbell 1999, no.31.

27 See photographs by Böhm (negs. 3173, 3415) and Alinari (negs.12533, 12535). See Ruskin's comments in Shapiro 1972, p.202; see also Horatio Brown, quoted Norwich 1990, p.232.

28 Warrell 1995, pp.97–8.

29 B&J 402, which includes the more muddled, alternative version of these lines, which appeared in some copies of the catalogue. Existing copies suggest the version given here was the more usual.

30 Samuel Carter Hall, The Book of Gems: The Poets and Artists of Great Britain, 1838. See Gage 1969, pp.145–6. It is interesting to note that a connection with Shelley was discernible to Turner's contemporaries, for when the painting was later displayed at the National Gallery one reviewer commented that it was 'a poem founded on Italian experiences, but dreamy and ideal, and of the seventh heaven as much as if it were a scene from Shelley's "Alastor"' (Athenaeum, 15 November 1856, p.1407).

31 17 June 1843, p.570.

32 Art Union, June 1843.

33 Adrian Stokes quoted in Plant 1996, pp.158–60; see also B&J 402 for Stuckey's suggestion that the boat is a self-portrait.

34 See Epilogue, n.5 below.

35 Shapiro 1972, p.202.

36 TB CCCXVI 23 (Stainton 1985, pl.72), 30 (Stainton 1985, pl.71), 31 (Stainton 1985, pl.79).

37 Finberg 1930, pp.125–6.

38 Warrell 1995, pp.101–2.

39 Quoted in Plant 2003, p.61.

12. Away from the City

1 Collins Baker 1920, no.586.

2 Compare Martineau and Robison 1994, p.98.

3 Laven 2002, pp.50, 96, 100–2.

4 E.g. Shanes 1990, pp.69, 120–1, 203, 271.

5 Warrell 1995, p.98.

6 W 1484 has also been linked with Venice. This was photographed by J. Hogarth when it was 'in the collection of Henry Vaughan' as 'A Storm, Venice'. As this work is not otherwise known to have belonged to Vaughan, this may seem to be a simple confusion of titles with the watercolour now at Edinburgh (fig.255). However, that work was also photographed by Hogarth: the print is dated 1862 and titled, 'Venice from the Lagoon, Squally Weather (Trieste Steamer going into Venice)'.

7 See Egerton 1995; Rodner 1997; Warrell 1997, pp.64–6, 86.

8 Constable and Links 1976, nos.365–6; Morassi 1973, nos.615–17.

9 Engraved by Ruskin for Modern Painters, vol.V (1860; Works, vol.VII, pl.67, opposite p.149).

10 He may have been recalling the feluccas of the Neapolitan coast (TB CCLXXX 143, 167).

11 Stainton 1985, p.34.

12 Ruskin Works, vol.XIII, pp.498–9; Shapiro 1972, p.205; Bradley 1955, p.112.

13 James 1872, pp.52–3; see also Gowing 1966, pp.17–19.

14 Stainton 1985, p.26.

15 B&J 385, 400.

16 Trevor-Roper 1970, pp.92–3. Howard Hodgkin has spoken perceptively about the British unease with strong colour, noting that 'I think the reason that so few British artists have used colour since the pre-Raphaelites is that the British regard it as slightly pornographic. Look at Turner's sunsets – they're the colour of tumescence really.' Interview, Financial Times, 17 August 2002, p.7.

17 See Gage 1984.

18 Warrell 1995, pp.115–16.

19 Finberg 1909, p.1020. Finberg (1930, p.159) lists a work entitled 'Approach to Venice', which had been sold at Christie's, 26 March 1920 (lot 48). This measured 24.2 x 30.4 cm, and was presumably painted on one of the sheets of Ansell paper of these dimensions that occur in the Bequest.

20 However, see Stainton 1985, no.83. For an equally vibrant eastern sky at sunset see Munday 1996, colour pl.116.

21 See Canto IV, stanza XXVII. Turner misquoted the same passage for his 1839 exhibit, Modern Rome – Campo Vaccino (B&J 379), though there he preserved the word 'divides'. See Alfrey 2000.

22 It could serve as an illustration of stanza II, lines 1–4.

23 R 679.

24 The Times, 8 May 1844, p.7; Spectator, 11 May, p.451.

25 Ruskin Works, vol.III, p.250.

26 Ruskin Works, vol.XIII, p.166.

27 Finberg 1930, p.126.

28 B&J, p.266.

29 For commentaries on all these works, and those of 1846, see B&J, pp.263–7; Butlin 2001.

30 Spectator, 24 May 1845, p.498.

31 Lloyd 1880, p.22.

32 Ruskin Works, vol.XIII, pp.140–1.

33 Thornbury 1877, p.124.

34 Oxford Companion, pp.185–6.

35 See B&J 415.

36 B&J 414, 415.

37 Morning Chronicle, 7 May 1845.

38 Hitherto identified as Venice from the Public Gardens (see Butlin 2001, p.24).

39 Gage 1980, pp.207–8.

40 Gage 1980, p.200. See the letter by Wethered to Etty, probably written in the autumn of 1844, B&J 412. In this Wethered seeks a work which will 'overawe and keep [the] Turner in subjection'.

41 Gage 1980, pp.201–2; see Warrell 1999.

42 Gage 1986, p.6, no.274a.

43 Shapiro 1972, p.171 n.2, a partial transcription of the letter in the Ruskin Library at Lancaster. It may be significant that Ruskin senior talks of 'J McCracken', whom Shapiro identifies as John McCracken of the firm of Francis McCracken & Co. This would complicate the commission of the Venice picture still further. However, it is possible that the elder Ruskin was mistakenly thinking of James McCracken, who was one of two brothers who packed and shipped works for the Royal Academy, a slip easily made in the circumstances (see Macleod 1996, pp.447–8).

44 Punch, vol.VIII, June 1845, p.233. The sketch of 'Venice by gaslight', if read in reverse, is almost a direct transcription of fig.265.

45 The Times, 6 May 1845, p.6.

46 Spectator, 10 May 1845, p.450.

47 Gage 1980, p.208.

48 See Warrell 1995, pp.152–3. The sale of the pictures from Windus is the root of the ensuing confusion of titles and dates. When the canvases were auctioned by Christie's in 1853 they were mistakenly identified as the 1846 pair, even though the exhibit numbers cited in the auction catalogue are actually those of 1845 (i.e. nos.117 and 162; see 20 June 1853, lots 1 and 2).

49 Gage 1980, pp.213–14. These identify Wethered as the projected owner of '(St Martino) returning from the Ball – and not (St Martha) going to the Ball which is for Mr Macracken of Belfast'.

50 T.S. Cooper, My Life, 1890, vol.II, pp.2–3.

51 B&J 423, 425.

52 Spectator, 9 May 1846, p.452.

53 Art Union, June 1846; quoted B&J, p.267.

54 The double campanile is the most striking feature of the image as there are few churches in Venice with more than one. The church on the island of San Servolo is another example, but the surrounding buildings in Turner's view do not fit the real topography, even if the dome and campanile on the right are then thought of as San Pietro di Castello, a similarly problematic solution.

55 Though if the island of San Giorgio in Alga is accepted as the subject of the San Martino painting of 1845, it would lie behind the viewer in this picture.

56 See Michiel 1829, vol.II, pp.219ff.; Lorenzetti 1926, p.561; Giordani 2002, p.564; Sammartini and Resini 2002, p.237.

57 Constable and Links 1989, no.360.

58 If Turner had wanted to make this point more directly, he could have paired Santa Marta with the church of Santa Maria dell'Anconetta, on the island of the same name near Marghera, not far to the west of these subjects.

59 1846; undated cutting in A.J. Finberg's papers (Tate Prints and Drawings Room).

60 8 August 1846; see Apollo, vol.85 (1967), p.42, letter IV.

61 Gage 1980, pp.214–15.

62 This point was noted by Evelyn Joll but not taken further (B&J, p.267). Since this section was written a similar solution has been proposed by David Hill in a lecture at the Paul Mellon Centre.

Epilogue: The Legacy of Turner's Venice

1 Finberg 1930, p.vii.

2 Ruskin Works, vol.III, pp.245–58.

3 Ruskin Works, vol.XIII, pp.231–316.

4 Shapiro 1972, p.202.

5 See Hewison 1978, p.40 and Hewison, Warrell and Wildman 2000, pp.68–9, for his four copies of The Sun of Venice; see Diaries, vol.I, p.337 for his sketched recollections of St Benedetto (17 May 1846) and the earlier entry, p.263 (8 February 1841).

6 See B&J 397, 402, 406, 412.

7 Shapiro 1972, p.202; Ruskin Works, vol.XIII, pp.164–5; Bradley 1955, p.112.

8 Hewison 1978.

9 Hewison, Warrell and Wildman 2000, no.107.

10 Bradley 1955, p.112.

11 Warrell 1995, pp.21–8.

12 Ruskin Works, vol.XIII, pp.557–60.

13 Probably quite recent acquisitions, they appear at the end of the list of Ruskin's collection in Thornbury's Life (vol.II, p.396). They may relate to a payment of £1,600 on 15 March 1861 for an unidentified group of 'Turner Drawings', though this would suggest that they were bought specifically to be given away (Account Book, Ruskin Library, Lancaster: MS 29).

14 See Away from the City n.9 above.

15 Murray 1847, p.311; Plant 2003, pp.109–11.

16 Munday 1996, pp.151–92.

17 For Roberts's version of the 1833 picture of Canaletti Painting, see Apollo, July 1968. Another version was made by William Callow, see Apollo, March 1974. Photographs of both in Witt Library.

18 Bettagno 1997, pp.286–7; Anderson 1998, pp.121–3, 139, 146.

19 Clark 1980, p.9.

20 Morand 1996, pp.238–42, 246–51.

21 See Martigues 1995.

22 Quoted in Gage 1969, pp.192–3; Smith 2000, p.11.

23 Ibid. p.193.

24 Ibid.

25 House 2001, no.25.

26 Paris 1963, nos.63–5, 71.

27 Patin in Bettagno 1997, pp.146–53.

28 Wildenstein 1996, nos.1742, 1751–4, 1768–9.

29 Clark 1974, pp.276–7.

30 Schulz 1980, p.416; Plant 1996, p.162.

31 B&J 414–15, 423, 426.

32 Gage 1980, p.203; Upstone 1993, pp.52–4.

33 See Wilton 1987, p.229.

34 Illustrated London News, 12 October 1844, p.228; The Times, 9 October 1844, p.4.

Bibliography

Alfrey 2000
Nicholas Alfrey, 'Reading into Turner', *Turner Society News*, no.85, Aug. 2000, pp.6–10

Anderson 1998
Nancy K. Anderson (ed.), *Thomas Moran*, exh. cat., National Gallery of Art, Washington 1998

Armstrong 1902
Walter Armstrong, *Turner*, London 1902

Ashton 1997
Geoffrey Ashton, *Pictures in the Garrick Club: A catalogue of the paintings, drawings, watercolours and sculpture*, ed. Kalman A. Bunim and Andrew Wilton, London 1997

Asleson and Bennett 2001
Robyn Asleson and Shelley M. Bennett, *British Paintings at the Huntington*, New Haven and London 2001

Baetjer and Links 1989
Katharine Baetjer and J.G. Links (eds.), *Canaletto*, exh. cat., Metropolitan Museum of Art, New York 1989

Bailey 1997
Anthony Bailey, *Standing in the Sun: A Life of J.M.W. Turner*, London 1997

Battiliana 1981
Marilla Battiliana, *The English Writers in Venice, Scrittori Inglesi a Venezia 1350–1950*, trans. Dario Calimani, Venice 1981

Beckett 1967
R.B. Beckett (ed.), *John Constable's Correspondence: V: Various Friends, with Charles Boner and the Artist's Children*, Suffolk Records Society, XI, Ipswich 1967

Beddington 2001
Charles Beddington, *Luca Carlevarijs's Views of Venice*, exh. cat., Timken Museum of Art, San Diego 2001

Berlin 1998
Claude Keisch, Peter-Klaus Schuster and Moritz Wullen (eds.), *Fontane und die bildende Kunst*, exh. cat., Nationalgalerie, Berlin 1998

Bettagno 1997
Alessandro Bettagno (ed.), *Venice da Stato a Mito*, exh. cat., Fondazione Giorgio Cini, Venice 1997

Bicknell and Guiterman 1987
Peter Bicknell and Helen Guiterman, 'The Turner Collector: Elhanan Bicknell', *Turner Studies*, vol.7, no.1, Summer 1987, pp.34–44

Black 1992
Jeremy Black, *The British Abroad: The Grand Tour in the Eighteenth Century*, Stroud, Gloucestershire 1992

Blessington 1840
Marguerite, Countess of Blessington, *The Idler in Italy*, 3 vols., London 1840

Bomford and Finaldi 1998
David Bomford and Gabriele Finaldi, *Venice through Canaletto's Eyes*, exh. cat., National Gallery 1998

Bond 1990
Steve Bond, *James Holland: The Forgotten Artist*, Leek 1990

Bower 1990
Peter Bower, *Turner's Drawing Papers: A Study of the Manufacture, Selection and Use of his Drawing Papers 1787–1820*, exh. cat., Tate Gallery 1990

Bower 1999
Peter Bower, *Turner's Later Papers: A Study of the Manufacture, Selection and Use of his Drawing Papers 1820–1851*, exh. cat., Tate Gallery 1999

Bradley 1955
John Lewis Bradley, *Ruskin's Letters from Venice 1851–2*, New Haven 1955, reprinted 1978

Bromberg 1993
Ruth Bromberg, *Canaletto's Etchings. Revised and Enlarged Edition of the Catalogue Raisonné*, San Francisco 1993

Brown 1981
David Blayney Brown, *Augustus Wall Callcott*, exh. cat., Tate Gallery 1981

Brown 1992
David Blayney Brown, *Turner and Byron*, exh. cat., Tate Gallery 1992

Busetto 1995
Giorgio Busetto, *Cento Scene di Vita Veneziana: Pietro Longhi e Gabriel Bella alla Querini Stampalia*, exh. cat., Palazzo Grassi-Palazzo Aperto, Venice 1995

B&J
Martin Butlin and Evelyn Joll, *The Paintings of J.M.W. Turner*, 2 vols., London and New Haven 1977, revised 2nd ed. 1984

Butlin 1996
Martin Butlin, 'Turner and Tradition', *Turner Society News*, no.74, Dec. 1996, pp.8–11

Butlin 2001
Martin Butlin, *Turner's Venice: Going to the Ball (San Martino); Returning from the Ball (St. Martha)*, exh. cat., Mallett & Son, London 2001

Butlin, Luther and Warrell 1989
Martin Butlin, Mollie Luther and Ian Warrell, *Turner at Petworth: Painter and Patron*, London 1989

Calimari 1981
Dario Calimari (ed.), *English Writers and Venice 1350–1950*, Venice 1981

Campbell 1993
Mungo Campbell, *Turner in the National Gallery of Scotland*, Edinburgh 1993

Chateaubriand c.1840
François-René, Vicomte de Chateaubriand, *Mémoires d'outre-tombe*, Paris c.1840

Clark 1974
Kenneth Clark, *Another Part of the Wood: A Self-Portrait*, London 1974

Clark 1980
Carol Clark, *Thomas Moran: Watercolours of the American West*, Austin, Texas 1980

Clegg 1981
Jeanne Clegg, *Ruskin and Venice*, London 1981

Collins Baker 1920
C.H. Collins Baker, *A Catalogue of the Petworth Collection of Pictures in the Possession of Lord Leconfield*, London 1920

Constable and Links 1976
W.G. Constable, rev. J.G. Links, *Canaletto: Giovanni Antonio Canal 1697–1768*, 2 vols., 2nd ed., Oxford 1976 (3rd ed., with supplement by J.G. Links, Oxford 1989)

Cooper 1838
James Fenimore Cooper, *Excursions in Italy*, Paris 1838

Cosgrove 1982
Denis Cosgrove, 'The Myth and the Stones of Venice: An historical geography of a symbolic landscape', *Journal of Historical Geography*, vol.2, 1982, p.164

Crary 1990
Jonathan Crary, *Techniques of the Observer. On Vision and Modernity in the Nineteenth Century*, Cambridge (Mass.) and London 1990

Cubberley, Herrmann and Scott 1992
Tony Cubberley, Luke Herrmann and Valerie Scott, *Twilight of the Grand Tour. A Catalogue of the Drawings by James Hakewill in the British School at Rome Library*, Rome 1992

Cundall 1908
H.M. Cundall (ed.), *William Callow: An Autobiography*, London 1908

Cunningham 1843
Allan Cunningham, *The Life of Sir David Wilkie*, 3 vols., London 1843

Daru 1817/19
Pierre Daru, *Histoire de la République de Venise*, Paris 1817/19

Davies 1992
Maurice Davies, *Turner as Professor: The Artist and Linear Perspective*, exh. cat., Tate Gallery 1992

Dawson 1988
Barbara Dawson, *Turner in the National Gallery of Ireland*, Dublin 1988

Dickens 1846
Charles Dickens, *Pictures from Italy*, London 1846 (Everyman ed., London and Rutland, Vermont 1997, ed. Leonée Ormond)

Dickens Letters
Kathleen Tillotson (ed.), *The Letters of Charles Dickens*, vol.4 (1844–6), Oxford 1977

Dorment and MacDonald 1994
Richard Dorment and Margaret F. MacDonald (eds.), *James McNeill Whistler*, exh. cat., Tate Gallery 1994

Dupret 1989
Dupret, Marcel-Etienne, 'Turner's "Little Liber"', *Turner Studies*, vol.9, no.1, Summer 1989, pp.32–47

Egerton 1995
Judy Egerton, *Making and Meaning: Turner, The Fighting Temeraire*, exh. cat., National Gallery 1995

Eglin 2001
John Eglin, *Venice Transfigured: The Myth of Venice in British Culture, 1660–1797*, Palgrave, New York and Basingstoke 2001

Eustace 1813
Revd John Chetwode Eustace, *A Tour through Italy*, 2 vols., London 1813

Evans 1992
Mark Evans, *Impressions of Venice from Turner to Monet*, exh. cat., National Museum of Wales, Cardiff 1992

Farington *Diary*
The Diary of Joseph Farington, I–VI, ed. Kenneth Garlick and Angus Macintyre; VII–XVI, ed. Kathryn Cave, New Haven and London 1978–84

Farr 1958
Dennis Farr, *William Etty*, London 1958

Finberg 1909
A.J. Finberg, *A Complete Inventory of the Drawings of the Turner Bequest*, 2 vols., London 1909

Finberg 1930
A.J. Finberg, *In Venice with Turner*, London 1930 (copies at the Tate and in the British Museum Print Rooms have manuscript annotations by C.F. Bell)

Finberg 1961
A.J. Finberg, *The Life of J.M.W. Turner*, Oxford 1939 (2nd ed., revised by Hilda Finberg, Oxford 1961)

Finley 1980
Gerald Finley, *Landscapes of Memory: Turner as Illustrator to Scott*, London 1980

Forrester 1996
Gillian Forrester, *Turner's 'Drawing Book': The Liber Studiorum*, exh. cat., Tate Gallery 1996

Francis 1847
J.G. Francis, *Notes from a Journal kept in Italy and Sicily, during the years 1844, 1845 and 1846*, London 1847

Franzoi 1991
Umberto Franzoi, *Palaces and Churches on the Grand Canal in Venice*, Venice 1991

Frost and Reeve 1865
W.E. Frost and H. Reeve, *A Complete Catalogue of Paintings, Water-Colour Drawings, and Prints, in the Collection of the late Hugh Andrew Johnstone Munro, Esq., of Novar, at the time of his death deposited in his house, no.6 Hamilton Place, London; with some additional paintings at Novar*, London 1865

Gage 1969
John Gage, *Colour in Turner: Poetry and Truth*, London 1969

Gage 1974
John Gage, 'Turner and Stourhead: The Making of a Classicist', *Art Quarterly*, vol.37, 1974, pp.83–4

Gage 1980
John Gage (ed.), *The Collected Correspondence of J.M.W. Turner*, Oxford 1980

Gage 1984
John Gage, 'Turner's Annotated Books: "Goethe's Theory of Colours"', *Turner Studies*, vol.4, no.2, Winter 1984, pp.34–52

Gage 1986
John Gage, 'Further Correspondence of J.M.W. Turner', *Turner Studies*, vol.6, no.1, Summer 1986, pp.2–9

Gage 1987
John Gage, *J.M.W. Turner: 'A Wonderful Range of Mind'*, New Haven and London 1987

Gage 1987a
John Gage, 'Turner in Venice', in J.C. Eade (ed.), *Projecting the Landscape*, Humanities Research Centre, Australian National University, Canberra 1987, pp.72–7

Gage 1999
John Gage, *Colour and Meaning, Art, Science and Symbolism*, London 1999

Gallo and Spadavecchia
Andrea Gallo and Fiorella Spadavecchia, *Chiesa del Redentore: arte e devozione*, Venice 1994

George 1970
Hardy George, 'Turner in Venice', unpublished MA thesis, Courtauld Institute of Art, London 1970

George 1971
Hardy George, 'Turner in Venice', *Art Bulletin*, vol.53, March 1971, pp.84–7

George 1984
Hardy George, 'Turner in Europe in 1833', *Turner Studies*, vol.4, no.1, Summer 1984, pp.2–21

George 1996
Hardy George, 'Turner, Lawrence, Canova and Venetian art: Three previously unpublished letters', *Apollo*, vol.164, no.416, October 1996, pp.25–32

Giordani 2002
Paolo Giordani, *Venice: Thirty Walks to Explore the City*, Venice 2002

Godfrey 2001
Richard Godfrey, *James Gillray. The Art of Caricature*, exh. cat., Tate Britain 2001

Gowing 1963
Lawrence Gowing, 'Turner's Pictures of Nothing', *Art News*, vol.62, October 1963, pp.30–3

Gowing 1966
Lawrence Gowing, *Turner: Imagination and Reality*, exh. cat., Museum of Modern Art, New York 1966

GPdiV
Gazzetta Privilegiata di Venezia

Greenacre 1988
Francis Greenacre, *Francis Danby*, exh. cat., Tate Gallery 1988

Greenacre and Stoddard 1991
Francis Greenacre and Sheena Stoddard, *W.J. Muller 1812–45*, exh. cat., Bristol Art Gallery 1991

Greenfield 1939
Kent Roberts Greenfield, 'Commerce and New Enterprise at Venice, 1830–1848', *The Journal of Modern History*, vol.11, 1939, pp.313–33

Grieve 2000
Alastair Grieve, *Whistler's Venice*, New Haven and London 2000

Gross 1992
John Gross, *Shylock: Four Hundred Years in the Life of a Legend*, London 1992

Guiterman 1989
Helen Guiterman '" The Great Painter": Roberts on Turner', *Turner Studies*, vol.9, no.1, Summer 1989, pp.2–9

Habert and Volle 1992
Jean Habert and Nathalie Volle (eds.), *Les Noces de Cana de Veronèse: une oeuvre et sa restauration*, exh. cat., Musée du Louvre, Paris 1992

Hale 1956
J.R. Hale (ed.), *The Italian Journal of Samuel Rogers*, London 1956

Halsby 1990
Julian Halsby, *Venice. The Artist's Vision: A Guide to British and American Painters*, London 1990

Hamber 1996
Anthony J. Hamber, 'A Higher Branch of the Art': Photographing the Fine Arts in England, 1839–1880, Amsterdam 1996

Hamilton 1997
James Hamilton, *Turner: A Life*, London 1997

Hartley 1984
Craig Hartley, *Turner Watercolours in the Whitworth Art Gallery*, Manchester 1984

Haskell 1960
Francis Haskell, 'Francesco Guardi as Vedutista and some of his patrons', *Journal of the Warburg and Courtauld Institutes*, vol.23, 1960, pp.266ff.

Haskell 1967
Francis Haskell, 'Some Collectors of Venetian Art at the end of the Eighteenth Century', *Studies in Renaissance and Baroque Art presented to Anthony Blunt*, London and New York 1967

Haskell 1976
Francis Haskell, *Rediscoveries in Art: Some aspects of taste, fashion and collecting in England and France*, Oxford 1976

Haskell 1987
Francis Haskell, *Past and Present in Art and Taste. Selected Essays*, New Haven and London 1987

Haskell 2000
Francis Haskell, *The Ephemeral Museum: Old Master Paintings and the Rise of the Art Exhibition*, New Haven and London 2000

Haydon *Diary*
Benjamin Robert Haydon, *Diary*, ed. Willard B. Pope, 5 vols., Cambridge (Mass.) 1960–3

Hayes 1992
John Hayes, *British Paintings of the Sixteenth Through Nineteenth Centuries, The Collections of National Gallery of Art Systematic Catalogue*, National Gallery of Art, Washington and Cambridge University Press 1992

Heath 1993
John Heath, *The Heath Family Engravers 1779–1878. Vol.2. Charles Heath (1875–1848) and his sons Frederick Heath (1810–78) and Alfred Heath (1812–96)*, Aldershot 1993

Herrmann 1968
Luke Herrmann, *Ruskin and Turner: A Study of Ruskin as a Collector of Turner, based on his Gifts to the University of Oxford; Incorporating a Catalogue Raisonné of the Turner Drawings in the Ashmolean Museum*, Oxford 1968

Herrmann 1990
Luke Herrmann, *Turner Prints: The Engraved Work of J.M.W. Turner*, Oxford 1990

Herrmann 2001
Luke Herrmann, 'Venice', in Joll, Butlin and Herrmann, *The Oxford Companion to J.M.W. Turner*, Oxford 2001, pp.358–63

Hewison 1978
Robert Hewison, *Ruskin and Venice*, exh. cat., J.B. Speed Art Museum, Louisville 1978

Hewison, Warrell and Wildman 2000
Robert Hewison, Ian Warrell and Stephen Wildman, *Ruskin, Turner and the Pre-Raphaelites*, exh. cat., Tate Gallery 2000

Hill 2000
David Hill, *Joseph Mallord William Turner: Le Mont-Blanc et la Vallée d'Aoste*, exh. cat., Museo Archaeologico Regionale, Aosta 2000

Hills 1999
Paul Hills, *Venetian Colour*, New Haven and London 1999

Hobhouse 1859
John Cam Hobhouse (Baron Broughton), *Italy: Remarks made in Several Visits from the Year 1816 to 1854*, 2 vols., London 1859

Holcomb 1969
Adele M. Holcomb, 'A Neglected Classical Phase of Turner's Art: His vignettes to Rogers' *Italy*', *Journal of the Warburg and Courtauld Institutes*, vol.32, 1969, pp.405–10

Holcomb 1972
Adele M. Holcomb, '"Indistinctness is my fault": A Letter about Turner from C.R. Leslie to James Lennox', *Burlington Magazine*, vol.114, 1972, pp.557–8

Holcomb 1988
Adele M. Holcomb, 'Turner and Rogers' *Italy* Revisited', *Studies in Romanticism*, vol.27, 1988, pp.63–95

Hollier 1831
Richard Hollier, *Glances at Various Objects, during a Nine Weeks' Ramble through Parts of France, Switzerland, Piedmont, Austrian Lombardy, Venice, Carinthia, the Tyrol, Schaffhausen, the Banks of the Rhine, and Holland*, London 1831

Honour 1965
Hugh Honour, *The Companion Guide to Venice*, London 1965 (and subsequent eds.)

House 2001
John House, *Paul Signac: Travels in France*, exh. cat., Courtauld Institute Gallery 2001

Howard 2000
Deborah Howard, *Venice and the East: The Impact of the Islamic World on Venetian Architecture 1100–1500*, New Haven and London 2000

Howard 2002
Deborah Howard, *The Architectural History of Venice*, revised ed., New Haven and London 2002

Humfrey 1993
Peter Humfrey, *The Altarpiece in Renaissance Venice*, New Haven and London 1993

Hyde and Wilcox 1988
Ralph Hyde and Scott B.Wilcox, *Panoramania! The Art and Entertainment of the 'All-Embracing' View*, exh. cat., Barbican Art Gallery 1988

Jaffé 2003
David Jaffé (ed.), *Titian*, exh. cat., National Gallery, London 2003

James 1873
Henry James, 'From Venice to Strassburg', *Nation*, vol.16, March 1873, republished in *Italian Hours*, 1909 (Penguin ed., New York and London 1992)

James 1882
Henry James, 'Venice', *Century Magazine*, XXV, November 1882, republished in *Italian Hours*, 1909 (Penguin ed., New York and London 1992)

Joll, Butlin and Herrmann 2001
Evelyn Joll, Martin Butlin and Luke Herrmann, *The Oxford Companion to J.M.W. Turner*, Oxford 2001

Kitson 1988
Michael Kitson, 'Turner and Rembrandt', *Turner Studies*, vol.8, no.1, Summer 1988, pp.2–19

Kowalczyk 2001
Bozena Anna Kowalczyk (with Monica da Cortà Fumei), *Bernardo Bellotto 1722–1780*, exh. cat., Museo Correr, Venice 2001

Krause 1997
Martin F. Krause, *Turner in Indianapolis. The Pantzer Collection of Drawings and Watercolours by J.M.W. Turner and His Contemporaries at the Indianapolis Museum of Art*, Indianapolis 1997

Kriz 1997
Kay Dian Kriz, 'Dido versus the pirates: Turner's Carthaginian paintings and the sublimation of colonial desire', in M. Rosenthal, Christiana Payne and Scott Wilcox (eds.), *Prospects for the Nation: Recent Essays in British Landscape, 1750–1880*, New Haven and London 1997, pp.231–60

Kroeber 1974
Karl Kroeber, 'Experience as History: Shelley's Venice, Turner's Carthage', *ELH*, vol. 41, 1974, pp.321–9

Laven 2000
David Laven, 'The Age of Restoration', in John A. Davis (ed.), *The Short Oxford History of Italy: The Nineteenth Century*, Oxford 2000, pp.51–73

Laven 2002
David Laven, *Venice and Venetia under the Habsburgs 1815–1835*, Oxford 2002

M. Laven 2002
Mary Laven, *Virgins of Venice: Enclosed Lives and Broken Vows in the Renaissance Convent*, London 2002

Leslie 1860
Charles Robert Leslie, *Autobiographical Recollections*, (ed. Tom Taylor), 2 vols., London 1860; reprinted in one vol., with an introduction by Robin Hamlyn, Wakefield 1978

Liebreich 1872
R. Liebreich, 'Turner and Mulready. On the Effect of Certain Faults of Vision on Painting, with Especial Reference to their Works', lecture delivered at the Royal Institution, 8 March 1872, published in *Macmillan's Magazine*, 1872, pp.499–508

Links 1966
J.G. Links, *Venice for Pleasure*, London 1966 (and subsequent eds.)

Links 1971
J.G. Links, *Views of Venice by Canaletto engraved by Antonio Visentini*, New York 1971

Links 1994
J.G. Links, *Canaletto*, London 1994

Links 1997
J.G. Links, *A Supplement to W.G. Constable's Canaletto. Giovanni Antonio Canal 1697–1768*, London 1997

Liversidge and Farington 1993
Michael Liversidge and Jane Farington (eds.), *Canaletto and England*, Birmingham 1993

Lloyd 1880
Mary Lloyd, 'A Memoir of J.M.W. Turner, R.A. by "M.L."', privately printed as *Sunny Memories*, London 1880; reprinted in *Turner Studies*, vol.4, no.1, Summer 1984, p.22

Lockett 1985
Richard Lockett, *Samuel Prout (1783–1852)*, London 1985

London 1972
The English in Venice, exh. cat., Parkin Gallery, London 1972

London 1974
Turner 1775–1851, exh. cat., Royal Academy of Arts 1974

Lorenzetti 1926
Giulio Lorenzetti, *Venezia ed il suo Estuario*, Milan 1926 (and subsequent eds.; English trans. 1961)

Lutyens 1965
Mary Lutyens (ed.), *Effie in Venice: Unpublished Letters of Mrs John Ruskin written from Venice between 1849–1852*, London 1965 (published in New York 1965 as *Young Mrs Ruskin in Venice: Her Pictures of Society and Life with John Ruskin 1849–1852*)

Lyles 1992
Anne Lyles, *Turner: The Fifth Decade 1830–40*, exh. cat., Tate Gallery, London 1992

MacDonald 2001
Margaret F. MacDonald, *Palaces in the Night: Whistler in Venice*, Aldershot 2001

Macleod 1996
Dianne Sachko Macleod, *Art and the Victorian Middle Class: Money and the Making of Cultural Identity*, Cambridge 1996

Mangini 1974
Nicola Mangini, *I teatri a Venezia*, Milan 1974

Martigues 1995
Felix Ziem 1821–1911, exh. cat., Musée Ziem, Martigues 1995

Marchand 1976
Leslie A. Marchand (ed.), '*The Flesh is Frail*', *Byron's Letters and Journals*, vols.5 (1816–17) and 6 (1818–19), London 1976

Martineau and Hope 1983
Jane Martineau and Charles Hope (eds.), *The Genius of Venice 1500–1600*, exh. cat., Royal Academy of Arts 1983

Martineau and Robison 1994
Jane Martineau and Andrew Robison (eds.), *The Glory of Venice: Art in the Eighteenth Century*, exh. cat., Royal Academy of Arts 1994

Melville 1964
Robert Melville, 'Pictures of Nothing', *New Statesman*, 27 November 1964, pp.847ff

Michiel 1829
Giustina Renier Michiel, *Le Origine delle Feste Veneziane*, 5 vols., Venice 1817–27; 6 vols., Milan 1829

Milhous 1999
Judith Milhous, 'Painters and Painting and the Pantheon Opera 1790–1792', *Theatre Research International*, 24 (1999) pp.54–70

Milhous 2001
Judith Milhous, Gabriella Dideriksen, Robert D. Hume, *Italian Opera in Late Eighteenth Century London. Vol.II The Pantheon Opera and its Aftermath 1789–1795*, Oxford 2001

Milner 1990
Frank Milner, *Turner Paintings in Merseyside Collections*, National Museums and Galleries on Merseyside, Liverpool 1990

Moore 1853–6
Memoirs, Journal and Correspondence of Thomas Moore, ed. Lord John Russell, 8 vols., London 1853–6

Moore 1860
Memoirs, Journal and Correspondence of Thomas Moore, condensed ed. selected by Lord John Russell, London 1860

Morand 1996
Anne Morand, with Joan Carpenter Troccoli, *Thomas Moran: The Field Sketches, 1856–1923*, University of Oklahoma Press, Norman and London 1996

Morassi 1973
Antonio Morassi, *Guardi: Antonio e Francesco Guardi. L'opera completa*, 2 vols., Venice 1973

Morris 1960
James Morris, *Venice*, London 1960 (and subsequent eds.)

Moschini 1815
Giannantonio Moschini, *Guida per la Città di Venezia all'Amico della Belle Arte*, 2 vols., Venice 1815 (French ed. 1819)

Munday 1996
John Munday, *Edward William Cooke 1811–1880. A Man of his Time*, Woodbridge 1996

Murray 1835
Lady Murray, *A Journal of a Tour in Italy*, V, London 1835

Murray 1847
Murray's Guide to North Italy, 3rd ed., London 1847

Musolino 1962
Giovanni Musolino, *Chiesa e Monastero di San Biagio e Cataldo alla Giudecca*, Istituto Tipografico Editoriale San Nicolo di Lido, Venice 1962

Nepi Scirè 1998
Giovanna Nepi Scirè (ed.), *The Accademia Galleries in Venice*, Milan 1998

Nicholson 1980
Kathleen Nicholson, 'Turner's "Appulia in Search of Appulus" and the Dialectics of Landscape Tradition', *Burlington Magazine*, vol.120, 1980, pp.679–86

Nicholson 1990
Kathleen Nicholson, *Turner's Classical Landscapes: Myth and Meaning*, Princeton and Oxford 1990

Noon 1991
Patrick Noon, *Richard Parkes Bonington: 'On the Pleasure of Painting'*, exh. cat., Yale Center for British Art, New Haven 1991

Norwich 1982
John Julius Norwich, *A History of Venice*, Harmondsworth 1982

Norwich 1990
John Julius Norwich (ed.), *A Traveller's Companion to Venice*, London 1990

Nugent and Croal 1997–8
Charles Nugent and Melva Croal, *Turner Watercolours from Manchester*, exh. cat., Memphis Brooks Museum of Art, Indianapolis Museum of Art, Joslyn Art Museum, Omaha, Whitworth Art Gallery, Manchester 1997–9

Oxford Companion
See Joll, Butlin and Herrmann 2001

Oxford 1990
Italia al Chiaro di Luna. Italy by Moonlight: The Night in Italian Painting 1550–1850, exh. cat., Ashmolean Museum, Oxford 1990

Palgrave 1842
F.T. Palgrave, *Hand-book for Travellers in Northern Italy: States of Sardinia, Lombardy and Venice, Parma and Piacenza ... as far as the Val d'Arno. With a Travelling Map*, London 1842

Paris 1963
Marie-Thérèse Lemoyne de Forges, *Signac*, exh. cat., Musée du Louvre, Paris 1963

Paris 1983
John Gage, Evelyn Joll and Andrew Wilton et al., *J.M.W. Turner*, exh. cat., Grand Palais, Paris 1983

Paris 1993
Jean-Pierre Cuzin and Marie-Anne Dupuy (eds.), *Copier Créer. De Turner à Picasso: 300 oeuvres inspirées par les maîtres du Louvre*, exh. cat., Musée du Louvre, Paris 1993

Pedrocco 2001
Filippo Pedrocco, *Titian: The Complete Paintings*, London 2001

Pemble 1999
John Pemble, *Venice Rediscovered*, Oxford 1999

Perkins 1990
Diane Perkins, *Turner: The Third Decade 1810–20*, exh. cat., Tate Gallery, London 1990

Petworth 2002
Christopher Rowell, Ian Warrell and David Brown, *Turner at Petworth*, exh. cat., Petworth House, Sussex 2002

Phillips 1833
Thomas Phillips, *Lectures on the History and Principles of Painting*, London 1833

Piggott 1993
Jan Piggott, *Turner's Vignettes*, exh. cat., Tate Gallery 1993

Plant 1996
Margaret Plant, 'Venetian Journey', in Michael Lloyd (ed.), *Turner*, exh. cat., National Gallery of Australia, Canberra 1996, pp.145–63

Plant 2003
Margaret Plant, *Venice: Fragile City*, New Haven and London 2002 (issued 2003)

Pointon 2000
Marcia Pointon, 'Museums, Shrines and J.M.W. Turner', lecture delivered at Tate Britain, 19 October 2000 (one of the Paul Mellon lecture series *Brilliant Effects: Jewellery and its Image in English Visual Culture 1700–1880*)

Powell 1982
Cecilia Powell, 'Topography, Imagination and Travel: Turner's Relationship with James Hakewill', *Art History*, vol.5, no.4., December 1982, pp.408–25

Powell 1983
Cecilia Powell, 'Turner's Vignettes and the Making of Rogers' "Italy"', *Turner Studies*, vol.3, no.1, Summer 1983, pp.2–13

Powell 1987
Cecilia Powell, *Turner in the South: Rome, Naples, Florence*, New Haven and London 1987

Powell 1989
Cecilia Powell (ed.), 'Henry James on Ruskin and Turner', *Turner Society News*, no.51, Feb. 1989, pp.9–10

Powell 1991
Cecilia Powell, *Turner's Rivers of Europe: The Rhine, Meuse and Mosel*, exh. cat., Tate Gallery 1991

Powell 1995
Cecilia Powell, *Turner in Germany*, exh. cat., Tate Gallery 1995

Price 1987
Curtis Price, 'Turner at the Pantheon Opera House, 1791–2', *Turner Studies*, vol.7, no.2, Winter 1987, pp.2–8

Quill 2000
Sarah Quill and Alan Windsor, *Ruskin's Venice: The Stones Revisited*, Aldershot 2000

Rawlinson 1908–13
W.G. Rawlinson, *The Engraved Work of J.M.W. Turner*, 2 vols., 1908 and 1913

Redford 1996
Bruce Redford, *Venice and the Grand Tour*, New Haven and London 1996

Reise c.1960
Barbara Reise, manuscript material prepared for a thesis on Turner's interest in Venice, intended to be submitted to Columbia University, late 1960s; now in the Tate Archives

Reynolds's Discourses
Sir Joshua Reynolds, *Discourses on Art*, ed. Robert R. Wark, New Haven and London 1975

Ritter 1994
Dorothea Ritter, *Venice in Old Photographs 1841–1920*, London 1994

Rodner 1997
William S. Rodner, *J.M.W. Turner: Romantic Painter of the Industrial Revolution*, Berkeley and Los Angeles 1997

Romanelli 1988
Giandomenico Romanelli, *Venezia Ottocento, L'Architettura, L'Urbanistica*, Venice 1988, pp.229–36

Romanelli 1997
Giandomenico Romanelli (ed.), *Dai Dogi agli Imperatori. Le fine della Repubblica tra storia e mito*, exh. cat., Palazzo Ducale, Museo Correr, Venice 1997

Rossi Bortolatto 1974
Luigina Rossi Bortolatto, *L'opera completa di Francesco Guardi*, Milan 1974

Ruskin *Diaries*
Joan Evan and John Howard Whitehouse (eds.), *The Diaries of John Ruskin*, 3 vols., Oxford 1956 (I: 1835–47), 1958 (II: 1848–1873), 1959 (III: 1874–1889)

Ruskin *Works*
E.T. Cook and Alexander Wedderburn (eds.), *The Works of John Ruskin*, Library Edition, 39 vols., London 1903–12

Russell 1996
Francis Russell, 'Guardi and the English Tourist', *Burlington Magazine*, vol.138, Jan. 1996, pp.4–11

Sammartini and Resini 2002
Tudy Sammartini and Daniele Resini, *Venice from the Bell Towers*, London 2002

Sand 1966
George Sand, *Correspondance*, II, 1832–Juin 1835, Paris 1966

Sand *Lettres*
George Sand, *Lettres d'un Voyageur* (first published in book form in 1837), trans. Sacha Rabinovitch and Patricia Thomson, Harmondsworth 1987

Sass 1818
Henry Sass, *A Journey to Rome and Naples ... in 1817, giving an account of the present state of society in Italy; and containing observations on the fine arts*, London 1818

Scharf 1968
Aaron Scharf, *Art and Photography*, London 1968, revised ed. 1974

Schulz 1980
Max F. Schulz, 'Turner's Fabled Atlantis: Venice, Carthage, and London as Paradisal Cityscape', *Studies in Romanticism*, vol.19, no.3, Fall 1980, pp.395–417

Shanes 1990
Eric Shanes, *Turner's Human Landscapes*, London 1990

Shanes 1990a
Eric Shanes, *Turner's England 1810–38*, London 1990

Shanes 1997
Eric Shanes, *Turner's Watercolour Explorations 1810–42*, exh. cat., Tate Gallery 1997

Shanes 2000
Eric Shanes, with Evelyn Joll, Ian Warrell and Andrew Wilton, *Turner. The Great Watercolours*, exh. cat., Royal Academy of Arts 2000

Shapiro 1972
Harold I. Shapiro (ed.), *Ruskin in Italy: Letters to his Parents 1845*, Oxford 1972

Shelley 1913
The Diary of Frances, Lady Shelley 1787–1817 (1818–73), edited by her Grandson, Richard Edgcumbe, 2 vols., London 1912–13

Shelley 1964
The Letters of Percy Bysshe Shelley, ed. Frederic L. Jones, II, *Shelley in Italy*, Oxford 1964

Smith 2000
Richard Smith, 'Turner in the Work of the Goncourt Brothers', *Turner Society News*, no.86, Dec. 2000, pp.10–12

Smith 2002
Greg Smith (ed.), *Thomas Girtin: The Art of Watercolour*, exh. cat., Tate Britain 2002

Solari 1824
Catherine Govion Boglio Solari (writing as 'A Lady of Rank'), *Italy under the yoke of France and Austia: with memoirs of the courts, governments and people of Italy*, 2 vols., London 1824

Solkin 2001
David H. Solkin (ed.), *Art on the Line: The Royal Academy Exhibitions at Somerset House 1780–1836*, New Haven and London 2001

Solly 1875
Neal Solly, *Memoir of the Life of William James Müller*, London 1875

Stainton 1985
Lindsay Stainton, *Turner's Venice*, London 1985

Staley 1968
Allen Staley (with Frederick Cummings), *Romantic Art in Britain. Paintings and Drawings 1760–1860*, exh. cat., Detroit Institute of Arts and Philadelphia Museum of Art 1968

Sutton 1972
Denys and Anthony Sutton, *Venice Rediscovered*, exh. cat., Wildenstein, London 1972

Taft and Loukes 1998
Sarah Taft and Andrew Loukes, *Moonlight and Firelight: Watercolours from the Turner Bequest*, exh. checklist, Tate Gallery 1998

Tanner 1992
Tony Tanner, *Venice Desired*, Oxford and Cambridge (Mass.) 1992

Taylor 1841
Catharine Taylor, *Letters from Italy to a Younger Sister*, 2 vols., London 1841

Thornbury 1862
Walter Thornbury, *The Life of J.M.W. Turner, R.A., Founded on Letters and Papers Furnished by his Friends and Fellow Academicians*, 2 vols., London 1862; single vol. revised ed., London 1877 (an annotated copy of the 1862 edition, with corrections by H.A.J. Munro of Novar and George Jones, is in the Tate Print Room, the gift of Francis Haskell)

Toronto 2004
Katharine A. Lochnan (ed.), *Turner–Whistler–Monet*, forthcoming exh. cat., Art Gallery of Ontario, Toronto 2004

Townsend 1993
Joyce Townsend, *Turner's Painting Techniques*, exh. cat., Tate Gallery 1993

Treuherz 1986
Julian Treuherz, 'The Turner Collector: Henry McConnel, Cotton Spinner', *Turner Studies*, vol.6, no.2, Winter 1986, pp.37–42

Trevor-Roper 1970
Patrick Dacre Trevor-Roper, *The World through Blunted Sight. An inquiry into the Influence of Defective Vision on Art and Character*, London 1970, 1988

Upstone 1993
Robert Upstone, *Turner: The Final Years*, exh. cat., Tate Gallery 1993

Valcanover 1988
Francesco Valcanover, *Jacopo Tintoretto and the Scuola Grande of San Rocco*, Venice 1988

Van der Merwe 1979
Pieter van der Merwe, *The Spectacular Career of Clarkson Stanfield 1793–1867: Seaman; Scene-Painter; Royal Academician*, exh. cat., Tyne and Wear Museums, Sunderland 1979

Venice 1979
Ippolito Caffi, exh. cat., Musei Civici Veneziani, Venice 1979

Vianello 1993
Sabina Vianello, *Le chiese di Venezia*, Venice 1993

Vio 1999
Ettore Vio (ed.), *The Basilica of St Mark in Venice*, Florence 1999; English ed. 2001

Wark 1971
Robert R. Wark, *Ten British Pictures 1740–1840*, San Marino 1971

Warrell 1993
Ian Warrell, *J.M.W. Turner 1775–1851*, exh. cat., Fundación la Caixa, Barcelona and Madrid 1993

Warrell 1995
Ian Warrell, *Through Switzerland with Turner: Ruskin's First Selection from the Turner Bequest*, exh. cat., Tate Gallery 1995

Warrell 1997
Ian Warrell, *Turner on the Loire*, exh. cat., Tate Gallery 1997

Warrell 1999
Ian Warrell, *Turner on the Seine*, exh. cat., Tate Gallery 1999

Warrell 1999a
Ian Warrell, 'Turner's Late Swiss Watercolours – and Oils' in Leslie Parris (ed.), *Exploring Late Turner*, exh. cat., Salander-O'Reilly Galleries, New York 1999

Warrell 2002
Ian Warrell, *Turner et le Lorrain*, exh. cat., Musée des Beaux Arts, Nancy 2002 (includes Michael Kitson's 1982 essay, 'Turner and Claude')

Warrell 2003
Ian Warrell, 'Exploring the "dark side": Ruskin and the problem of Turner's erotica', *British Art Journal*, vol.4, no.1, Spring 2003, pp.5–46

Whitley Papers
Cuttings collected by W.T. Whitley, housed in the British Museum Print Rooms

Whittingham 1985
Selby Whittingham, review of Lindsay Stainton's *Turner's Venice*, *Turner Studies*, vol.5, no.2, Winter 1985, pp.50–1

Whittingham 1993
Selby Whittingham, 'Windus, Turner & Ruskin: New Documents', *J.M.W. Turner, R.A.*, no.2, Dec. 1993, pp.69–116

Wilcox 1980
Tim Wilcox (ed.), *Visions of Venice: Watercolours and Drawings from Turner to Procktor*, exh. cat., Bankside Gallery 1990

Wildenstein 1996
Daniel Wildenstein, *Monet. Catalogue Raisonné*, 4 vols., reprinted Cologne 1996

Wilkinson 1974
Gerald Wilkinson, *The Sketches of Turner, R.A: 1802–20: Genius of the Romantic*, London 1974

Wilton 1975
Andrew Wilton, *Turner in the British Museum: Drawings and Watercolours*, exh. cat., British Museum 1975

Wilton 1979
Andrew Wilton, *The Life and Work of J.M.W. Turner*, Fribourg and London 1979

Wilton 1982
Andrew Wilton, *Turner Abroad: France, Italy, Germany, Switzerland*, London 1982

Wilton 1987
Andrew Wilton, *Turner in his Time*, London 1987

Wilton 1989
Andrew Wilton, 'The "Keepsake" Convention: *Jessica* and Some Related Pictures', *Turner Studies*, vol.9, no.2, Winter 1989, pp.14–33

Wilton 1990
Andrew Wilton, 'Picture Note: Study for the Sack of a Great House? (Interior at Petworth)', *Turner Studies*, vol.10, no.2, Winter 1990, pp.55–9

Wilton 1995
Andrew Wilton, *Venise. Aquarelles de Turner*, Paris 1995; Italian ed., *Venezia. Acquerelli di Turner*, Paris 2001

Wilton and Bignamini 1997
Andrew Wilton and Ilaria Bignamini (eds.), *Grand Tour: The Lure of Italy in the Eighteenth Century*, London 1997 (see especially Ilaria Bignamini and Giorgio Marini, 'Venice', pp.186–7)

Wilton and Lyles 1993
Andrew Wilton and Anne Lyles, *The Great Age of British Watercolours 1750–1880*, exh. cat., Royal Academy of Arts 1993

Wilton and Turner 1990
Andrew Wilton and Rosalind Turner, *Painting and Poetry: Turner's Verse Book and His Work of 1804–1812*, exh. cat., Tate Gallery 1990

Zannier 1981
Italo Zannier, with Albert Moravia and Vittorio Sgarbi, *Venice: The Naya Collection*, Venice 1981

Ziff 1963
Jerrold Ziff, 'Backgrounds: Introduction of Architecture and Landscape', *Journal of the Warburg and Courtauld Institutes*, vol.21, 1963, pp.124–47

Ziff 1980
Jerrold Ziff, review of 'The Paintings of J.M.W. Turner' by Martin Butlin and Evelyn Joll, *Art Bulletin*, vol.62, 1980, p.170

Ziff 1982
Jerrold Ziff, 'But why "Medea" in Rome?', *Turner Studies*, vol.2, no.1, Summer 1982, pp.18–19

Ziff 1986
Jerrold Ziff, 'William Henry Pyne's "J.M.W. Turner, R.A.": A Neglected Critic and Essay Remembered', *Turner Studies*, vol.6, no.1, Summer 1986, pp.18–25

List of Works

Explanatory Notes:

Except where stated otherwise, all works are by Turner and are part of his bequest, as resolved in 1856, now housed at the Tate.

Measurements are given in centimetres, height before width.

All watercolours and pencil sketches were executed on white paper unless otherwise specified.

The term 'bodycolour' is used here in preference to gouache: this better reflects the nature of Turner's improvisatory use of his materials, where lead white was deployed in an *ad hoc* way to thicken his colours.

A list of abbreviated standard references will be found on p.4, opposite the Contents.

Details are correct at time of going to press.

A) WORKS BY OTHER ARTISTS

1 Richard Parkes Bonington (1802–1828)
Venice: Ducal Palace with a Religious Procession exhibited Salon 1827, British Institution 1828 **(fig.99)**
Oil on canvas, 114.3 x 162.6
Tate. Presented by Frederick John Nettlefold 1947 (N05789)

2 Richard Parkes Bonington (1802–1828)
Palazzi Manolesso-Ferro, Contarini-Fasan, and Contarini on the Grand Canal c.1826 **(fig.80)**
Oil on board, 36.8 x 47.6
Richard L. Feigen & Co, New York

3 Giuseppe Borsato (1771–1849)
The Arrival of Napoleon in Venice 1847 **(fig.28)**
Oil on canvas, 56 x 74
Pinacoteca Ambrosiana, Milan

4 Augustus Wall Callcott (1779–1844)
Murano ('The Old Part of Venice') exhibited Royal Academy 1836 **(fig.107)**
Oil on canvas, 74.9 x 109.9
Private collection (courtesy of Agnew's)
London only

5 William Callow (1812–1908)
The Grand Canal 3 September 1840 **(fig.89)**
Pencil and watercolour, 25.4 x 36.2
Private collection (courtesy of Agnew's)

6 Giovanni Antonio Canaletto (1697–1768)
Four Views of Venice: La Libreria V [top left]; La Piera del Bando. V [bottom left]; The Market on the Molo [top right]; Le Preson. V [bottom right] c.1735–40 **(fig.24, detail)**
Etching, 45 x 61; each image about 14.2 x 20.9
The British Museum, London
(1838-5-26-4 (15-18))

7 Giovanni Antonio Canaletto (1697–1768) and assistants
Venice: the Bacino di San Marco c.1735–44 **(fig.25)**
Oil on canvas, 71.3 x 187.7
Private collection

8 William Etty (1787–1849)
Window in Venice, during a Festa exhibited Royal Academy 1831 *(not reproduced)*
Oil on canvas, 61 x 50.2
Tate. Presented by Robert Vernon 1847 (N00364)
London only

9 William Etty (1787–1849)
The Bridge of Sighs exhibited Royal Academy 1835 **(fig.132)**
Oil on canvas, 80 x 50.8
York City Art Gallery
London only

10 Attributed to William Etty (1787–1849) after Jacopo Robusti, known as Tintoretto (1518–1594)
The Miracle of Saint Mark Freeing the Slave c.1823 **(fig.48)**
Oil on paper mounted on canvas, 40.6 x 59.7
National Gallery, London. Bequeathed by Lady Lindsey, 1912

11 James Gillray (1757–1815)
Titianus Redivivus; or the Seven Wise-Men consulting the new Venetian Oracle, – a Scene in the Academic Grove 1797 **(fig.34)**
Etching and watercolour, 54.9 x 42
The British Museum, London

12 Thomas Girtin (1775–1802) after Canaletto (1697–1768)
The Rialto Bridge c.1796–8 **(fig.22)**
Pen and ink, 37.4 x 51.1
The British Museum, London

13 James Hakewill (1778–1843)
The Rialto 1817 **(fig.29)**
Pencil, 14 x 21.5
The British School at Rome Library

14 James Hakewill (1778–1843)
The Grand Canal, with the Salute 1817 **(fig.32)**
Pencil, 14 x 21.5
The British School at Rome Library

15 James Duffield Harding (1797/8–1863)
The Grand Canal, Venice exhibited Royal Academy 1835 **(fig.100)**
Pencil, watercolour, bodycolour, pen and brown ink, with gum, on paper laid down on wood panel, 77.8 x 106
Yale Center for British Art, Paul Mellon Collection

16 James Holland (1799–1870)
The Church of Santa Maria dei Miracoli, Venice 30 September 1835 **(fig.86)**
Pencil, watercolour and bodycolour, 35.7 x 23.9
Whitworth Art Gallery, University of Manchester. Gift of A.E. Anderson, 1918 (D.1918.3)

17 John Frederick Lewis (1805–1876)
The Rialto Bridge 1827 **(fig.97)**
Watercolour, bodycolour and gum arabic, 21.5 x 34.4
Trustees of the Cecil Higgins Art Gallery, Bedford

18 William Marlow (1740–1813)
Capriccio: St Paul's Cathedral and the Grand Canal c.1795–7 **(fig.27)**
Oil on canvas, 129.5 x 104.1
Tate. Purchased 1954 (N06213)

19 Charles Mottram (1807–1876) after John Doyle (1797–1868)
Samuel Rogers at his Breakfast Table c.1830–50 **(fig.63)**
Engraving and mezzotint, 58 x 86.6
Tate. Presented by Dr David Blayney Brown 1996 (T04907)

20 William James Müller (1812–1845)
The Ca'd'Oro, 1834
(not reproduced; but see fig.84)
Pencil, 28.5 x 44.8
Birmingham Museums and Art Gallery

21 Gilbert Stuart Newton (1794–1835)
Shylock and Jessica, The 'Merchant of Venice' exhibited Royal Academy 1830 **(fig.60)**
Oil on canvas, 88.9 x 74.9
Yale Center for British Art, Paul Mellon Collection

22 Lady Susan Elizabeth Percy (1782–1847)
Venice, with the Salute 1834 **(fig.85)**
Chalk and watercolour on blue paper, 18.7 x 27.5
Tate. Purchased as part of the Oppé Collection with assistance from the National Lottery through the Heritage Lottery Fund 1996 (T10699)
London only

23 Samuel Prout (1783–1852)
The Pilastri Acritani in the Piazzetta, with the Campanile c.1824 **(fig.81)**
Pencil, heightened with white, 36.2 x 26
Birmingham Museums and Art Gallery. Bequeathed by J.R. Holliday, 1927

24 Samuel Prout (1783–1852)
The Rialto Bridge Venice, from the North possibly exhibited Old Water Colour Society 1827 **(fig.98)**
Watercolour, 74 x 114
Private collection

25 John Ruskin (1819–1900)
Court of the Ducal Palace, Venice May 1841 **(fig.92)**
Pencil, pen and ink, with wash, 34 x 46
Ashmolean Museum, Oxford. Ruskin School Collection

26 Clarkson Stanfield (1793–1867)
The Dogana and the Church of Santa Maria della Salute c.1830–1 **(fig.101)**
Watercolour and bodycolour with scratching-out, 22 x 31.5
The British Museum, London (S 109)

27 Clarkson Stanfield (1793–1867)
Venice from the Dogana exhibited Royal Academy 1833 **(fig.102)**
Oil on canvas, 130 x 165.4
Trustees of the Bowood Collection
London only

28 Ludovico Ughi 18th century
Iconografica rappresentatione della Inclita Città di Venezia 1729 **(fig.21)**
Engraving, 152 x 215
The British Library, London
London only

29 Unknown artist after Titian (c.1490–1576)
The Death of St Peter Martyr 17th century **(fig.40)**
Oil on canvas, 141 x 94
Collection of the late Sir Brinsley Ford

B) WORKS BY TURNER NOT PAINTED IN OR DEPICTING VENICE

30 *London from Lambeth, with Westminster Bridge c.1795–7* **(fig.26)**
Pencil and watercolour, 31.8 x 45.1
Private collection

31 *Holy Family* exhibited Royal Academy 1803 **(fig.45)**
Oil on canvas, 102.2 x 141.6
Tate (N00473; B&J 49)

32 *Vision of Medea* exhibited Rome 1828, Royal Academy 1831 **(fig.50)**
Oil on canvas, 173.7 x 248.9
Tate (N00513; B&J 293)

33 *Pilate Washing his Hands* exhibited Royal Academy 1830 **(fig.51)**
Oil on canvas, 91.4 x 121.9
Tate (N00510; B&J 332)

34 *Jessica* exhibited Royal Academy 1830 **(fig.59)**
Oil on canvas, 122 x 91.5
Accepted by H.M Government in lieu of tax and allocated to the Tate Gallery 1984; on deposit at Petworth House (T03887; B&J 333)
London only

35 *Bacchus and Ariadne* exhibited Royal Academy 1840 **(fig.55)**
Oil on canvas, 78.7 x 78.7
Tate (N00525; B&J 382)

C) TURNER'S OIL PAINTINGS OF VENICE

Paintings exhibited by Turner

36 *Bridge of Sighs, Ducal Palace and Custom-House, Venice: Canaletti painting* exhibited Royal Academy 1833 **(fig.103)**
Oil on canvas, 51.1 x 81.6
Tate; Presented by Robert Vernon 1847 (N00370; B&J 349; S 96)

37 *Venice (the Dogana and San Giorgio Maggiore)* exhibited Royal Academy 1834 **(fig.104)**
Oil on canvas, 91.5 x 122
National Gallery of Art, Washington, Widener Collection (1942.9.85; B&J 356)

38 *Keelmen heaving in Coals by Night* exhibited Royal Academy 1835 **(fig.105)**
Oil on canvas, 92.3 x 122.8
National Gallery of Art, Washington, Widener Collection (1942.9.86; B&J 360)

39 *Venice from the Porch of Madonna della Salute* exhibited Royal Academy 1835 **(fig.109)**
Oil on canvas, 91.4 x 122.2
Metropolitan Museum of Art, New York, Bequest of Cornelius Vanderbilt, 1899 (B&J 362)

40 *The Grand Canal, Venice* exhibited Royal Academy 1837 **(fig.58)**
Oil on canvas, 148 x 110.5
The Huntington Library, Art Collections and Botanical Gardens, San Marino (B&J 368)
London only

41 *Venice, from the Canale della Giudecca, Chiesa di S. Maria della Salute, &c* exhibited Royal Academy 1840 **(fig.110)**
Oil on canvas, 61.2 x 91.8
Sheepshanks Bequest 1857, Victoria and Albert Museum (B&J 384; S 100)
London only

42 *Venice, the Bridge of Sighs* exhibited Royal Academy 1840 **(fig.113)**
Oil on canvas, 68.6 x 91.4
Tate (N00527; B&J 383; S 99)

43 *Ducal Palace, Dogano, with Part of San Georgio, Venice* exhibited Royal Academy 1841 **(fig.197)**
Oil on canvas, 63.5 x 93
Allen Memorial Art Museum, Oberlin College, Ohio. Mrs F.F. Prentiss Bequest, 1944 (B&J 390)

44 *The Dogana, San Giorgio, Citella, from the Steps of the Europa* exhibited Royal Academy 1842 **(fig.220)**
Oil on canvas, 61.6 x 92.7
Tate: Presented by Robert Vernon 1847 (N00372; B&J 396; S 101)

45 *Campo Santo, Venice* exhibited Royal
Academy 1842 **(fig.257)**
Oil on canvas, 61.2 x 91.2
Lent by the Toledo Museum of Art;
Gift of Edward Drummond Libbey
(B&J 397; S 102)

46 *St Benedetto, looking towards Fusina*
exhibited Royal Academy 1843 **(fig.211)**
Oil on canvas, 62.2 x 92.7
Tate (N00534; B&J 406)

47 *The Sun of Venice going to Sea* exhibited
Royal Academy 1843 **(fig.248)**
Oil on canvas, 61.6 x 92.1
Tate (N00535; B&J 402; S 103)

48 *Venice – Maria della Salute* exhibited Royal
Academy 1844 **(fig.230)**
Oil on canvas, 61.3 x 92.1
Tate (N00539; B&J 411)

49 *Approach to Venice* exhibited Royal
Academy 1844 **(fig.263)**
Oil on canvas, 62 x 94
National Gallery of Art, Washington,
Andrew W. Mellon Collection
(1937.1.110; B&J 412)

50 *Venice Quay, Ducal Palace* exhibited Royal
Academy 1844 **(fig.238)**
Oil on canvas, 62.2 x 92.7
Tate (N00540; B&J 413)

51 *Venice, Evening, going to the Ball* exhibited
Royal Academy 1845 (formerly listed
as 'Going to the Ball (San Martino),
RA 1846') **(fig.264)**
Oil on canvas, 61 x 91.4
Private collection (B&J 416/421)

52 *Morning, returning from the Ball, St Martino*
exhibited Royal Academy 1845 (formerly
listed as 'Returning from the Ball
(St Martha) RA 1846') **(fig.265)**
Oil on canvas, 61 x 91.4
Private collection (B&J 417/422)

53 *Going to the Ball (San Martino)* exhibited
Royal Academy 1846 (formerly listed
as 'Morning, returning from the Ball,
St Martino, RA 1845') **(fig.266)**
Oil on canvas, 61.6 x 92.4
Tate (N00544; B&J 417/421)

54 *Returning from the Ball (St Martha)*
exhibited Royal Academy 1846
(formerly listed as 'Venice, Evening,
going to the Ball, RA 1845') **(fig.268)**
Oil on canvas, 61.6 x 92.4
Tate (N00543; B&J 416/422; S 104)

Paintings found in Turner's Studio after his Death

55 *Venice, the Piazzetta, with the Ceremony of
the Doge Marrying the Sea* c.1835 **(fig.108)**
Oil on canvas, 91.4 x 121.9
Tate (N04446; B&J 501; S 98)

56 *Scene in Venice, probably looking down
the Grand Canal from alongside the Palazzo
Mocenigo* c.1844 **(fig.168)**
Oil on canvas, 62.2 x 92.7
Tate (N05488; B&J 503)
London only

57 *Venice with the Salute* c.1844 **(fig.178)**
Oil on canvas, 62.2 x 92.7
Tate (N05487; B&J 502)

58 *Riva degli Schiavoni, Venice: Water Fete*
c.1843–5 **(fig.242)**
Oil on canvas, 72.4 x 113
Tate (N04661; B&J 507)

59 *The Arrival of Louis-Philippe at Portsmouth,
8 October 1844* c.1844–5 (formerly listed as
'Festive Lagoon Scene, Venice c.1845') **(fig.276)**
Oil on canvas, 90.8 x 121.3
Tate (N04660; B&J 506)
London only

60 *The Disembarkation of Louis-Philippe at
Portsmouth, 8 October 1844* c.1844–5
(formerly listed as 'Procession of Boats,
with Distant Smoke, Venice c.1845') **(fig.277)**
Oil on canvas, 90.2 x 120.6
Tate (N02068; B&J 505; S 105)
London only

D) TURNER'S SKETCHBOOKS AND WATERCOLOURS OF VENICE

Watercolours of Venice from c.1818 up to the visit in 1840

61 *The Rialto, from the Albergo Leon Bianco, after
a Drawing by James Hakewill* c.1818 **(fig.30)**
Pencil and watercolour, 18.2 x 26.6
Tate (TB CCCXVI 7; D32144; S 60)

62 *Venice: The Ducal Palace, for Samuel Rogers's
'Italy'* c.1826–7 **(fig.64)**
Watercolour, 24 x 30.6
Tate (TB CCLXXX 193; D27710)

63 *Venice (The Rialto – Moonlight), for Samuel
Rogers's 'Poems'* c.1830–2 **(fig.67)**
Watercolour, 24.2 x 30.7
Tate (TB CCLXXX 196; D27713)

64 *Study of the Piazza San Marco, Venice: possibly
for Samuel Rogers's 'Italy' or 'Poems'* c.1826–32
(fig.68)
Watercolour, 20.4 x 24.1
Tate (TB CCLXXX 2; D27519)

65 *Venice from Fusina* c.1821 **(fig.94)**
Watercolour, 28.6 x 40.6
Private collection (W 721)

66 *The Rialto, Venice* c.1820 **(fig.95)**
Watercolour and bodycolour on
off-white paper, 28.6 x 41.3
Indianapolis Museum of Art, Gift in
memory of Dr. and Mrs Hugo O. Pantzer
by their Children (W 718)

67 *The Grand Canal, with the Palazzo Grimani,
from below the Rialto Bridge* c.1820 **(fig.96)**
Pencil and watercolour, 28.3 x 40.7
National Gallery of Ireland (W 725)
Not exhibited

68 *The Punta della Dogana, with San Giorgio
Maggiore beyond* 1833 or 1840 **(fig.82)**
Pencil, watercolour and bodycolour on
grey paper, 19.5 x 28.1
Tate (TB CCCXVII 22; D32207; S 35)

69 *Looking down the Grand Canal towards Santa
Maria della Salute, from near the Accademia*
c.1833 or 1840 **(fig.172)**
Pencil, watercolour and bodycolour on
grey paper, 19.1 x 28.2
Tate (TB CCCXVII 25; D32210)

70 *The Mouth of the Grand Canal, with the Steps of
Santa Maria della Salute* c.1833 or 1840 **(fig.180)**
Pencil, watercolour and bodycolour on
grey paper, 18.4 x 27.8
Tate (TB CCCXVII 23; D32208; S 34)

71 *The Dogana, Campanile of San Marco and the
Doge's Palace* c.1833 or 1840 **(fig.189)**
Pencil, watercolour and bodycolour on
grey paper, 19.3 x 28.1
Tate (TB CCCXVII 20; D32205; S 32)

72 *Boats in front of the Dogana and Santa Maria
della Salute* c.1833 or 1840 **(fig.190)**
Pencil, watercolour and bodycolour
on grey paper, using a pen dipped in
watercolour for details, 19 x 28.1
Tate (TB CCCXVII 21; D32206; S 33)

Bound Sketchbooks

73 'Studies in the Louvre' sketchbook
Copy after Titian's 'Crowning with Thorns'
1802 **(fig.38)**
Pencil and watercolour, 12.9 x 11.4
Tate (TB LXXII f.52; D04340)

74 'Calais Pier' sketchbook
*Composition study for 'Venus mourning the
Dead Adonis'* c.1802–3 **(fig.42)**
Pencil and chalk on blue paper, 43.3 x 27.2
Tate (TB LXXXI f.52; D04954)
London only

75 'Route to Rome' sketchbook
*Copies of 'The Crucifixion' and other pictures by
Tintoretto in the Scuola Grande di San Rocco*
1819 **(fig.49)**
Pencil, 8.7 x 11.7 each
Tate (TB CLXXI ff.25 verso, 26; D13906,
D13907)
London only

76 'Milan to Venice' sketchbook
*The Cannaregio Canal, with the Palazzo Labia
and San Geremia on the Left, with the Ghetto
in the Distance; also a
Group of Gondolas* 1819 **(fig.72)**
Pencil, 11.2 x 18.5 each
Tate (TB CLXXV ff.87 verso, 88;
D14482, D14483)

77 'Venice to Ancona' sketchbook
*The Bacino looking East, with Sketches of
the Sky* 1819 **(fig.76)**
Pencil, 11.1 x 18.4 each
Tate (TB CLXXVI ff.20 verso, 21;
D14526, D14527)
London only

78 'Vienna up to Venice' sketchbook
*Views of the Punta della Dogana and Santa
Maria della Salute from the Hotel Europa* 1833
(fig.83)
Pencil, 11.3 x 18.4 each
Tate (TB CCCXI ff.80 verso, 81;
D31573, D31574)
London only

79 'Venice' sketchbook
*Two views of the Bridge of Sighs, with a study
of the Doge's Palace* 1833 **(fig.112)**
Pencil, 10.9 x 20.3 each
Tate (TB CCCXIV ff.30 verso, 31;
D31985, D31986)

80 'Venice up to Trento' sketchbook
*Views on the Grand Canal: the steps of Santa
Maria della Salute; and a view towards the
Rialto bridge* 1833 **(fig.8)**
Pencil, 10.9 x 20.3 each
Tate (TB CCCXII ff.2 verso, 3; D31600,
D31601)
London only

81 'Rotterdam to Venice' sketchbook
*The Porta della Carta of the Doge's Palace; and
various views of the Piazzetta* 1840 **(fig.116)**
Pencil, 14.9 x 8.9 each
Tate (TB CCCXXX ff.87 verso, 88;
D32434, D32435)
London only

82 'Venice and Bozen' sketchbook
*Sketches on the Giudecca Canal near Santa
Marta, the Gesuati and Santi Biagio e Cataldo*
1840 **(fig.11)**
Pencil, 12.3 x 17.3 each
Tate (TB CCCXIII ff.32 verso, 33;
D31853, D31854)

83 'Venice: Passau to Würzburg' sketchbook
Two Views of the Palazzo Foscari 1840 **(fig.87)**
Pencil, 12.6 x 19.8 each
Tate (TB CCCX ff.4 verso, 5;
D31284, D31285)
London only

Leaves from the 'Como and Venice' sketchbook, 1819

84 *San Giorgio Maggiore – Early Morning* 1819
(fig.74)
Watercolour, 22.3 x 28.7
Tate (TB CLXXXI 4; D15254)

85 *The Punta della Dogana, with the Zitelle in the
Distance* 1819 **(fig.75)**
Watercolour, 22.3 x 28.5
Tate (TB CLXXXI 6; D15256)

86 *Venice: Looking East towards San Pietro di
Castello – Early Morning* 1819 **(fig.77)**
Watercolour, 22.3 x 28.7
Tate (TB CLXXXI 5; D15255)

87 *The Campanile of San Marco and the Doge's
Palace* 1819 **(fig.78)**
Pencil and watercolour, 22.3 x 28.7
Tate (TB CLXXXI 7; D15258)

Leaves from the 'Grand Canal and Giudecca' sketchbook, 1840

88 *On the Grand Canal, looking towards the Palazzi
Mocenigo, with the Palazzo Foscari beyond* 1840
(fig.169)
Pencil and watercolour, 22.1 x 32
Tate (TB CCCXV 1; D32117)

89 *The Rialto Bridge from the North* 1840 **(fig.156)**
Watercolour, 22.1 x 32
Tate (TB CCCXV 3; D32119)

90 *Shipping in the Bacino, with the Entrance to the
Grand Canal* 1840 **(fig.243)**
Watercolour, 22.1 x 32.1
Tate (TB CCCXV 4; D32120)

91 *The Steps of Santa Maria della Salute, looking up
the Grand Canal* 1840 **(fig.182)**
Pencil and watercolour, with details
added using a pen dipped in watercolour,
22.1 x 32.3
Tate (TB CCCXV 5; D32121; S 45)

92 *Looking down the Grand Canal to Palazzo Corner
della Ca'Grande and Santa Maria della Salute*
1840 **(fig.174)**
Pencil and watercolour, 22.1 x 32.5
Tate (TB CCCXV 6; D32122; S 47)

93 *The Palazzo Grimani and the Palazzo Corner-
Contarini dei Cavalli on the Grand Canal, with
the Rio San Luca* 1840 **(fig.162)**
Pencil and watercolour, 22.1 x 32.4
Tate (TB CCCXV 7; D32123)

94 *The Upper End of the Grand Canal, with San
Simeone Piccolo; Dusk* 1840 **(fig.151)**
Watercolour and bodycolour, with pen and
ink, 21.9 x 32
Tate (TB CCCXV 8; D32124; S 46)

272

95 *A Boat near Santa Marta* 1840 **(fig.206)**
Watercolour, 22.2 x 32.1
Tate (TB CCCXV 9; D32125; S 43)

96 *Venice by Moonlight* 1840 **(fig.207)**
Watercolour, 22 x 31.9
Tate (TB CCCXV 10; D32126; S 48)

97 *The Giudecca Canal, looking towards Santa
Maria della Salute* 1840 **(fig.199)**
Watercolour, bodycolour and coloured
crayons, with details added using a pen
dipped in watercolour, 22.2 x 32.1
Tate (TB CCCXV 11; D32127; S 49)

98 *The Western End of the Giudecca Canal, from
near the Convent of Santi Biagio e Cataldo*
(fig.208)
Watercolour, coloured crayon, and details
added using a pen dipped in watercolour,
22.1 x 32.2
Tate (TB CCCXV 12; D32128; S 50)

99 *The Giudecca Canal, looking towards Fusina at
Sunset* 1840 **(fig.210)**
Pencil, watercolour, and bodycolour with
coloured crayons, 22 x 32.3
Tate (TB CCCXV 13; D32129; S 51)

100 *Sunset over Santa Maria della Salute and the
Dogana* 1840 **(fig.227)**
Watercolour, 22.1 x 32.1
Tate (TB CCCXV 14; D32130; S 52)

101 *The Grand Canal from near the Accademia,
with Santa Maria della Salute in the Distance*
1840 **(fig.171)**
Pencil and watercolour, 22.3 x 32.5
Tate (TB CCCXV 15; D32131)

102 *The Punta della Dogana at Sunset, with
the Domes of Santa Maria della Salute*
1840 **(fig.228)**
Watercolour, 22.1 x 32.2
Tate (TB CCCXV 17; D32133; S 53)

103 *The Grand Canal from the Traghetto di San
Felise, with Ca'Corner della Regina and
Ca'Pesaro on the left* 1840 **(fig.155)**
Pencil and watercolour, 22.2 x 32.4
Tate (TB CCCXV 19; D32135)

104 *The Grand Canal, from the Palazzo Balbi
and the Palazzo Mocenigo to the Rialto Bridge*
1840 **(fig.88)**
Pencil and watercolour, 22.3 x 32.8
Tate (TB CCCXV 20; D32136; S 55)

105 *The Grand Canal, looking towards the Palazzo
Grimani* 1840 **(fig.160)**
Pencil and watercolour, 22.2 x 32
Tate (TB CCCXV 21; D32137; S 54)

Leaves from the 'Storm' sketchbook, c.1840

106 *The Accademia from the Grand Canal*
1840 **(fig.173)**
Pencil and watercolour, using a pen
dipped in watercolour for details, with
some scraping-out, 21.7 x 31.8
Ashmolean Museum, Oxford.
Presented by John Ruskin, 1861
(W 1366; Herrmann 57; S 91)

107 *The Grand Canal, with the Salute* 1840 **(fig.177)**
Pencil, watercolour and bodycolour, using
a pen dipped in watercolour for details,
21.5 x 31.5
Ashmolean Museum, Oxford.
Presented by John Ruskin, 1861
(W 1363; Herrmann 56; S 93)

108 *Venice: The Riva degli Schiavoni* 1840 **(fig.239)**
Watercolour, with some scratching-out,
and details added using a pen dipped in
watercolour, 21.7 x 31.8
Ashmolean Museum, Oxford.
Presented by John Ruskin 1861
(W 1364; Herrmann 58; S 69)

109 *Storm at Venice* 1840 **(fig.188)**
Watercolour, with details added using
a pen, 21.8 x 31.8
British Museum (Sale Bequest;
W 1354; S 87)

110 *The Doge's Palace from the Bacino* 1840 **(fig.234)**
Pencil and watercolour, with scratching-
out and details added using a pen dipped
in watercolour, 22.2 x 32.3
Walker Art Gallery, Liverpool. Board of
Trustees of the National Museums and
Galleries on Merseyside (W 1373)
London only

111 *The Mouth of the Grand Canal* 1840 **(fig.184)**
Watercolour, with details added using a
pen, 21.9 x 31.8
Yale Center for British Art, Paul Mellon
Collection (W 1360)

112 *The Grand Canal, with Santa Maria della Salute,
from near the Hotel Europa* 1840 **(fig.183)**
Pencil, watercolour and bodycolour, with
some scraping-out, 22 x 31.8
Private collection (W 1368; S 94)
Not exhibited

113 *Venice: looking towards the Dogana and San
Giorgio Maggiore, with a Storm Approaching*
1840 **(fig.187)**
Watercolour, with details added using
a pen dipped in watercolour, 22 x 32
Private collection (courtesy of
Richard Green; W 1355)

114 *San Giorgio Maggiore at Sunset* c.1840 **(fig.216)**
Pencil, watercolour and bodycolour,
with details added using a pen dipped in
watercolour, 22 x 32
Private collection

Other Watercolours, c.1840
(arranged by paper type; see comments on
pages 258–9)

115 *The Piazzetta and the Doge's Palace from the
Bacino* c.1840 **(fig.115)**
Watercolour and bodycolour on grey paper,
19.3 x 27.9
Tate (TB CCCXVII 1; D32180)

116 *The Giants' Staircase in the Doge's Palace*
c.1840 **(fig.117)**
Watercolour and bodycolour on grey paper,
19.1 x 28
Tate (TB CCCXVII 2; D32181)

117 *The Campanile of San Marco, with the
Pilastri Acritani, from the Porta della Carta*
1840 **(fig.119)**
Pencil, watercolour and bodycolour on
grey paper, 28.2 x 19.1
Tate (TB CCCXVII 19; D32204; S 30)

118 *The Arcades of the Procuratie Nuove and
the Palazzo Reale, with the Piazza beyond*
1840 **(fig.128)**
Watercolour and bodycolour on grey paper,
15.5 x 22.4
Tate (TB CCCXIX 7; D32255)

119 *The Church of Santo Stefano, from the Rio del
Santissimo* 1840 **(fig.129)**
Pencil, watercolour and bodycolour on
grey paper, 27.8 x 19.1
Tate (TB CCCXVII 32; D32217; S 41)

120 *The Punta della Dogana, with Santa Maria
della Salute, from the Traghetto del Ridotto*
1840 **(fig.139)**
Watercolour, bodycolour, with ink wash
on grey paper, 22.3 x 30.4
Tate (TB CCCXVIII 13; D32232; S 17)

121 *The Rialto Bridge on the Grand Canal from near
the Palazzo Grimani* c.1840 **(fig.161)**
Pencil, watercolour and bodycolour
on grey paper, using a pen dipped in
watercolour for details, 19.6 x 28.1
Tate (TB CCCXVII 27; D32212; S 36)

122 *The Church of San Luca and the Back of the
Palazzo Grimani from the Rio San Luca* 1840
(fig.165)
Pencil, watercolour and bodycolour
on grey paper, using a pen dipped in
watercolour for details, 19.4 x 27.9
Tate (TB CCCXVII 30; D32215; S 40)

123 *The Rio San Luca alongside the Palazzo Grimani,
with the Church of San Luca* 1840 **(fig.166)**
Pencil, watercolour and bodycolour
on grey paper, using a pen dipped in
watercolour for details, 19.1 x 28.1
Tate (TB CCCXVII 29; D32214; S 37)

124 *Looking down the Grand Canal towards
the Palazzo Pisani-Moretta and the
Palazzo Barbarigo, from near the Palazzo
Grimani* 1840 **(fig.167)**
Pencil, watercolour and bodycolour
on grey paper, using a pen dipped in
watercolour for details, 19.1 x 28.1
Tate (TB CCCXVII 28; D32213; S 38)

125 *The Dogana and the Salute, with the Entrance to
the Grand Canal, at Twilight* 1840 **(fig.231)**
Pencil, watercolour and bodycolour on
grey paper, 18.8 x 27.9
Tate (TB CCCXVII 16; D32201)

126 *The Entrance to the Grand Canal, with the
Campanile and the Doge's Palace* 1840 **(fig.232)**
Pencil, watercolour and bodycolour on
grey paper, 18.8 x 28
Tate (TB CCCXVII 5; D32184; S 31)

127 *Orange Sunset over the Lagoon* 1840 **(fig.256)**
Bodycolour on grey paper, 18.5 x 28
Tate (TB CCCXVII 18; D32203)

128 *Reclining Nude on a Bed* 1840 **(fig.137)**
Watercolour and bodycolour on a textured
grey wove paper, 21.6 x 28.4
Tate (TB CCCXVIII 17; D32236)

129 *The Interior of San Marco, looking into the North
Transept* 1840 **(fig.121)**
Watercolour and bodycolour on
grey-brown paper, 29.6 x 22.3
Tate (TB CCCXVIII 7; D32226; S 14)

130 *The Piazzetta, with San Marco and its
Campanile; Night* 1840 **(fig.123)**
Watercolour and bodycolour on
grey-brown paper, 15 x 22.8
Tate (TB CCCXVIII 1; D32220; S 8)

131 *San Marco and the Piazzetta* 1840 **(fig.124)**
Watercolour and bodycolour on
grey-brown paper, 14.9 x 22.8
Tate (TB CCCXIX 8; D32256)

132 *The Piazzetta with the Campanile; Night*
1840 **(fig.125)**
Watercolour and bodycolour on
grey-brown paper, 14.1 x 22.5
Tate (TB CCCXIX 10; D32258)

133 *San Marco and the Piazzetta, with San Giorgio
Maggiore; Night* 1840 **(fig.126)**
Watercolour and bodycolour on
grey-brown paper, 14.8 x 22.8
Tate (TB CCCXIX 2; D32250; S 9)

134 *The Bridge of Sighs; Night* 1840 **(fig.131)**
Watercolour and bodycolour on
grey-brown paper, 22.8 x 15.2
Tate (TB CCCXIX 5; D32253; S 27)

135 *A Study of Firelight* 1840 **(fig.135)**
Watercolour and bodycolour on
grey-brown paper, 22.6 x 29.4

136 *The Interior of San Marco: the Atrium, looking
North* 1840 **(fig.120)**
Watercolour and bodycolour on red-brown
paper, 24.3 x 30.4
Tate (TB CCCXVIII 22; D32241)

137 *The Campanile and San Marco, from the Atrio
of the Palazzo Reale* 1840 **(fig.127)**
Watercolour and bodycolour on red-brown
paper, 31.9 x 23.8
Tate (TB CCCXVIII 26; D32245; S 24)

138 *The Salute from the Traghetto del Ridotto*
1840 **(fig.138)**
Watercolour and bodycolour on red-brown
paper, 25 x 30.7
Tate (TB CCCXVIII 11; D32230)

139 *Santa Maria della Salute, Night Scene with
Rockets* 1840 **(fig.140)**
Watercolour and bodycolour on red-brown
paper, 24 x 31.5
Tate (TB CCCXVIII 29; D32248; S 29)

140 *Venice: Women at a Window* 1840 **(fig.136)**
Watercolour and bodycolour on red-brown
paper, 23.6 x 31.5
Tate (TB CCCXVIII 20; D32239; S 21)

141 *The Campanile of San Marco, from the Roof of
the Hotel Europa: Moonlight* 1840 **(fig.149)**
Watercolour and bodycolour on red-brown
paper, 24.2 x 30.7
Tate (TB CCCXVIII 5; D32224; S 13)

142 *Lightning behind the Campanile of San
Marco, from the Roof of the Hotel Europa* 1840
(fig.150)
Watercolour and bodycolour on red-brown
paper, 15.8 x 23.2
Tate (TB CCCXIX 6; D32254; S 12)

143 *Venice: The Interior of a Theatre* 1840 **(fig.134)**
Watercolour and bodycolour on a warm
buff paper, 22.4 x 29.3
Tate (TB CCCXVIII 18; D32237; S 20)

144 *The Porta della Carta, Doge's Palace* c.1840
(fig.118)
Pencil, watercolour and bodycolour on
pale buff paper, with some stopping-out,
30.5 x 23.4
Tate (TB CCCXVIII 28; D32247; S 25)

145 *Turner's Bedroom in the Palazzo Giustinian
(the Hotel Europa)* 1840 **(fig.141)**
Watercolour and bodycolour on pale buff
paper, 23 x 30.2
Tate (TB CCCXVII 34; D32219; S 42)

146 *On the Grand Canal near the Rialto, with the
Fabbriche Nuove and the Campanile of San
Giovanni Elemosinario* 1840 **(fig.158)**
Pencil and watercolour on pale buff paper,
22.5 x 30
Tate (TB CCCXVI 12; D32149)

147 *Isola di San Giorgio Maggiore* 1840 **(fig.214)**
Watercolour on pale buff paper, with
detail added using a pen dipped in
watercolour, 23 x 30
Tate (TB CCCXVI 11; D32148)

148 *The Punta della Dogana and the Campanile,*
from the Giudecca Canal 1840 **(fig.224)**
Watercolour on pale grey-white paper,
22.2 x 29.9
Tate (TB CCCXVI 14; D32151)

149 *The Approach to Venice* 1840 **(fig.262)**
Watercolour and bodycolour on pale
grey-white paper, 23 x 32.2
Tate (TB CCCXVI 16; D32153; S 70)

150 *Looking north from the Hotel Europa, with the*
Campaniles of San Marco, San Moise, and Santo
Stefano 1840 **(fig.144)**
Pencil and watercolour, 19.8 x 28.2
Tate (TB CCCXVI 3; D32140; S 56)

151 *Venice at Sunrise from the Hotel Europa, with*
the Campanile of San Marco 1840 **(fig.145)**
Watercolour, 19.8 x 28
Tate (TB CCCLXIV 106; D35949; S 85)

152 *View over the rooftops towards the Giardini Reale*
and the Campanile of San Marco 1840 **(fig.146)**
Pencil, watercolour and bodycolour,
19.3 x 28
Tate (TB CCCXVI 42; D32179)
London only

153 *Venice from the Hotel Europa; Looking East over*
the Rooftops towards the Campanile, the Doge's
Palace and San Giorgio Maggiore 1840 **(fig.147)**
Watercolour, 18.8 x 28.4
Tate (TB CCCLXIV 43; D35882)

154 *San Giorgio Maggiore from the Hotel Europa, at*
the Entrance to the Grand Canal 1840 **(fig.148)**
Watercolour, 19.5 x 27.6
Whitworth Art Gallery, University of
Manchester. Gift of John Edward Taylor,
1892 (D.1892.114)

155 *San Giorgio Maggiore at Sunset, from the Hotel*
Europa 1840 **(fig.215)**
Pencil, watercolour and bodycolour,
19.3 x 28.1
Tate (TB CCCXVI 28; D32165; S 78)

156 *The Punta della Dogana, and Santa Maria della*
Salute at Twilight, from the Hotel Europa 1840
(fig.222)
Pencil and watercolour, with pen, 19.4 x 28
Tate (TB CCCXVI 29; D32166)

157 *Fishermen on the Lagoon, Moonlight* 1840 **(fig.252)**
Watercolour, 19.2 x 28
Tate (TB CCCLXIV 334; D36192)

158 *Venice: An Imaginary View of the Arsenale*
c.1840 **(fig.130)**
Watercolour and bodycolour, 24.3 x 30.8
Tate (TB CCCXVI 27; D32164; S 75)

159 *Among the Chimney-pots above Venice; the*
Roof of the Hotel Europa, with the Campanile
of San Marco 1840 **(fig.143)**
Pencil, watercolour and bodycolour,
24.5 x 30.6
Tate (TB CCCXVI 36; D32173; S 74)

160 *Santa Maria della Salute from near the Traghetto*
San Maurizio 1840 **(fig.175)**
Pencil and watercolour, 24.2 x 30.4
Tate (TB CCCXVI 1; D32138; S 58)

161 *Boats Moored alongside the Punta della Dogana,*
with the Doge's Palace beyond 1840 **(fig.193)**
Watercolour, 24.6 x 30.7
Tate (TB CCCXVI 35; D32172; S 82)

162 *Looking up the Giudecca Canal, with Santa*
Maria della Salute on the Right 1840 **(fig.194)**
Pencil and watercolour, 24.5 x 30.5
Tate (TB CCCXVI 26; D32163)

163 *Santa Maria della Salute from the Bacino* 1840
(fig.195)
Pencil and watercolour, 24.4 x 30.7
Tate (TB CCCXVI 37; D32174)

164 *Santa Maria della Salute, the Campanile*
of San Marco, the Doge's Palace and San
Giorgio Maggiore, from the Giudecca Canal
1840 **(fig.196)**
Watercolour, 24.5 x 30.8
Tate (TB CCCXVI 8; D32145)

165 *On the Giudecca Canal beside the Redentore,*
looking towards San Giorgio Maggiore 1840
(fig.201)
Pencil and watercolour, 24.4 x 30.7
Tate (TB CCCXVI 4; D32141)

166 *San Giorgio Maggiore at Sunset, from the Riva*
degli Schiavoni 1840 **(fig.217)**
Watercolour, 24.4 x 30.6
Tate (TB CCCXVI 24; D32161; S 77)

167 *The Doge's Palace and the Riva degli Schiavoni,*
from the Bacino 1840 **(fig.236)**
Pencil, watercolour and bodycolour,
with details added using a pen dipped
in watercolour, 24.3 x 30.4
Tate (TB CCCXVI 17; D32154; S 63)

168 *Looking back on Venice from the Canale di San*
Marco to the East 1840 **(fig.247)**
Watercolour, with details added using
a pen dipped in watercolour, 24.5 x 30.6
Tate (TB CCCXVI 18; D32155; S 64)

169 *Shipping off the Riva degli Schiavoni, from near*
the Ponte dell'Arsenale 1840 **(fig.249)**
Watercolour, 24.3 x 30.6
Tate (TB CCCXVI 20; D32157; S 67)

170 *Looking across the Bacino di San Marco at*
Sunset, from near San Biagio 1840 **(fig.250)**
Watercolour, with details added using
a pen dipped in watercolour, 24.4 x 30.4
Tate (TB CCCXVI 21; D32158; S 65)

171 *Looking along the Riva degli Schiavoni, from*
near the Rio dell'Arsenale 1840 **(fig.251)**
Pencil and watercolour, 24.6 x 30.4
Tate (TB CCCXVI 22; D32159)

172 *The Zitelle, Santa Maria della Salute, the*
Campanile and San Giorgio Maggiore, from
the Canale della Grazia 1840 **(fig.254)**
Pencil and watercolour, with details
added using a pen dipped in watercolour,
24.3 x 30.5
Tate (TB CCCXVI 19; D32156; S 62)

173 *Boats on the Lagoon, near Venice* c.1840
(fig.258)
Watercolour, 24.6 x 30.6
Tate (TB CCCLXIV 137; D35980)

174 *Looking across the Lagoon at Sunset*
c.1840 **(fig.259)**
Watercolour, 24.4 x 30.4
Tate (TB CCCXVI 25; D32162; S 83)

175 *An Open Expanse of Water on the Lagoon, near*
Venice c.1840 **(fig.260)**
Watercolour, 24.8 x 30.7
Tate (TB CCCLXIV 332; D36190)

176 *Venice: Moonlight on the Lagoon* 1840 **(fig.261)**
Watercolour and bodycolour, 24.5 x 30.4
Tate (TB CCCXVI 39; D32176; S 81)

E) BOOKS, ENGRAVINGS AND OTHER
MATERIAL

177 Antonio Visentini (1688–1782) after
Canaletto (1697–1768)
A Regatta on the Grand Canal 1836 **(fig.23)**
(plate 3 of *Trente Huit Vues Choisies de la Ville*
de Venise Dessinées par Antoine Canaletto et
Gravées par Antoine Visentini à Venise
published by Joseph Battaggia, 1836)
Etching, 38.7 x 54.7
The British Museum, London

178 John Pye (1782–1874) after Turner
The Rialto 1820 **(fig.31)**
(from James Hakewill's *Picturesque Tour of*
Italy 1818–20)
Engraving from Turner's own copy,
published volume 14.3 x 22 (image)
on sheets 28.7 x 38.7
Private collection

179 J. Tingle after Samuel Prout (1783–1852)
Palace of Foscari, looking south towards
Accademia 1830 **(fig.70)**
(plate 20 of the *Landscape Annual for* 1830;
also known as *The Tourist in Switzerland and*
Italy by Thomas Roscoe)
Engraving, published volume, 14 x 20.3
Private collection

180 R. Wallis after Clarkson Stanfield
(1793–1867)
Church of San Pietro di Castello 1832 **(fig.71)**
(plate 13 of *Heath's Picturesque Annual for*
1832; also known as *Sketches in the North*
of Italy, the Tyrol, and on the Rhine by
Leitch Ritchie)
Engraving, published volume, 13.5 x 20.4
Private collection

181 Edward Finden (1791/2–1857) after a
watercolour by Turner (W 1225), based
on a sketch by T. Little
The Bridge of Sighs 1832 **(fig.66)**
(from *Byron's Life and Works*, vol.XI, 1832)
Line engraving, published volume,
17.7 x 10.7
Dr Jan Piggott (R 421)

182 William Miller (1796–1882) after a
watercolour by Turner (W 1105)
The Campanile 1835 **(fig.69)**
(from *Scott's Prose Works*, vol.X, 1835)
Line engraving, published volume,
16.5 x 20.5
Dr Jan Piggott (R 528)

183 George Hollis (1793–1842) after Turner
St Mark's Place, Venice: Juliet and her Nurse
1842 (*not reproduced; see* fig.61)
Engraving, 41.9 x 56.3 (image);
53.5 x 65 (plate mark)
Tate. Purchased 1988 (T05188; R 654)

184 J.T. Willmore (1800–1863) after Turner
Venice – Bellini's Pictures being Conveyed to the
Church of the Redentore 1858
(*not reproduced; see* fig.205)
Engraving, 39.2 x 61
Tate. Purchased 1988 (T05192; R677a/668)

185 Anonymous
Model of Bragozzo, 19/20th century
(*not reproduced; see* fig.246)
Wood, 110 x 110 x 20
Museo Storico Navale, Venice

Lenders

Public Collections

Bedford, Cecil Higgins Art Gallery
Birmingham, Birmingham City Art Gallery
Indianapolis, Indianapolis Museum of Art
Liverpool, Walker Art Gallery
London, The British Library
London, The British Museum
London, National Gallery
London, National Trust
London, Victoria and Albert Museum
Manchester, Whitworth Art Gallery
Milan, Pinacoteca Ambrosiana
New Haven, Yale Center for British Art
New York, Metropolitan Museum of Art
Oberlin, Allen Memorial Art Museum
Oxford, Ashmolean Museum
Petworth, Petworth House
Rome, British School at Rome Library
San Marino, Huntington Library, Botanical Gardens and Art Collection
Toledo, Toledo Museum of Art
Washington, National Gallery of Art
York, York City Art Gallery
Venice, Museo Storico Navale

Private Collections

Trustees of the Bowood Collection
Lord and Lady Egremont
Richard Feigen & Co., New York
Collection of the late Sir Brinsley Ford
Dr Jan Piggott
Private Collection (Courtesy of Agnew's)
Private Collection (Courtesy of Richard Green)
Private Collection

Photographic Credits

Courtesy of Agnew's, London *10, 107, 198, 233*
© Allen Memorial Art Museum *197*
© Arkansas Arts Center *274*
The Art Archive/Garrick Club *62*
© Biblioteca Ambrosiana *28*
The Ashmolean Museum, Oxford *92, 173, 177, 239*
Russell Bell
Birmingham Museums and Art Gallery *81*
© 2003 The Museum of Fine Arts, Boston *79*
Bridgeman Art Library *20, 47*
The British Library, London *1, 21*
© Copyright The British Museum *6, 22, 23, 24, 34, 101, 181, 188*
© Cameraphoto Arte *2*
Photograph © National Gallery of Canada *18*
© Christie's Images Limited, 2003 *25, 43, 84, 133, 183, 198*
M. Lee Fatheree *216*
Richard L. Feigen, New York *80*
Fitzwilliam Museum, University of Cambridge *46, 213, 219, 253*
Courtesy of Richard Green Gallery, London/The Antique Collector's Club *269*
Courtesy of Richard Green Gallery, London *245*
Trustees, Cecil Higgins Art Gallery, Bedford, England *97*
The Huntington Library Art Collection and Botanical Gardens, San Marino, California/Powerstock *58*
Indianapolis Museum of Art *95*
Jane Inskipp *212*
© Courtesy of the National Gallery of Ireland *96, 186, 218, 235,*
Isabella Stewart Gardner Museum, Boston *56*
Grahame Jackson *94*
National Museums, Liverpool/Walker Art Gallery *234*
Robert Lorenzon *33*
© The National Gallery, London *44, 48, 54, 152*
© National Maritime Museum, Greenwich *73, 275*

Courtesy of Marlborough Fine Art *205*
Photograph © 1988 The Metropolitan Museum of Art *109*
Courtesy of Estudio Moltedo *61*
Museo Storico Navale, Venice *246*
National Museum of Photography Film and Television/Science and Society Picture Library *93*
Derek Parker for Bowood House *102*
Photographic Survey, Courtauld Institute of Art *7*
The Royal Collection © 2003, Her Majesty Queen Elizabeth II *106, 122*
Ruskin Foundation (Ruskin Library, University of Lancaster) *270*
Salamon, Milan, Italy *20*
© 1990, Photo SCALA *52, 204*
© The National Gallery of Scotland, Edinburgh *10, 90, 114, 179, 244, 255*
Courtesy of Sotheby's *98, 185, 273*
Sotheby's Picture Library *271, 272*
Staatliche Museen zu Berlin – Preußisher Kulterbesitz Gemäldgalerie. Photography: Jörg P. Anders *267*
Taft Museum of Art, Cincinnati, Ohio *57*
Tate Photography *63, 91, 111, 209, 240*
Tate Photography/Marcus Leith and Andrew Dunkley *40*
Tate Photography/Caroline Shuttle *5*
Tate Photography/Rodney Tidnam *3, 8, 11, 12, 15, 16, 26, 29, 30, 31, 32, 35, 36, 37, 38, 39, 41, 42, 49, 64, 66, 67, 68, 69, 70, 71, 72, 74, 75, 76, 77, 78, 82, 83, 85, 87, 88, 112, 115, 116, 117, 118, 119, 120, 121, 123, 124, 125, 126, 127, 128, 129, 130, 131, 134, 135, 136, 137, 138, 139, 140, 141, 142, 143, 144, 145, 146, 147, 149, 150, 151, 154, 155, 156, 158, 159, 160, 161, 162, 163, 164, 165, 166, 167, 169, 170, 171, 172, 174, 175, 176, 180, 182, 189, 190, 191, 192, 193, 194, 195, 196, 199, 200, 201, 202, 203, 206, 207, 208, 210, 214, 215, 217, 222, 224, 225, 226, 227, 228, 231, 232, 236, 237, 242, 243, 247, 249, 250, 251, 252, 254, 256, 258, 259, 260, 261, 262, 266*

Tate Picture Library *5, 19, 27, 45, 50, 51, 53, 55, 59, 99, 103, 108, 113, 168, 178, 211, 220, 230, 238, 241, 248, 268, 276, 277*
Thaw Collection, The Pierpont Morgan Library, New York/Joseph Zehavi *58*
The Toledo Museum of Art *257*
Andrew Tullis for 'Insight' *264, 265*
V&A Picture Library *110*
The Trustees of the Wallace Collection, London *221*
© 2003 Board of Trustees, National Gallery of Art, Washington *104, 105, 229, 263*
The Whitworth Art Gallery, The University of Manchester *86, 148*
Yale Center for British Art/Richard Caspole *9, 60, 100, 184*
York Museums Trust (York Art Gallery) *132*

Index

Supporting Tate

Tate relies on a large number of supporters – individuals, foundations, companies and public sector sources – to enable it to deliver its programme of activities, both on and off its gallery sites. This support is essential in order to acquire works of art for the Collection, run education, outreach and exhibition programmes, care for the Collection in storage and enable art to be displayed, both digitally and physically, inside and outside Tate. Your donation will make a real difference and enable others to enjoy Tate and its Collections both now and in the future. There are a variety of ways in which you can help support the Tate and also benefit as a UK or US taxpayer. Please contact us at:

The Development Office
Tate Millbank
London SWIP 4RG
Tel: 020 7887 8942
Fax: 020 7887 8738

Tate American Fund
1285 Avenue of the Americas (35th fl)
New York NY 10019
Tel: 001 212 713 8497
Fax: 001 212 713 8655

Donations
Donations, of whatever size, from individuals, companies and trusts are welcome, either to support particular areas of interest, or to contribute to general running costs.

Gifts of Shares
Since April 2000, we can accept gifts of quoted shares and securities. These are not subject to capital gains tax. For higher rate taxpayers, a gift of shares saves income tax as well as capital gains tax. For further information please contact the Campaigns Section of the Development Office.

Tate Annual Fund
A donation to the Annual Fund at Tate benefits a variety of projects throughout the organisation, from the development of new conservation techniques to education programmes for people of all ages.

Gift Aid
Through Gift Aid, you can provide significant additional revenue to Tate. Gift Aid applies to gifts of any size, whether regular or one-off, since we can claim back the tax on your charitable donation. Higher rate taxpayers are also able to claim additional personal tax relief. Contact us for further information and a Gift-Aid Declaration.

Legacies
A legacy to Tate may take the form of a residual share of an estate, a specific cash sum or item of property such as a work of art. Legacies to Tate are free of Inheritance Tax.

Offers in lieu of tax
Inheritance Tax can be satisfied by transferring to the Government a work of art of outstanding importance. In this case the rate of tax is reduced, and it can be made a condition of the offer that the work of art is allocated to Tate. Please contact us for details.

Tate American Fund and Tate American Patrons
The American Fund for the Tate Gallery was formed in 1986 to facilitate gifts of works of art, donations and bequests to Tate from United States residents. United States taxpayers who wish to support Tate on an annual basis can join the American Patrons of the Tate Gallery and enjoy membership benefits and events in the United States and United Kingdom (single membership $1000 and double $1500). Both organisations receive full tax exempt status from the IRS. Please contact the Tate American Fund for further details.

Membership Programmes
Tate Members enjoy unlimited free admission throughout the year to all exhibitions at Tate Britain, Tate Liverpool, Tate Modern and Tate St Ives, as well as a number of other benefits such as exclusive use of our Members' Rooms and a free annual subscription to Tate Magazine.

Whilst enjoying the exclusive privileges of membership, you are also helping secure Tate's position at the very heart of British and modern art. Your support actively contributes to new purchases of important art, ensuring that the Tate's Collection continues to be relevant and comprehensive, as well as funding projects in London, Liverpool and St Ives that increase access and understanding for everyone.

Patrons
Tate Patrons are people who share a keen interest in art and are committed to giving significant financial support to the Tate on an annual basis, specifically to support acquisitions. There are four levels of Patron, including Associate Patron (£250), Patrons of New Art (£500), Patrons of British Art (£500) and Patrons Circle (£1000). Benefits include opportunities to sit on acquisition committees, special access to the Collection and entry with a family member to all Tate exhibitions.

Corporate Membership
Corporate Membership at Tate Modern, Tate Liverpool and Tate Britain, and support for the Business Circle at Tate St Ives, offer companies opportunities for corporate entertaining and the chance for a wide variety of employee benefits. These include special private views, special access to paying exhibitions, out-of-hours visits and tours, invitations to VIP events and talks at members' offices.

Corporate Investment
Tate has developed a range of imaginative partnerships with the corporate sector, ranging from international interpretation and exhibition programmes to local outreach and staff development programmes. We are particularly known for high-profile business to business marketing initiatives and employee benefit packages. Please contact the Corporate Fundraising team for further details.

Charity Details
The Tate Gallery is an exempt charity; the Museums & Galleries Act 1992 added the Tate Gallery to the list of exempt charities defined in the 1960 Charities Act. The Friends of the Tate Gallery is a registered charity (number 313021). Tate Foundation is a registered charity (number 1085314).

TATE BRITAIN DONORS TO THE CENTENARY DEVELOPMENT CAMPAIGN

Founder
The Heritage Lottery Fund

Founding Benefactors
Sir Harry and Lady Djanogly
The Kresge Foundation
Sir Edwin and Lady Manton
Lord and Lady Sainsbury of Preston Candover
The Wolfson Foundation

Major Donors
The Annenberg Foundation
Ron Beller and Jennifer Moses
Alex and Angela Bernstein
Lauren and Mark Booth
Ivor Braka
The Clore Duffield Foundation
Maurice and Janet Dwek
Bob and Kate Gavron
Sir Paul Getty KBE
Nicholas and Judith Goodison
Mr and Mrs Karpidas
Peter and Maria Kellner
Catherine and Pierre Lagrange
Ruth and Stuart Lipton
William A Palmer
John and Jill Ritblat
Barrie and Emmanuel Roman
Charlotte Stevenson
Tate Gallery Centenary Gala
The Trusthouse Charitable Foundation
David and Emma Verey
Clodagh and Leslie Waddington
Mr and Mrs Anthony Weldon
Sam Whitbread

Donors
The Asprey Family Charitable Foundation
The Charlotte Bonham-Carter Charitable Trust
The CHK Charities Limited
Sadie Coles
Giles and Sonia Coode-Adams
Alan Cristea
Thomas Dane
The D'Oyly Carte Charitable Trust
The Dulverton Trust
Tate Friends
Alan Gibbs

Mr and Mrs Edward Gilhuly
Helyn and Ralph Goldenberg
Richard and Odile Grogan
Pehr and Christina Gyllenhammar
Jay Jopling
Howard and Lynda Karshan
Madeleine Kleinwort
Brian and Lesley Knox
Mr and Mrs Ulf G. Linden
Anders and Ulla Ljungh
Lloyds TSB Foundation for England and Wales
David and Pauline Mann-Vogelpoel
Nick and Annette Mason
Viviane and James Mayor
Anthony and Deidre Montague
Sir Peter and Lady Osborne
Maureen Paley
Mr Frederik Paulsen
The Pet Shop Boys
The P F Charitable Trust
The Polizzi Charitable Trust
Mrs Coral Samuel CBE
David and Sophie Shalit
Mr and Mrs Sven Skarendahl
Pauline Denyer-Smith and Paul Smith
Mr and Mrs Nicholas Stanley
The Jack Steinberg Charitable Trust
Carter and Mary Thacher
Mr and Mrs John Thornton
Dinah Verey
Gordon D. Watson
The Duke of Westminster OBE TD DL
Mr and Mrs Stephen Wilberding
Michael S. Wilson
and those donors who wish to remain anonymous

TATE COLLECTION

Founders
Sir Henry Tate
Sir Joseph Duveen
Lord Duveen
The Clore Duffield Foundation
Heritage Lottery Fund
National Art Collections Fund

Founding Benefactors
Sir Edwin and Lady Manton
The Kreitman Foundation
The American Fund for the Tate Gallery
The Nomura Securities Co Ltd

Benefactors
Gilbert and Janet de Botton
The Deborah Loeb Brice Foundation
National Heritage Memorial Fund
Patrons of British Art
Patrons of New Art
Dr Mortimer and Theresa Sackler Foundation
Tate Members

Major Donors
Aviva plc
Edwin C Cohen
Lynn Forester de Rothschild
Noam and Geraldine Gottesman
The Leverhulme Trust
Hartley Neel
Richard Neel
New Opportunites Fund

Donors
Howard and Roberta Ahmanson
Lord and Lady Attenborough
The Charlotte Bonham-Carter Charitable Trust
Mrs John Chandris
Brooke Hayward Duchin
GABO TRUST for Sculpture Conservation
The Gapper Charitable Trust
The Getty Grant Program
Calouste Gulbenkian Foundation
HSBC Artscard
Lord and Lady Jacobs
The Samuel H Kress Foundation
Leche Trust
Robert Lehman Foundation
William Louis-Dreyfus
The Henry Moore Foundation

Friends of the Newfoundland Dog and Members of the Newfoundland Dog Club of America
Peter and Eileen Norton, The Peter Norton Family Foundation
The Radcliffe Trust
The Rayne Foundation
Mr Simon Robertson
Lord and Lady Rothschild
Mrs Jean Sainsbury
The Foundation for Sports and the Arts
Stanley Foundation Limited
Mr and Mrs A Alfred Taubman
and those donors who wish to remain anonymous

Tate Collectors Forum
Lord Attenborough Kt CBE
Colin Barrow
Ricki Gail Conway
Madeleine Kleinwort
Jonathan Marland
Keir McGuinness
Frederick Paulsen
Tineke Pugh
Virginia Robertson
Roland and Sophie Rudd
Andrew and Belinda Scott
Dennis and Charlotte Stevenson
Sir Mark Weinberg
and those donors who wish to remain anonymous

TATE BRITAIN DONORS

Major Donors
The Bowland Charitable Trust
Mr and Mrs James Brice
The Henry Luce Foundation
The Henry Moore Foundation
The Horace W Goldsmith Foundation
John Lyon's Charity

Donors
Howard and Roberta Ahmanson
Blackwall Green
Mr and Mrs Robert Bransten
The Calouste Gulbenkian Foundation
Ricki and Robert Conway
The Glass-House Trust
ICAP plc
ICI
The Stanley Thomas Johnson Foundation
Kiers Foundation
The Kirby Laing Foundation
London Arts
The Paul Mellon Centre for Studies in British Art
The Mercers' Company
The Peter Moores Foundation
Judith Rothschild Foundation
Keith and Kathy Sachs
The Wates Foundation
and those donors who wish to remain anonymous

TATE CORPORATE MEMBERS

Accenture
American Express
Aviva plc
Bank of Ireland GB
The Bank of New York
BNP Paribas
Clifford Chance
Deloitte & Touche
Drivers Jonas
EDF Energy
EMI
Ernst & Young
Freshfields Bruckhaus Deringer
GAM
GLG Partners
Hugo Boss
Lehman Brothers
Linklaters
Mayer, Brown, Rowe & Maw
Merrill Lynch
Nomura
Pearson
Reckitt Benckiser
Scottish Power
Simmons & Simmons
Standard Chartered
Tishman Speyer Properties
UBS

TATE BRITAIN SPONSORS

Founding Sponsors
BP p.l.c
  Campaign for the creation of Tate
  Britain (1998–2000)
  BP Displays at Tate Britain
  (1990–2007)
  Tate Britain Launch (2000)
BT
  Tate Online (2001–2006)
Channel 4
  The Turner Prize (1991–2003)
Ernst & Young
  Cézanne (1996)
  Bonnard (1998)

Benefactor Sponsors
Egg Plc
  Tate & Egg Live (2003)
GlaxoSmithKline plc
  Turner on the Seine (1999)
  William Blake (2000)
  *American Sublime: Landscape
  Painting in the United States,
  1820–1880* (2002)
Prudential plc
  *The Age of Rossetti, Burne-Jones
  and Watts: Symbolism in Britain
  1860–1910* (1997)
  The Art of Bloomsbury (1999)
  Stanley Spencer (2001)
Tate & Lyle plc
  Tate Members (1991–2000)
  Tate Britain Community Education
  (2001–2004)

Major Sponsors
Barclays PLC
  Turner and Venice (2003)
The British Land Company PLC
  Joseph Wright of Derby (1990)
  Ben Nicholson (1993)
  Gainsborough (2002)
The Independent Newspapers
  Media Partner for *William Blake*
  (2000)
  Media Partner for *Stanley Spencer*
  (2001)
  Media Partner for *Exposed:
  The Victorian Nude* (2001)

Morgan Stanley
  *Visual Paths: Teaching Literacy
  in the Gallery* (1999–2002)
Tate Members
  Exposed: The Victorian Nude (2001)
  Bridget Riley (2003)
UBS
  Lucian Freud (2002)
Volkswagen
  *Days Like These: Tate Triennial
  of Contemporary Art* (2003)

Sponsors
B&Q
  Michael Andrews (2001)
Classic FM
  Media Partner for *Thomas Girtin:
  The Art of Watercolour* (2002)
The Daily Telegraph
  Media Partner for *American
  Sublime* (2002)
The Economist
  James Gillray: The Art of Caricature
  (2001)
The Guardian
  Media Partner for *Wolfgang
  Tillmans if one thing matters,
  everything matters* (2003)
  Media Partner for *Bridget Riley*
  (2003)
Hiscox plc
  Tate Britain Members Room
  (1995–2001)
John Lyons Charity
  *Constable to Delacroix: British Art
  and the French Romantics* (2003)